OBJECT PERCEPTION

Structure and Process

OBJECT PERCEPTION
Structure and Process

Edited by

Bryan E. Shepp
Brown University

Soledad Ballesteros
Universidad Nacional de Educacion a Distancia

LAWRENCE ERLBAUM ASSOCIATES, PUBLISHERS
1989   Hillsdale, New Jersey   Hove and London

Lawrence Erlbaum Associations, Inc., Publishers
365 Broadway
Hillsdale, New Jersey 07642

Library of Congress Cataloging-in-Publication Data
Object perception: structure and process / edited by Bryan E. Shepp,
    Soledad Ballesteros.
        p.   cm.
    Bibliography: p.
    Includes index.
    ISBN 0-8058-0060-3.   ISBN 0-8058-0333-5 (pbk.)
    1. Visual perception.   I. Shepp, Bryan E.   II. Ballesteros.
Soledad.
    BF241.025 1988
    152.1'4—dc19

Printed in the United States of America
10   9   8   7   6   5   4   3   2   1

For
Wendell R. Garner
who led the way

CONTENTS

7   ON PERCEIVING OBJECTS: HOLISTIC VERSUS
FEATURAL PROPERTIES   *203*
Bryan E. Shepp

8   SOME DETERMINANTS OF PERCEIVED STRUCTURE:
EFFECTS OF STIMULUS TASKS   *235*
Soledad Ballesteros

9   CATEGORY BOUNDS AND STIMULUS
VARIABILITY   *267*
Gregory R. Lockhead

PREFACE

This book presents the lectures given at a conference entitled *Object Perception: Structure and Process* that was held in Madrid, Spain from May 18–20, 1987. The conference was organized in the Spring of 1986 by Soledad Ballesteros on behalf of the United States–Spanish Committee for Cultural and Educational Cooperation. The goal was to arrange a meeting in which researchers from the United States and Spain could exchange views on current research and theory on issues in object perception.

After consulting with U.S. colleagues, Soledad Ballesteros invited twelve U.S. and two Spanish investigators to participate and arranged for Bryan Shepp and Jose Luis Fernandez Trespalacios to serve, respectively, as the U.S. and Spanish Directors of the conference. These three individuals collaborated in the preparation of an Institutional Cooperation Grant between Brown University and the Universidad Nacional de Educacion a Distancia. After the U.S.–Spanish Committee approved the grant to support the conference, the final arrangements were made. We are most grateful to the Committee for its support. We are also indebted to Brown University for assistance in organizing the conference, and to the Universidad Nacional de Educacion a Distancia for providing the facilities in which the conference met.

The topics covered in this book, faithful to its title, address structure and process in object perception, and they range from the automatic effects of preattentive organization to the consequences of deliberate strategies in category learning. In some instances there are themes that are common to several chapters, for example, the operation of Gestalt principles or holistic versus analytical perception, but even in such cases each chapter deals with a special aspect of a particular issue. Most of the participants accept some form of an information processing approach, however, and within this context, characterize an aspect of object perception or the relation between perception and one or more cognitive processes.

The book begins on a philosophical note. Jose Fernandez Trespalacios, noting a revival of phenomenology, offers a clarification of the relation between the phenomenological and the scientific study of perception. He sees two problems as central: mistaking perception for other processes and defining perception by the performance in a task that is not just a perceptual task. He proposes that an experimental phenomenology will yield definitions of perception that will assist in the selection of tasks that are exclusively perceptual. No one doubts the importance of phenomenology in the informal selection of tasks to study perception, but for many a formal status is not as yet clear.

Howard Egeth, Charles Polk, and Paul Mullin ask whether preattentive processing of stimuli occurs in parallel and independently of other cognitive resources. They pursue these questions in a variety of tasks, and generally the answers to both are affirmative. When subjects search for a target that differs from the distractors on but a single dimension, there is clear support for parallel processing with unlimited capacity. Similar support was obtained for digit-letter classification, but when the classification was based on word meaning capacity was substantially limited. Taken together, their results, contrary to early selection theories, indicate that simple and some complex information are analyzed on spatially parallel channels, but, contrary to late selection theories, word meaning is not processed in this fashion.

Several chapters consider the perception of shape or aspects of shape, and some investigate the role of Gestalt principles in shape perception. Steve Palmer addresses the question, how do people know that two objects have the same shape despite variations in other properties of the objects, for example, orientation? He tests several theories that are formulated to explain the selection of reference frames, which serve to preserve shape equivalence while eliminating the transformations that are produced in the objects by other properties such as a change in orientation. Several series of experiments are reported, and although each theory is successful with some of the data, none is entirely successful. He proposes that the most promising theoretical direction for these perceptual phenomena is offered by the new connectionist models.

Lynn Cooper tackles another fundamental problem in object perception. She notes that although we perceive a well organized, meaningful world, our ordinary encounters with objects provide only partial information about the layout and structure of the objects. She argues that the partial information either specifies the important properties of hidden surfaces and/or is used in the construction of mental models of the objects. In one set of experiments, subjects were given a problem solving task with orthographic projections, followed by an isometric recognition task. Subjects were quite successful in the recognition task, which Cooper takes to mean that a mental model of the three dimensional object was constructed from the two dimensional projections. Cooper believes that these and related experiments can establish the relations between the aspects of an object that can be predicted or generated and the mental models that perform these computations.

Chapter 3 by Jim Pomerantz, Edward Pristach, and Cathy Carson and Chapter 6 by Maria Lasaga introduce the concept of configural stimuli and the processing that such stimuli allow. Configural stimuli arise when components, for example, contours, combine to yield emergent features. Thus, configural stimuli are one type of holistic organization, but the emergent feature may be perceptually independent of either the whole or other components of the stimulus.

After reviewing the evidence for configural stimuli, Pomerantz et al. go on to discuss two kinds of interference, Garner and Stroop, that such stimuli may yield. Garner interference is attributable to variation on an irrelevant dimension; Stroop interference results when the trial-specific contents on an irrelevant dimension give rise to a competing response. The authors describe the conditions that lead to each type of interference, and propose a model to account for such effects.

Maria Lasaga reports a series of experiments that identify some of the factors that affect local/global precedence. If a large S is generated by a pattern of small Os, the S is the global property while the Os are the local property. Precedence occurs if, in the generation of a percept, information about one set of properties is available earlier than information about the other set. Her research shows that when stimuli are generated by physically disconnected local units, global and local properties are generated in parallel and that the local/global precedence is determined by their relative discriminabilities within a stimulus. When, on the other hand, the stimuli are generated by physically connected local units, global properties have precedence.

Another variety of holistic versus analytic organization contrasts the perception of objects as wholes with the perception of their constituent features. The contrast arises from comparisons of integral and separable dimensions, and is discussed by Bryan Shepp, Soledad Ballesteros, and Deborah Kemler Nelson. Integral stimuli, for example, hue versus saturation, are perceived holistically, whereas separable stimuli, for example, size of circle versus angle of a radial line, are perceived as aggregates of features. Each of these types of stimulus is well behaved; the perceptual organization identified with either type of stimulus rarely occurs, and then only weakly, with the other.

A major theoretical problem arises, however, because many physically integral stimuli, for example, color and form, appear to be processed holistically in some speeded tasks, but are psychologically separable in unspeeded tasks. Such results have led to the view that there is a continuum of integrality on which dimensions vary in their analyzability.

Shepp argues that integral dimensions should be distinguished from separate dimensions. The latter present spatially separated features that are invariably perceived as aggregates of features; they are not perceived holistically at any level of processing. The former, however, are first perceived holistically, and depending on their analyzability may be decomposed into their constituent features. This view is tested in several speeded tasks with shape and size presented either as integral or as separate stimuli. Shepp also argues that the analysis of integral stimuli is facilitated when searches are initiated by name codes rather than visual codes. The results strongly converge on his claims.

Kemler Nelson takes the view that overall similarity relations (holistic processing) are pervasive in a variety of tasks for integral and separable stimuli alike, and she discusses the basis for distinguishing between holistic processing and several analytic alternatives. Importantly, she also makes the distinction between two forms of nonselective holistic processing, one strong and the other weak, and nonselective analytic processing.

In both forms of holistic processing, the stimulus representations are accessed as wholes, not simply a concatenation of independent features. Wholes rather than features are the primary unit of processing. When stimuli are compared, they are compared as wholes and the relation that is internally computed is overall similarity. The difference between the weak and the strong forms of holistic processing is based on the input to the "overall similarity computer." In the weak form, the inputs to the computer are the dimensional or feature specific encoding, but they are not directly accessed. In the strong form, there is no psychological reality of dimensions or features even as inputs to the computer. In nonselective analytic processing, the observer attends to all of the features of a stimulus and uses these properties in making mental comparisons and response decisions. In this mode direct access to dimensional properties is achieved. Overall similarity may guide responses, but it is a consequence rather than the psychological basis for comparison and decision. Kemler Nelson reviews the evidence for each type of processing, and although she acknowledges some difficulty in distinguishing between the nonselective analytic mode and the weak version of the holistic mode, she presents a convincing case that the evidence converges on the primacy of holistic organization in object perception.

Soledad Ballesteros examined the relation between task demands and object perception. She tested the hypothesis that dimensions typically classified by dimensional relations would be classified by overall similarity under conditions that would favor holistic perception. Three reference sets of dimensions were used: size versus shape, length versus orientation, and value versus chroma. Subjects were asked to perform a speeded restricted classification task in which two of three stimuli could be classified systematically according to either overall similarity or dimensional relations. Her task demands included the salience of the relations in the triads, instructions to respond on the basis of either first impressions or precisely, and duration of the stimulus. Generally, value and chroma were classified by overall similarity regardless of demand, whereas size and shape as well as length and orientation yielded fewer dimensional classifications under conditions that favored holistic perception.

The holistic versus analytic issue also has figured prominently in recent discussions of the development of perceived structure and its relation to cognitive development. Several participants in the conference (Kemler Nelson, Shepp, and L. Smith) have been directly involved in establishing the developmental trend that dimensions that are perceived as separable by the older child and adult are perceived as integral by the young child. Two points about this work are important. The first is general. This research, and other developmental work as well, reveals some of the constraints to be placed on theories of adult perception and cognition; it also indicates more specifically the kinds of changes that occur during development. The second is specific and speaks to the development of perceived structure. The research now indicates that the developmental trend from holistic to analytic perception may involve more than a simple change in perceptual organization. Kemler Nelson and Shepp would certainly argue that there are some differences in perceived structure across age; such differences may be more easily detected in speeded tasks. But Smith and Evans show that a model that assumes equivalent object perception across age, combined with a developmental change in attention and valued identity, can speak impressively to the details of unspeeded classification.

The final chapters focus on categories or category learning. Greg Lockhead is concerned with the conditions that affect the placement of category boundaries and how readily a stimulus is assigned to an experimenter-determined category. In both kinds of situations, response variability was directly proportional to the variability of the stimuli. In the just noticeable boundary task, more variable stimulus sets were placed farther apart than were less variable sets. Moreover, the greater the stimulus variability, the greater the variability in boundary judgments. Similarly, in both absolute identification and speeded sorting, an increase in stimulus variability produced greater response variability and resulted in poorer performance. These conclusions hold for several domains of stimuli including intervals of time and space, loudness, sizes of rectangles, and animal names.

Many recent investigations of category learning have used stimuli by which category membership is not usually defined by a criterial attribute but rather by a family resemblance structure that is most appropriately characterized as holistic. This newer work stands in contrast to the traditional approach in concept identification in which membership is based on a criterial attribute within a structure that is more clearly analytic. The chapters by Kemler Nelson, David Smith, and Tom Ward discuss current issues in category learning. Many modern theories of category learning do adopt the view that such learning proceeds through an encoding of the stimuli in a holistic fashion, but as Smith points out such theories are often a curious mixture of holistic and analytic concepts. They are not holistic in either the weak or strong sense of Kemler Nelson, and as some of her evidence suggests category learning is sometimes achieved in the strong sense of holistic processing. What is not entirely clear are the circumstances that control holistic versus analytic organization. Smith describes results where holistic processing occurs when learning is incidental or when subjects are performing a concurrent task, but with no constraints or with speeded practice learning tended to be analytic. In contrast to the views of Kemler Nelson and Smith, Ward argues for an analytical view of category learning and the evidence from his experiments, including incidental learning, show analytical responding. It is perhaps case, as Smith suggests, that some incidental learning situations well as other task demands promote an analytical approach and learning may proceed by components. On balance, however, the holistic view should prevail. Holistic models, particularly ones that assume weak holistic processing, can address learning by components. But it is not clear when learning is unmistakably holistic how an analytic model can address such a finding.

The editors would like to express their appreciation to the many individuals who helped in the preparation of this book. We are grateful to our colleagues for their prompt revisions and responses to editorial chores. We are also indebted to Donald Blough and Peter Eimas for their editorial comments on selected chapters. Kristi Erdal carefully proofread all of the chapters. We are especially indebted to Lara Baskin who assisted in many of the editorial chores including the preparation of the subject index. Finally, thanks are due to Michele Barchi and Janice Viticonte for their assistance in the preparation of the author index and for typing selected manuscripts.

1 OBJECT PERCEPTION AND PHENOMENOLOGY

J. L. Fernández Trespalacios
Universidad Nacional de Educacion a Distancia, Madrid

INTRODUCTION

Research on perception is not, nor has it been, the kind of endeavor that leads either to a corpus of accumulated, firmly established knowledge or to a universally accepted theory and research methodology. On the contrary, there are several theoretical approaches and research methodologies that address the psychology of perception. Typically, the superiority of one approach or methodology over another does not seem to be based on well-established results but on the dominance of certain theories among the members of some groups of scientists.

I have previously documented this view by examining the variety of approaches used by contemporary investigators of visual information processing (Fernández Trespalacios, 1985, 1986), and, more recently, Cutting (1987) has made a similar argument about studies of perception and information.

In general terms, the main research trend currently focuses on the study of information provided in the structure of stimuli. This study is carried out by means of several approaches and methods. Some examples are the theory of structural information and what Cutting (1987) called group theory, according to which the amount of perceptual information provided depends on the number of members in a symmetry group. Other approaches deal with the information supplied by Fourier components in the analysis of spatial frequencies. There are even some attempts to work out an optic system that, by measuring visual angles, should permit a geometrical study of the amount of information supplied by visual stimuli.

Be that as it may, any study of perceptual information should consider the percept or perceptual result. And it is precisely at this stage that a study of the percept in itself seems impossible and seems feasible only by indirect means; that is, by observing reaction time or accuracy in performing a task that presumably defines the perceptual process.

At this point, a somewhat naive question may arise: Why, then, is it not possible to study the percept or perceptual result even if we have some experience about it? We could ask ourselves whether it may be valid (although in a different sense from that in Barry Loewer, 1987) to pass from information to intentionality. Therefore a study of intentionality has been the aim of phenomenology.

Phenomenology is said to be in fashion again. Indeed, philosophy has seen the resurgence of existentialist studies, and sociologists are working on the phenomenological perspectives of sociological analysis. As for psychology, Jennings (1986) wrote about the relationship between psychology and phenomenolgy.

However, the reason that I am dealing with object perception and phenomenology in this chapter is not this revival of phenomenology. I have chosen this topic because I believe that perhaps we could consider two previous steps concerning the scientific study of perception. In the first place, we should go back to the thing itself; we must focus on the percept we experience directly because the study of intentionality is to phenomenology what the study of information is to science. Secondly, we should bracket all our epistemological and scientific prejudices if a study of intentionality is to be made possible.

I should make it clear that my intention is neither to solve the scientific problem of perception, nor to replace a scientific approach by a phenomenological one in the study of perception. My only aim is to clarify the possible relation between a phenomenological and a scientific position in the study of perception. I will try, then, to solve two problems: the problem of mistaking other (cognitive) processes for the perceptual process, and the problem of defining the perceptual process in terms of the performance of a task that, in fact, is not just a perceptual task.

THE PROBLEM OF MISTAKING OTHER (COGNITIVE) PROCESSES FOR THE PERCEPTUAL PROCESS

Modern science has stressed analysis and discrimination. A knowledge of complex things has never been reached through a study of complexity directly, but by analyzing and sifting out the smaller, more simple components. Analysis leads to discrimination, which keeps us from mistaking some things for others. Therefore, the best method of studying perception should be one that allows us to study such a perceptual process—or, if you like, such type of processing—by distinguishing it from other processes or types of processing.

European psychologists, who are phenomenologists or phenomenology-oriented, have always differentiated between perceptual configuration and perceptual categorization. Among the Gestaltists, Köhler tried, as early as 1929, (Köhler, 1929) to make such a distinction. The Belgian psychologist Michotte (1927) observed two stages in the process of apprehension: the presence of a form and the meaning conferring act. According to Michotte, an individual can perceive a form along with its inner structure or figural features without yet knowing what the object is. The French phenomenologist Merleau-Ponty (1945) has written a whole book on this subject. The Italian philosopher Cornelio Fabro (1961), in addressing the phenomenology of perception, pointed out that reality is first seen then classified. Recently, Kanizsa (1985) once more emphasized the radical differences between seeing and thinking. To support his claims, he offered a series of demonstrations based on personal experience—a sort of experimental phenomenology. The demonstrations illustrated perceptions as opposed to learning, the perception of a figure before any categorization, and the different ways in which we complete, perceptually or conceptually, an incomplete object.

It is quite obvious that for all these European psychologists and phenomenologists, the perceptual process consists of the configuration of a visual object as a form distinct from the rest of the scene. Meaning is something conferred to what is previously configured. It is in this sense that these European researchers insist that we can perceive distinct and steady forms without perceptual ambiguity, but still be unable to classify them under any specific category. For example, seeing an object is phenomenologically, and hence originally, a process different from classifying, judging, or inferring.

As opposed to this phenomenological position, one version of traditional psychological empiricism has been to consider perception as an "unconscious inference". To put it briefly, starting from proximal stimulation and with the help of past experiences and cognition, we could solve the problem of configuring the object we perceive with all its characteristic features. In terms of modern American psychology, perception (according to that traditional empiricist idea) must have "top-down" components, as Cutting (1987) recently pointed out. Generally speaking, I would argue that any author (e. g. Rock, 1983) who considers perception as categorization, hypothesis checking, or problem solving does not make a real distinction between a perceptual process and a logical or thought process.

The problem with such ideas on perception is that some rules or principles peculiar to logical or thought processes are also applied to the perceptual process (Brunner, 1957). But if the perceptual process is a "bottom-up" process without reasoning or thought components, and, if the perceptual process consists of the structural organization of sensorial wholes, we should not assume that logical or thought processes are perceptual processes. Such an assumption set would make it even more difficult to know the rules or principles of perceptual organization. As we see later on in this chapter, the aim of analysis and phenomenological description is precisely the discrimination of different processes so that we can study these processes, phenomenologically or scientifically, without any misunderstanding that could impede our understanding of such processes.

THE PROBLEM OF STUDYING PERCEPTION BY MEANS OF STUDYING TASK-PERFORMANCE

Garner's (1981) approach to the study of perception, which has inspired much of the work in this book, is very different from that of the cognitive models I have mentioned so far. This approach, which I have called (following Cutting [1987]) "group theory", also constitutes, as Garner himself points out, an analytic study of perception. This analytic approach does not deny the fact that what we perceive are "unitary wholes", just that the way we perceive these "unitary wholes" can be analyzed. To put it briefly, the issue is to analyze perception—which is naturally holistic—in a scientific way.

Due to the stress placed on the analysis of perceptual stimuli, Garner's approach to the study of perception differs widely from those cognitive ideas referred to in the previous section. However, the "group theory" maintains that it is not plausible, at least in daily life situations, that every explanation of perceptual phenomena is based on the stimulus. A certain degree of intervention from the subjects must be admitted. Perceptual information appears in many forms, and the perceiving subject must choose or combine these forms.

The evidence suggests, however, that the subject's choice or combination is determined by the features of the stimulus. Integral stimuli, for example, are combined in one way, whereas separable stimuli are combined in another. Unfortunately, the usual way to determine whether stimulus dimensions are integral or separable is to study the performances in tasks that make particular demands such as selective or divided attention.

Garner's approach has made considerable contributions to the study of perception, and I do not intend to criticize it. But I do want to consider the difficulties that, from a phenomenological perspective, the study of perception by means of a task-performance analysis may entail.

The epistemological position of phenomenology claims that a truly scientific study of perception should begin with observation of the object itself. The analytical approach to perception to which I am referring, however, maintains a thoroughly opposed epistemological position. It claims that a scientific study of perception requires that we study task performances rather than percepts. Percepts can be studied only by indirect means; we must infer the way percepts act or influence our behavior. This means that the behavior under study must be an indicator of the specific nonbehavioral phenomenon, and it is at this point that a serious problem arises. There is no biunique correspondence between a nonbehavioral phenomenon and a behavior, nor can behavior permit a study of all the characteristics belonging to the nonbehavioral phenomenon.

A phenomenological position necessarily differs from the analytic approach to perception; not because the latter is analytic and phenomenology is not, but because the aim of phenomenology is a direct study of perception, whereas the aim of the analytic approach is a direct study of task performance—that is, of behaviors. The phenomenological method is, in its essence, analytical. To define an object phenomenologically requires analysis. This does not mean that phenomenological psychologists perform all the necessary analyses, but it cannot be said that phenomenological methods reject analysis. What phenomenology rejects is not analysis, but the position of natural scientists who consider as subjective every datum from experience that cannot be publicly observed, and who only admit nonbehavioral phenomena as an explanation to behavioral phenomena, but not considered in themselves.

Nevertheless, no one can deny the importance of the analysis of stimulus features that is obtained through an analytic approach. In my opinion, it has been most relevant to have positively defined configurational features as relations between component features. Thus, instead of defining the features of the stimulus in themselves, they are defined according to the type of processing or perception to which they lead. But this involves an evaluation of the role that the features of the stimulus play on the perceptual result. Such an evaluation is obtained by means of converging operations. The reason for this is not only the need to prove that different performances might be due to different features in the stimulus, but also that these differences in performance measure the degree to which such differences are the result of configurational features in the stimulus and not of component features; configurational features coexist with component ones.

In other words, it is difficult to prove that a certain type of processing or perception is the result of a certain configurational feature. It is with this aim that converging operations are used.

But the problem lies in the fact that such converging operations are obtained by means of performing very different tasks. If we are dealing with a perceptual phenomenon, the tasks must define the phenomenon, and they must belong to this phenomenon and it alone. Is this the case with classification tasks, same–different tasks, and other tasks commonly used in this line of research? Phenomenologists think it is not. Classification, for instance, involves a categorization not only specific to the perceptual process, but to cognitive processes as well. In short, according to phenomenology, this method of studying perception confounds what it is and what it is not. This is precisely what phenomenological analysis tries to avoid, and the reason that it points to two basic aims: to give a discrete definition of what perception is, and to study the process directly.

THE ECOLOGIC ALTERNATIVE

It is funny that in his autobiography, Gibson eventually compares himself with a phenomenologist. Gibson (1967) said that the Belgian psychologist Albert Michotte, a phenomenologist, had reached the same conclusions as himself: "We got the same results. That is what counts" (p. 143). I must confess that such a statement stirs my curiosity; how is it possible that Gibson reached the same conclusions as a phenomenologist?

I will not address the correctness or incorrectness of Gibson's views. I will just try to make clear what Gibson meant by saying that he and Michotte have obtained the same results. Nor will I try to give a full explanation of it as if my intention was to prove a thesis. My only aim is to express what, in my opinion, Gibson meant.

To begin with, Gibson's aforementioned statement cannot be understood in the sense that he is a phenomenologist. Phenomenology starts from the study of the phenomena of personal experience. But Gibson, as I see it, considers consciousness as something parallel, an epiphenomenon, and not able to determine our behavior. Hence, consciousness is not worthy of study. In this respect, Gibson's position is closely related to behaviorism. According to Skinner (1985), if perception is a representation of consciousness, "we do not see the world, we see copies of it" (p. 292). To see copies of the world instead of the world itself is most opposed to Gibson's position. As a result, consciousness is to be disregarded when we study perception. Quite obviously, a phenomenologist does not consider consciousness as exclusively a representation, but as an experience of the world, although direct experience plays an all-important role in phenomenology.

According to the theory of direct perception, information is not obtained from, or built upon, data. Data constitute the information itself. Perceptual stimuli are informational stimuli, not data on which information can be elaborated following a particular procedure. Perceptual organization is originally in the stimulus, in reality. That is why the theory of direct perception is an ecological approach.

But what does the ecological approach mean? It means that perceptual organization and its contents are originally in the environment. But not in a physical one; that is, not the environment "in itself", but the ecological one; in other words, the environment "for itself", for the animal living in it. What we perceive are "affordances", and these we perceive directly. What is perceived and who perceives are aspects of the same reality, a result of evolution.

Direct perception permits a "return to things themselves", which is the basis of a phenomenological position, albeit following different ways from that of the ecological approach. Furthermore, according to the ecological approach, the environment is a "for the animal" environment, not a physical "in itself" environment. In phenomenology, the perceptual object is a "for itself", not an "in itself". The world would be the "in itself", and the "for itself" would be the direct experience of that world,—consciousness considered *noematically*. For Gibson (1979), the "in itself" is the physical world, the "for itself" is the ecological environment in its relation to the perceptor as well as to what is perceived. For phenomenology, the "in itself" is the world, the "for itself" is the experience of the world in its relation to the perceptor as well as to what is perceived.

From these emphases Gibson's statement referred to at the beginning of this section becomes understandable. In my opinion, we could also understand why phenomenology and the theory of direct perception find it so difficult to be adapted to experimental techniques. Perceptual organization, along with its rules and principles, is, for Gibson, something belonging to the field of ecological physics, whereas for phenomenology it belongs to direct experience as it appears phenomenologically in consciousness. Maybe the same results can be reached from apparently very different positions.

GESTALT PSYCHOLOGY AND PHENOMENOLOGY

What is a phenomenological psychology of perception? Metelli (1982) pointed out that the first feature of the investigations on perception carried out by the Gestalt psychologists is the need for observation and phenomenological description. The Gestalt school took the phenomenon according to its phenomenological description, but explained it in terms of the neural activity supposed to underlie the perceptual process.

In short, if the approach of information processing starts from the task in an attempt to observe the process indirectly, the Gestalt point of departure was the phenomenon in order to describe the process and find a neurophysiological explanation. This focus on a phenomenal description has led to the conclusion that Gestalt psychology's methods were phenomenological. This methodology, according to Boring (1942), has been retrospectively called "experimental phenomenology". But the question remains: Was Gestalt psychology based on phenomenology?

The relationship between Gestalt psychology and phenomenology cannot be denied. Disregarding historical connections the demonstrations of the perceptual phenomena that they developed can be taken as an application of the phenomenological method. Thus, Gestalt psychologists were able to describe perceptual phenomena, discover some new ones, offer solutions to those problems that seemed unsolvable, and describe the principles regulating such phenomena. All this was done by providing phenomenological demonstrations.

However, phenomenology was only a point of departure for Gestaltists. The Gestalt school did not elaborate a philosophy comparable to the French philosopher Merleau-Ponty's (1945) phenomenology of perception. Gestaltists wanted to make a science, a scientific psychology like any other natural science. But the method applied to natural sciences has not been phenomenology. What Gestalt psychology did was to start from the phenomenon and try to build on it a scientific psychology of perception. For this reason, as I have previously asserted (Fernández Trespalacios 1974), Gestalt psychology's theoretical basis is not phenomenology.

Neither do Gestalt psychology's basic scientific principles hold any relation to phenomenology, nor is the Gestalt view a philosophical doctrine; nor is its ultimate theoretical reference framework phenomenological philosophy. Let us consider briefly each of these points.

The basic scientific principles of Gestalt psychology are not related to phenomenology. That is made clear in three fundamental points of Gestalt psychology: (a) its holistic position as opposed to mentalistic elementalism, (b) its attitude toward introspection, and (c) its claim of autochthonous, determinant principles of perception previous to the observer's past experience.

Gestalt psychology's opposition to sensorial elementalism was due to the belief that sensations or other psychic elements do not exist as real phenomena; that is, they can not be directly observed, but only indirectly as artificial, sophisticated elaborations. Gestaltist do not reject analysis as a technique of the scientific method; they affirm that analysis should reach the limit of real phenomena. It is in this sense that we must understand Köhler's (1969) complaint against Ebbinghaus because the latter admitted the existence of psychological atoms, although he confessed uncertainty that such atoms were authentic data.

As a result, Gestalt psychologists disregarded sensorial atoms and searched for other principles to explain perception. They believed to have found these principles in those dynamic fields in which energies are organized; these fields have been studied in the physics of electricity. For Gestaltists, energy fields—and not sensorial atoms—provide the principles to explain perceptual phenomena, among which the Gestalt school chose the "phi phenomenon" as a prototype.

Gestalt psychologists criticized introspectionists because they did not abide by direct experience but restricted it to only what was acceptable in terms of their epistemological prejudices, that is, Cartesian subjectivism and objectivism.

For Gestalt psychologists, the introspectionist's position was a philosophical rather than a scientific one, and that is the reason that they adopted direct experience and disregarded the epistemological problem of subjectiveness and objectiveness. When Wertheimer (1925/1938) spoke of a new method for psychology, he openly referred to the new science, not to any philosophical issue. Clearly, what drew the attention of Gestalt psychologists concerning the method was a scientific alternative—dynamic fields instead of mechanic atoms—, and not a philosophical alternative.

Finally, consider the existence of some principles that determine perception and are previous to past experience. To do so, we must once more resort to those dynamic principles of energy physics. Gestalt psychologists have never used the concept of innate as something that depends on the genetic code. Complex activities, even the genetic activity itself, are governed by the simpler laws of physics and chemistry. Evolution implies a change in all the universe, but, in order for something to change, it is necessary—as Köhler (1969) pointed out—that something remains the same. Biological beings change by evolution, but, in all of them, the laws of physics remain unchanged.

Consequently, Gestalt psychologists intend to explain some complex phenomena and organizational processes—such as perceptual phenomena—by means of more simple, basic principles that undergo no change throughout evolution; that is, by means of principles ruling the physical dynamics of energy fields.

I believe that the foregoing arguments show quite clearly that the basic principle of Gestalt theory is not based on phenomenological philosophy but on physical science; more precisely, on the physics of electricity, which, at the beginning of this century, showed a spectacular development.

All these arguments also prove the second statement that was made at the beginning of this chapter, namely, that Gestalt psychology is not a philosophical doctrine. However, Gurwitsch (1957) stated that Gestalt theoretical principles are contained in phenomenology. Of course, Gestalt psychologists maintained a close relationship with many phenomenological philosophers, but this does not prove that Gestalt psychology is in fact a philosophical doctrine; that is perhaps why Gurwitsch does not give much importance to this association. The main argument alleged is that Gestalt psychologists denied the "constancy hypothesis", a position that, for Gurwitsch, implies a phenomenological reduction. But, by denying the "constancy hypothesis", Gestaltists denied a mechanistic association. This view cannot be taken as a phenomenological reduction, because Gestaltists bracket neither real physical objects— they speak of physical *gestalten*—nor natural science; in fact, their position is the opposite, as we have previously seen.

But, most of all, for Gestalt psychology to be a phenomenological psychology, it should be reduced to a merely descriptive level and must abandon any sort of explanation. This is not the case, however, since the "constancy hypothesis" is replaced by the "isomorphism hypotheses", by means of which they give a neurphysiological explanation to perceptual phenomena.

Finally, we can say that Gestalt theory has, as any other theory, an ultimate philosophical reference framework. But, to confirm my third statement about Gestalt psychology, it is not a phenomenological philosophy. Instead, the framework is the dynamicist philosophy developed by Leibnitz between the 17th and 18th centuries, and not the phenomenological one developed by Husserl at the beginning of this century. Boring, as early as 1929 (Boring, 1929), referred to the relation between Gestalt psychology and Leibnitz's philosophy. In fact, what is basic for Leibnitz is energy, or dynamic physics. But it is through this physics that Leibnitz's influence reaches Gestalt psychology. For Leibnitz, it is energy that remains throughout its many forms, not a number of atoms and the quantity of movement as advocated by Cartesian mechanism. Therefore, Gestalt psychology's theory of dynamic fields has Leibnitz as its antecedent and ultimate source.

What I have said is also true for the present Gestalt scientific attitude. Gestalt theory aims to be a scientific theory and, as such, holds no relation with phenomenology. But, before this scientific attitude, Gestalt psychology had a phenomenological attitude, which consisted in the description of the phenomena under study. The description of the "phi phenomenon" or the principles of perceptual organization is phenomenological. Contemporary science has defended an exact correspondence between the stimulus and elemental perception as well as a constant connection between them. But direct experience—the phenomenon—shows, for example, that two objectively equal figures are perceived as different if some auxiliary lines are added. Gestalt psychologists abided by direct experience and did not reject it searching for explanations *ad hoc* in the influence of cognitive processes, for example, evaluating, thinking, and so on.

But phenomenological description was just a point of departure. Phenomenology was immediately abandoned by Gestaltist who then moved on to science. The neurophysiological explanation they gave to phenomena or direct experience aimed to be a scientific one. Surprisingly, Gestalt psychology was quite successful in its first aim, but not in the second one. Their success is the reason that those phenomena described by Gestaltists have been, and still are, so interesting to most of the psychologists who study perception.

SOME REMARKS ON THE PHENOMENOLOGICAL METHOD

A description of the phenomenological method is too extensive and complex to be summed up briefly. Therefore, I do not make such an attempt, but just offer some remarks on those points of phenomenological method relevant to my purpose.

Although the phenomenological method has several interpretations, the essence of the method is the "return to things themselves"; that is, things are not studied either by means of signs or as a series of epistemological or scientific prejudices that make one see them according to one's subjective experience. Rather things must be studied in their purity, the way they appear.

Perception in its purity shows itself in direct experience. But, in order to achieve this experience, a strategy is necessary. This strategy consists of *reduction*. The phenomenological method applies several types of reduction, but here I am dealing only with phenomenological reduction.

In this phenomenological reduction, there is a first step that is negative, and consists of the "epoché," or bracketing. What is bracketed?

Everything that is not the thing itself: every epistemological position, every scientific theory, every attitude accepting or not accepting the natural existence of the world, and all the artificial introspections of consciousness. It is necessary to point out that the "epoché" does not consist of doubts about science or the existence of the world, but in bracketing our attitudes towards science, epistemology, philosophy, what we think about the world, and so one.

But the "epoché", disregarding everything but the phenomenon itself, gives the method a positive character; that is, it makes us limit ourselves to the thing itself (not to the essence of the thing, because that would be the result of aeidetic reduction, and would lead us to a philosophical position).

But reduction, as San Martín (1986) pointed out, means not only to limit oneself to the thing, but also to adopt a new attitude that implies our seeing the phenomenon originally. To observe the origins is to discover the operations of which the phenomenon itself consists.

We can analyze these operations by distinguishing what is noematic in the phenomenon (that is, the operant intentionality) from what is noetic (that is, subject's constructive activity). Thus, in the study of perception, reduction leads us also to analyze what is the perceptual process in the phenomenon, and to make it explicit.

Therefore, by means of reduction, the aim of the phenomenological method is to study perception as it appears in immediate experience. To this purpose, reduction brackets the prejudice that science requires perception to be studied indirectly through behavior. It also brackets the subjectivism of introspection, because we do not have to deal with an individual's subjective experience, a time, a culture or a race. Neither must we deal with a noetic analysis that explains perception in terms of a subject's constructive activity. In phenomenology, the issue is to describe the experienced world, whereas for introspectionist subjectivism, the main point is to build up the world with the help of sensorial data.

The phenomenological attitude is not subjectivist, because it is not a noetic analysis of the way in which the subject shapes what is perceived and he or she who perceives. But we cannot say either that the phenomenological attitude is empiricism or objectivism, because it does not reject direct experience. It is a noematic attitude and its point of departure is our life in this world. The world is experienced; it is not built up according to a certain type of knowledge. But neither am I opposed to the world as if I were an alien to it. Only the world pre-exists, but I am I in the world. There is no inner man, nor outer world; the man is man in the world.

I feel compelled to draw your attention once more to the parallelism between the phenomenological attitude and the ecological approach in the study of perception. Perhaps the principal difference between them lies in the fact that phenomenology begins with the need for leaving behind subjectivism and objectivism in philosophy, whereas the ecological approach starts from the scientific theory of evolution as an origin of the world and the animal. For this reason, phenomenology studies intentionality. I do not refer to the intentionality of the fact—such as the intention of an opinion or of an act of will—, but rather to the operant intentionality; that is, the unity of world and man in life. This is the reason that intentionality is defined by saying that every consciousness is consciousness of something. We are dealing with our experience, our direct experience, before any activity of cognitive processes.

The phenomenological method—whose relation with psychology has been characterized by Kruger (1981), and Weintraub (1975), among others—plays a fundamental role in the study of perception. It does so by leading us to study perception itself rather than behavioral indicators. Moreover because the phenomonological description makes perception explicit, perception is distinguished from cognitive processes which are not perceptual.

SCIENTIFIC PSYCHOLOGY AND PHENOMENOLOGY

Science considers the physical as something natural and, hence, governed by natural laws. For this reason, natural science has attempted to reduce mental events to physical ones. Many scientists have based their reduction of every sort of event to the level of physical events, intending to study the mental event by means of the experimental study of a physical event. For instance, many psychologists study perception by studying performances in particular kinds of tasks.

Phenomenological philosophy reacted strongly against this naturalistic perspective. As a result of this reaction, phenomenological philosophy has accused scientific psychology of studying behaviors instead of perception. Phenomenologists have criticized the use of reaction time to study mental processes, and have argued that those psychologists study the characteristics of responses, but not immediate experience. Consequently, these philosophers have advocated the phenomenological method to study immediate experience.

But that which is valid for philosophical thinking cannot be used in experimental science, and philosophy cannot replace science in the study of perception. The question, at least in regard to the study of perception, is to find a fruitful relation between scientific psychology and the phenomenological method. As Weintraub (1975) has pointed out:

"For me, the phenomenological aspects are an appealing aspect of the study of perception. . . . For the investigators involved, I propose the title, Experimental Phenomenologist" (p. 281).

Phenomenology is not opposed to experimental research in psychology. Rather it aims to use immediate experience as the ultimate reference, and to clarify the experimental study of perception. For a long time, it was assumed that the environment provided sensory organs with messages processed in such a way that, once decoded, their original texts were reproduced in the perceiver. This process was not attributed to direct experience but to the constancy hypothesis; that is, the exact correspondence between the external stimulus and the percept. Gestalt psychology argued that such an exact correspondence was against direct experience. Two objectively equal lines can be perceived as different in some contexts. Therefore, Gestaltists disregarded elements or sensations to fix their attention on perceptual organization. In this sense, and from a phenomenological position, Merleau-Ponty (1945) pointed out that the capacity of being affected by context is a feature peculiar to what is perceived. Experimental psychology must study those regularities according to which perception is modeled, and must discover the appropriate principles. But it is necessary to work on perception itself, and to distinguish the perceptual process from any other processes. Phenomenological description is required to achieve these ends.

In this sense, the objective of phenomenology is to describe and clearly define perception as a direct experience and as a process different from other processes. Contemporary experimental psychologists usually begin their arguments by admitting the phenomenological aspects of perceptual experience, but they do not bother to give a phenomenological description of the process; therefore, when they want to describe a process by means of a task, they do not base their arguments on the phenomenological analysis.

This last point is really an urgent and important one. If the experimental tasks under study do not define perception, mistaking other processes for the perceptual process, an experimental study of perception will be defective from the start. Experimental techniques may be highly sophisticated, but, if they are not really applied to the study of perception but to the performance that confounds perception and other processes, we will face an endless chain of investigations that are radically wrong. Consequently, we will be unable to acquire a scientific knowledge of perception. It is therefore most urgent to pay attention to the phenomenological aspects of perception. This is perhaps what Weintraub (1975) meant when he called for the investigation of those aspects of perception, which he calls experimental phenomenology.

Clearly, the point is not to replace experimental psychology by phenomenological psychology, but to apply the phenomenological method that can lay the foundations of the experimental study of perception. Such an application does not mean a return to introspectionism or subjectivism, because the question is neither to study an individual's contents of consciousness here and now, nor to base perception on the subject's constructive activity, but to describe the basic, particular characteristics of percepts and of the perceptual process.

CONCLUSIONS

From the foregoing arguments, it follows that there are some aspects of perception that require a phenomenological analysis. Those who accept this view believe that the study of perception demands an authentic experimental phenomenology. The basic role of this phenomenology would be not only to describe what is perceived, but also, to define clearly and discretely the nature of the perceptual process.

From a phenomenological-philosophical position, Merleau-Ponty (1945) specified this objective. According to the French philosopher, we have long thought to know what perceiving is, but now we realize that defining perception is a problem. Perhaps we have not managed to solve this problem yet. If this is the case, instead of using behavioral indicators to reveal the perceptual process, it would be necessary—in terms of phenomenology—to go back to those experiences we call perception in order to obtain a definition.

The phenomenological analysis has yielded some fruits in this respect. Merleau-Ponty (1945) pointed out that pure sensations are imperceptible, because qualities are never experienced immediately. For instance, we cannot perceive "red," but the "furry red" of a rug. Kanizsa (1985), with the help of phenomenological data, has recently shown that "seeing" and "thinking" work according to different rules. Therefore, it is necessary to distinguish the perceptual process from the thinking process. Previously Gestaltists took a positive step toward a phenomenological definition of perception by pointing out that simple feature-defined perception is not the mere sensation, but the figure–background structure. We find an example of the distinction between perception and thought in the so-called impossible figures. Kanizsa (1979) has phenomenologically shown that Penrose and Penrose's impossibles figures (1958) are impossible only for thought, but not for perception. Accordingly, these figures should be considered as unthinkable rather than perceptually impossible. In this vein, our experiments have shown that subjects with diminished thought, but with normal perception, make a lot of mistakes when considering Penrose and Penrose's figures as impossible; the rate of mistakes is higher for these subjects than the rate for those who do not show diminished thought. We have found this effect in schizophrenics (Fernández Trespalacios, Luna, & Bermúdez, 1979) and in subjects with a serious school retardation (Fernández Trespalacios & Grzib, 1980).

But, if perceiving and thinking differ phenomenologically, and we can get experimental results to support phenomenological analyses, then we can achieve a very important conclusion in the study of perception; namely, that those tasks used as behavioral indicators of perception cannot be the same ones as the behavioral indicators of thinking. In other words, if the task performed by the subject does not define perception and only perception, we will not be able to know which process is generating the results we obtain.

A distinction between perceptual processes and other processes is absolutely necessary if a scientific study of perception is to be made possible. Scientific research has always obtained an important benefit not only from comparing the similarities between perception and other processes, but also from specifying the differences between them.

In the study of perception, it seems necessary to take three consecutive steps: to describe, in a phenomenological way, the object under study; to make an experimental investigation of its functional relations; and, finally, to formulate a theory that serves as an explanation. The first of these three steps is phenomenological analysis.

ACKNOWLEDGMENT

I am grateful to Professor Bryan E. Shepp for the comments to the early version of the manuscript.

REFERENCES

Boring, E. G. (1929). *History of experimental psychology*. New York: Appleton.
Boring, E. G. (1942). *Sensation and Perception in the history of experimental psychology*. New York: Appleton-Century-Crofts.
Bruner, J. (1957). On perceptual readiness. *Psychological Review, 64*, 123–152.
Cutting, J. E. (1987). Perception and information. *Annual Review of Psychology, 38*, 61–90.
Fabro, C. (1961). *La fenomenologia della percezione (2nd ed.)*. Brescia: Morcelliana.
Fernández Trespalacios, J. L. (1974). *El fundamento teórico de la Gestalt*. Madrid: Fragua.
Fernández Trespalacios, J. L. (1985). Parametros estimulares en el estudio de la perception. In J. Mayor (Ed.), *Actividad humana y procesos cognitivos* (pp. 65–79). Madrid: Alhambra Universidad.

Fernández Trespalacios, J. L. (1986). *Psicología general I*. Madrid: Gráficas Maravillas.
Fernández Trespalacios, J. L., Luna, M. D., & Bermúdez, J. (1979). *Modificatión psicológica de la conducta perceptual en esquizofrénicos*. Madrid. Universidad Nacional de Educación a Distancia.
Fernández Trespalacios, J. L., & Grzib, G. (1980). Modificación de conducta mediante las leyes perceptuales. *Informe del Instituto de Ciencias de la Educación de la Universidad Nacional de Educación a Distancia*. Madrid.
Garner, W. R. (1981). The analysis of unanalyzed perceptions. In M. Kubovy & J.R. Pomerantz (Eds.), *Perceptual organization (pp. 119–139)*. Hillsdale, New Jersey: Lawrence Erlbaum Associates.
Gibson, J. J. (1967). Autobiography. In E.G. Boring & G. Lindzey (Eds.), *A history of psychology in autobiography*. Volume 5. (pp. 127–143) New York: Appleton-Century-Crofts.
Gibson, J. J. (1979). *The ecological approach to visual perception*. Boston: Houghton Mifflin.
Gurwitsch, A. (1957). *Théorie du champ de la conscience*. Paris: Desclée de Brouwer.
Jennings, J. L. (1986). The forgotten distinction between psychology and phenomenology. *American Psychologist, 41*, 1231–1240.
Kanizsa, G. (1979). *Organization in vision*. New York: Praeger.
Kanizsa, G. (1985). Seeing and thinking. *Acta Psychologica, 59*, 23–33.
Köhler, W. (1929). *Gestalt psychology*. New York: Liveright.
Köhler, W. (1969). *The task of gestalt psychology*. Princeton: Princeton University Press.
Kruger, D. (1981). *An introduction to phenomenological psychology*. Pittsburgh: Duquesne University Press.
Loewer, B. (1987). From information to intentionality. *Synthese, 70*, 287–317.
Merleau-Ponty, M. (1945). *Phénoménologie de la perception*. Paris: Gallimard.
Metelli, F. (1982). Some characteristics of gestalt-oriented research in perception. In J. Beck (Ed.), *Organization and representation in perception* (pp. 219–233). Hillsdale, New Jersey: Lawrence Erlbaum Associates.
Michotte, A. (1927). Rapport sur la perception des formes. *Proceedings and papers of the VIII International Congress of Psychology* (166–175). Groningen, Netherlands.
Penrose, L. S., & Penrose, R. (1958). Impossible objects: A special type of illusion. *British Journal of Psychology, 49*, 31–33.
Rock, I. (1983). *The logic of perception*. Cambridge, MA: MIT Press.
San Martín, J. (1986). *La estructura del método fenomenológico*. Madrid: Universidad Nacional de Educación a Distancia.
Skinner. B. F. (1985). Cognitive science and behaviorism. *British Journal of Psychology, 76*, 291–301.
Weintraub, D. J. (1975). Perception. *Annual Review of Psychology, 26*, 263–289.
Wertheimer, M. (1938). Gestalt theory. In W.D. Ellis (Ed. and Trans.) *A source book of Gestalt Psychology* (pp. 1–11). London. Routledge and Kegan Paul Ltd. (Über Gestalttheorie [an address before the Kant Society] Erlaugen, West Germany, 1925).

2 SPATIAL PARALLELISM IN THE PROCESSING OF LINES, LETTERS, AND LEXICALITY

Howard E. Egeth
Charles L. Folk
Paul A. Mullin
The Johns Hopkins University

INTRODUCTION

Human vision appears to operate in two rather different modes. One involves processing that requires the allocation of cognitive resources (i.e., attention). This "attentive" mode is generally assumed to operate in a serial fashion. The other mode involves processing that can proceed independently of cognitive resources and in a spatially parallel fashion. Preattentive processing occurs first and provides the basic input for further attentive processing.

The characterization of the preattentive mode as spatially parallel and unlimited in capacity seems to be widely accepted. What is controversial, however, is the functional role that preattention plays in visual processing. According to early selection theorists, preattention segregates the visual field into perceptual units that are then operated on by focal attentive processes to achieve full analysis and interpretation (e.g., Broadbent, 1971; Neisser, 1967, Treisman, 1964). In contrast, late selection theorists argue that preattentive processing permits full semantic analysis of information in the visual field (e.g., Deutsch & Deutsch, 1963; Duncan, 1980; Norman, 1968). On this account, capacity is limited for behavioral action (e.g., Keele, 1973), or for awareness (e.g., Duncan, 1980), but *not* for the derivation of form or meaning.

The purpose of this chapter is to explore performance in a variety of different stimulus-task domains in an effort to clarify the functional role of preattentive processing. We begin with brief reviews of the literature concerning three widely studied tasks: (a) low-level tasks involving the detection or discrimination of simple visual features, (b) tasks in which a correct response requires the integration of information from two or more separable features, and (c) tasks in which responses are dependent on meaning. We then provide a more intensive and focused discussion of recent research in our laboratory, which has been concerned with the first and third of the aforementioned topics.

BACKGROUND

Simple Visual Features

A substantial literature suggests that highly discriminable feature differences can be processed in parallel across the visual field. Some of the evidence for this conclusion comes from studies of visual search in which subjects are asked to determine whether or not a display contains a specific target element where the target, when it is present, differs from the remaining elements of the display with respect to a single simple feature (e.g., a red target among blue nontargets; a horizontal line segment among vertical line segments). Several studies have shown that the time required to detect the presence of such a target is virtually independent of the number of nontargets that are present (e.g., Egeth, Jonides, & Wall, 1972, Exp. 2; Egeth, Virzi, & Garbart, 1984; Treisman & Gelade, 1980; Treisman & Souther, 1985). Additional evidence comes from studies of *same–different* discriminations. In discrimination tasks, subjects are typically instructed to indicate if all of a set of stimuli are the same or whether one of them is different. Several studies have shown that with stimuli defined in terms of simple features, the time to respond *same* or *different* is essentially independent of the number of stimuli in the display (e.g., Connor, 1972; Donderi & Zelnicker, 1969; Egeth, Jonides, & Wall, 1972, Exp. 1).

We should note here that it can be a difficult matter to decide whether processing is parallel or serial. As Townsend has pointed out in a series of important papers (e.g., Snodgrass & Townsend, 1980; Townsend, 1971; 1972), certain limited-capacity parallel models can produce mean reaction time (RT) predictions that are indistinguishable from those for serial models. However, it is difficult for a psychologically plausible serial model to account for data that show mean RT to be independent of the number of stimuli. It is for this reason that we have (conservatively) adopted as one signature of a parallel process independence of RT and display size.

Some additional evidence concerning processing mode is available from another paradigm in which redundant targets are displayed. Several studies have shown that when all stimuli are targets, the time required to identify a target decreases as the number of targets present in a display is increased (e.g., Van der Heijden, 1975; Van der Heijden, La Heij, & Boer, 1983). In the study by Van der Heijden et al (1983), subjects had to discriminate Es from Fs; this task might well be construed as requiring the determination of whether a simple feature (a horizontal line segment at the bottom of the character) was present or absent. Subjects had to press a response key when one or more Es were present and refrain from responding when one or more Fs were present. (Es and Fs were never shown on the same display.) Subjects responded most slowly to one-element displays, somewhat faster to two-element displays, and most quickly to three-element displays. Such a redundancy gain is compatible with self-terminating processing models, but not those that assume exhaustive processing. It also appears to be incompatible with models that assume limited-capacity processing (this includes the entire class of serial models). In fact, what remains plausible in the face of this result is a parallel, self-terminating, unlimited capacity model. However, Snodgrass and Townsend (1980) suggested that the word "unlimited" may be too strong. It may be possible to devise parallel models with some degree of capacity limitation that could still predict a redundancy gain. However, the degree of limitation would have to be less than that of two well-known parallel models that cannot predict a redundancy gain. One of these assumes a fixed capacity that is divided among the target elements present on a trial; the other is similar except that as targets finish processing, capacity that was devoted to them is reallocated to the remaining items. For the sake of simplicity, in the remainder of this paper we interpret a redundancy gain to mean that capacity is unlimited; however, it should be understood that some degree of capacity limitation may still be compatible with the obtained results. This is an issue that will have to be addressed in further, more detailed, research.

The preceding studies demonstrate a capacity for parallel processing of featural information. When does parallel processing of featural information *not* obtain? One circumstance in which parallel processing may not occur involves the special case where the target of search is distinguished by the *absence* of a feature that is present in all of the nontargets (Treisman & Souther, 1985; see also Neisser, 1963). Thus, if the target is a circle with an intersecting line (like the tail of a Q) in a background of plain circles, search time is independent of the number of nontarget plain circles. But, if the target is a plain circle and the nontargets are all circles with intersecting lines, then search time increases with the number of nontargets. Treisman and Souther (1985) show how this interesting asymmetry can be accounted for in terms of feature-integration theory (see the following section), which assumes parallel processing of featural information. Thus, this finding does not really challenge the general conclusions concerning attentive and preattentive processing discussed earlier in this chapter.

A more provocative failure to obtain evidence for parallel processing of feature information was reported by Sagi and Julesz (1985a; see also 1985b). They examined the nature of processing in three different tasks. One, like several of the tasks described earlier, required a *same–different* discrimination; the stimuli to be discriminated were horizontal and vertical line segments. The displays consisted of a few "targets" (the horizontal and vertical line segments) embedded in a texture composed of diagonal line segments that were all oriented in the same direction. Subjects had to indicate whether all of the targets were of the same orientation (all horizontal or all vertical) or whether one of them was in a different orientation (e.g., one vertical among three horizontal). Stimuli were presented briefly and followed by a pattern mask. Performance was measured in terms of accuracy at different stimulus onset asynchronies (SOAs). For the discrimination task, the SOA required to achieve 95% accuracy increased linearly with the number of targets; the mean slope was 16.6 ms per target element. (At the end of the paper it was briefly mentioned that a similar set of results had been obtained in the color domain.) In striking contrast to the studies discussed earlier, Sagi and Julesz (1985a) concluded, on the basis of these findings, that discrimination, even of highly discriminable single features, is *not* a spatially parallel process, but is instead accomplished serially. It is important to recognize that their findings about discrimination cannot be dismissed on the grounds that orientation discrimination is difficult and cannot be handled preattentively. There is, in fact, a substantial body of evidence indicating that the required discrimination is a particularly easy one (e.g., Beck & Ambler, 1972; Olson & Attneave, 1970; Pomerantz & Sager, 1976).

The procedures employed by Sagi and Julesz differ in possibly important respects from those used in most of the experiments mentioned earlier. It is important to note that the inclusion of the background diagonals may change the nature of the task. In an ordinary discrimination task, the stimuli would contain just horizontals and/or verticals; the subject can respond *different* as soon as any difference in orientation is noted. When background line segments are introduced, it is no longer possible to respond *different* as soon as a difference in orientation is noticed because all targets differ from the background in orientation. We presume that it is for this reason that Sagi and Julesz say that their task requires *identification* of individual targets.

One of the chief purposes of the empirical research described in this chapter is to attempt to clarify the reason(s) for the disparity between the findings of Sagi and Julesz and those of other investigators.

Conjunctively Defined Targets

There is a well-known series of studies by Treisman and her colleagues that has been interpreted as demonstrating serial processing when subjects search for a target defined as a conjunction of features (e.g., Treisman & Gelade, 1980; Treisman, Sykes, & Gelade, 1977). Thus if targets are defined as red squares and the nontargets are a mix of red circles and blue squares, reaction time will increase markedly with the number of items in the display. The increase for negative (target absent) RTs is about twice as great as for positive (target present) RTs, a finding that implies that the search is self-terminating.

Treisman's account of these results (and of the finding of parallel processing for simple features) is known as feature-integration theory. According to Treisman and Gelade (1980), the basic idea is that:

> . . . features are registered early, automatically, and in parallel across the visual field, while objects are identified separately and only at a later stage, which requires focal attention. We assume that the visual scene is initially coded along a number of separable dimensions, such as color, orientation, spatial frequency, brightness, direction of movement. In order to recombine these separate representations and to ensure the correct synthesis of features for each object in a complex display, stimulus locations are processed serially with focal attention. (p. 98)

The finding that RT for conjunctively defined targets is strongly dependent on display size is easy to replicate (e.g., Quinlan & Humphreys, 1987). However, in view of recent findings, the interpretation of this finding is not as straightforward as when feature-integration was first proposed. Pashler (1987) found that the 2:1 ratio of negative to positive slopes is due to a range effect involving display size. When small display sizes (up to eight elements) are used, the display-size functions are parallel (see also Houck & Hoffman, 1986 for a similar result). This might suggest that search is serial and exhaustive, but additional data (a reduction of positive RT when redundant targets were added to displays) suggests that search is not exhaustive here. The data appear to be consistent with a limited-capacity parallel processing model of the self-terminating variety. Pashler proposes that when large displays are presented, subjects may search clumps of up to eight items at a time. The parallel self-terminating within-clump searches are embedded in a molar serial search process.

There are some additional problems for feature-integration theory. For one, not all combinations of (seemingly separable) features yield the expected result. Nakayama and Silverman (1986) examined performance with the dimensions of motion and color; RT increased with display size. However, they also found that when one of the dimensions in a conjunctive search is stereo disparity and the other is either color or motion, RT does *not* increase with display size. Another problem is raised by the results of a study by Egeth, Virzi, and Garbart (1984), who showed that subjects to not search unselectively and serially through display elements in an effort to find the target; there is evidence that they search through subsets of stimuli (e.g., all the red items) and ignore other subsets. Thus, many stimuli may be rejected in parallel (see also Treisman, 1985).

Finally, there are two reports that it is possible to correctly conjoin features even under circumstances where it is reasonable to assume that focal attention has not been brought to bear (Allport, Tipper, & Chmiel, 1985; Houck & Hoffman, 1986).

A simple summary statement seems imprudent at this time; search for conjunctively defined targets seems more complex than is suggested by Treisman's feature integration theory, but it is not yet clear what new theory will prevail.

Semantic Tasks

The question at issue in this section is whether or not it is possible to apprehend the meanings of two or more stimuli in parallel. More specifically, our inquiry is focused on what should be the most demanding stimulus domain—alphanumeric symbols and words. When one deals with natural stimuli from the real world, it is at least possible that meaning is carried directly by just a few perceptual attributes. For example, teeth, claws, and thorns are all sharp; this may directly signify "danger" or some other such meaning. If that is the case, then the principles discussed in the preceding sections may possibly suffice to account for the ability or inability to process such meanings preattentively. However, with verbal stimuli this is not the case. In general, there are no perceptual features that distinguish among categories of words or other alphanumeric symbols. Thus, the *words* "tooth," "claw," and "thorn" are no more alike than, say, "trout," "crow," and "hedge" Moreover, fairly detailed visual processing is required to ascertain the meaning of a word (compare, e.g., "arc" and "are"). For these reasons it is difficult to believe that parallel processing of semantically defined targets is possible. Be that as it may, there are at least four lines of evidence that lead us to suspect that discriminations beyond the level of single features *can* be made in parallel.

For one, Egeth, Jonides, and Wall (1972) gave subjects the task of detecting the presence of a single target defined as any digit in a background consisting of several different letters. Reaction time to detect a target was unaffected by the number of nontargets, which suggests that display characters were examined in parallel. The digit–letter classification is not unique; Schneider and Shiffrin (1977) have shown that after extensive consistent-mapping practice, search for arbitrary target sets is similarly unaffected by the number of nontargets in a display.

A second line of evidence is provided by Pashler and Badgio (1985). They devised a task that required exhaustive processing to the point of identification. Subjects had to name the highest digit present in any array of digits. The effect of display size was additive with the effect of visual quality (clear vs. degraded). This result implies that subjects did not serially examine the displays to find the highest digit; if they had, then the effect of visual quality would have interacted with display size, as each comparison would have been slowed down by the same amount in the degraded condition. As it stands, however, the data might only indicate that a very early stage, involved perhaps in the "clean up" of degraded stimuli, was executed in parallel. This interpretation is contraindicated by the additional finding that visual quality interacted with response factors (e.g., the identity of the highest digit). The authors argue that the overall pattern of results is consistent with parallel encoding of the entire display.

Third, there are some interference effects that occur at the semantic level that might be taken as evidence of parallel processing. A suggestive example comes from a paradigm first developed by Bjork and Murray (1977). They demonstrated the existence of perceptual interference effects between simultaneously presented letters that varied as a function of the similarity of the letters (see also La Heij & Van Der Heijden, 1983). Maximum similarity, created by repetition of the same letter (e.g., AA), led to the poorest performance. Egeth and Santee (1981) further showed that repetition at the name level (e.g., Aa) also led to interference. Although not definitive, this finding is at least compatible with the hypothesis that interference is due to similarity of meaning. Moreover, exposures are brief, typically around 50 ms, and followed my a mask; these conditions may make parallel processing more likely.

Additional relevant evidence comes from Stroop-like interference effects. In the usual Stroop interference condition, subjects name a color while trying to ignore the meaning of a color word. Both the color and the word carry meaning; the interference effect can thus be construed as evidence for parallel processing of meaning.

Finally, Mozer (1983) and McClelland and Mozer (1986) have explored interactions, specifically letter migrations, between simultaneously presented strings of letters. A stimulus might consist, for example, of the side by side presentation of SAND and LANE, which might then be followed by a poststimulus cue indicating which of the two words to report. Subjects make a variety of errors. Especially interesting are migration errors. Thus, in the example above, when cued to report the word on the left, they might respond "sane" or "land." The frequency of such errors depends on whether the letter strings form words or not. The explanation offered for the pattern of results assumes that both strings simultaneously access high-level structural knowledge about what sequences of letters form familiar words.

Although these lines of evidence suggest that parallel processing of semantic information is possible, none of them is completely convincing. As Pashler and Badgio (1985) pointed out, the problem with studies like that of Egeth, Jonides, and Wall (1972) is that they do not require the processing of non-target items to the point of identification. Instead, they permit a response upon detection of the target. Thus, conclusions about parallel processing at the level of category or meaning are inappropriate. If we consider the Pashler and Badgio (1985) study, although it is important as far as it goes, it does not speak to the ability to process words in parallel. The problem with interference studies such as those based on the Stroop effect is that although they do establish that mandatory processing of irrelevant information sometimes occurs, they are not designed in such a way as to permit the conclusion that relevant and irrelevant material were processed simultaneously and independently. Indeed, Kahneman and Chajczyk (1983) accounted for data from a Stroop task with a capture model that assumed that subjects attended to just one word at a time. Finally, the theoretical interpretation offered for the Mozer (1983) and McClelland and Mozer (1986) studies appears to implicate parallel processing, but only for lexical status (i.e., whether a string of letters is a word or a nonword). It is not clear that word meaning is processed in this way. In view of the inconclusiveness of the existing literature, one of the aims of the empirical research reported in the next section is to come up with an alternative research design that may afford a cleaner test of processing mode with verbal stimuli.

EMPIRICAL RESEARCH

In this section, we present a series of six experiments concerned with the proposal of Sagi and Julesz (1985a,b) that identification of features requires serial processing. We then present a series of three experiments designed to explore whether word meaning can be processed in parallel from more than a single spatial location.

Experiment 1: Discrimination vs. Identification

It is possible that the difference between the Sagi and Julesz findings and the earlier findings is due to the fact that the stimuli in those studies did not contain anything comparable to the diagonal texture elements of Sagi and Julesz. There are several possible ways in which texture might affect performance. For example, the diagonal lines may to some extent stimulate detectors whose tuning curves are centered on horizontal and vertical, thus using up processing capacity that might otherwise be devoted to target elements. This could lead to the increase in processing time with increasing numbers of targets, possibly by inducing serial processing, as Sagi and Julesz (1985a) suggest. Another possibility is that diagonal texture elements change the task from one that can be solved by the detection of any feature difference into one that requires identification of specific values of orientation.

The first experiment was conducted in an effort to determine simply if the addition of a textured background to a normal *same–different* task does indeed result in a qualitative change in performance. The basic design of the Sagi and Julesz discrimination task experiment was recast in a fairly standard "chronometric" paradigm; RT was measured after a 150 ms exposure that was not preceded or followed by any kind of mask, and trials were mixed rather than blocked with respect to target numerosity. Displays with and without texture-forming background elements were presented to subjects in separate blocks.

Method

Subjects. Eight paid volunteers were tested initially. Two of these subjects produced data that were markedly slower and more variable than that of the other subjects in this or in any of the subsequent experiments. These two subjects were replaced by two new subjects.

Stimuli. Displays consisted of line segments placed in the imaginary cells of a 6 × 6 matrix that subtended 7 cm vertically and horizontally. Line segments were 8mm long and had a stroke width of approximately 0.7mm. There were drawn in black ink on white cardboard cards with a Digital LVP16 plotter. At the viewing distance of 91.5 cm, the matrix subtended approximately 4.37 deg. of visual angle horizontally and vertically, and the line segments subtended approximately 0.44 deg.

   Targets were defined as line segments that were either horizontal or vertical; they were distributed randomly among the 36 cells of the matrix with the constraint that no two targets could appear in cells that were either horizontally, vertically, or diagonally adjacent. Target numerosity was varied randomly from trial to trial. On any given trial, two, three, or four targets could appear with equal probability. On half of the trials in each background condition (i.e., no-texture and texture), the targets had the same orientation (all vertical or all horizontal); on the other half of the trials, one target differed in orientation from the others (e.g., three vertical and one horizontal). On half of the *same* trials, the targets were vertical; on the other half of the *same* trials, the targets were horizontal. On half of the *different* trials, the discrepant target element was vertical; on the other half of those trials, it was horizontal.

   In the texture condition, cells that did not contain targets contained a negatively sloped diagonal line segment. In the no-texture condition, cells that did not contain a target were left blank. Sample stimuli are shown in Fig. 2.1.

Procedure.   Displays were presented for 150 ms in a Gerbrands four-channel tachistoscope. The subject's task was to indicate whether all of the targets had the same orientation, or if one differed from the others, by pressing with their index fingers one of two appropriately labelled buttons. Reaction time was recorded to the nearest millisecond. The assignment of response buttons to hands was balanced across subjects.

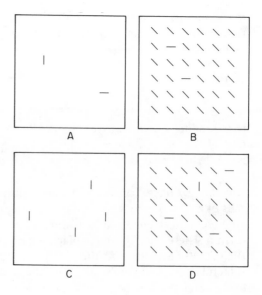

FIGURE 2.1. Sample stimuli with (B and D) and without (A and C) background texture.

A fixation point was visible at the center of the field whenever a stimulus was not being presented. The sequence of events on a trial was as follows. The experimenter initiated a trial manually. One half-second after initiation of a trial, a warning tone sounded for 250 ms; 500 ms after the offset of the tone, the stimulus was presented for 150 ms.

The two background conditions were blocked and the order of the conditions was balanced across subjects. In each condition, subjects received 16 practice trials followed by two sixty-trial blocks of experimental trials. Thus, in both the no-texture and texture conditions, there were 20 *same* and 20 *different* trials for each of the three levels of target numerosity (2, 3, and 4). There were short breaks between blocks and between conditions.

Results and Discussion

Mean RTs and error rates are shown in Fig. 2.2. For each condition, the function relating reaction time to target numerosity was subjected to a trend analysis, the results of which are presented in Table 2.1 along with the best fitting slopes, intercepts, and the percentage of variance attributable to the linear component.

As indicated in Table 2.1, none of the functions relating mean to RT to target numerosity had a slope that differed significantly from zero. Analysis of variance of the reaction time data showed that the 133 ms main effect of background (no-texture vs. texture) was significant, $F(1,7) = 338.35$, $p < .001$, as was the 40 ms main effect of trial type (*same* vs. *different*) trials, $F(1,7) = 9.18$, $p < .02$. Neither the main effect

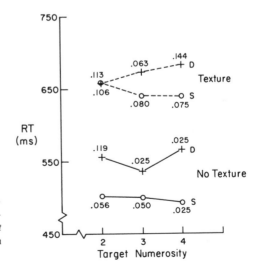

FIGURE 2.2. Mean RT and error rate as a function of target numerosity for *same* and *different* trials with and without texture in Experiment 1.

TABLE 2.1
Summary Statistics for Functions Relating Reaction Time to Target
Numerosity in Each Condition of Experiments 1–4

Exp.	Background	Response	Slope	Intercept	Significance of Linear Component	Percentage Linear
1	No Texture	Same	−4.8	513	n.s.	—
		Different	4.7	539	n.s.	—
	Texture	Same	−9.9	676	n.s.	—
		Different	13.3	631	n.s.	—
2	No Texture	Same	9.3	419	<.05	67.9
	Texture	Same	−16.1	630	n.s.	—
3	No Texture	Same	1.0	521	n.s.	—
		Different	6.5	531	n.s.	—
4	Texture	Same	24.8	554	n.s.	—
		Different	37.1	583	<.05	97.8

of target numerosity (2, 3, or 4) nor any of the interactions was significant.

The mean error rate across conditions was less than 8%. There does not appear to be much evidence of a speed–accuracy tradeoff in these data, as speed and accuracy were positively correlated across conditions. Specifically, the correlation of mean error rate and mean RT was $r(10) = .66$, $p < .05$. In other words, conditions with longer mean RTs had higher error rates.

This first experiment indicates that although the presence of a textured background significantly slows overall reaction time, there is no suggestion that it induces serial processing of display elements. The only hint of such an effect is that in the texture condition, the slope on *different* trials was 13.3 ms per target element—however, this slope was not significantly different from zero.

Experiment 2: A Variation in Response Mode

Experiment 1 suggests that texture alone can not explain the discrepancy between the results of Sagi and Julesz (1985a) and those of other investigators; however, our results were not entirely compelling. For one thing, we felt obliged to replace two seemingly aberrant subjects. For another, even though a slope of 13.3 ms was obtained in one condition, it was not significant. In Experiment 2, an attempt was made to reduce the variability in the data by requiring a go-no go response. Subjects were instructed to respond when all targets were the same but to refrain from responding when one target differed in orientation from the others. (The *same* response would appear to require exhaustive processing, and hence would be more likely to show an effect of target numerosity than would *different* responses.)

Method

Subjects. Eight students at the Johns Hopkins University participated in this experiment.

Procedure. The experiment was essentially the same as Experiment 1 with the following exceptions. Subjects were instructed to respond only on *same* trials by pressing a button with the index finger of their preferred hand. In both the texture and no-texture conditions, there were 16 practice trials followed by two blocks of 75 experimental trials. Of the experimental trials, 60% (45) in each block were *same* and 40% (30) were *different*. Thus in both the texture and no-texture conditions, there were 90 *same* trials, 30 for each number of target elements (2,3, and 4) and 60 *different* trials, 20 for each number of target elements.

Results and Discussion

Mean RTs and error rates are shown in Fig. 2.3; results of trend analyses and summary statistics for the best-fitting straight lines for the different conditions appear in Table 2.1.

It is worth noting that our effort to reduce variability by introducing a go-no go response seems to have worked; the mean within-condition

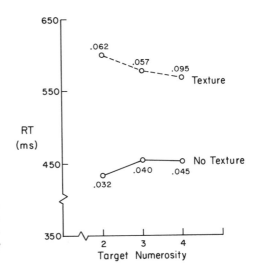

FIGURE 2.3. Mean RT and error rate as a function of target numerosity for texture and no texture trials in Experiment 2. Only *same* responses were required.

standard deviation was 89.2 ms in this experiment, down from 109 ms in Experiment 1, $t(14) = 2.36$, $p<.025$.

In the presence of a texture, the function relating mean RT to number of targets had a nonsignificant negative slope of 16.1 ms per item. With no texture, the 9.3 ms per item slope was positive and significant. The reaction time data were subjected to a within-subjects analysis of variance with background (no-texture vs. texture), and target numerosity (2, 3, or 4) as factors. The only clearly significant effect was the 135 ms main effect of background, $F(1,7) = 49.10$, $p <.001$. However, the interaction between target numerosity and background almost achieved a conventionally acceptable level of significance, $F(2,14) = 3.58$, $p <.06$.

The mean error rate across conditions was approximately 6%. There is little indication that subjects traded speed for accuracy as the correlation of mean error rate with mean RT was positive, although not significantly so, $r(4) = .74$, p.>.05.

This experiment, just like Experiment 1, showed that texture produces an increment in overall reaction time, but again there was no indication that the presence of a textured background causes serial processing of target elements. If anything, there is a hint in the data that texture may produce a *negative* slope in the function relating *same* reaction time to target numerosity. (In other experiments we have, in fact, observed significant negative slopes in this condition.) It is difficult to know what to make of the significant positive slope in the no-texture condition. Including pilot work, we have examined approximately 20 functions relating RT to number of targets in no-texture conditions. We have found one significant positive slope (the present study), one significant negative slope, and the rest near zero and nonsignificant. We suspect that the true value is close to zero; the present result may well be Type I error.

Experiment 3: Range Effects in Discrimination

The results of Experiments 1 and 2 make it clear that the difference between the results of Sagi and Julesz (1985a) and those of previous studies is not due simply to the use of textured backgrounds. We turned our attention next to another aspect of their experiment that differed from what might be considered standard chronometric procedures. The number of target elements (2, 3, and 4) was blocked in the Sagi and Julesz experiment. In most studies in which reaction time is the dependent variable of chief interest display size is normally randomly mixed within blocks of trials. Egeth, Jonides, and Wall (1972, pp. 688–690) have previously demonstrated that such a design difference can have a major impact on the results of visual search experiments. Specifically, they found that when display size varied randomly from trial to trial, reaction time on target-present trials was virtually independent of display size. However, when display size was blocked (actually, different size displays were presented to different subjects), reaction time increased significantly with display size. For a more complete discussion of range effects, see Poulton (1982).

In the present experiment we used the standard *same–different* discrimination task (i.e., no textured background), but with target number blocked (within subjects).

Method

Six subjects served in this experiment. The stimuli were the same as in Experiment 1.

Procedure. Each subject was given three blocks of trials, one for each of the three levels of number of targets (i.e., 2, 3, and 4). The order of these conditions was determined by a 3 x 3 Latin Square that was replicated once. (The natural design here with six subjects would be to use all possible orders of the three conditions. A Latin Square was used because the experiment being reported here was embedded in a larger experiment. The results from the other conditions in that larger experiment will be reported in a subsequent publication.)

Each block of trials consisted of 16 practice trials followed by 60 experimental trials, half *same* and half *different*. There were short breaks between blocks. Subjects indicated *same* with their preferred hand and *different* with their other hand.

Results

Mean RTs and error rates are shown in Fig. 2.4; results of trend analyses and summary statistics for the best-fitting straight lines for the different conditions appear in Table 2.1.

The difference between *same* and *different* RTs was not significant at the .05 level, $F(1, 5) = 4.67$. More important, neither the number of targets nor the interaction of *same–different* and number of targets was significant, both $Fs < 1.0$. We conclude that the independence of mean RT and display size found when simple features are discriminated (e.g., Donderi & Zelnicker, 1969) obtains when display size is blocked as well as when it is mixed.

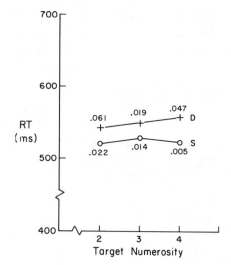

FIGURE 2.4. Mean RT and error rate as a function of target numerosity for *same* and *different* trials in Experiment 3. There were no texture elements, and target numerosity was blocked.

Experiment 4: Range Effects in Identification

We turn now to a chronometric version of the Sagi and Julesz discrimination task in which number of targets is blocked as in their original experiment.

Method

Subjects Twelve subjects participated in this experiment.

Stimuli. Stimuli were constructed in the same manner as in the first three experiments. All displays contained background texture elements.

Procedure. As in Experiments 1 and 3 (but unlike Experiment 2), two buttons were provided for the response, one for *same* trials, the other for *different* trials. The subject's preferred hand was always used to indicate that targets were the same. The temporal sequence of events on individual trials was identical to that used in the first two experiments. Subjects were presented with three blocks of 60 trials. Within a given block, *same* and *different* trials were equiprobable. Each block was preceded by 16 practice trials. There were short breaks between blocks. The number of target elements was constant throughout a 60-trial block (and its concomitant set of practice trials). The order in which the three levels of target numerosity (2,3, or 4) were presented was balanced across subjects, as all possible orders were used equally often.

Results

Mean RTs and error rates are shown in Fig. 2.5; summary statistics for the best-fitting straight lines and trend analyses in Table 2.1

Both the *same* and *different* functions are positively sloped. The 37.1 ms/element slope of the *different* function differs significantly from zero, $F(1,11) = 6.69$, $p <.05$, however the 24.8 ms/element slope of the *same* function does not, $F(1,11) = 2.87$, $p >.05$.

Trial type did not interact with target numerosity, $F < 1$. Thus the slopes of the *same* and *different* functions did not differ significantly when target numerosity was blocked.

The mean error rate across conditions was just over 3%. Again there is little evidence of a speed–accuracy tradeoff as the correlation of mean error rate, and mean RT was $r(10) = .76$, $p<.01$.

The results of Experiment 3 suggest that we have been able, under certain conditions, to obtain results similar to those of Sagi & Julesz using a reaction time paradigm. In the presence of texture, with blocked presentation mode, RT increased directly with target numerosity. (This was clearly the case for *different* trials; the slope for *same* trials, although substantial, did not differ significantly from zero.)

Discussion

Despite the linearity of the relation between RT and number of targets (at least for *different* trials), it is not clear that our results unambiguously support the contention that the identification of orien-

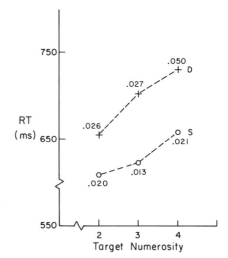

FIGURE 2.5. Mean RT and error rate as a function of target numerosity for *same* and *different* trials in Experiment 4. Stimuli contained textured backgrounds; target numerosity was blocked.

tation required the serial allocation of focal attention. It has been pointed out that increases in reaction time with display size are not a unique signature of a serial process (Townsend, 1971; Snodgrass & Townsend, 1980), Other models of this *same–different* search task could give rise to increases in reaction time with display size. For example, a parallel limited-capacity search, or a parallel unlimited-capacity search that is exhaustive (and that has nonzero variances for its component subprocesses), could give rise to increasing RT functions.

Experiment 5: A Further Testing of Serial Processing

The purpose of this experiment was to test for evidence of spatially serial processing in feature identification. More specifically, it tested the hypothesis, proposed by Sagi and Julesz (1985a), that the variation in performance as a function of target number with textured stimuli is due to serial allocation of focal attention.

The design and logic are similar to that used in the study by Pashler and Badgio (1985) that was described earlier in this chapter (see BACK-GROUND). In their experiment, Pashler and Badgio attempted to distinguish between parallel and serial models of alphanumeric character identification. They had subjects perform detection tasks in which the size (i.e., the number of stimuli) and the visual quality (e.g., contrast) of the display were varied factorially. The authors reasoned that if identification of alphanumeric characters requires a serial, element by element scan, then any increase in processing time due to contrast reduction should be added to each item in turn, resulting in a multiplicative interaction of visual quality with display size. If, however, the identification process is parallel, then visual quality should be strictly additive with display size. The results indicated a highly significant main effects of display size and visual quality, but no interaction between the two factors. These results could not be accounted for by a serial model and were consistent with a parallel, limited-capacity model of character identification.

As in Experiment 4, subjects in the present experiment made *same–different* decisions about the orientations of horizontal and vertical line segments embedded in diagonal texture elements, with number of targets a blocked variable. In addition to varying the number of targets, the visual quality of the displays was manipulated by superimposing visual noise (a dot mask) on half of the trials. If the increase in reaction time between two and four targets observed in Experiment 4 (at least on *different* trials) is due to the serial encoding of feature identity, and visual noise affects the efficiency of this encoding process, then the effect of visual quality should be overadditive with display size, yielding an inter-action between those two variables.

Method

Subjects.   Eight subjects participated in this experiment.

Stimuli and Apparatus.   For this experiment, displays were similar to those of the preceding experiments, however, they were generated by an IBM AT computer and displayed for 200 ms on a Hewlett Packard 1345A digital display module with a P31 phosphor (for further details about these displays, see Folk, 1987).

Procedure.   As in previous experiments, the subject's task was to deter-mine if the non-diagonal targets in a display were all the same orienta-tion or not. Only two levels of target number were used—two and four.

Both visual quality and target numerosity were blocked. Half the sub-jects received the masked condition first and the unmasked condition second, half the opposite order. Within each visual quality condition, subjects received four blocks of trial. Each block consisted of 12 practice trials and 60 experimental trials. There were two blocks at each level of target numerosity. The two blocks of each target number were always contiguous (e.g., 2244 or 4422, but not 2424). The order of target num-ber was counterbalanced across subjects.

Results

Mean correct reaction time and error rates for *same* and *different* re-sponses at each level of target number and visual quality are shown in Figure 2.6. Mean correct RTs for each subject were entered into a within-subjects analysis of variance with response type (*same* vs. *differ-ent*) target number (two vs. four) and visual quality (masked vs. un-masked) as factors. The dot mask proved effective in influencing pro-cessing, as the 92 ms main effect of visual quality was highly significant, $F(1,7) = 20.31$, $p <.005$. The main effect of response type was also highly significant, $F(1,7) = 49.20$, $p, <.001$, indicating that *same* re-sponses were faster than *different* responses. Finally, responses to dis-plays with four targets took significantly longer than responses to dis-plays with only two targets, as the main effect of target number was highly significant $F(1,7) = 45.60$, $p <.001$.

The only interaction that approached significance was that of re-sponse type by target number, $F(1,7) = 5.0$, $p <.06$, reflecting the fact that across the two levels of visual quality, *different* responses were af-

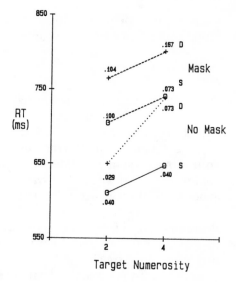

FIGURE 2.6. Mean RT and error rate as a function of target numerosity for *same* and *different* trials in Experiment 5. Data points from the low visual quality condition (superimposed noise mask) are connected by dashed lines, that from the high visual quality condition (no mask) are connected by solid lines.

fected to a greater extent by an increase in target number than *same* responses.

Similar analyses were performed on the error data. The results revealed a significant main effect of visual quality, $F(1,7) = 10.07$, $p < .02$, a marginal effect of response type, $F(1,7) = 4.78$, $p < .07$, and a significant interaction between response type and target number $F(1,7) = 9.85$, $p < .02$. Overall, there is little indication of a speed–accuracy trade-off as error rates were positively correlated with reaction time, $r = 0.87$.

Discussion

The results of this experiment are important in two respects. First, they replicate the results of Experiment 4. With target number blocked, reaction time to respond *same* or *different* increased with target number. Moreover, the effect of target number is again greater for *different* trials than for *same* trials. Second, the lack of interaction between target number and visual quality suggests that if masking the stimulus did indeed affect the extraction of target identity, then this process proceeds in parallel. If the increase in reaction time with target number was due to a serial process, then the effects of visual quality should have been overadditive with target number. There is no hint in the data of such overadditivity. Thus, the results of the present experiment suggest that feature identification does not involve a serial process as Sagi and Julesz have contended.

This result, standing alone, cannot be considered definitive, because one could argue that the mask affected a stage of processing operating prior to the processing of feature identity. However, one model of feature identification that *can* be unambiguously rejected on the basis of the present results is one in which focal attention operates serially on the actual degraded display elements or some low-level, veridical representation or "primal sketch" (Marr, 1982) of the degraded display.

Experiment 6: Redundancy Gain in Identification

Experiment 6 suggests that identification can be carried out in parallel. However, as mentioned previously, the results cannot be considered definitive. This suggests the need for a fresh approach to the question of whether feature identification is a serial or parallel process. An approach that recommends itself is the redundancy gain paradigm mentioned earlier (e.g., Van der Heijden, La Heij, & Boer, 1983, among others).

This experiment was modeled closely after the research of Van der Heijden *et al.* (1983), in which subjects had to discriminate Es from Fs; in our study, horizontal and vertical line segments take the place of Es and Fs. A possibly important difference between the Van der Heijden et al. (1983) study and this one is that we are requiring subjects to distinguish between two levels of a dimension, whereas in the earlier research, subjects might have been responding on the basis of the presence or absence of a feature (cf. Garner 1978). Note also that in the present experiment, there are no diagonal background elements. This permits a valuable simplification of the subject's task. Recall that it was argued that the background texture may force identification of stimuli in Sagi and Julesz's version of a *same–different* task because one cannot respond simply on the basis of whether or not a feature gradient is detected. For all its simplicity, the present task shares that virtue. No display contains a "feature gradient", as all of the stimuli in a display are identical in orientation; correct response requires identification of that orientation.

Method

Subjects.   Eight subjects participated in this experiment.

Stimuli and apparatus.   The equipment was the same as in Experiment 5, as was the timing of events on each trial. On each trial the stimuli were one, two, or three vertical line segments or one, two, or three horizontal line segments. The centers of the line segments were located on an imaginary circle 1.3 deg. in diameter. The locations used were at 12:00, 4:00, and 8:00.

Procedure. There were six blocks of 54 trials each. The first block was considered practice. In each block, half of the trials contained only vertical stimuli, the other half contained only horizontals. There were equal numbers of trials with one, two, or three stimuli. Stimuli appeared equally often at each of the three possible locations, equally often in each condition. Stimuli were randomized within blocks, and thus all factors were mixed rather than blocked.

Half of the subjects were instructed to respond with a dominant-hand button press when vertical lines were shown and to refrain from responding when horizontal lines were shown; the other half of the subjects were instructed to respond only when horizontal stimuli were displayed. (Reasons for the use of a go-no go response are provided by Van der Heijden et al., 1983.)

Results

The mean RTs for one, two, and three targets were 451, 435, 410 ms, respectively. These means differed significantly, $F(2, 14) = 87.44$, $p < .001$, suggesting that processing of the displays was parallel and of unlimited capacity. No analysis of errors could be carried out, as there were only five errors in the entire experiment.

It is not sufficient to simply compare overall mean RTs, as there are certain artifacts that can produce a similar pattern of results. Suppose, for example, that for each subject there is a particular favored position in the display that is processed more quickly than others, perhaps because it is inspected first in a serial scan. The greater the number of targets, the greater the probability that one of them will be in the favored position, and thus the faster the mean RT. (Similar artifacts have been discussed with respect to other domains; see e.g., Biederman & Checkosky, 1970; Santee & Egeth, 1982.)

If the obtained redundancy gain exceeds that expected on this artifact, then the mean RT on three-target trials should be faster than the mean RT for the fastest position (determined separately for each subject). However, as Van der Heijden et al. (1983) point out, this comparison is biased against finding a redundancy gain. It is appropriate only if there is a fixed favored position. To determine if this analysis was appropriate, we analyzed the data for single-target trials. Specifically, for each subject we compared the mean RT for his or her fastest position with the mean RT for the fastest subset that resulted when trials were divided randomly ito three subsets. There was no significant difference, which we take to be direct evidence that there was no fixed favorite position. (In other words, the data suggest that the "fastest position" was not really any faster than one would expect on the basis of random variability.)

An even more insidious artifact is possible; there may be a favored position that is not fixed, but varies randomly across trials. For displays with a single target, that target will be in the favored position on about one third of the trials. On this fraction of trials, a relatively fast response can be expected. The greater the number of targets, the greater the probability that one of them will be in the favored position (whichever that happens to be on a given trial), and thus the faster the mean RT. An analysis suitable for testing this artifact was suggested by Van der Heijden et al. (1983). They note that for displays with three targets, there is a target in the favored position on every trial, and these trials should not contain any particular subset of fast trials. Thus if the RTs in that condition are ordered from slowest to fastest and then divided into three equal-sized subsets (slowest third, intermediate third, and fastest third), then the differences among the means of those three subsets should simply reflect random variation. For the one-target displays, the variability among the means might or might not reflect just trial-by-trial variability. The alternative is that the fast subset is fast because of the random favored-position artifact. If that were the case, there ought to be more variability among the subset means for one-target than for three-target displays.

By way of analysis, for each subject we ordered the 45 RTs in the one-target condition from slowest to fastest and then partitioned them into three equal sized subsets and calculated the means of these subsets. We did the same for the three-target displays. These means are shown in Table 2.2.

The difference between the mean RTs of the one-target and three-target trials is significant even when just the fast subsets are considered, $(F(1,7) = 92.41, p, < .001$. However, the differences increases as we move from the fast subset through the medium subset to the slow subset, $F(2, 14) = 15.96, p < .001$. This pattern is consistent with the random favored-position artifact. Thus, although the redundancy gain observed in this experiment may well be real (the significant and large effect for the fast subset data is suggestive here), we cannot rule out the possibility that the data indicate only a random favored-position artifact.

(We have done a Monte Carlo simulation of the parallel unlimited-capacity model. Under conditions like those of Experiment 6, we found that RTs diverge, just as in the top section of Table 2.2, even when no favored position is assumed. For this reason we offer the analysis based on the work of Van der Heijden et al. [1983] somewhat tentatively; it is not clear to us that an ideal test of the random favored-position artifact has been devised yet.)

The results of this study are somewhat ambiguous because of the possibility that the data can be explained in terms of a random favored-

TABLE 2.2
Mean Reaction Times of Subsets for
the Random Favored Position Analysis
in Experiments 6, 7, and 9

Exp.	Number of Targets	Fast	Intermediate	Slow
6	1	384	441	532
	3	354	399	474
7	Digits			
	1	434	501	618
	3	419	480	588
	Letters			
	1	469	543	649
	3	461	525	621
9	1	447	—	580
	2	439	—	566

Note. Reaction times were ordered for each subject from fastest to slowest and then partitioned into as many subsets as there were target locations.

position artifact. However, in view of the results of the preceding experiment and the lack of any clear evidence for a random favored-position artifact in the following experiments, our best guess is that feature identification is a spatially parallel process that has unlimited capacity. One might well wonder if the results would be different if we had included the diagonal texture elements used by Sagi and Julesz (1985a,b) and in several experiments in this chapter. We replicated the present experiment but with texture elements instead of a blank background. The results were essentially identical.

Discussion

One issue that is in need of clarification is the nature of the differing capacity limits suggested by Experiments 5 and 6. The redundancy gain in Experiment 6 suggests unlimited capacity, while the increase in RT with target numerosity in Experiment 5 suggests limited capacity (although not so limited as to require serial processing). One possible resolution is suggested by Folk's (1987) claim that the RT increase found in a discrimination task when target numerosity is blocked and a textured background is present, as in Experiment 5, is due to decision-level effects. In brief, the argument is that subjects solve the discrimination task by comparing the amount of activity in horizontal and vertical "maps" (the map terminology is borrowed from Treisman & Souther, 1985, among others). Each horizontal and vertical target contributes activation to its corresponding map. Applying the principle of coarse coding (e.g., Hinton, McClelland, & Rumelhart, 1986), it is further assumed that each diagonal contributes some relatively small degree of activation to both of those maps (as well as a much larger contribution to the diagonal map, of course). When two targets are present, there should be equal activity in the horizontal and vertical maps on *different* trials and unequal activity in those maps on *same* trials. Reaction time depends on how long it takes the subject to compare the activation in the two maps. When four targets are present, the level of activity in the horizontal and vertical maps is unequal for both *same* and *different* trials. (Recall that a *different* trial consisted of three stimuli of one orientation and one of the other orientation.) Reasonable assumptions about the amount of activation contributed to the two maps by target and texture elements lead to the expectation that the difference in activation levels between *same* and *different* trials should be harder to resolve when there are four targets than when there are two targets, thus accounting for the increase in mean RT as target numerosity increases. The reader is referred to Folk's (1987) thesis for a fuller description of the decision-level account. The model accounts for the independence of mean RT and target numerosity when there is no background; it also accounts for the absence of increasing functions when target numerosity is mixed. Nevertheless, at this point his model is qualitative; further quantification is necessary.

Experiment 7: Digit vs. Letter Categorization

We turn now to a series of three studies, all of which presumably require a response based on a more abstract property than the orientation of a line segment. The question is whether any of them permit spatially parallel processing. In the first of these three studies, subjects indicated whether characters were digits or letters.

Method

Subjects. Thirty-two students participated in this experiment.

Equipment. Stimuli were displayed on a green monochrome monitor controlled by an IBM XT computer with a Hercules Graphics adapter. Responses were made by pressing the space bar on the computer keyboard. Millisecond timing was accomplished with the computer's internal clock.

Stimuli and Procedure. On each trial one, two, or three letters or one, two, or three digits were displayed for 150 ms. A go-no go task was used; half of the subjects were to press a response key when the display contained letters and to refrain from responding when the display contained digits; the other half of the subjects reponded when the display contained digits. The set of digits used was 2,4,5,6,8; the set of letters used was B,G,K,S,Z. The digits and letters were matched on similarity. It is important to note that all of the characters on a given display were identical. Thus a display might consist, for example, of G or 44 or BBB, but not 245 or BGK or 2K5.

The centers of the characters were located on an imaginary circle 2.14 deg. in diameter. The locations used were at 12:00, 4:00, and 8:00. Individual characters were light on a dark background; they were 0.3 deg. in height and 0.2 deg. in width.

Each subject received 20 randomly selected practice trials followed by 360 experimental trials that were divided equally between letter and digit presentations. For both letter and digit displays one-, two-, and three-character presentations were equally frequent. The various characters and possible display locations were also used equally often. Because of the difficulty of the required discriminations, subjects received error feedback.

Results

The data were analyzed separately for subjects who responded to letters and those who responded to digits. Mean RTs for the one-, two-, and three-letter displays were 553, 535, and 535 ms respectively, and 517, 506, and 495 ms for the corresponding digit displays. There was a significant effect of number of redundant targets, both $Fs(2,30) > 13.00$, $ps < .001$. Errors tended to decrease as target numerosity increased; for both letters and digits, $p < .05$.

Analysis of the data for single-target conditions, as described in Experiment 6, showed no evidence of a fixed favored-position, and thus the analysis in terms of a fixed favored-position artifact was not carried further.

The redundancy gain was tested against the random favored-position hypothesis, as in the preceding experiment. The mean RTs for the subset analysis appear in Table 2.2. There was, of course, a significant effect of number of targets. More instructive is the lack of any interaction between subset and number of targets. For both letters and digits, $Fs < 1.5$. Thus, the random favored-position hypothesis cannot account for the observed redundancy gain.

Our conclusion is that the most natural accounting of these results is in terms of unlimited capacity parallel processing.

Explicit in our introduction of the letter–digit classification task is the assumption that it is categorical and not solvable by detecting one or another specific feature. This assumption has been made before, but it is controversial. For example, Krueger (1984) has claimed that the control for featural differences has been incomplete in most studies of digit–letter classification. When he matched letters and digits with respect to featural differences, the "category effect" disappeared. More recently, however, Dixon and Shedden (1987) have countered that similarity of items between categories may have biased observers against using category information in Krueger's task. When this problem was eliminated, a category effect reemerged. This controversy is, we are sure, not over yet. The problem with digits and letters is that there are relatively few of them. An ingenious advocate can always find some small set of features that could conceivably be used to distinguish stimuli drawn from the two categories. However, if a similar effect could be demonstrated with words, the possibility of such a featural analysis would be very unlikely.

Experiment 8: Semantic Categorization

Having found that parallel processing is possible in the categorization of characters as digits or letters, it seemed a plausible extension to see if it would also be possible in a task that requires semantic categorization of words.

Method

Subjects.   Twelve students participated in this experiment.

Equipment.   The equipment was the same as in the preceding experiment.

Stimuli and Procedure.   A total of 40 different four-letter words was used. Individual words were 0.6 deg. in height and 1.2 deg. in width, and were located 0.6 deg. above or below fixation.

On each trial, either one or two words were presented for 150 ms; when one was presented; it was equally likely to be above or below fixation. When two words were presented, they were in fact two physically identical copies of the same word (e.g., LION and LION, one above the other).

Each subject received a total of 640 experimental trials, divided into four equal blocks. In each 160-trial block, subjects made a different categorical decision. For example, in one block, a subject might respond to animal names and refrain from responding to names of tools, while in another block that same subject might respond to names of articles of clothing and refrain from responding to vehicle names. There were four target categories to which subjects were to respond by pressing the space bar (animals, body parts, birds, clothing), and four nontarget categories for which subjects were to refrain from responding (tools, vehicles, furniture, fruits and vegetables). Each category contained five words. The specific combinations of the four positive and four negative categories were balanced in a Latin Square design.

Each 160-trial block consisted of equal numbers of one-word and two-word displays, and equal numbers of positive and negative trials. Within each block, the order of presentation of trials was random.

Results and Discussion.

Mean positive RTs for one-target and two-target trials were 547 and 545 ms, respectively, $F(1,11) = 0.45$. The error rates for the two conditions were 4.2% and 3.5%, respectively, which did not differ significantly. There is obviously, no effect of redundancy in this experiment, and so no further analyses were required.

It should be noted first that there is no evidence that subjects were using an exhaustive processing rule in this task. If they had, then mean RT would have increased with display size. In fact, mean RT was uninfluenced by display size. This suggests the existence of a capacity limit for word categorization. Whether processing is serial or parallel cannot be determined.

The different between Experiments 7 and 8 is intriguing. One possible reason for the discrepancy is simply that there were too many letters on the screen on Experiment 8. There were four or eight characters on the screen in that experiment, as compared to a maximum of three in the previous experiment. In addition, the characters in Experiment 8 were packed together to form words; lateral interactions among adjacent letters may have impaired performance. Then again, there may be something about word categorization that imposes heavier demands on capacity than digit–letter categorization. It may even be the case that word analysis is inherently serial.

Experiment 9: Lexical Decision Task

To begin to explore the reasons for the difference between the results of Experiments 7 and 8, the stimuli in Experiment 9 included the same target words as were used in Experiment 8, but they were used in a different task. Word trials were mixed with nonword trials; subjects had to respond to words and refrain from responding to nonwords. The equipment was also the same as in the preceding experiment.

Method

Subjects. Twelve students participated in this experiment.

Stimuli. The stimuli were the same as in the preceding experiment except that the 20 words from the four nontarget categories were converted to pronounceable nonwords by changing one letter of each word; e.g., raft became reft. The four letter positions served about equally often as the locus of the change.

There were 640 trials divided into eight equal blocks. However, here the purpose of the blocks was simply to provide subjects with opportunities to rest; the blocks did not correspond to a change in any substantive factor. Thus, the appearance of any particular kind of word was not restricted to a particular block (e.g., the animal names did not all appear in one block). Words and nonwords were selected randomly with the constraint that each item appeared equally often. As before, when two stimuli were presented on a trial, they were identical.

Results

The overall positive mean RTs for the one- and two-target conditions were 518 and 504 ms, respectively, $F(1,11) = 38.64, p, <.001$. The corresponding error rates were 5.6% and 3.0%, respectively, $F(1,11) = 13.5, p < .01$. (Note that this is the opposite of a speed–accuracy tradeoff.) The redundancy gain was reliable, but further analysis was necessary to determine if the effect might be due to a favored-position artifact.

Once again, analysis of the data from the single-target trials showed no evidence of a fixed favored-position, and so no further analysis along these lines was carried out. The test for the random favored-position hypothesis was analogous to the one in Experiment 6. The relevant data for fast and slow random subsets are shown in Table 2.2. The difference between one- and two-target trials is not significantly larger for the slow than the fast subset; for the interaction $F(1,11) <1.0$. Thus, a random favored-position artifact does not seem to account for the data.

Discussion

The processing mode suggested by the results of this experiment is unlimited capacity parallel processing. This result indicates that the difference between the digit–letter classification and semantic categorization studies is probably not due to such factors as the absolute number of letters in the display or lateral interactions among letters that form words. In the absence of further research, it is not possible to say with any confidence just what it is about the semantic categorization task that leads to results that are so different from that of digit–letter classification and lexical access. This is obviously an interesting area for further research.

CONCLUSIONS

One of the major issues addressed in this chapter concerns the ability to process in parallel individual stimuli that differ with respect to a single dimension. This was the topic of Experiments 1–6. Our conclusion is that parallel processing is indeed possible, even in tasks that appear to require "identification" of the levels of each target on the critical dimension and do not permit a response simply upon detection of a feature gradient. This conclusion is broadly consistent with the thinking of a variety of researchers who have written about preattentive processing (e.g., Beck, 1982; Julesz, 1986, Treisman, 1985). We see the contributions of our research as twofold. First, we feel we have in large part clarified the challenge to current theorizing posed by the work of Sagi and Julesz (1985a,b). In particular, we conclude that their finding that performance deteriorated linearly with number of targets does not require the assumption that processing is serial. Second, by the use of a broad range of tasks and experimental conditions (e.g., textured background and no background conditions; blocked and mixed presentation modes; search and redundant-target paradigms; clear and degraded stimuli) we have substantially broadened the empirical basis for theories of preattentive processing.

The other major issue addressed in this chapter concerns the ability to process in parallel stimuli that differ with respect to their meaning. This was the topic of Experiments 7 and 8, and, depending on how one thinks the lexical decision task is accomplished, possibly Experiment 9 as well.

The results of the letter–digit classification task (Exp. 7) confirm the earlier finding of Egeth, Jonides, and Wall (1972) that processing in that task can be characterized as parallel with unlimited capacity. However, when the classification task was based on word meaning (Exp. 8), limited capacity processing was found; whether it was parallel or serial is not possible to determine at this time.

Perhaps the single most striking finding of the present set of nine experiments is that the lexical decision task (Exp. 9) permitted unlimited capacity parallel processing. On the one hand, this results should perhaps not be considered completely unexpected, as McClelland and Mozer (1986) have previously argued that two word strings can simultaneously achieve access to structural knowledge about word form. Note, however, that (a) their experiments did not provide a direct test of this hypothesis, and (b) the hypothesis does not require that processing capacity be unlimited. On the other hand, if one's point of departure is something like feature integration theory (according to which something as seemingly simple as finding a red circle in a field of red squares and blue circles requires serial processing), then the present result is very surprising indeed.

The redundancy-gain paradigm was introduced in the hope that it would provide a clear test of processing mode. However, it does suffer from one of the problems discussed in the BACKGROUND section in the beginning of this chapter. Because a response can be made as soon a single target is identified, it does not necessarily require *full* processing of all target items (Pashler & Badgio, 1985). It is possible, for example, that the redundancy gain is due to a "race" between low-level perceptual process. A process of stimulus categorization, whether semantic or otherwise, may then be applied just to the stimulus whose low-level processing finishes first. This argument may be countered by noting that a race among low-level processes should be just as beneficial in a semantic categorization task as a lexical-decision task. That there was no redundancy gain in the semantic task thus stands as at least some evidence against the application of Pashler and Badgio's (1985) argument to our lexical decision task.

Several interesting implications arise from the results of Experiments 7, 8 and 9. First, these results seem to imply, contrary to early selection theories, that complex structural information can be analyzed in a spatially parallel manner on independent channels. It is difficult to see how the lexical decision task could be performed without a detailed analysis of form. Second, these results seem to imply, contrary to late selection theories, that word meaning cannot be derived in a spatially parallel manner on independent channels.

Clearly, there is no easy resolution to these issues, and equally clearly, more research is required to determine whether these preliminary explorations are accurate portrayals of the processing architecture. However, it would appear that a compromise of some sort may be necessary between theories that assume that all interpretive analyses of visual stimuli can be conducted in parallel without capacity limitations and theories that assume only rudimentary analyses can be performed in this manner. At this point, it is somewhat unclear how detailed the structural analysis of visual stimuli can be before limitations are encountered. Our research suggests that simple features can be processed in parallel and independently, and in some instances, stimuli such as alphanumeric characters and even words can be processed in that way. An interesting enterprise would be to attempt to understand what it is about the processing system involved in semantic analyses of words that results in the observation of capacity limits.

ACKNOWLEDGMENTS

The research reported in this chapter was supported in part by a grant from the National Science Foundation (BNS-8420151) and in part by a grant from the Air Force Office of Scientific Research (87-0180). The authors would like to thank Alfonso Caramazza, Neal Cohen, Gary Hatfield, Michael McCloskey, Toby Mordkoff, Warren Torgerson, and Steve Yantis for helpful comments throughout this project. Reprint requests should be sent to Howard Egeth, Dept. of Psychology, Johns Hopkins University, Baltimore, MD 21218.

REFERENCES

Allport, D. A., Tipper, S. P., & Chmiel, N. R. J. (1985). Perceptual integration and postcategorial filtering. In M. I. Posner & O. S. M. Marin (Eds.), *Attention and performance XI* (pp. 107–132). Hillsdale, NJ: Lawrence Erlbaum Associates.

Beck, J. (1982). Textural segmentation. In J. Beck (Ed.), *Organization and representation in perception* (pp. 285–317). Hillsdale, NJ: Lawrence Erlbaum Associates.

Beck, J., & Ambler, B. (1972). Discriminability of differences in line slope and in line arrangement as a function of mask delay. *Perception & Psychophysics, 12,* 33–38.

Biederman, I., & Checkosky, S. F. (1970). Processing redundant information. *Journal of Experimental Psychology, 83,* 486–490.

Bjork, E.L., & Murray, J.T. (1977). On the nature of input channels in visual processing. *Psychological Review, 84,* 472–484.

Broadbent, D.E.J. (1971). *Decision and stress.* London: Academic Press.

Connor, J.M. (1972). Effects of increased processing load on parallel processing of visual displays. *Perception & Psychophysics, 12,* 121–128.

Deutsch, J.A., & Deutsch, D. (1963). Attention: Some theoretical considerations. *Psychological Review, 70,* 80–90.

Dixon, P., & Shedden, J.M. (1987). Conceptual and physical differences in the category effect. *Perception & Psychophysics, 42,* 457–464.

Donderi, D., & Zelnicker, D. (1969). Parallel processing in visual same–different decisions. *Perception & Psychophysics, 5,* 197.

Duncan, J. (1980). The locus of interference in the perception of simultaneous stimuli. *Psychological Review, 87,* 272–300.

Egeth, H., Jonides, J., & Wall, S. (1972). Parallel processing of multielement displays. *Cognitive Psychology, 3,* 647–698.

Egeth, H., & Santee, J.L. (1981). Conceptual and perceptual components of interletter inhibition. *Journal of Experimental Psychology: Human Perception and Performance, 7,* 506–517.

Egeth, H., Virzi, R.A., & Garbart, H. (1984). Searching for conjunctively defined targets. *Journal of Experimental Psychology: Human Perception and Performance, 10*, 32–39.

Folk, C.L. (1987). *Preattentive representation and processing of visual feature information.* Unpublished doctoral dissertation, Johns Hopkins University, Baltimore.

Garner, W.R. (1978). Aspects of a stimulus: Features, dimensions and configurations. In E. Rosch & B.B. Lloyd (Eds.), *Cognition and categorization* (pp. 99–133). Hillsdale, NJ: Lawrence Erlbaum Associates.

Hinton, G.E., McClelland, J.L., & Rumelhart, D.E. (1986). Distributed representations. In D.E. Rumelhart & J.L. McClelland (Eds.), *Parallel distributed processing* (pp. 77–109). Cambridge, MA: The MIT Press.

Houck, M.R., & Hoffman, J.E. (1986). Conjunction of color and form without attention: Evidence from an orientation-contingent color after effect. *Journal of Experimental Psychology: Human Perception and Performance, 12*, 186–199.

Julesz, B. (1986). Texton gradients: The texton theory revisited. *Biological Cybernetics, 54*, 464–469.

Kahneman, D., & Chajczyk, D. (1983). Tests of the automacity of reading: Dilution of Stroop effects by color-irrelevant stimuli. *Journal of Experimental Psychology: Human Perception and Performance, 9*, 497–508.

Keele, S.W. (1973). *Attention and human performance.* Pacific Palisades, CA: Goodyear.

Krueger, L.E. (1984). The category effect in visual search depends on physical rather than conceptual differences. *Perception & Psychophysics 35*, 558–564.

La Heij, W., & van der Heijden, A.H.C. (1983). Feature-specific interference in letter identification. *Acta Psychologica, 53*, 37–60.

Marr, D. (1982). *Vision.* San Francisco: W.H. Freeman and Company.

McClelland, J.L., & Mozer, M.C. (1986). Perceptual interactions in two-word displays: Familiarity and similarity effects. *Journal of Experimental Psychology: Human Perception and Performance, 12*, 18–35.

Mozer, M.C. (1983). Letter migration in word perception. *Journal of Experimental Psychology: Human Perception and Performance, 9*, 531–546.

Nakayama, K., & Silverman, G.H. (1986). Serial and parallel processing of visual feature conjunctions. *Nature, 309*, 264–265.

Neisser, U. (1963). Decision time without reaction-time. Experiments in visual scanning. *American Journal of Psychology, 76*, 376–385.

Neisser, U. (1967). *Cognitive psychology.* New York: Appleton-Century-Crofts.

Norman, D.A. (1968). Towards a theory of memory and attention. *Psychological Review, 75*, 522–536.

Olson, R., & Attneave, F. (1970). What variables produce similarity grouping? *American Journal of Psychology, 83*, 1–21.

Pashler, R. (1987). Detecting conjunctions of color and form: Reassessing the serial search hypothesis. *Perception & Psychophysics, 41*, 191–201.

Pashler, H., & Badgio, P. (1985). Visual attention and stimulus identification. *Journal of Experimental Psychology: Human Perception and Performance, 11*, 105–121.

Pomerantz, J.R., & Sager, L.C. (1976). Line-slope versus line-arrangement discrimination: A comment on Ambler and Finklea's paper. *Perception & Psychophysics, 20*, 220.

Poulton, E.C. (1982). Influential companions: Effects of one strategy on another in the within-subjects designs of cognitive psychology. *Psychological Bulletin, 91*, 673–690.

Quinlan, P.T., & Humphreys, G.W. (1987). Visual search for targets defined by combination of color, shape and size: An examination of the task constraints on feature and conjunction searches. *Perception & Psychophysics, 41*, 455–472.

Sagi, D., & Julesz, B. (1985a). "Where" and "what" in vision. *Science, 228*, 1217–1219.

Sagi, D., & Julesz, B. (1985b). Detection versus discrimination of visual orientation. *Perception, 14*, 619–628.

Santee, J.L., & Egeth, H.E. (1982). Independence versus interference in the perceptual processing of letters. *Perception & Psychophysics, 31,* 101–116.

Schneider, W., & Shiffrin, R.M. (1977). Controlled and automatic human information processing: I. Detection, search, and attention. *Psychological Review, 84,* 1–66.

Snodgrass, J.G., & Townsend, J.T. (1980). Comparing parallel and serial models: Theory and implementation. *Journal of Experimental Psychology: Human Perception and Performance, 6,* 330–354.

Townsend, J.T. (1971). A note on the identifiability of parallel and serial processes. *Perception & Psychophysics, 10,* 161–163.

Townsend, J.T. (1972). Some results on the identifiability of parallel and serial processes. *British Journal of Psychology, 25,* 168–199.

Treisman, A. (1964). Verbal cues, language, and meaning in selective attention. *American Journal of Psychology, 77,* 533–546.

Treisman, A. (1985). Preattentive processing in vision. *Computer Vision, Graphics and Image Processing, 31,* 156–177.

Treisman, A., & Gelade, G. (1980). A feature integration theory of attention. *Cognitive Psychology, 12,* 97–136.

Treisman, A., & Souther, J. (1985). Search asymmetry: A diagnostic for preattentive processing of separable features. *Journal of Experimental Psychology: General, 114,* 285–310.

Treisman, A., Sykes, M., & Gelade, G. (1977). Selective attention and stimulus integration. *Attention and Performance VI* (pp. 333–361). Hillsdale, NJ: Lawrence Erlbaum Associates.

Van der Heijden, A.H.C. (1975). Some evidence for a limited capacity parallel self-terminating process in simple visual search tasks. *Acta Psychologica, 39,* 21–41.

Van der Heijden, A.H.C., La Heij, W., & Boer, J.P.A. (1983). Parallel processing of redundant targets in simple visual search tasks. *Psychological Research, 45,* 235–254.

3 ATTENTION AND OBJECT PERCEPTION

James R. Pomerantz
Edward A. Pristach
Cathy E. Carson
State University of New York at Buffalo

INTRODUCTION

This chapter discusses the relationship between attention and object perception, and it contains two main foci. The first concerns how we perceive multidimensional stimuli, with an emphasis on stimuli that possess configural or Gestalt characteristics. The second concerns selective attention and the methods by which it is assessed.

These two foci are linked by a large body of research, some of it ours, that has used attentional selectivity as a tool to determine the effective perceived dimensions or components of stimuli. We assess the status of that approach and in so doing try to shed light on the nature of both object perception and selective attention.

To anticipate our conclusions, selective attention research can reveal much about how we perceive complex objects. But selective attention and the tasks used to assess it are not yet well understood. Subjects' performance on even the most basic selective attention tasks can be interpreted in more than one way, in part because selective attention can fail or appear to fail at many different levels of information processing. As a result, it is difficult to interpret performance on any single attentional task, and there are as yet no foolproof procedures to diagnose the effective, primitive features of visual stimuli.

Conceptions of Attentional Selectivity

The literature contains many proposed schemes by which attention could be allocated in the visual field. Among them there is some support for the notion that attention in vision acts like an adjustable-beam spot-light, with stimuli outside the spotlight receiving little or no processing save for their most primitive sensory features (Johnson & Dark, 1986). This metaphor helps explain why selectivity based on spatial location is so effective in most cases. Within the spotlight, attention is allocated to objects (Duncan, 1984; Rock & Gutman, 1981).

Formons and Attention to Objects

Objects often can be recognized from their silhouettes alone, in the ab-sence of information specifying color, lightness, texture, motion, or depth. Clearly, there can be nothing more important than contour for the recognition of visual objects. Both perceptual psychologists and those working on computer vision (e.g. Hoffman & Richards, 1984) have focused on segments of contiguous contour, referred to here as *parts*, as likely units of analysis for form perception. For example, many models for printed letter recognition have started with an analysis of the visual forms into oriented line segments or their intersections as primi-tive units.

A major challenge for such approaches is to identify which of many possible candidates for units of analysis have psychological reality. Meeting this challenge requires techniques for diagnosing the existence of such units. We refer to psychological units of visual forms as *formons*, a term analogous in some respects to *textons* in texture perception (Julesz, 1981) and to *codons* in image processing (Richards & Hoffman, 1985). We propose that the term formon be reserved for units with demonstrated psychological reality. We distinguish formons from codons or other units that might be perfectly valid for describing or con-structing forms and that might even be useful in machine vision but that have not been shown to be used by humans. The term *part* must be used with caution to avoid confusing its physical sense as a component of a form with its psychological sense as a unit of perceptual processing. As noted elsewhere (Pomerantz, 1986), there is little agreement on the definition of several common and key terms in form perception. For the sake of clarity, a brief glossary is included at the end of this chapter to help the readers (and the authors) stay consistent in their usage.

Attentional Spotlight
and the Identification of Formons

Formons would be easy to diagnose if attention were assigned to them in an all-or-none fashion. Perhaps the attentional spotlight could adjust itself in "shrink wrap" fashion to the minimum size needed to contain a formon and no smaller. Were this the case, the smallest empirically determined spotlight of selective attention would diagnose or operationally define the formons of the stimuli being processed. A number of researchers have pursued this approach, and the basic idea has been supported (Duncan, 1984; Kahneman & Henik, 1981; Pomerantz, 1981).

Stroop and Garner Measures of Selective Attention

Recent work in our laboratory has uncovered a measurement problem that must be resolved before the selective attention approach to identifying formons can proceed. We have been examining two of the most common selective attention tasks that have been used in this work and have determined that the two tasks are not equivalent, nor is either task well understood at this point. In the Stroop task, the subject responds to the relevant structural component (typically one or more line segments) of a stimulus while attempting to ignore an irrelevant component that is assigned to an incompatible response. In the Garner task, the subject attempts to ignore an irrelevant component that varies unpredictably from trial to trial. Thus, Stroop interference arises from the *contents* on the irrelevant component (e.g., what is present on any one trial), whereas Garner interference arises from the *variation* on the irrelevant component across trials. This chapter describes a number of empirical and theoretical differences between Stroop and Garner interference, and it presents some stimuli where these two measures of selective attention are in disagreement. We discuss possible loci of these two types of interference in the information processing sequence and show why it is inappropriate to think of either type as necessarily implying a failure (rather than a mere absence or intentional avoidance) of selective attention. Finally, we discuss the implications of this work for theories of object perception and theories of attention.

GROUPING AND FORMONS

Psychological Reality and the Identification of Formons

Stimuli can be described physically in an infinite number of ways. Psychological theories of perception assume, at least implicitly, that the perceptual system relies on a small number of representational schemes, perhaps only one, when it describes or encodes stimuli. If this assumption is correct, then there are only a small number of sets, perhaps only one, of primitive elements underlying the perception of forms by humans. In this chapter, we refer to those primitive elements as formons. It is possible that the perceptual system uses multiple sets of primitives, to be used for different purposes or purely for the sake of redundancy. In this case, there is no constraint that one and only one set have psychological reality, and so there may turn out to be multiple, overlapping sets of formons. Even in this case, however, the perceptual system will represent stimuli using only a few of the ways in which they *could* be represented, so most candidates for formons will prove not to be formons.

Although there is no fixed procedure for establishing the psychological reality of parts, there are a number of promising approaches (see Pomerantz, 1981). The most sound method would be one that relies on converging operations, and that avoids the commonly acknowledged pitfalls of intuition.

The approach pursued in this chapter is one that possesses these attributes. It is an approach that our laboratory has been pursuing for some time (Pomerantz, 1981, 1986), and it is based on the assumption that perceptual groups or primitives act as indivisible units in attentional tasks. Parts at a level more microscopic than formons surely may be described physically, but psychologically they are not represented independently or explicitly. Rather, they are said to be perceptually "grouped" into unitary configurations.

Put simply, selective attention should be difficult to achieve *within* a perceptual unit but should be easy *between* units. Conversely, divided attention should be easy to achieve within a unit but difficult between units. In the experimental tasks used, subjects are presented with stimuli that vary along experimenter-defined dimensions or units, and we attempt to determine if these are also the units that subjects use by seeing how subjects allocate their attention.

Claims Regarding Grouping

Four Claims.   Our first goal in this chapter is to review the current state of research on the identification of formons and to advance a set of claims that this research supports, both with respect to formons and to the methods by which they are isolated. These claims, which are explained in detail shortly, are as follows:

   1.   There are theoretical reasons to believe that the grouping of contours into unitary perceptual configurations should be identifiable through failures to find successful selective attention to component contours. There is strong empirical support for this notion as well.

2.   Despite the preceding claim, many apparent failures of selective attention to contours are not failures at all, but instead reflect deliberate attention to emergent features. There is little evidence for the existence of any perceptual glue binding together parts of a perceptual group.

3.   Absences of selective attention can be accounted for instead by the presence of emergent features to which subjects voluntarily attend. For emergent features to affect performance, they must be more salient than physical features and must be mapped onto response categories in a useful way.

4.   There presently exist no foolproof performance measures to diagnose the existence of perceptual grouping of contours or of emergent features.

We shall now explain and summarize the rationale for making these four claims.

Grouping and Failure of Selective Attention.   It is easy to demonstrate the failure (or absence) of selective attention to parts using the parenthesis stimuli shown in Figure 3.1 (Pomerantz & Garner, 1973). In the experiment, subjects are presented with parentheses, one pair at a time, and are required to make a speeded classification response (a button press) to each stimulus in the sequence. They are to base their responses on a classification rule that is specific to each task. Their performance is assessed in terms of reaction times (RTs) and error rates. The stimuli may be presented foveally or to the visual periphery, and they may be flashed briefly or left on the screen until a response is made; for the results reported here, these two factors do not matter except where noted.

Four types of speeded classification tasks are used in each experiment, and they are shown in Figure 3.2. These tasks are ones commonly employed in tests of dimensional integrality and separability. In the *control* conditions, only two stimuli, say () and)), are possible, and each is assigned to a single button. The task is thus merely to discriminate between two stimuli. Although the subject is not told what strategy to follow or what parenthesis (left or right) is relevant or should be attended, the classification rule for this example can be reduced to the orientation of the left parenthesis; the right parenthesis points the same way for both stimuli, and so its orientation is irrelevant to the task.

In the *filtering* conditions, the classification rule again can be reduced to the orientation of just one parenthesis, but now the orientation of the other parenthesis varies randomly from stimulus to stimulus, although of course it is still irrelevant to the task. If these experimenter-defined dimensions, namely, left and right parenthesis, are the same dimensions

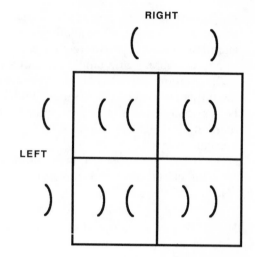

FIGURE 3.1. Normally oriented parentheses.

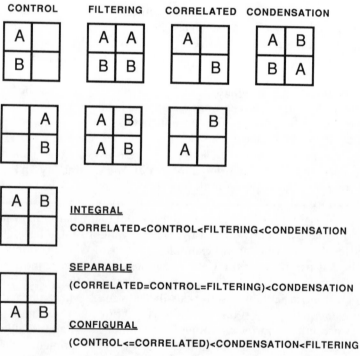

FIGURE 3.2. The experimental tasks used and the interpretation of their outcomes.

the subject uses and attends to selectively, then we would expect performance on the control and filtering conditions to be the same.

In the *correlated* conditions, the orientation of the two parentheses varies in a perfectly correlated manner throughout the sequence and so either the left or right parenthesis is relevant, although only one need be attended to perform the task. Finally, in the *condensation* condition, subjects must base their responses on the joint status of the two parentheses; attending to either alone will not suffice. This task is therefore sensitive to how well subjects can divide their attention.

There are a number of possible outcomes from such a set of tasks, and they have been discussed extensively elsewhere (Garner, 1974, 1983; Pomerantz, 1986; Treisman, 1986). For the present purposes, it is important merely to note just two effects that we have obtained repeatedly with these parenthesis stimuli. First, performance (RTs and error rates) is better in the control condition than in the filtering condition, despite the fact that they both can be performed by attending to just one parenthesis. Thus, variation on the irrelevant parenthesis hurts performance, a result referred to as *Garner interference* and whose meaning is discussed at length hereafter. Second, performance on the condensation condition is better than on the filtering condition. This shows that a task requiring divided attention is actually easier than one allowing (even encouraging) selective attention. These two results are part of a larger collection of outcomes that define *configural* interaction of dimensions, which can be distinguished from *integral* or *separable* dimensions. (Fig. 3.2 summarizes the defining criteria for each of these types of dimensional interaction, and further information is given about each later and in the glossary.)

When one of the two parentheses is rotated 90 deg., as in Figure 3.3, a drastically different pattern of results emerges. Specifically, Garner interference vanishes with these "misoriented" parentheses, and the condensation condition becomes much harder than the filtering condition. This is part of a larger collection of outcomes that define separable dimensions. At a phenomenological level, it appears that rotating one parenthesis destroyed the configuration, which resulted in the stimuli being perceived as two parentheses that happen to be placed near one another. Configural interaction can also be destroyed by moving the parentheses further apart (Pomerantz & Schwaitzberg, 1975), a result in keeping with phenomenology and with the Gestalt law of proximity (Pomerantz & Kubovy, 1986).

Configural interaction is not unique to parentheses. Fig. 3.4 shows a set of patterns formed by various orientations and positions of straight line segments. When asked to discriminate stimuli on the basis of the slope of a diagonal line or the position of a vertical line, subjects do not

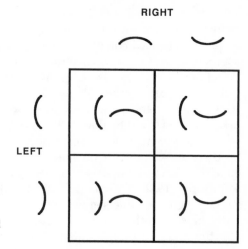

FIGURE 3.3. The misoriented
parentheses.

attend selectively to these line segments but attend rather to the shapes
of whole configurations, which, here, are arrows and triangles.

Perceptual Glue Hypothesis.   There are two sorts of explanations that
have been offered for these results and in particular for Garner interference, which is an essential diagnostic tool for configural interaction
(Pomerantz, 1986). One holds that parts that are grouped are attracted
by autochthonous forces or are otherwise bound together by some perceptual glue. The Gestalt psychologists discussed these forces in detail
(Boring, 1942; Kohler, 1920), and references to a metaphorical glue
continue to the present (Treisman & Paterson, 1984).

   According to the *perceptual glue hypothesis*, as this notion will hereafter
be called, Garner interference is mandatory. The drop in performance in

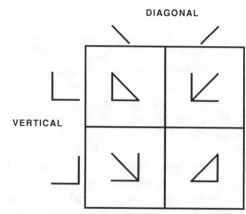

FIGURE 3.4.   Arrows and triangles constructed from horizontal,
vertical, and diagonal line segments.

the filtering conditions is explained either by subjects' being forced to deal with a four-to-two stimulus–response mapping task (i.e., to process four whole stimuli) or by subjects' taking the time to "unglue" whole configurations to access individual parts.

Emergent Feature Hypothesis and Attentional Strategies. An alternative to the perceptual glue hypothesis holds that Garner interference is due neither to glue nor to any mandatory force or process binding the elements together. Rather, it stems from subjects' voluntarily and preferentially attending to *emergent features* (Pomerantz, Sager, & Stoever, 1977) in the control conditions. Emergent features are relations among parts or other physical features or units that happen to be particularly salient to the human observer. For example, the symmetrical or parallel orientations of line segments could be emergent features for the parentheses, whereas closure could be an emergent feature for the triangles.

According to this *emergent feature hypothesis,* Garner interference does not represent a failure of selective attention at all. In fact, the very term "interference" is misleading. Rather, subjects in the control conditions are electing to discriminate () from)) by attending to emergent features of whole configurations rather than by attending just to the left parenthesis in this example. In the filtering conditions, where they must discriminate () and ((from)) and)(, the emergent features of symmetry or parallelism no longer are useful for performing the discrimination required because these features are not mapped onto response categories in a one-to-one fashion. Therefore, subjects either must attend to four whole configurations or must attend selectively to just the left parenthesis. Attending just to the left parenthesis is less efficient than attending to emergent features, not because any ungluing is required (as the perceptual glue hypothesis would claim), but because emergent features are more salient or discriminable from one another than are individual parentheses. This last claim is supported by results showing that () and)) are more easily discriminated from one another than are (and); this finding is known as a *configural superiority effect* (Pomerantz, Sager, & Stoever, 1977; see Fig.3.5).

Although the matter is not resolved completely, current evidence favors the emergent feature hypothesis over perceptual glue. A major piece of evidence comes from the stimulus set in Fig. 3.6 where, as in Fig. 3.4, horizontal, vertical, and diagonal segments combine to form arrows and triangles. One (nominal) dimension of variation is again the orientation of the diagonal, but the other dimension is now the joint position of the horizontal and vertical line, rather than just the vertical as in Fig. 3.4. The results from experiments in our laboratory using these

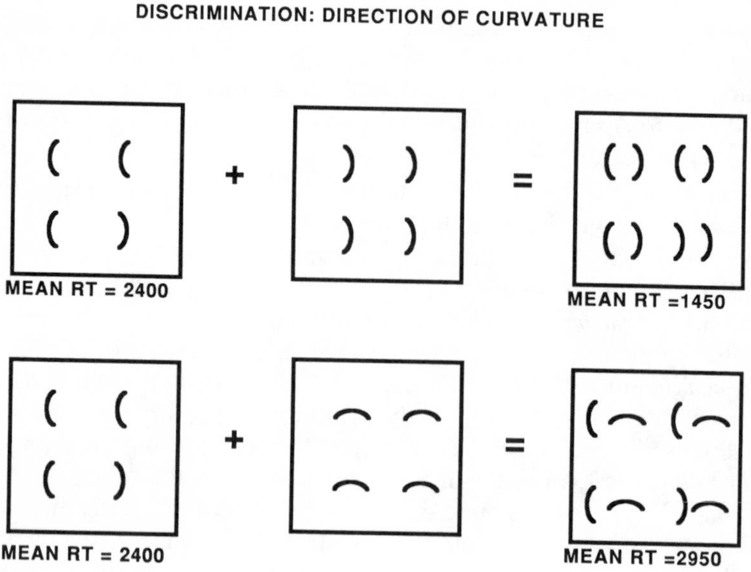

DISCRIMINATION: DIRECTION OF CURVATURE

((( )	**+**))))	**=** ( ) ( ) ( )))

MEAN RT = 2400   MEAN RT =1450

MEAN RT = 2400   MEAN RT =2950

FIGURE 3.5. Various configural superiority effects.

stimuli have shown that the arrows and triangles of Fig. 3.6 now are free of Garner interference and show very poor performance on the condensation task. In short, these line segments now appear to be separable, not configural.

The perceptual glue hypothesis would have to claim that the line segments of the arrows and triangles are equally well glued together in Fig. 3.4 and Fig. 3.6, so this striking difference in performance should not result. The emergent feature hypothesis, however, can accommodate this result without difficulty by noting that in Fig. 3.6 the emergent fea-

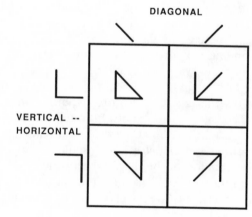

FIGURE 3.6. Arrows and triangles that show a separable pattern of results.

ture of arrow versus triangle is not correlated with response categories in the condensation task or in the control and filtering tasks where the horizontal and vertical lines constitute the nominally relevant dimension. Therefore, subjects would elect not to attend to this emergent feature in those tasks. For example, the condensation task involves discriminating one arrow and one triangle from another arrow and triangle. By contrast, in Fig. 3.4 this task involved discriminating two arrows from two triangles, so attending to the emergent feature of arrow versus triangle would be sufficient to perform the task there.

In the control and filtering tasks of Fig. 3.6, where the horizontal and vertical lines constitute the nominally relevant dimension, the emergent feature hypothesis would hold that subjects do in fact attend to these nominal dimensions. The absence of any Garner interference therefore indicates that the horizontal and vertical lines could be attended to or extracted from the arrows and triangles without cost. (In Pomerantz, 1983, Exp. 5, it is shown that the diagonal line can also be extracted without cost from arrows and triangles.) The emergent feature hypothesis would claim that when the diagonal lines were the nominal dimension, subjects would elect to attend instead to the arrow versus triangle distinction, because it is perceptually more salient than the diagonal line distinction.

Conclusions

The experimental approach just described begins with a set of experimenter-defined dimensions and evaluates whether these are also the dimensions that subjects actually use. If the dimensions show themselves to behave separably, this is strong evidence that the nominal dimensions are in fact the dimensions that subjects are perceiving. If the dimensions prove to be configural, this is strong evidence that an emergent feature is present and that subjects are attending to this emergent feature instead of to the nominal dimensions.

At this juncture, four points remain to be made concerning formons, emergent features, and selective attention.

Shortcomings of Diagnostic Tests. The first point follows directly from Fig. 3.6: Although emergent features are present in these stimuli, our selective and divided attention tasks failed to diagnose this fact, so we know that the diagnostics that these tasks provide can miss emergent features that we know to exist. One implication is that the misoriented parentheses of Fig. 3.3 may also contain emergent features that simply go undetected because they are not correlated with response categories in a useful way. It would appear quite unlikely that these diagnostics would issue a false positive, because there is no apparent way in which, for example, the condensation condition could lead to better performance than the filtering condition unless an emergent feature were present. Thus, these diagnostics would appear to err on the side of conservatism. In any case, they are not infallible, so it is not possible to say at this point that we have a foolproof web of diagnostics that can trap any type of emergent feature.

Evidence for Perceptual Glue.   Although the weight of the evidence leans toward the emergent feature hypothesis, there is still some evidence for perceptual glue. Perhaps the most significant result, not mentioned earlier, is that the filtering task is performed better with the misoriented parenthesis of Fig. 3.3 than with the normal parentheses of Fig. 3.1. This result would be expected if subjects performed the filtering tasks by attending to just the one relevant parenthesis in the filtering tasks, but they needed time to "unglue" the normally oriented parentheses to access an individual parenthesis. Prinzmetal (1981) has also provided evidence for perceptual glue by showing that feature migrations are much less likely to occur across boundaries than within boundaries of perceptual groups. Although it is possible to construct an explanation that avoids perceptual glue, these effects do give the notion of glue some element of plausibility.

Emergent Features and Formons.   If the emergent feature hypothesis is correct, then subjects are attending to emergent features in the control tasks, but are attending to the experimentally defined features or parts in the filtering tasks. According to this explanation, attention to parts is effortless for subjects if this is the strategy they opt to pursue.

From this reasoning, it follows that subjects can attend to any part they wish to without incurring any costs for ungluing, although some parts are inherently less salient perceptually and so subjects would never attend to them unless forced to do so. Thus, under the emergent feature hypothesis, there are no absolute formons in the sense of mandatory and indivisible primitives in vision. Instead, formons would refer to preferred, "natural" units of processing, with the understanding that, barring the future confirmation of perceptual glue, there are no such things as indivisible perceptual units.

Emergent Features and Wholistic Processing.   Finally, it is worth noting that emergent features are not spatially local features in the sense that parts are local. Symmetry, closure, and the like are properties that are distributed throughout a form. If attention is distributed in a spotlight fashion when emergent features are being processed, it follows that the spotlight should be expanded to cover the entire form. In a spatial sense, then, attention to emergent features is global, or "wholistic." In all other respects, however, an emergent feature is just like any other feature and captures only a limited amount of information about a stimulus. That is, emergent feature processing is informationally analytic rather than wholistic, and emergent features may behave separably with respect to other features, wholistic or otherwise, of the stimulus.

ASSESSING SELECTIVE ATTENTION: STROOP VS. GARNER INTERFERENCE

The first half of this chapter has concentrated on formons and how they might be identified. A major tool for isolating and identifying formons has been the selective attention task. Recent experiments from our laboratory have indicated that the apparent success of selective attention depends in part on how that selectivity is measured. We now turn our focus toward two different methods for assessing the success of selective attention.

Claims Regarding Selective Attention

Six Claims.   This section is devoted to comparing two measures of selective attention: Garner interference and Stroop interference. In particular, we wish to advance the following six claims:

1. Attention to irrelevant channels or stimuli is demonstrated by observed effects of:
   a) the presence
   b) the variation (Garner interference)
   c) the information contents (Stroop interference) of irrelevant stimuli on performance of selective attention tasks.
2. These indices of attentional selectivity are related but not equivalent. In some cases, they yield contradictory conclusions.
3. No stimuli have been found yet that show Stroop interference without Garner interference, although the converse is commonly found.
4. Both Stroop and Garner indices can and do reveal asymmetries between channels, but the magnitudes and even directions of these asymmetries can disagree.
5. Stroop effects can be inhibitory or facilitory, whereas Garner effects are only inhibitory.

6. Stroop and Garner effects may be explained within a unified model incorporating facilitory and inhibitory links.

Next, we elaborate on these six claims and summarize their rationale.

Distinguishing Stroop From Garner Interference.   Stroop and Garner interference are statistically independent measures of selective attention. They are based on orthogonal contrasts on the very same set of data, collected from experiments exactly like those described earlier in this chapter. Because of this, direct comparisons may be made between the two without the concerns that would arise if the two were based on different data collected in different experiments.

Garner interference is already a familiar quantity: It is the drop in performance in the filtering conditions (where the irrelevant dimension varies randomly) relative to the controls (where it remains constant). Thus, Garner interference is a *between conditions* filtering loss attributable to *variation* on the irrelevant dimension.

Stroop interference is also familiar from the famous effect of J.R. Stroop (1935), in which RTs to name ink colors increase dramatically if the colored stimulus happens to be a word that names a different color from the ink color (e.g., the word RED printed in green ink). Here we use the term Stroop interference generically to refer to a drop in performance attributable to the irrelevant dimension being incongruent with (calling for the opposite response to) the relevant dimension. Thus, Stroop interference is a *within condition* filtering loss attributable to the trial-specific *contents* on the irrelevant dimension. Fig. 3.7 illustrates the computation of Stroop and Garner interference.

In the following sections we review some experiments that reveal various relationships between Stroop and Garner interference and that lay down the base for a model that specifies how each operates. The experiments differ from each other only in the stimulus sets used or the manner of presentation employed (e.g., foveal vs. peripheral stimulus presentation). In the interests of space, only a few, representative stimulus sets will be described. In most cases, however, there are many other sets that demonstrate the same point.

Example Stimulus Sets

Stimuli Showing Both Garner and Stroop Interference   One set of stimuli that shows both types of interference is shown in Fig. 3.8. Stimuli of this sort have been used by a number of researchers (Kinchla, 1974; Lasaga, chapter 6 of this volume; Navon, 1977; Pomerantz, 1983; Pomerantz & Sager, 1975) to investigate the perception of local versus global struc-

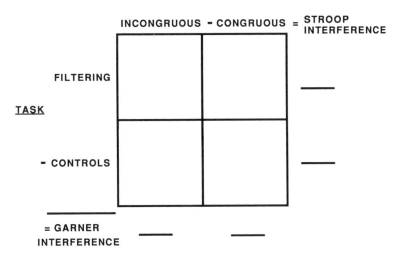

FIGURE 3.7.   Computation of Stroop and Garner interference.

ture of visual patterns. Subjects presented with these compound letters may be asked to classify them on the basis of the smaller, local letters while ignoring the larger, global letters, or vice versa. Garner interference would reveal itself if performance were worse in the filtering conditions, where the irrelevant level varies compared with the controls, where it stays constant. Stroop interference would reveal itself within the filtering or control conditions if those trials on which the local and global letter conflicted led to poorer performance than those on which they agreed.[1]

When the compound letters of Fig. 3.8 were presented to subjects' visual peripheries and the local letters were the relevant dimension, both Stroop and Garner interference appeared. That is, the global letter interfered with the local for both measures. So here is one example of a stimulus set showing both forms of interference. (See Pomerantz, 1983 for discussion of additional examples.)

Stimuli Showing Neither Garner nor Stroop.   When the experiment just described was repeated, again with peripheral presentation but this time

---

[1]Stroop interference can also be assessed as a between conditions effect by comparing performance on the two different conditions with correlated dimensions, as outlined in Fig. 3.2. One of these involves a discrimination between two stimuli with congruent dimensions, whereas the other involves two stimuli with incongruent dimensions. Although we do not discuss these conditions in this chapter, they are included in our experiments to test for redundancy gains, a defining feature of integral dimensions.

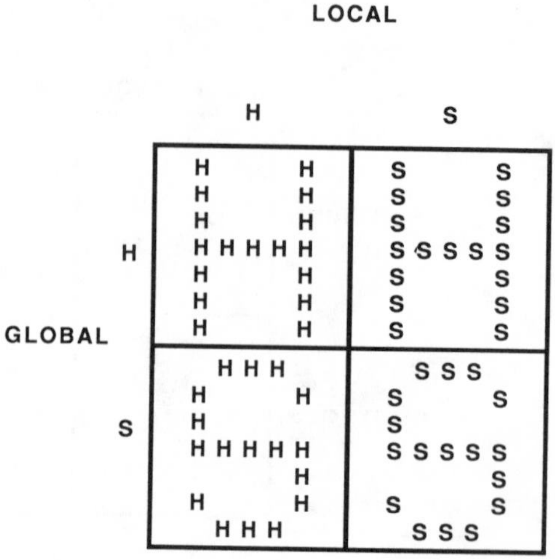

FIGURE 3.8. Compound letter stimuli with global and local dimensions.

with the global letters as the relevant dimension, neither Stroop nor Garner interference appeared. That is, the local letters did not interfere with the global letter by either measure. (This asymmetric effect is referred to as global precedence.) Or when the compound letters were presented foveally, neither form of interference occurred, regardless of whether the local or the global letter was relevant. Here then are examples of stimuli showing neither Stroop nor Garner interference. One would expect this pattern of results with fully separable dimensions where it simply is not possible for subjects to attend to both dimensions simultaneously.

It is of considerable interest to know why the compound letters show global precedence when they are presented peripherally and why they do not when presented foveally. Some general causes of interference are discussed in a later section of this chapter, and some specific causes of interference for these stimuli have been discussed elsewhere (Pomerantz, 1983). The important point for now, however, is that in all of these experiments with compound letters, the Stroop and Garner measures have been in agreement. Let us turn now to cases where they disagree.

Stimuli Showing Garner Without Stroop.   One stimulus set showing Garner without Stroop interference is the normally oriented parentheses of Fig. 3.1. These parenthesis pairs may be described as two individual parentheses, side by side, that agree or disagree in orientation. As explained earlier, these stimuli show sizable Garner interference, whether they are presented foveally or in the periphery. However, they show no Stroop interference under any testing conditions. Some possible reasons are presented later. For now it is sufficient just to note that parentheses show Garner but not Stroop interference.

Asymmetries and Other Complex Effects   So far, we have seen all combinations of Stroop and Garner interference save one: Stroop interference without Garner interference. This missing combination is of considerable importance and is discussed in a separate section later in this chapter. Before turning to that, however, let us consider some additional, more complex relationships between Stroop and Garner interference that we have uncovered.

First, note that in all of our experiments, we look for interference effects going in both directions between the two stimulus dimensions being tested. Usually, these effects are symmetric, so that the first dimension interferes with the second as much as the second does with the first. For example, when the left parenthesis reveals Garner interference on the right parenthesis, the right shows a similar effect on the left. When the left shows no Stroop effect on the right parenthesis, the right in turn shows no effect on the left. Occasionally asymmetries arise, as we saw with the compound letters of Fig. 3.8 presented in the periphery, where for both Stroop and Garner measures the global letter interfered more with the local than vice versa. Such asymmetries have been discussed at length by Garner (1983).

We have now found several instances where Stroop and Garner interference differ with respect to these asymmetries and so reveal an asymmetry of asymmetries. One example is shown in Fig. 3.9, where the letters A and N have been substituted for the left and right parentheses of Fig. 3.1. These letter pairs show both Stroop and Garner interference, but whereas the Stroop interference is roughly *symmetric*, the Garner is massively *asymmetric*: Variation in the left letter produces 199 msec of interference on responses to the right letter, but variation on the right produces only 24 msec of interference on the left. The corresponding interference levels for Stroop interference are 48 msec and 28 msec, respectively. These data come from trials with stimuli presented to the periphery, but a similar pattern holds with foveal presentation.

Some possible explanations of this asymmetry of asymmetries are presented later, but the immediate point is that the Garner measure is revealing a striking left–right asymmetry that the Stroop measure misses entirely.

A different but equally potent effect surfaced with the stimuli of Fig. 3.10. These were displays in which short vertical line segments move upward or downward within a rectangular window, which itself moved either upward or downward. Thus, the direction of motion of the local lines and of the global window could agree or disagree. These stimuli

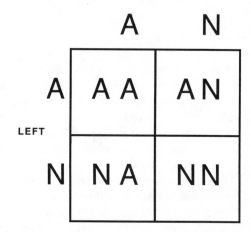

FIGURE 3.9.   Letter pair stimuli.

showed both Stroop and Garner effects, and both these effects were asymmetric. But the directions of the asymmetry were opposite for the two: The Garner measure showed more interference from the global dimension, whereas the Stroop showed more interference from the local dimension. Again, the interpretation of this result is discussed later. The immediate implication, however, is that Stroop and Garner effects can differ in compelling but subtle ways.

The Missing Combination: Stroop Without Garner

We have conducted a large number of experiments searching specifically for stimulus dimensions that show Stroop interference but not Garner. We have focused our efforts on dimensions that, for various reasons, ought to show this combination if any do. Despite these efforts, none have been found.

Efforts to Find Stroop Without Garner.   Our most promising efforts have involved stimuli previously tested but modified in ways that should reduce levels of Garner interference while increasing Stroop interference. For example, we added vertical lines to each parenthesis of the parenthesis pairs, as shown in Fig. 3.11. Recall that the original parentheses show Garner but not Stroop. We reasoned that the Garner interference stemmed from the pairs being perceived as a single configuration with emergent features such as symmetry, parallelism and closure. Although adding the verticals still leaves symmetry and parallelism, the latter may be rendered less salient. Further, by adding the verticals, we create two closed forms placed side by side that seem more likely to be perceived as two separate objects. Similarly, Stroop interference may have failed to

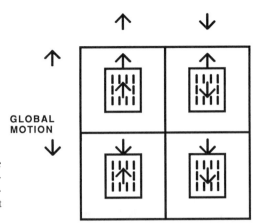

FIGURE 3.10. Moving line stimuli with global and local dimensions. The arrows indicate direction of motion and are not themselves part of the stimulus.

appear with the original parentheses because they are perceived as a single object, not as two contours that are congruent or incongruent. Thus, one might expect the modified parentheses of Fig. 3.11 to show Stroop but not Garner interference. Contrary to this reasoning, these stimuli show over 100 msec of Garner interference but under 10 msec of Stroop, whether presented foveally or in the periphery. Thus, adding the vertical segments does not alter the pattern of results.

To recount another effort, we modified the letter pair stimuli in an attempt to break the configural properties of the pairs and make it more likely they would be perceived as two letters, side by side, that were ei-

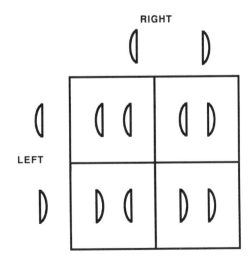

FIGURE 3.11. Modified parentheses: Vertical segments added.

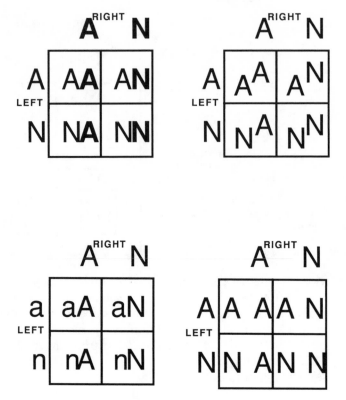

FIGURE 3.12. Letter pair stimuli modified in various ways. The thicker letters in the upper left panel represent letters that were presented in increased intensity (luminance).

ther same or different. As shown in Fig. 3.12, we attempted to do this by: a) making the two letters differ in intensity; b) offsetting the two vertically; c) making the case of the letters different; and d) separating the two letters horizontally. In no case did the manipulation produce the missing result of Stroop without Garner interference.

Many other stimulus sets have been tested. Some results reported by Kimchi and Palmer (1985) suggested that under the right circumstances, texture and form might produce this result, but several experiments carried out in our laboratory failed to do so. Some experiments using the original Stroop color–word stimuli are now under way, but they also look unlikely to supply the missing result.

Conclusion. It is of course impossible to prove the universal negative that no dimensions exist that show Stroop interference without Garner, but all efforts targeted at finding them in our laboratory or in the literature have been unsuccessful. We venture a speculation that the universal negative, despite its inability to be falsified, seems likely to be correct in this instance.

Differences Between Stroop and Garner

Overview of Differences. A number of differences between Garner and Stroop interference have been described at this point. Let us now summarize these, plus some other differences not mentioned earlier.

First, Fig. 3.13 presents a scattergram representing data from 63 separate experiments in our laboratory that measured Garner and Stroop interference simultaneously. From inspection, there is no obvious correlation between the two measures. It is also clear, as noted earlier, that there are no data points indicating high levels of Stroop interference along with low levels of Garner interference.

Second, note that the overall levels of Garner interference are much larger than those for Stroop. For those experiments included in Fig.

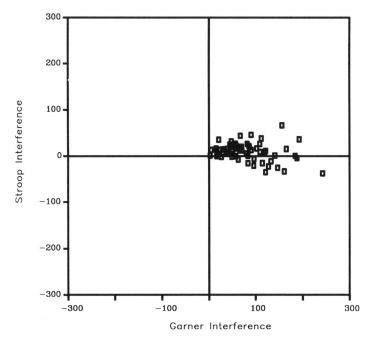

FIGURE 3.13. Scattergram of net Stroop interference plotted against net Garner interference over 63 separate experiments from our laboratory.

3.13, Garner interference averages 82 msec compared with only 9 for Stroop.

Third, note that the Stroop interference levels shown in Fig. 3.13 sometimes go negative; that is, reveal a *facilitation* effect rather than an interference effect. This does not reflect measurement error around a mean of zero: The effect occurs too often and when it occurs it is replicable. Some explanations for this result are offered below, but at this point we wish only to note its occurrence.

Fourth, notice that Garner interference never goes negative. That is, variation on an irrelevant dimension never seems to facilitate performance: It either has no effect or it hurts. The fact that these data are free of negative levels of Garner makes it even more clear that the negative levels found for Stroop are not mere noise.

Fifth and last, both Stroop and Garner measures are capable of detecting asymmetries between dimensions, but as we have seen, the two do not necessarily agree on the presence of or direction of these asymmetries. Fig. 3.14 shows, for each of the same 63 experiments in Fig. 3.13, the levels of Stroop interference from the first dimension to the second plotted against the same levels from the second to the first. (Which dimension is regarded as first is arbitrary and immaterial here.) All points that deviate from the positive diagonal indicate an asymmetry. As we have seen, some of these asymmetries are quite large and reliable. Fig. 3.15 shows the same scattergram for Garner interference. Note that both of these figures show a sizable linear relationship, meaning that dimensions tend to behave symmetrically, but the departures are real and possibly reveal significant aspects not only of these particular dimensions but of the Stroop and Garner measures.

Figure 3.16 shows the asymmetry of asymmetries referred to before, that is, a scattergram revealing levels of Stroop *asymmetry* plotted against Garner *asymmetry* for each experiment. Note that here there is virtually no relationship revealed in the scattergram: Knowing whether the Garner measure has detected an asymmetry in one particular direction tells you nothing about what the Stroop measure would show, or vice versa.

Theoretical Interpretation of Differences.   It is clear that significant differences exist between Stroop and Garner interference. It is also clear that the two forms of interference are not entirely unrelated, because if they were, then Stroop could occur without Garner. Although Stroop interference evidently does not occur without Garner, and although when Stroop does occur it is generally smaller in magnitude than Garner, it would be a mistake to think of Stroop interference as being equivalent to but merely less sensitive than Garner. We have seen fine-grained differences between the two measures, particularly with respect to dimen-

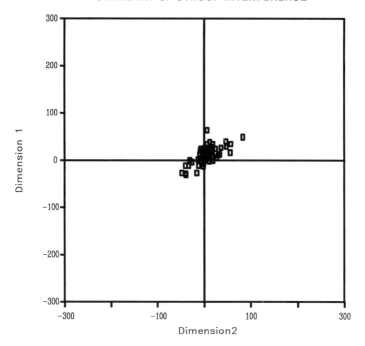

FIGURE 3.14. Stroop asymmetries: A scattergram of Stroop interference from Dimension 1 to Dimension 2 plotted against Stroop interference in the opposite direction (from Dimension 2 to Dimension 1) from the same experiments as in Fig. 3.13. The labeling of dimensions as 1 and 2 is arbitrary, but is consistent for the abscissa and the ordinate.

sional asymmetries, and we have seen that Stroop facilitation can occur whereas Garner facilitation does not.

We speculate that Stroop and Garner share a common set of origins, but for Stroop effects to arise, some additional conditions must be met. If the prerequisites for Stroop included all those for Garner plus more, that would explain why Stroop effects cannot occur without Garner.

Following, we introduce the outlines of a model that could account for Stroop and Garner effects.

EXPLAINING STROOP AND GARNER INTERFERENCE

Outlines of a Model

What a Model Must Explain.   Before turning to the model itself, let us first outline eight basic facts that any model must explain:

SYMMETRY OF GARNER INTERFERENCE

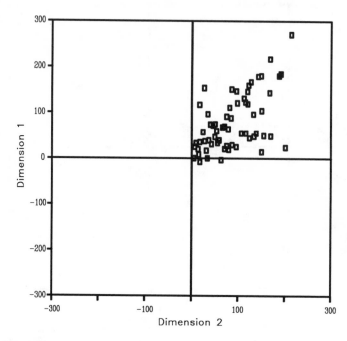

FIGURE 3.15.   Garner asymmetries: A scattergram of Garner interference from Dimension 1 to Dimension 2 plotted against Garner interference in the opposite direction (from Dimension 2 to Dimension 1) from the same experiments as in Fig. 3.13.

1. The existence of separable dimensions; that is, dimensions that show neither Garner nor Stroop interference.
2. Why Garner interference occurs, but not facilitation.
3. How Garner asymmetries arise.
4. Why Stroop interference and facilitation both occur.
5. Why Stroop effects do not appear without Garner.
6. How Garner interference can occur without Stroop.
7. How asymmetric Stroop effects arise.
8. How Stroop and Garner asymmetries can go in opposite directions.

Basic Elements of a Model   The model we sketch here is intended to indicate how information can interact between two channels to produce apparent failures of selective attention as witnessed by Stroop and Garner interference. First, the model must account for separable dimensions, where selective attention is successful, in that neither Stroop nor Garner interference appears. The basic situation for separable dimensions is

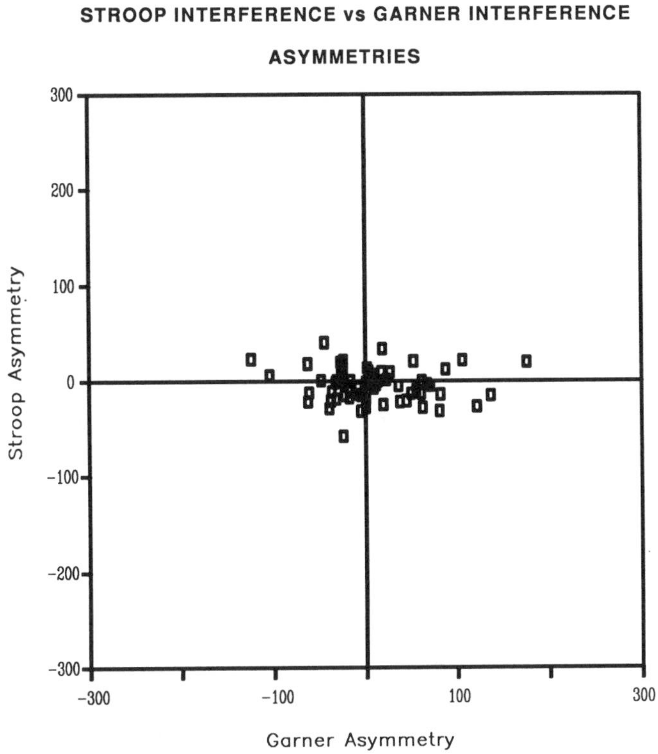

STROOP INTERFERENCE vs GARNER INTERFERENCE

ASYMMETRIES

FIGURE 3.16. Differences between Stroop and Garner asymmetries: A scattergram of asymmetric Stroop interference plotted against asymmetric Garner interference from the same experiments as in Fig. 3.13. For purposes of this graph, greater interference from Dimension 1 to Dimension 2 is considered positive, and greater interference in the other direction is considered negative.

shown in Fig. 3.17. Here, two experimentally manipulated dimensions, D_1 and D_2, are registered by separate sensory detectors, processed by separate intervening modules or stages, and emit their own separate responses, with no crosstalk, intentional or otherwise, between channels. Neither Stroop nor Garner effects could arise in this situation.

Explaining Garner Interference. Second, the model must explain how Garner interference occurs and why Garner facilitation does not arise. Garner interference is handled in the model in two different ways. One is through a voluntary or controlled process (Shiffrin, 1988) and is shown in Fig. 3.18. Here an emergent feature, EF, is available and subjects opt to process this EF because that is more efficient than processing D_1 or D_2, that is, the EF discrimination is easier than the D_1 or D_2 dis-

Independent channels: separable dimension

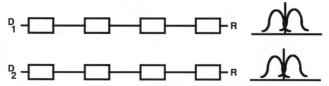

FIGURE 3.17.   Outlines of a model for explaining Stroop and Garner interference. Here, the two nominal stimulus dimensions are processed by two independent channels with no crosstalk between them and no emergent feature being processed. So configured, this model explains separable dimensions.

crimination. As we saw earlier on page 61, this can lead to faster performance in the control conditions where subjects are processing EFs than in the filtering conditions where they are forced to process D_1 or D_2. This in turn leads directly to Garner interference.

The other route by which Garner interference can occur is through crosstalk or other leakage of information, probably involuntary and automatic, between channels, as shown in Fig. 3.19. In the model, crosstalk is equivalent to the failure of selective attention. When no crosstalk occurs, as in Fig. 3.17, the subject has only to discriminate between the two alternative levels that can occur on the relevant dimension (say between left- and right-pointing parentheses). However, if information from the irrelevant channel leaks into the information path for the relevant channel, then in the filtering condition, where all four stimuli do occur, the subject is forced to discriminate among up to four levels on the relevant channel, as indicated by the four overlapping distributions in the figure. In the control conditions, however, there are just two stimuli to be discriminated whether crosstalk occurs or not. Discriminating among samples drawn from four distributions is clearly

Emergent feature processing

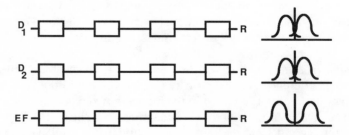

FIGURE 3.18.   Modification of the model to handle Garner interference resulting through attention to emergent features.

Symmetric crosstalk

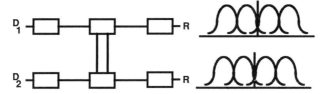

FIGURE 3.19. Modification of the model to handle Garner interference through crosstalk.

more time-consuming and error-prone than discriminating between just two (Garner, 1962), so Garner interference arises.

To make this concrete, suppose the subject is classifying rectangles differing nominally in height and width, as in Fig. 3.20 (see Felfoldy, 1974). Suppose that the subject had no separate detectors for height and width, so that whatever channels the subject could use were sensitive to both of these dimensions. Suppose, for example, the subject had an "area detector" that responded to the *product* of height and width. In the

EMERGENT FEATURE: AREA

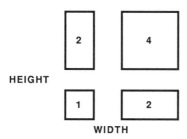

EMERGENT FEATURE: HEIGHT / WIDTH RATIO

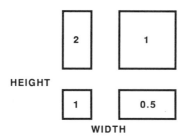

FIGURE 3.20. Rectangle stimuli differing in height and width.

Asymmetric crosstalk

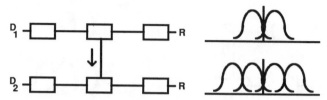

FIGURE 3.21. Modification of the model to handle asymmetric Garner interference through crosstalk channels running in one direction only.

control conditions, the subject would be discriminating just two different levels of area, but in the filtering conditions there would be three or four levels of area (depending on the values of height and width chosen), and these levels would not necessarily be linearly separable (see Smith & Evans, Chapter 11 of this volume). The resulting increase in difficulty would appear as Garner interference. A similar situation would arise if subjects were sensitive only to the *ratio* of height to width.

There is no way that either of these routes could lead to Garner facilitation rather than to interference: Emergent features cannot benefit the filtering conditions more than they do the control conditions; and discriminating among three or four alternatives is always more difficult than between just two.

The third effect the model must explain is asymmetric Garner interference. These asymmetries arise in two different ways. The first comes from asymmetries in direction of flow of crosstalk. Fig. 3.21 shows an extreme example where crosstalk flows from D_1 to D_2 but not vice versa because no path exists for the latter direction of flow. A less extreme asymmetry can be achieved by allowing paths in both directions but by adjusting the relative magnitudes of information flow in the two directions.

The second way in which Garner asymmetries can arise is through emergent feature processing. If emergent features are present in the stimulus set but are uncorrelated with either D_1 or D_2, as in Fig. 3.4, subjects will attend to the EF in all the control conditions and so all the control conditions will show equal performance. But they will attend to D_1 or D_2 as appropriate in the filtering conditions because the EF does not correlate with the required responses there. If D_1 and D_2 are not equally discriminable, then the two filtering tasks will not yield equivalent performance, and so a Garner asymmetry will arise.

Explaining Stroop Interference. The fourth result to be explained by the model involves Stroop effects and why they can involve facilitation as well as interference. The crosstalk mechanism for Garner interference just described is a between-conditions phenomenon that rests on a larger number of alternative stimuli being possible in the filtering than in the control condition. Stroop interference, by contrast, is a within-condition effect in which the level of the irrelevant dimension on any given trial affects performance. In the model, Stroop effects arise when the information leaking in from the irrelevant channel on a particular trial calls for the opposite response to the information in the relevant channel, and as a result a decision is delayed or ends up being in error. So in contrast to Garner interference, where crosstalk is regarded as noise, Stroop interference results from the polarity of the crosstalk from the irrelevant channel clashing with the polarity of the signal arising in the relevant channel.

Stroop interference thus arises over the same channels as Garner interference, which accounts for the fifth result to be explained: why Stroop cannot occur without Garner. But for Stroop to occur, the relevant and irrelevant channels also must contain incongruent information. If they are congruent or neutral with respect to one another, no Stroop interference will occur, which provides one account of the sixth result to be explained by the model; how Garner interference can occur without Stroop. Another, independent account applies to situations in which there is no crosstalk. Here, Garner interference results solely from emergent feature processing, but Stroop cannot arise because there is no path available for crosstalk.

Whether the information flowing through the relevant and irrelevant channels is congruent or incongruent depends in part on the stimulus and in part on the wiring of the system. In fact, this wiring can be configured in a way that permits Stroop facilitation or interference to occur. To illustrate both of these possibilities, consider a conventional Stroop stimulus, the word GREEN printed in red ink. The subject's task is to attend to the ink color channel and so produce the response "red," but crosstalk somewhere in the system from the word channel leaks into the ink channel, biases that channel toward the response "green" and so delays the "red" response. If the irrelevant word were RED, no such delay would occur. This is the model's approach to Stroop interference.

Suppose the stimulus were altered to consist of a disk of one color surrounded by a ring or annulus of another color, as shown in Fig. 3.22. The subject's task is to name the color of the disk and ignore the annulus. We might expect that if the disk is red and the annulus is green, Stroop interference will again arise. However, we know from the opponent process wiring of the color channels in vision that a green surround may actually amplify the system's response to the red disk. Here, then, we might predict faster responses to the disk when the annulus is of an incongruent color. This is the model's approach to Stroop facilitation.

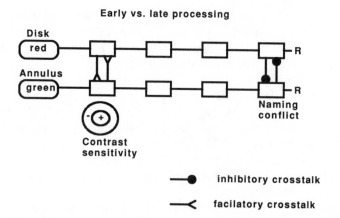

FIGURE 3.22. Modification of the model to explain how Stroop effects can be inhibitory or facilitory. Here, facilitation is achieved through color opponency.

Although this color example is hypothetical, we have obtained equivalent effects based on opponent process coding with motion configuration stimuli. For example, if the subject's task is to decide if a dot is moving upward or downward, an opposite direction of motion in irrelevant flanking dots would be facilitory rather than inhibitory (via the phenomenon of induced motion) and so lead either to Stroop facilitation or at least to lower levels of Stroop interference than one would expect otherwise.

Traditional Stroop color–word interference is usually regarded as a "late" effect arising toward the response end of the information processing sequence (Dyer, 1973). According to the model presented here, Stroop effects considered generically can occur anywhere in the system, early or late. Opponent process interactions are common in early stages of perception, but in principle could occur anywhere. For that reason, the model makes no claims about the locus of either Stroop or Garner effects: In principle, either can occur at any location or even at multiple locations.

To illustrate the latter claim, consider the parentheses once again, as shown in Fig. 3.23. At an early level of contour coding, the pairs with parallel parentheses [((and))] would be regarded as *congruent* because the contours have the same orientation. At a later, hypothetical level of shape representation, however, these same parenthesis pairs could be regarded as *incongruent*, because one parenthesis traces out a convex edge and the other a concave edge of the whole, closed form. Recall that the parentheses show no net Stroop effect; that is, neither interference nor facilitation. As noted earlier, this could be because subjects are processing emergent features such as symmetry, and so are not attending to two separate contours. But it could also be that the pairings that are incongruent at one level are congruent at another, and so no net Stroop effect emerges. Thus, the absence of Stroop effects does not necessarily mean that attention is selective. Indeed, considerable crosstalk could be taking place but with no net interference or facilitation arising. By contrast, the model holds that the absence of Garner interference unambiguously implies that attention is selective and thus that information flows through the dimensional channels independently.

The last two phenomena to be explained from our list of eight are asymmetric Stroop interference and how it arises independently from Garner asymmetry. Recall that Garner asymmetries are postulated to result from asymmetries in crosstalk between the two channels. Because Stroop effects arise from the same crosstalk that can create Garner interference, one might expect Stroop and Garner asymmetries to be related. But as Fig. 3.16 made clear, there is no apparent relationship between the two.

The answer lies once again in analyzing which pairings of irrelevant and relevant dimension are regarded as congruent and which as incongruent. Although the details of these interactions are conceivably complicated, one can imagine a situation in which the *amount* of crosstalk from D_1 to D_2 is greater than from D_2 to D_1, thus giving rise to a Garner asymmetry; but the coding of these channels is based on opponency or contrast, and so what might have appeared as greater Stroop *interference* from D_1 to D_2 than vice versa ends up being greater *facilitation*. This would lead to the Stroop measure showing the opposite direction of asymmetry to the Garner measure.

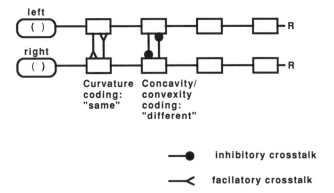

FIGURE 3.23. Demonstration of how parenthesis pairs could lead to Stroop interference, facilitation, or both, depending on whether the representation of contours codes orientation, convexity, or both.

The model predicts that if there is no Garner interference going from D_1 to D_2 (or vice versa), then there can be no Stroop interference or facilitation in that same direction. The reason is simply that the absence of Garner interference implies the absence of any crosstalk (as well as the absence of emergent features), and this same crosstalk is a prerequisite for any Stroop effects. The data from the same 63 experiments shown earlier in Fig. 3.13 corroborate this prediction.

Remaining Questions

The model just outlined is clearly preliminary and is intended only to suggest how the range of effects already established can be accommodated. As wide as this range is, we may not assume that all possible differences between Stroop and Garner have been found yet. For example, Stroop and Garner could differ with respect to spatial extent, such that the width or even the shape of the attentional spotlight might vary depending on which measure were used. The two might respond differentially to arousal level, fatigue, or concurrent processing loads. We do have good evidence that moving stimulus presentations from the periphery to the fovea produces identical effects on Stroop and Garner. But the two might have different sensitivities in instructional manipulations and to a host of other possible factors known to affect attention. In short, we do not claim to have explored all or even most of the terrain referenced in this chapter.

CONCLUSIONS

Summary

This chapter had two main goals: to show how selective attention can be used to diagnose the effective units or formons of visual form recognition, and to show how different ways of assessing attentional selectivity can lead to different conclusions.

With respect to formons, we have seen attentional selectivity does indeed provide a window into the effective units of analysis in form perception. In particular, emergent features can be diagnosed through a network of converging operations centered around absence of selective attention assessed through Garner interference and successful divided attention; and supplemented by absence of redundancy gains and the presence of configural superiority effects. Although these converging operations can successfully reveal the presence of emergent features, they are not completely foolproof and so can miss emergent features under some circumstances.

We have also seen that perceptual grouping should probably be thought of more as the creation of emergent features rather than the loss of parts. That is, there is scant evidence for the existence of perceptual glue binding together and making inaccessible individual parts of configurations.

With respect to selective attention, we have seen that Stroop and Garner effects can be assessed simultaneously and so can be compared against one another directly. Although there are commonalities between them, Stroop and Garner effects can differ at both a macroscopic and microscopic level. At the macroscopic level, we see stimuli like the parentheses that show large Garner interference but no Stroop interference at all. At a more microscopic level, we see stimuli that show asymmetric Garner interference running in one direction, whereas Stroop shows an opposite asymmetry.

The relationship between Stroop and Garner interference is thus complicated, but it appears explainable within a unitary model manifesting channels for emergent features and both inhibitory and facilitory crosstalk between channels. The failure to find Stroop interference without Garner interference is explained by basing Stroop and Garner both on the presence of crosstalk between channels but requiring an additional element for Stroop, namely that the information in the relevant and irrelevant channels must call for congruent or incongruent responses. Asymmetries in the levels of crosstalk are responsible for asymmetric Stroop and Garner effects. Garner interference can arise either through attention to emergent features or through crosstalk between the relevant and irrelevant channels, but Garner facilitation cannot arise in the model. Stroop interference arises when the relevant and the irrelevant channels are incongruent, whereas Stroop facilitation occurs when the channels are linked via an opponent process such that nominally conflicting information on the irrelevant channel ends up facilitating performance.

Immediate Implications

Although much work remains to be done on both problems addressed in this chapter, there are some immediate lessons to be learned. Perhaps the most obvious is that Stroop and Garner measures cannot be used interchangeably to assess attentional selectivity. Faced with a choice between the two, experimenters should consider given priority to Garner because it is a less complex measure (in that it depends on fewer requisite conditions) and a more robust measure (in that it typically produces much larger effects) than Stroop. Unlike with Stroop, a zero level of Garner interference does in fact indicate selective attention. Many researchers are interested in selective attention, not so much in its own right as in its applications for understanding other cognitive process such as form perception, the effects of arousal on performance, and certain clinical conditions. If these researchers based their conclusions solely on either Stroop or Garner measures, they clearly would be creating a distorted image of how attention is allocated. Certainly, an exclusive reliance on Stroop would overestimate the selectivity of attention. On the other hand, the Stroop measure can provide a window on coding processes that Garner cannot.

A second immediate implication is that given our current set of diagnostics, we cannot know with certainty whether a given set of stimuli possesses emergent features. This means that the search for formons must proceed with caution. It might be tempting to conclude, for example, that the misoriented parentheses of Fig. 3.3 do not configure, but in reality we have no way of knowing that for sure at this time.

Identifying formons remains a major problem, perhaps *the* major problem of form recognition by humans. By studying our diagnostic procedures as closely as we study our stimuli, we may eventually learn how emergent features can be identified in a sensitive yet foolproof fashion.

GLOSSARY

Asymmetric interference.   A situation in which the interference (Stroop or Garner) from one dimension to a second is greater in magnitude than the corresponding interference from the second to the first dimension.

Condensation condition.   A condition in a speeded classification experiment in which both dimensions vary orthogonally throughout the task and both dimensions must be attended to for successful performance.

Configural dimensions.   Stimulus dimensions that show a form of perceptual interaction characterized by Garner interference, absence of systematic redundancy gains, and divided attention performance that is superior to selective attention.

Control condition.   A condition in a speeded classification experiment in which the level presented on the irrelevant dimension stays constant throughout the entire block of trials.

Emergent feature hypothesis.   The notion that Garner interference is due (at least in part) to subjects' voluntarily and preferentially attending to emergent features in control conditions and thereby showing better performance there than in the filtering conditions.

Emergent features.   Relational features such as symmetry, colinearity, parallelism, and closure that for human observers are as or more salient than the more elementary physical features on which they are defined.

Filtering condition. A condition in a speeded classification experiment in which the level presented on the irrelevant dimension varies orthogonally to the relevant dimension throughout the entire block of trials.

Formons. Segments of contour or regions of a form that have demonstrated psychological reality, for example by acting as a single unit in attentional tasks. All regions that interact with one another in the perceptual process (i.e. are perceptually dependent) belong to the same formon, whereas regions acting independently of one another belong to different formons.

Garner interference. Loss in performance (increase in reaction time or error rate) attributable to the irrelevant dimension varying orthogonally to the relevant within a block of trials compared with the irrelevant dimension staying constant. It is calculated between conditions by subtracting performance on control tasks from that on filtering tasks. Unlike Stroop, Garner interference never appears to assume negative values (i.e. Garner facilitation does not occur).

Integral dimensions. Stimulus dimensions that show a form of perceptual interaction characterized by Garner interference, systematic redundancy gains, and divided attention performance that is inferior to selective attention.

Parts. Segments of contiguous contour in a visual form. No psychological reality is implied. Some tolerance for gaps is allowed, so that a dotted line could be considered as a part. However, regions separated widely or bisected by an occluding object cannot be regarded as single parts, although they could be single formons.

Perceptual glue hypothesis. The notion that Garner interference is due (at least in part) to automatic forces binding together the parts of a configuration and thereby preventing selective attention to the parts.

Separable dimensions. Stimulus dimensions that show a form of perceptual interaction characterized by the absence of Garner interference, absence of systematic redundancy gains, and divided attention performance that is inferior to selective attention.

Stroop interference. Loss in performance (increase in reaction time or error rate) attributable to the irrelevant dimension being incongruent with (calling for the opposite response to) the relevant dimension, compared with being congruent (calling for the same response). It is calculated within conditions by subtracting performance on consistent trials from that on inconsistent trials. Occasionally, Stroop interference turns out to have a negative value, indicating that a facilitation effect has occurred.

REFERENCES

Boring, E.G. (1942). *Sensation and perception in the history of experimental psychology.* New York: Appleton-Century-Crofts.

Duncan, J. (1984). Selective attention and the organization of visual attention. *Journal of Experimental Psychology: General, 113,* 501–517.

Dyer, F.N. (1973). The Stroop phenomenon and its use in the study of perceptual, cognitive and response processes. *Memory & Cognition, 1*, 106–120.

Felfoldy, G.L. (1974). Repetition effects in choice reaction time to multidimensional stimuli. *Perception & Psychophysics, 15*, 453–459.

Garner, W.R. (1962). *Uncertainty and structure as psychological concepts.* New York: Wiley.

Garner, W.R. (1974). *The processing of information and structure.* Hillsdale, NJ: Lawrence Erlbaum Associates.

Garner, W.R. (1983). Asymmetric interactions of stimulus dimensions in perceptual information processing. In T.J. Tighe & B.E. Shepp (Eds.), *Perception, cognition and development: Interactional analyses.* (pp. 1–38). Hillsdale, NJ: Lawrence Erlbaum Associates.

Hoffman, D.D., & Richards, W.A. (1984). Parts of recognition. *Cognition, 18*, 65–96.

Johnson, W.A. & Dark, V.J. (1986). Selective attention. *Annual Review of Psychology, 37*, 43–75.

Julesz, B. (1981). Textons, the elements of texture perception, and their interactions. *Nature, 290*, 91–97.

Kahneman, D. & Henik, A. (1981). Perceptual organization and attention. In M. Kubovy & J.R. Pomerantz (Eds.), *Perceptual organization,* (pp. 181–211). Hillsdale, NJ: Lawrence Erlbaum Associates

Kimchi, R. & Palmer, S.E. (1985). Separability and integrality of global and local levels of hierarchical patterns. *Journal of Experimental Psychology: Human Perception and Performance, 11*, 673–688.

Kinchla, R.A. (1974). Detecting target elements in multi-element arrays: A confusability model. *Perception & Psychophysics, 15*, 225–231.

Kohler, W. (1920). *Die physischen Gestalten in Ruhe und im stationaren Zustand.* Braunschweig: Vieweg.

Navon, D. (1977). Forest before trees: The precedence of global features in visual perception. *Cognitive Psychology, 9*, 353–383.

Pomerantz, J.R. (1981). Perceptual organization in information processing. In M. Kubovy & J.R. Pomerantz (Eds.), *Perceptual organization.* (pp. 141–180). Hillsdale, NJ: Lawrence Erlbaum Associates.

Pomerantz, J.R. (1983). Global and local precedence: Selective attention in form and motion perception. *Journal of Experimental Psychology: General, 112*, 516–540.

Pomerantz, J.R. (1986). Visual form perception: An overview. In E.C. Schwab & H.C. Nusbaum (Eds.), *Pattern recognition by human and machines, Vol 2: Visual Perception.* (pp. 1–30). New York: Academic Press.

Pomerantz, J.R. & Garner, W.R. (1973). Stimulus configuration in selective attention tasks. *Perception & Psychophysics , 14*, 565–569.

Pomerantz, J.R. & Kubovy, M. (1986). Theoretical approaches to perceptual organization. In K. Boff, L. Kaufman & J. Thomas (Eds.), *Handbook of perception and human performance. (pp. 36-1–36-46). New York: Wiley.*

Pomerantz, J.R. & Sager, L.C. (1975). Asymmetric integrality with dimensions of visual pattern. *Perception & Psychophysics, 18*, 460–466.

Pomerantz, J.R., Sager, L.C., & Stoever, R.J. (1977). Perception of wholes and of their component parts: Some configural superiority effects. *Journal of Experimental Psychology: Human Perception and Performance, 3 ,* 422–435.

Pomerantz, J.R., & Schwaitzberg, S.D. (1975). Grouping by proximity: Selective attention measures. *Perception & Psychophysics, 18*, 355–361.

Prinzmetal, W. (1981). Principles of feature integration in visual perception. *Perception & Psychophysics, 30*, 330–340.

Richards, W.A., & Hoffman, D.D. (1985). Codon constraints on closed 2D shapes. *Computer Vision, Graphics, and Image Processing, 31*, 265–281.

Rock, I., & Gutman, D. (1981). The effect of inattention on form perception. *Journal of Experimental Psychology: Human Performance and Perception, 7*, 275–285.

Shiffrin, R.M. (1988). Attention. In R.C. Atkinson, R.J. Herrnstein, G. Lindzey & R.D. Luce (Eds.), *Stevens' handbook of experimental psychology*. New York: Wiley & Sons.

Stroop, J.R. (1935). Studies of interference in serial verbal reactions. *Journal of Experimental Psychology, 18*, 643–662.

Treisman, A. (1986). Properties, parts and objects. In K. Boff, L. Kaufman & J. Thomas, Eds.), *Handbook of perception and human performance*. (pp. 35-1–35-70). New York: Wiley.

Treisman, A., & Paterson, R. (1984). Emergent features, attention and object perception. *Journal of Experimental Psychology: Human Perception and performance, 10*, 12–31.

4 MENTAL MODELS OF THE STRUCTURE OF VISUAL OBJECTS

Lynn A. Cooper
Columbia University

INTRODUCTION

One of the most obvious yet significant features of our perceptual experience is that it is organized and meaningful. That is, rather than experiencing a world consisting of fleeting, elementary units of sensation, we perceive a coherent world of integrated, three-dimensional objects and of unified temporal events, This observation becomes even more challenging when we realize that, in our ordinary perceptual encounters with the world, we generally operate on the basis of incomplete information concerning the layout and the structure of objects and events. The information acquired in a single glance or even in multiple samples involving eye fixations and observer movement rarely provides projections of either all surfaces of objects in the environment or the relationships among the surfaces of one or many such objects. Nonetheless, behavior proceeds in a relatively uninterrupted fashion; rarely do we collide with the hidden surfaces of three-dimensional objects or register surprise as previously concealed aspects of object structure are revealed. Clearly, the partial information available for object structure effectively specifies the important properties of hidden surfaces, and/or this partial information is used as a basis for the ongoing construction of a mental model of the objects and their relationships in the immediate environment.

One time-honored explanation of how the perception of objects is accomplished is to regard this activity as "inferential" (or, in more contemporary parlance, "computational") in nature. In one formulation of this position—commonly referred to as "unconscious inference" after von Helmholtz (1866)—the premises of the inference are both partial sensory information (usually regarded as provided by the retinal image) and learned constraints in the physical world. These learned constraints embody relationships between object attributes and attributes of sensory stimulation, and the application of rules derived from the constraints allows the inference or computation of object structure from the structure of sensory information. To quote Hochberg's (1985) paraphrase of this account, "we perceive just that state of affairs in the world that would, under normal conditions, be most likely to produce the pattern of sensory responses that we receive" (p. 257).

There are a number of implications of and questions arising from this proposal that perception is an activity analogous to inference. Such an account implies that there is some level of information in the world that is important to the organism and that there is an internal model or representation of that information that is computed by the perceptual process. It is the rules derived from constraints in the world that provide mapping relations between external information and internal representations of that information. Given this formulation of the perceptual process, a number of questions naturally arise: What is the nature of the mapping relations between structure in the world and the mental structures that guide our actions? From what do the constraints that specify the mappings arise? Of all of the possible aspects of structure that could be specified by the mappings, which ones are selected, under what conditions, to be preserved by the perceptual process? And, under what circumstances are the selected mapping relations or correspondences between the world and mental representations of the world more or less adequate? In the specific case of perceiving objects, what aspects of object structure are preserved in mental models of objects?

All of these questions have been addressed to some extent by recent theoretical and empirical work in the field of perception. Cutting (1986), for example, has presented a compelling case—buttressed by substantial experimental results—that the mapping relations between information in the world and perceptual representations of that information are many to one. That is, Cutting (1986) argues that multiple sources of information exist for perceiving certain properties of objects, and perceivers may find one source useful in some situations and other sources useful under different conditions. With respect to the question of the genesis of internalized constraints, several investigators, most notably Shepard (1984), have argued that these constraints are a product of the evolutionary history of the organism.

The research reported here is addressed to the latter two questions, namely, to the selective aspects of mappings between object structure and internal representations of that structure and to the conditions under which mental representations of structure in the world correspond well to aspects of that external structure. The research program discussed has two distinct lines that share certain features. In both lines of research, observers are given partial information about the structure of a three-dimensional object, and they are asked to make judgments that require extrapolation, generation, prediction, or confirmation of other aspects of object structure that are not explicitly contained in the information provided. The forms of partial information are not of the sort requiring tachistoscopic presentation or very low levels of stimulus luminance. Rather, the information is of the sort that might be sampled as an observer has a relatively natural perceptual encounter with the world.

In the first line of work to be discussed, information about some but not all projections of the surfaces of a three-dimensional object is provided, and observers are asked to make judgments about the structure of surfaces not explicitly presented. In the second line of work, observers view a continuous spatial transformation of a perspective view of a three-dimensional object. Following an interruption of the transformation, judgments concerning the probable continuation of the transformation are obtained. There is a single idea motivating both of these lines of research. It is that knowing something about which aspects of object structure can be generated or predicted in the absence of continuous external information might provide a clue as to the nature of the mental structures or models that underlie the prediction. In particular, the concern is with the degree to which the constructed mental representations embody key elements of the external objects and events that they represent.

RECOGNITION OF HIDDEN SURFACES
OF CONSTRUCTED MENTAL REPRESENTATIONS
OF THREE-DIMENTIONAL OBJECTS

The first line of research exploring the forms of object structure that are preserved in mental representations of objects arose, initially, from an interest in the strategies that people use to solve complex spatial problems requiring the manipulation of visual information. (See Cooper, 1988, for details of the problem-solving task and results pertaining to alternative strategies for performance.) The experimental situation required observers to reason about the structure of objects from two-dimensional projections of object surfaces. Following this problem-solving task, the nature and extent of information about three-dimensional object structure available from the mental representation generated during reasoning was assessed via a surprise recognition procedure.

The methods of depicting objects that were used are orthographic projection—in which three different views of an object are displayed at right angles to each other by dropping perpendiculars from each side of the object—and isometric projection—in which three surfaces of an object are displayed in a single plane, with the projectors perpendicular to the picture plane and the three principal axes making equal angles with the plane. Figs. 4.1 and 4.2 illustrate the correspondence between isometric and orthographic projections of a single three-dimensional object. In Fig. 4.1, orthographic views of five surfaces of the object shown in isometric form are displayed, projected from the corresponding sides of the object. Note that only three sides of the object are visible in the isometric view. All but the bottom view are shown in orthographic form. Note, also, that various drawing conventions are used in orthographic projection, the most important of which is that dashed lines rep-

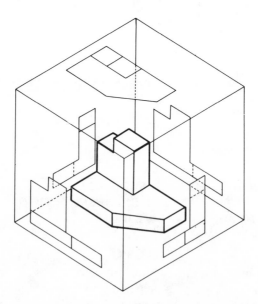

FIGURE 4.1.   Illustration of relationships among isometric and orthographic views of the same three-dimensional object. Orthographic views are shown projected from corresponding surfaces of the isometric.

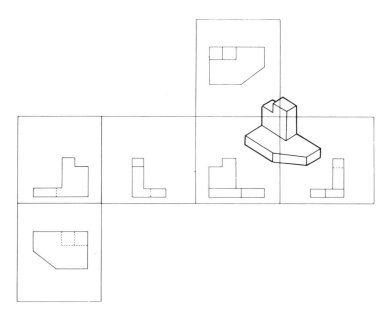

FIGURE 4.2. Orthographic views of the three-dimensional object shown in isometric projection "unfolded" from the corresponding surfaces of the isometric.

resent hidden edges of the depicted object. In Fig. 4.2, all six sides of the object shown in isometric projection are displayed as "unfolded" from the representation given in Fig. 4.1. Fig. 4.3 displays two three-dimensional objects, shown in isometric projection on the left and in orthographic projection on the right. Note, in particular, the labeling of the object surfaces that correspond in the two forms of projection.

The observers in the experiments were students enrolled in beginning mechanical engineering courses at the University of Arizona. The problems posed to them were similar to certain exercises encountered in class. The actual problem-solving situation is illustrated schematically in Fig. 4.4. It is somewhat more difficult than simple comparison of isometric and orthographic views of objects. The first level of increased difficulty comes from introducing a temporal separation between parts of the problem, and a second level of difficulty is achieved by removing isometric projections from the task altogether. As shown in Fig. 4.4, observers were asked to determine the possibility or "compatibility" of two sets of orthographic views of potentially realizable three-dimensional objects. That is, given two orthographic views and an empty "placeholder" indicating the location of a missing third view, a judg-

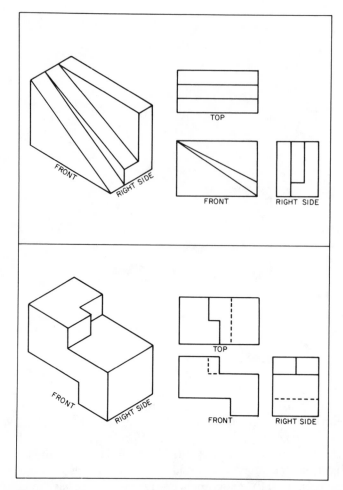

FIGURE 4.3. Isometric (left) and orthographic (right) views of two three-dimensional objects. Corresponding sides of the two sets of projections are labeled.

ment of the possibility, correctness, or compatibility of that third view—displayed immediately after the two "given" views—was required.

Two features of the problems and the task structure are important. First, at no time were observers ever shown isometric projections of objects during the reasoning task. They were simply shown sets of orthographic views and were required to determine their compatibility, with no reference to corresponding isometric views.

Second, for the majority of the problems, the three-dimensional object corresponding to the orthographics presented was uniquely determined from the two initial orthographic views, given the constraints of

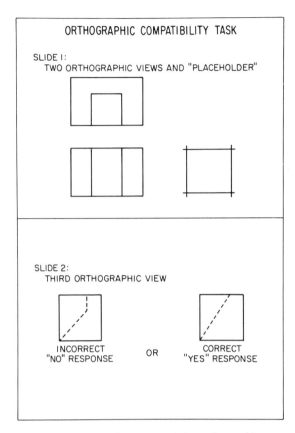

FIGURE 4.4. Schematic illustration of the orthographic compatibility task.

the task environment. That is, it was possible to generate a mental model of the object corresponding to the initial set of two orthographics and simply to check this model against the ensuing third, or test, orthographic view. In the actual experimental procedure, observers were allowed to alternate between the two parts of each of 20 to 35 problems (depending on the particulars of a given experimental context) as frequently as they desired before giving the "yes–no" response. In addition, they were required to provide verbal protocols (of various sorts, depending on the experiment) concerning how they believed they had gone about solving the problems.

Of particular importance is a second, incidental task that followed the orthographic problem solving. Observers were shown a series of surprise recognition items at the end of the experimental session. These items consisted of isometric views that corresponded to objects that had or had not been presented in the form of orthographic projections during the earlier, problem-solving phase of the experiment. Observers were required to choose which of two isometric views—a target and a distractor view—corresponded to any object that had been displayed earlier in orthographic form. Fig. 4.5 provides a schematic illustration of both a problem-solving trial and a subsequent isometric recognition trial.

In the experiments considered here, the distractor isometrics were generated according to an orderly procedure. For each target isometric, four distractors were constructed so that each distractor shared one or-thographic view in common with the target isometric. In addition, any salient feature present in the target structure—such as a large, angled protrusion—was not totally absent in the distractor. An independent group of observers rated each target/distractor pair on a 1 to 7 scale, and the data were normalized by converting each value to a z-score. A single

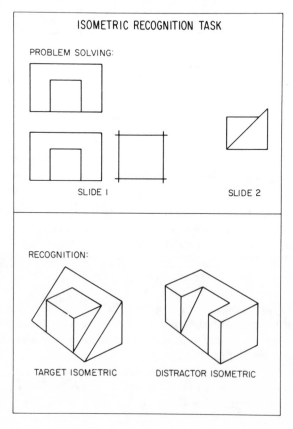

FIGURE 4.5. Schematic illustration of the isometric recognition task.

distractor was chosen for each target isometric by selecting that structure of the four rated with an average z-score nearest .5, corresponding
to an intermediate rating of similarity to the appropriate target isometric.

The purpose of the incidental recognition task was to probe, retrospectively, the nature of the mental models or representations that observers constructed during the course of solving these spatial problems.
Initially, the expectation was that performance on the recognition task
would be related to the strategy used during problem solving (assessed
by other methods that are not of concern here). Certain features of the
results of early experiments showed relationships between recognition
latency and problem-solving strategy, but in general, the overall recognition results are representative of the date of individual subjects, and by
now have been replicated several times.

The central features of the recognition results from a typical experiment (Cooper, Mumaw, and Morrow, 1984), and the relationship between problem solving and recognition performance are shown in the
top row of Table 4.1. They can be summarized as follows: Overall accuracy on solving orthographic compatibility problems was 76.5%, and
average solution time was 45 seconds. Average accuracy in discriminating target isometric views from distractors was high—85.5%. Furthermore, accuracy on the problem solving and recognition tasks were not
independent, $X^2(1) = 8.58$, $p<.01$. The rightmost cell in Table 4.1
shows that the probability of correctly recognizing an isometric view of

TABLE 4.1
Summary of Results from a Variety of Problem Solving
and Incidental Recognition Experiments

Problem Solving Task	Accuracy, Latency Problem Solving	Recognition Task	Accuracy, Latency Recognition	PCC/PCI
Orthographic Compatibility	76.5%	Isometric Views	85.5%	.90
				$(t_9 = 2.29 \ p < .05)$
	45.0 sec.		9.3 sec.	.72
Orthographic Compatibility	86%	Orthographic Views	89.5%	.90
				NS
	48.9 sec		13.7 sec.	.85
Isometric Comparison	72.5%	Isometric Views	96%	.96
				NS
	21.8 sec.		3.8 sec.	.97
Isometric Comparison	73.5%	Orthographic Views	75.5%	.75
				NS
	21.6 sec.		26.1 sec	.79

an object, given that the corresponding orthographic compatibility problem had been solved correctly, was .90. The probability of correct recognition, given an incorrect problem solution, was .72; and, these two recognition probabilities are significantly different, $t(9) = 2.29$, $p<.05$.

What might this pattern of results mean? It has been interpreted (Cooper, Mumaw & Morrow, 1984) as consistent with the idea that solving orthographic compatibility problems is accomplished by the construction of an internal or mental model of a three-dimensional structure—permitting later recognition of isometric views—even though the form in which the problem was originally presented contained only flat, separated views of individual sides of a visual structure. This conclusion is supported, first, by the generally high level of recognition. More importantly, the significantly superior later recognition of isometrics deriving from problems that had been solved correctly than from problems that were solved incorrectly, provides stronger evidence for the claim that the solution process was mediated by a mental representation of a three-dimensional object, rather than by the orthographic views presented in the problems. This follows from the fact that retention of information about individual orthographic views need not be affected by whether or not a given problem is solved correctly or incorrectly. However, retention of information about corresponding isometric representations of objects should be strongly affected by problem solving accuracy. This is because, by hypothesis, it is the mental construction of a representation corresponding to a three-dimensional object that underlies the process of problem solution.

Initially, the results displayed in Table 4.1 seemed quite surprising. Recall that the isometric recognition test, in essence, requires the observer to discriminate between representations of objects never seen before in precisely the surface form provided at the time of recognition. The fact that recognition performance is relatively good suggests that the mental representation constructed and used during problem solving itself is "objectlike", or, more properly, contains structural information similar to that displayed in an isometric projection, even though such a projection has never been encountered before, or only viewed in a much different surface form.

These results (referred to hereafter as the "isometric recognition effect") are reminiscent of findings in other perceptual and cognitive domains. In particular, they seem related to the general class of phenomena that demonstrate cognitive abstraction from individual or particular exemplars of meaningful categories and/or the effective integration of partial or unordered information. Thus, research like that of Posner and Keele (1968), showing that visual prototypes are abstracted from individual instances of categories even though the prototypes are never displayed, and studies like those of Bransford and Franks (1971), showing that gist or meaning is abstracted from the surface form of linguistic information, may be tapping the same kind of cognitive/representational principles as those tapped here. Another domain with seeming similarities to the phenomenon obtained here is the linear ordering literature (e.g., Potts, 1972, 1974), in which it has been demonstrated that piecemeal presentation of individual relations may lead to the construction of an integrated mental model in which all of the relations are represented directly. The results in Table 4.1 extend these sorts of findings by demonstrating that meaningful mental representations of three-dimensional objects are constructed from separate surface projections, even when viewers have no expectation that information in isometric-like form will be required for or relevant to the task, and even though the central problem-solving task can be completed on the basis of exclusively two-dimensional information (cf., Cooper, 1988).

There are several directions in which this initial finding has led the program of research, but only one is directly related to the concerns of this paper. Briefly, one of the other directions involves demonstrating that the isometric recognition findings cannot be accounted for wholly by reference to internal representations that do not incorporate aspects of three-dimensional structure. The results shown in the bottom three rows of Table 4.1 are taken from a series of experiments in which different problem-solving formats and recognition formats (orthographic–isometric, orthographic–orthographic, isometric–isometric, and isometric–orthographic) were examined. The pattern of results taken together suggests that although some two-dimensional information may be available for use at the time of recognition, the ability to discriminate isometric from distractor structures following reasoning with flat projections does indeed rely on the construction of a mental model of a three-dimensional object. Another direction that the research program has taken concerns why it is that viewers construct mental representations of three-dimensional objects in tasks for which two-dimensional information will suffice. That is, what aspects of the structure of three-dimensional mental models make them useful problem-solving tools? A third and related research line involves examining the range of reasoning situations over which results like these might apply. That is, what are the conditions under which three-dimensional spatial models are more effective than two-dimensional equivalents?

The central direction in which the isometric recognition effect has led the research program involves using the isometric recognition task to ask questions concerning the aspects of object structure that are preserved in the mental models constructed during problem solving. The isometric recognition effect itself indicates only that constructed mental representations of objects contain structural information adequate to discriminate isometric views of objects presented in orthographic form from isometric views of other, albeit structurally related, objects. That is, the constructed object representations are more like isometrics than like isometrics of other structures.

The specific question concerning structural characteristics of constructed representations of objects, to which the following series of experiments is directed, concerns whether the mental representations contain information about three-dimensional structure that is specific to a particular point of view or whether the accessible information in these representations is more general, in the sense of being view-independent. Stated somewhat differently, the question of interest in these experiments concerns how accessible non-depicted or "hidden" surfaces of a target isometric might be at the time of recognition. To what extent can the structure of object surfaces not explicitly presented in orthographic form at the time of problem solving be induced from the structure of the mental representation mediating isometric recognition? Note that the results of experiments addressed to such questions might, in addition to articulating further the nature of the mental models used in spatial reasoning tasks, be relevant to the question of the accessibility of different levels of perceptual representation postulated by Marr (1982).

Observers were again required to solve orthographic compatibility problems and then to engage in incidental recognition of isometrics. However, unlike the earlier experiment, the isometric recognition pairs were of eleven different types, divided into four separate experiments. The relationship among the target isometric structures for three of the four experiments is shown in Fig. 4.6. The depicted isometric views all correspond to the same three-dimensional object that would be constructed by combining the orthographic views shown in the center of the figure. They differ, however, in *which* surfaces of the object are visible and in *how* the visible surfaces correspond to the three given views displayed in orthographic form. Note that the isometrics in Fig. 4.6 can share all three (the standard isometric view), two, one, or no surfaces in common with the three orthographic views explicitly presented in the problem-solving task. That is, although the target isometrics shown in Fig. 4.6 all correspond to the same three-dimensional object, the point of view from which the object is depicted in the cases of two-, one-, and zero-shared-views reveals one or more surfaces that are not explicitly presented in the orthographic problem, and hides one or more of the surfaces that are explicitly given in the problem.

In the first experiment, forced-choice surprise recognition pairs consisted of standard isometric views, along with the associated

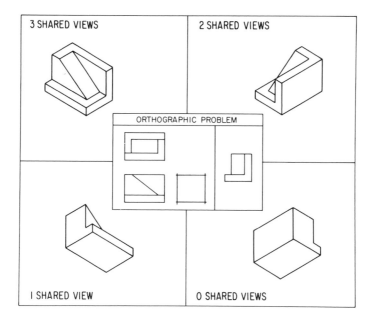

FIGURE 4.6. Illustration of the types of isometric views used in the present series of experiments. Isometrics sharing three, two, one, and no views with the orthographic views given during problem solving are shown.

distractors, or of isometric/distractor pairs that shared only two views in common with the surfaces presented in orthographic form. In the second experiment, recognition pairs consisted of standard target/distractor isometric views and of corresponding sets of isometrics that shared only one surface in common with those presented as orthographics. In the third experiment, standard isometric pairs were intermixed with pairs of target/distractor isometrics that displayed no views in common with the previously presented orthographic projections.

In the cases of Experiments 1 and 2, containing isometrics that share two or one view(s) with the standard isometric, three sorts of corresponding structures are possible. All three were used in the experiments. Fig. 4.7 illustrates the three ways in which two views can be shared between transformed and standard isometric recognition items, as well as illustrating each target structure paired with the associated distractor. The correspondences shown are between front and right, top and right, and top and front views. Fig. 4.8 illustrates the three ways in which one view can be shared between transformed and standard isometrics by virtue of correspondence between front, right, or top surfaces of the specified three-dimensional object. Distractors are also shown paired with the appropriate target isometric. The single way in which no views are

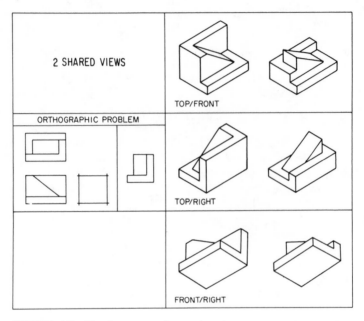

FIGURE 4.7. The three types of "two-shared-views" target/distractor iso-metric recognition items.

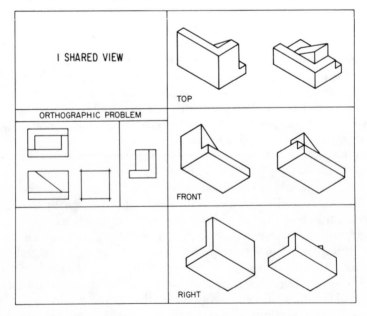

FIGURE 4.8. The three types of "one-shared-view" target/distractor iso-metric recognition items.

shared between standard and transformed isometrics can be seen by referring to Fig. 4.6.

In addition to the three experiments comparing performance on standard and viewpoint-transformed isometric recognition items, a fourth experiment assessed performance on standard isometrics and performance on the same isometric view, but rotated 60°, 120°, or 180° in the picture plane. Fig. 4.9 illustrates the isometric views with corresponding distractors that result from this set of transformations. The idea behind including this final experiment was to enable comparisons between recognition performance on isometrics that have undergone structure-revealing transformations around one or more axes in depth and those that have undergone picture-plane transformations that do not result in the presentation of previously hidden surfaces.

In summary, separate groups of twelve observers participated in each of the four experiments. The novel feature of this set of experiments is that surprise recognition is assessed not only for isometrics that correspond in their portrayed point of view to the surfaces given in the orthographic problem, but also for isometrics shown from a point of view other than that of the isometric that would have been constructed from the three surfaces shown in orthographic projection during problem solving. In addition to variations in points of view, items depicting

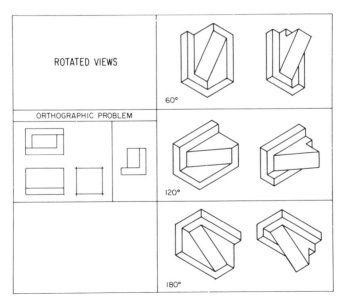

FIGURE 4.9. Isometric recognition items displaying target/distractor views rotated 60°, 120°, and 180° from the picture-plane orientation of the standard isometric view.

structure-preserving plane rotations of the standard isometrics are included.

What results might be expected from these experiments concerning the accessibility of non-depicted, or "hidden", surfaces of constructed mental representations of three-dimensional objects? Two extreme sets of outcomes seemed possible. At one extreme, it could be that constructed mental representations of objects are more or less strictly confined to representing three-dimensional structure from a particular point of view. Under this account, the various recognition pairs sharing two, one, or no views with the standard should not differ from each other and should yield substantially poorer recognition performance than pairs showing isometrics in the standard orientation. At the other extreme, it could be that all structural information in a constructed mental representation is equally available; that is, that the representation is "orientation-free" or "object-centered", in Marr's (1982) terminology. If this is the case, then the overall level and pattern of recognition performance should be the same for all types of transformed views, and these views should not differ in performance from the standard orientations of the test isometrics.

The overall results of these experiments, shown in Table 4.2, fall somewhere between these two extremes, and several interesting patterns are apparent. Table 4.2 presents accuracy and latency measures for both problem solving and recognition separately for each of the five

TABLE 4.2
Summary of Problem Solving and Incidental Recognition Results
from Experiments in Which Structural Relations Between Standard
and Test Isometrics Were Varied

Recognition View Type	Accuracy, Latency Problem Solving	Accuracy, Latency Recognition	PCC/PCI
3 Shared Views	84% 55 sec.	86% 9.6 sec.	.89 .77
2 Shared Views	82% 71 sec.	83% 15.9 sec.	.85 .83
1 Shared View	85% 63 sec	67% 13.7 sec.	.67 .65
0 Shared Views	81% 68 sec.	60% 15.5 sec.	.57 .53
Rotated Views	85% 69 sec.	82% 15.6 sec.	.85 .67

types of target/distractor isometric pairs—standard views, views containing two, one, or no shared surfaces with the standard, and rotated isometric views. In addition, probabilities of correct recognition given correct and incorrect problem solution are shown. (For purposes of simplifying presentation, data for the standard or "three-shared-views" case are taken from an independent experiment, making all comparisons between conditions also between subject groups.)

Consider, first, the problem-solving results shown in the leftmost column in Table 4.2. Little variation in either accuracy or latency of problem solving is apparent over the various experiments, and the results shown here are consistent with those obtained in earlier experiments. This is comforting, as it suggests that there are no sampling differences from one experiment to another and that there are no artifacts of training that could interact with subsequent recognition.

Overall recognition performance, shown in the middle column of Table 4.2, does clearly differ among the five types of recognition items. Specifically, recognition accuracy for standard (three), rotated, and two shared views is high, but accuracy for no shared views approaches chance with the one-shared-view condition falling in between. The pattern of latencies is somewhat different, in that the most substantial decrement in performance is obtained between the standard three-shared-views condition and all of the others. In general, the conditional recognition probabilities shown in the rightmost column of Table 4.2 reflect the pattern of overall recognition rates. However, the standard and the rotated cases are the only ones for which the probability of correct recognition given correct versus incorrect problem solution differ substantially. This pattern in the standard condition replicates earlier findings, and there is reason to question the stability of the estimated probabilities of correct recognition given incorrect problem solution for the other cases. This is because a substantial number of subjects solved all of the problems corresponding to the appropriate recognition items correctly, so the conditional probabilities had to be estimated by regression techniques. An experiment is currently in progress in an attempt to provide more stable estimates of the probabilities of correct recognition, given incorrect problem solution, for the zero-, one-, and two-shared-views conditions.

The picture that emerges from the overall pattern of data suggests that some degree of non-explicit (or "hidden") structural information can be accessed from mental representations of three-dimensional objects, but the extent of the accessibility is limited, and access—even when possible—requires additional time. Thus, although the accuracy with which isometrics sharing two views in common with standard isometrics compares well with accuracy for recognizing the standard views themselves, the time needed to make the recognition response is significantly longer than for recognizing standard isometric views.

In the extreme case of no shared surfaces between the standard and test isometrics, latency is long and accuracy is close to chance, indicating that access to object structure that is completely concealed is virtually impossible. That is, the mental representation of an object formed from separate, flat, orthographic projections may contain accessible information concerning the structure of immediately adjacent surfaces, but no accessible structural information is available concerning completely concealed views. Note, in addition, that recognition of isometrics rotated in the picture plane is as high as recognition of standard isometric views. Thus, a transformation that does not reveal previously hidden structure has virtually no effect on recognition accuracy, but even this structure-preserving transformation increases the amount of time needed to access the structural information and, thus, to achieve recognition.

There are additional features of the data from these experiments that are too detailed to present here, but that may provide insight into the conditions under which concealed structure can and cannot be accessed from mental representations of three-dimensional objects. These features include variations in recognition accuracy depending on which of the two or one object surface(s) are shared with the standard isometric view, and how much information for object structure the particular portrayed surfaces contain. These data are currently being examined closely in an effort to determine what kinds of explicitly presented surface information might provide the richest indications of structure contained from other points of view.

In summary, the overall results of these experiments suggest that constructed mental representations of three-dimensional objects are neither strictly viewer-centered (2 $\frac{1}{2}$ =/D) nor object centered (fully 3-D) in Marr's (1982) representational scheme, but somewhere in between. At present, the incidental recognition technique continues to provide a revealing method for probing the nature of the mental representation of three-dimensional objects and, specifically, for addressing the question of what forms of structural information are available in such constructed mental models.

EXTRAPOLATION OF PERCEPTUALLY DRIVEN SPATIAL TRANSFORMATIONS ON DEPICTIONS OF THREE-DIMENSIONAL OBJECTS

A second line of experimental work has been initiated that will hopefully complement the incidental recognition research, described heretofore, in providing evidence about the nature and extent of structural information about external objects and events that are preserved in corresponding mental representations. The experimental paradigm on which this work is based was initially introduced by me and Robert Vallone (see Shepard & Cooper, 1982 for a brief summary of initial results), but it has only recently been developed fully. The experiments in this research line differ from the incidental recognition work in several ways, the most important of which is that viewers are explicitly required to make predictions or to generate expectations concerning the continuing structure of a transforming object, rather than to make judgments about the structure of an object in an unanticipated, retrospective fashion.

The experimental situation is as follows: Observers view computer-generated drawings of three-dimensional objects undergoing a specified continuous spatial transformation at a constant rate. In the case of initial experiments, the spatial transformations have been confined to rigid rotations in depth or in the picture plane about a single axis. At some unpredictable moment during the continuously portrayed rotation, the transformation is interrupted by the display going blank. After an again unpredictable period of time, the object reappears—still undergoing the same transformation at the same rate as displayed before the blackout. The observer must then judge whether the point of reappearance of the object is at the correct position in the transformational trajectory, had the rotation continued smoothly during the blank interval. That is, observers are being asked to generate expectations concerning the continuing appearance of a transforming object during a period of time when the object and its transformation are momentarily obscured. Fig. 4.10 provides a schematic illustration of the experimental situation.

Although the present procedure—in which observers are asked to extrapolate internally a continuous external transformation of an object that is momentarily interrupted—is superficially quite different from the incidental recognition experiments—in which the availability of information about the structure of hidden surfaces of an object is probed retrospectively—the underlying logic in the two cases is actually quite similar. In both situations, the goal is to determine experimentally what aspects of the structure of the external objects and events is represented internally when only incomplete external information is available. As in the isometric recognition experiments, the main objective of the initial experiments on interrupted transformations has been to determine, if possible, the range of conditions under which extrapolation is easily computed by the perceptual system as well as conditions under which performance breaks down.

In the following set of experiments, a single object–a parallel projection of a cube, with hidden lines removed—and a single rate of

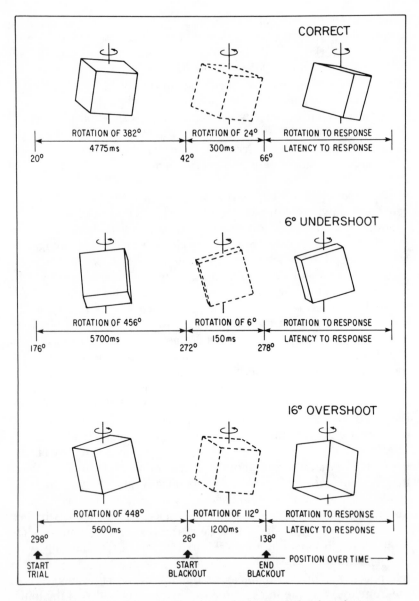

FIGURE 4.10. Schematic illustration of three types of trials in the interrupted transformation experiments. The top panel shows a trial on which the object reappeared in the correct position following the blackout interval. The middle panel shows a trial on which the reappearance undershot the correct position, and the bottom panel shows a trial on which the reappearance overshot the correct position.

rotation—80° per second—were used. The arbitrarily selected 0° position of the cube, which displayed the object tilted 15° on the x-axis and
5° on the z-axis, is illustrated in Fig. 4.11 along with other portrayed
orientations. Both starting positions and blackout positions of the
rotating object occurred randomly within the first and second complete
360° rotations, respectively. Three separate experiments were run, one
displaying a large cube (visual angle = 7.2°) rotating about the y-axis in
depth, one displaying a small cube (visual angle = 3.6°) rotating about
the same axis, and one displaying the large cube rotating about the
z-axis in the picture plane. In each of the three experiments, both the
duration of the blackout interval (150, 300, 600, 1200 ms) and the extent of angular displacement of the point of reappearance from the correct reappearance position (0°, ± 6°, ± 16°, ± 26°, ± 36°) were manipulated. For those cases in which the reappearance position was not
at the correct position in the transformational trajectory, undershoots
and overshoots appeared equally often.

Some of the data from this initial set of experiments are displayed in
Figs. 4.12, 4.13, 4.14, and 4.15. Fig. 4.12 shows mean percent of "correct" responses (i.e., judgments that the displayed object reappeared at
the correct position in the transformational trajectory) as a function of

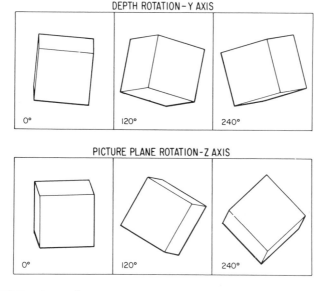

FIGURE 4.11.   Illustration of the arbitrarily selected 0° position of the object used in the interrupted transformation experiments. Rotations of the object in depth (top panel) and in the picture plane (bottom panel) are also
shown.

the angular extent of displacement or "shift" of the object's point of reappearance from the objectively correct location. Thus, only responses
at the 0° position are accurate; all other responses are false positive errors. Fig. 4.13 shows the same data, plotted separately for each of the
four durations of the blackout interval. The data in both figures come
from conditions in which the portrayed rotation was about the y-axis in
depth. In addition, the plotted points represent averages over size of the
object, as this factor had no effect on performance.

Not surprisingly, the data in Fig. 4.12 indicate that performance on
the task, for those cases in which the point of reappearance is shifted
from the correct location, becomes more accurate (i.e., there is less of a
tendency to judge that displaced onsets are the correct position of reappearance) as the angular size of the shift increases in either a forward or
a backward direction. However, both the shift value at which this function peaks and the asymmetry in the function for forward and backward
directions of displacement are noteworthy. In particular, Fig. 4.12
clearly reveals that undershoots—cases in which the object reappeared
after the blackout at a position backward (in terms of the ongoing transformation) from the correct point of reappearance—are uniformly less
detectable than are overshoots–cases in which the object reappeared in
a position ahead of the correct point of reappearance. And, this ten-

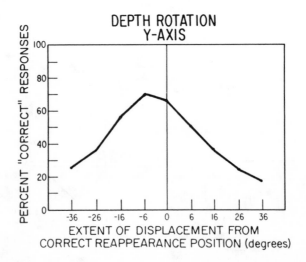

FIGURE 4.12.   Mean percentage of "correct" responses as a function of
the angular extent of displacement of the position of reappearance from the
correct location, from the depth rotation version of the interrupted transformation experiments. The plotted points represent averages over subjects,
stimulus size, and duration of the blackout interval.

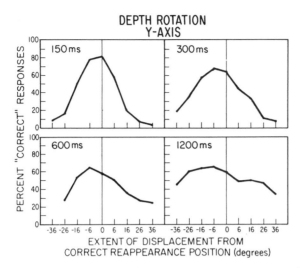

FIGURE 4.13. Data corresponding to those shown in Fig. 4.12, plotted separately for each of the durations of the blackout interval.

dency for false positive judgments to occur to undershoots is more marked for the smaller angles of displacement. Indeed, the average percentage of "correct reappearance" judgments is actually greater for 6° undershoots than it is for the 0° position, in which the object reappeared in the objectively correct location!

The data in Fig. 4.13 indicate that performance on correct reappearances and both undershoots and overshoots with large displacements from the correct location is better for shorter durations of the blackout interval. The asymmetry in judgments to undershoots and overshoots is apparent for all blackout durations, and only at the shortest blackout interval is the tendency to respond "correct" to objectively correct reappearances greater than the tendency to respond "correct" to small (−6°) undershoots.

Fig. 4.14. shows average data for the experiment in which rotations of the object were about the z-axis in the picture plane. Fig. 4.15 presents these same data plotted separately for each of the four durations of the blackout interval. Comparison of Figs. 4.12 and 4.13, for depth rotations, with Figs. 4.14 and 4.15, for picture plane rotations, shows striking similarity. For rotations and blackouts in the picture plane, as well as in depth, the marked asymmetry in judgments to undershoots and to overshoots is readily apparent. The similarity between these two sets of data is somewhat surprising, because the projected structure of an object transforming in the picture plane remains the same before and after an interruption of the transformation, while the projection of an object before, during, and after the interruption of a transformation in depth can be radically different. Hence, it might be expected that judgments about reappearances of objects obscured during a transformation in depth would be less accurate or based on different information than judgments about reappearances following the interruption of a picture-plane rotation. However, equivalent performance under conditions of depth and picture-plane rotations has been commonly reported for studies of mental rotation (Shepard & Cooper, 1982; Shepard & Metzler, 1971).

Given some of the unexpected results shown in Figs. 4.12–4.15, in particular the striking asymmetry of the functions, it seems appropriate to question whether the observers were in fact carrying out the task as they had been instructed. That is, could observers have been engaging in some strategy other than attempting to extrapolate, internally, the rotation of an object in three dimensions during the blackout interval? And, could the use of some alternative strategy produce the obtained pattern of results? There are reasons to be confident that observers were attempting to perform the task as instructed, which can be described only briefly here.

First, the near equivalence of patterns of performance for the depth and the picture-plane rotations/interruptions suggests that judgments were not being affected by peculiarities or particular properties of projections of the object in depth before or after the blackout interval. Indeed, an analysis of accuracy of judgment at different positions of object

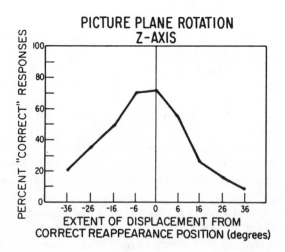

FIGURE 4.14. Mean percentage of "correct" responses as a function of the angular extent of displacement of the position of reappearance from the correct location, from the picture-plane rotation version of the interrupted transformation experiments. The plotted points represent averages over subjects and duration of the blackout interval.

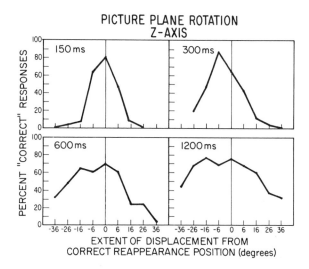

PICTURE PLANE ROTATION
Z-AXIS

EXTENT OF DISPLACEMENT FROM
CORRECT REAPPEARANCE POSITION (degrees)

FIGURE 4.15.   Data corresponding to those shown in Fig. 4.14, plotted separately for each of the durations of the blackout interval.

reappearance in the depth rotation case showed no systematic relationship between performance and the projection of the object when it reappeared. Second, an effort was made to articulate and to test an alternative strategy for performance based on following the movement of one particular point or corner of the object translating with accelerating and decelerating speed. Two different expressions of this strategy—for which judgment accuracy should be related to transformational distance in two dimensions—failed to account for significant amounts of variance in the judgments, compared to a model based on extrapolated distance over a three-dimensional trajectory. Thus, it appears that the data in Figs. 4.12–4.15 do reflect patterns of judgments produced by an internal process that extrapolates object transformation in three-dimensional space.

How, then, can the systematic error of accepting as "correct" reappearances slight backward displacements of test objects be explained? It would appear that the mental process of extrapolation "slows down" during the blackout or that some source of variability in the rate of the extrapolation is introduced that distorts the location of the anticipated point of reappearance in a backward direction.

It should be noted that directional distortions in similar sorts of judgments have been reported by Freyd and her associates (Freyd, 1983; Freyd & Finke, 1984; Freyd & Johnson, 1987) for a related perceptual/cognitive task. (Note, however, that others, most notably Cooper, 1976, have found a remarkable degree of accuracy when subjects are required to make judgments about a shape that appears in an expected versus unexpected position during the process of mental rotation.) The phenomenon that Freyd has described, termed *representational momentum*, is the tendency of memory for the final position of a static display in which directional motion is implied to be shifted forward, in the direction of the implied movement. That is, observers are likely to make false positive responses to objects presented in positions ahead of the position that is accurate, presumably owing to the implied dynamic properties of otherwise static displays.

The data from the present experiments reveal a directional judgment distortion intriguingly similar to the "representational momentum" effect, but in the opposite direction. That is, while the representational momentum experiments show bias in a forward direction, consistent with the implied trajectory of motion in static displays, the present results show bias in the reverse direction of the presented and extrapolated motion of dynamic displays. It must be noted that there are substantial differences in both the displays and the tasks used in the present studies and those of Freyd (1983; Freyd & Finke, 1984; Freyd & Johnson, 1987). In the present studies, the displays depict real motion (except during the blackout interval), the objects are portrayed as three-dimensional and the transformations are in depth, and observers are explicitly asked to extrapolate the transformation and to anticipate the point at which the object will reappear. In the representational momentum work, the displays are static (with motion implied by presenting an ordered sequence of objects), the objects and transformation are generally two-dimensional), and observers are asked to judge whether the position of a test object is the same as the position of the last object in the sequence—not to make judgments requiring mental extrapolation of real or implied motion.

Experiments are in progress in an effort to determine whether there is any relationship between the representational momentum findings and the results from the interrupted transformation studies and, if so, what factors might be controlling the difference in the direction of the two effects. One speculative but interesting possibility (about which data are currently being collected) centers around the velocities of the displays used by Freyd and her associates and those used in the present research. The implied velocities in the representational momentum work have generally been considerably slower than the 80°-per-second rate of rotation of the interrupted transformation displays. And, the work of Freyd and Johnson (1987) shows that, after a retention interval of about 100 ms, the amount of memory shift resulting from representational momentum decreases and changes direction as implied velocity increases. (For very short retention intervals, the amount of memory shift appears to be proportional to the implied velocity of the display.) It is intriguing to suppose that for intervals that exceed some critical value, the perceptual system might have internalized a preferred, natural rate of mental transformation. For internalized transformations of external rotations that exceed that rate, errors in the direction of the undershoots reported here might result, and for transformations that are slower than that rate, overshoots or momentum might be found. Results of experiments in which a range of velocities is examined using the interrupted transformation paradigm should shed light on this speculation.

In addition to evaluating the possibility discussed previously and elucidating the relationship between the present findings and other phenomena such as representational momentum, the interrupted transformation technique appears to provide a rich experimental situation for studying correspondences between the perceived structure of external objects and their transformations and the forms of object and transformational structure most readily preserved in constructed mental representations. Extensions of this work currently planned include examining the extrapolation of portrayed transformations about multiple axes and additional structure-preserving, as well as nonrigid transformations on various sorts of objects. The research approach is predicated on the idea that determining which classes of transformations (under which particular conditions) are most easily extrapolated in the absence of continuous perceptual information will provide insight into the nature of the internal system that anticipates the results of perceived transformations on objects in space.

CONCLUDING REMARKS

The richness and structure of our perceptual experience of the world is a commonplace, and it is sometimes surprising to realize that our mental models of objects and events are based on discrete samples of partial external information. Such considerations have led various perceptual theorists to liken the process of perception to a computation or an inference. Using this metaphor, information from the environment and constraints in the form of rules about relationships that hold in the world can be viewed as premises, and expectations or structured anticipations about likely states of affairs can be viewed as the outcomes of the computations, or the conclusions of the inference. To take a somewhat more concrete example, information about the structure of an object in various positions and the application of rules about possible transformations on the object in space can allow the perceptual system to anticipate how that object would look from points of view that reveal previously concealed information about object structure and about where and how the structure of the object might change while undergoing a transformation that is not continuously visible.

This account of the perception of objects and their transformations as computational or analogous to inference raises a host of questions concerning the nature of the mappings between structure available in the environment and structure preserved in representations of information in the environment, as well as questions concerning the selectivity of the system that performs the mappings. In this chapter, an approach to studying the structure preserved in mental representations of objects and transformations has been suggested. The approach is primarily an empirical one, and it relies on developing experimental procedures that are sensitive enough to reveal what aspects of external structure are accessible from internal representations of the structure. Two techniques that seem capable of providing this sort of evidence have been described. Although the general program of research is largely empirical in nature, the outcomes of experiments based on these techniques promise to have potential theoretical impact. That is, determining the forms of information about object and transformational structure that are incorporated in mental representations of objects and transformations may provide the raw material for constructing a theory of the architecture of the system doing the representing.

ACKNOWLEDGMENTS

The research reported here was funded in part by contract N0014-81-C-5032 from the Office of Naval Research, and in part by a Biomedical Research Support Grant from the University of Arizona. The author thanks Lyn Mowafy, Joe Stevens, Brad Gibson, and Doug Tataryn for substantive contributions to the program of research and Mark Bakarich, Ron Johnson, and Bruce Helming for technical assistance.

REFERENCES

Bransford, J.D., & Franks, J.J. (1971). The abstraction of linguistic ideas. *Cognitive Psychology, 2*, 331–350.

Cooper, L.A. (1976). Demonstration of a mental analog of an external rotation. *Perception & Psychophysics, 19*, 296–302.

Cooper, L.A. (1988). The role of spatial representations in complex problem solving. In S. Schiffer & S. Steele (Eds.), *Cognition and Representation*. Boulder, CO: Westview Press.

Cooper, L.A., Mumaw, R.J., & Morrow, L. (1984). *Probing the nature of the mental representation of visual objects*. Paper presented at the 25th annual meeting of the Psychonomic Society, San Antonio, Texas.

Cutting, J.E. (1986). *Perception with an eye for motion.* Cambridge, MA: The MIT Press.

Freyd, J.J. (1983). The mental representation of movement when static stimuli are viewed. *Perception & Psychophysics, 33,* 575–581.

Freyd, J.J., & Finke, R.A. (1984). Representational momentum. *Journal of Experimental Psychology: Learning Memory, and Cognition, 10,* 126–132.

Freyd, J.J., & Johnson, J.Q. (1987). Probing the time course of representational momentum. *Journal of Experimental Psychology: Learning, Memory, and Cognition, 13,* 259–268.

Hochberg, J. (1985). Visual perception of real and represented objects and events. In N. Smelser & D. Gerstein (Eds.), *Behavioral and social sciences: Fifty years of discovery.* Washington, DC: National Academy Press.

Marr, D. (1982). *Vision.* San Francisco, CA: W.H. Freeman Company.

Posner, M.I., & Keele, S.W. (1968). On the genesis of abstract ideas. *Journal of Experimental Psychology, 77,* 353–363.

Potts, G.R. (1972). Information processing strategies used in the encoding of linear orderings. *Journal of Verbal Learning and Verbal Behavior, 11,* 727–740.

Potts, G.R. (1974). Storing and retrieving information about ordered relationships. *Journal of Experimental Psychology, 103,* 431–439.

Shepard, R.N. (1984). Ecological constraints on internal representation: Resonant kinematics of perceiving, imagining, thinking, and dreaming. *Psychological Review, 92,* 417–447.

Shepard, R.N., & Cooper, L.A. (1982). *Mental images and their transformations.* Cambridge, MA: The MIT Press.

Shepard, R.N., & Metzler, J. (1971). Mental rotation of three-dimensional objects. *Science, 171,* 701–703.

von Helmholtz, H. (1866). *Physiological optics* (Vol. 3, 3rd ed., J.P.C. Southall, Trans., 1925). Menasha, WI: The Optical Society of America.

5 REFERENCE FRAMES IN THE PERCEPTION OF SHAPE AND ORIENTATION

Stephen E. Palmer
University of California, Berkeley

The research described in this chapter concerns the role of reference frames in perceiving the shape and orientation of objects. Ultimately, I describe some experiments I have done to understand how the human visual system might define these reference frames, but before I do this, I want to motivate the problem with some theoretical background concerning why one would postulate perceptual reference frames in the first place. Perhaps the easiest way to do this is to present reference frames as one possible solution to the problem of shape equivalence and then to describe some evidence that favors this hypothesis. Finally, I describe my own research testing three theories of how reference frames are selected.

REFERENCE FRAMES AND THE PROBLEM OF SHAPE EQUIVALENCE

How do people know that two different objects have the same shape? This is something that people do quite easily under most circumstances, yet perceptual psychologists do not yet fully understand how it is accomplished.

The problem of shape equivalence can be stated most precisely in terms of a transformational analysis. To see how, consider the example shown in Fig. 5.1. Roughly speaking, people see all of these triangles as having the same "shape" or "form", even though they differ in several

122   PALMER

respects: namely position, orientation, size, sense (mirror-image reflection), or some combination of these characteristics. This observation
suggest that the visual system factors incoming stimulus information
about perceptual objects into (at least) five fundamentally different but
interrelated domains: shape, position, orientation, size, and sense. All
except shape turn out to be intimately linked to simple geometric transformation groups. Figures that differ only in position are related by
translations along a line, those that differ in orientation are related by
rotations about a point, those that differ in size are related by *dilations*
(radial expansions and contractions) about a point, and those that differ
in sense are related by *reflections* about a line. The role that these particular transformations play in two-dimensional shape equivalence implies
a fundamental link to the *Euclidean similarity group*, which consists of
just this set of transformations: translations, rotations, dilations, reflections, and their composites.

There are two classes of theories about how shape equivalence might
be detected, both of which are fundamentally related to the transformational view described previously, but in somewhat different ways. I call
them the *invariant features* hypothesis and the *reference frame* hypothesis,
for reasons that become obvious once they have been described. We
consider each of them in turn.

The Invariant Features Hypothesis

The invariant feature hypothesis assumes that shape perception is mediated by detecting those geometrical properties of figures that do not
change (are invariant) when the figure is transformed in particular
ways. Any given set of transformations partitions the total set of figural
properties into two subsets: those that change when the figure is trans-

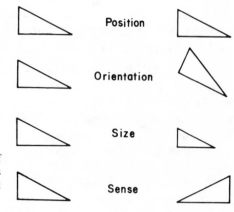

FIGURE 5.1. Examples of
shape equivalence over differences
in position, orientation, size, and
sense (mirror reflection).

formed in these ways, and those that do not. For example, when a figure is rotated through an arbitrary angle, the orientations of lines change, but the number of lines and the sizes of angles between them do not. Therefore, line number and angle size are invariant features of the group of rotations. In fact, they both are invariant features under the whole Euclidean similarity group, because neither property changes when figures are subjected to arbitrary translations, rotations, dilations, reflections, or any combination of these. Table 5.1 shows some examples of figural properties that are invariant over various transformation groups. The groups are ordered from those containing fewest transformations (at the top) to most transformations (at the bottom). These groups form a nested hierarchy, so that each group is a subgroup of the ones below it (e.g., the similarity group is a subgroup of the projective and the topological groups). This means that a given group includes all the transformations of the groups listed *above* it (e.g., the similarity group includes all of the congruences, which includes all of the displacements, etc.). As a consequence, all the properties listed *with or below* the group are invariant properties at that group (e.g., the invariant features of the similarity group include colinearity and continuity, the invariants of the projective and topological groups, as well as angle size).

The invariant features hypothesis, then, suggests that shape is represented by detecting just those properties of objects that do not change over the relevant set of transformations. As argued previously, the set of transformations that seems to underlie shape equivalence of two-dimensional figures is just the similarity group. Thus, number of lines, angle size, relative length of lines, number of angles, closedness, connectedness, and the like are possible candidates for invariant features of perceived shape because they are all invariant over the similarity group. This fact guarantees that any pair of figures that are related by a transformation from this group will necessarily be identical with respect to these features. To the extent that shape equivalence is indeed tied to the similarity group, these invariant features will solve the problem of shape equivalence.

TABLE 5.1
Invariants of Geometrical Groups

Geometrical Group	Invariant Property
Identity Group	Point Position
Displacement Group	Line Orientation
Congruence Group	Line Length
Similarity Group	Angle Size
Projective Group	Colinearity
Topological Group	Continuity

In some form or other, the invariant features hypothesis has dominated psychological theories of shape perception for a long time. Explicitly or implicitly, its assumptions underlie the Gestalt theory of shape perception, J.J. Gibson's theory of shape constancy, and the classical "feature set theories" of pattern recognition proposed by Selfridge and Neisser (1963) and many others. Such theories are attractive, at least in part, because of their structural simplicity: Shape is represented as a simple set (or list) of attributes. These can be weighted by importance and augmented by transformationally variant features (e.g., line orientation), but the basic proposal is always that a simple list of features is sufficient to explain shape perception. The question of how these features might get selected—phylogenetically through evolution of the species or ontogenetically through perceptual learning by the individual organism—is an interesting one, but it does not concern us here. We are interested in whether, or to what extent, the invariant features hypothesis is correct. If it is, we want to know which features are actually used to represent shape.

Unfortunately, there is some fairly compelling evidence that the invariant features hypothesis is wrong. It comes from counterexamples to the "similarity group hypothesis" concerning shape equivalence. Perhaps the simplest and most elegant demonstration is Mach's (1959) observation that when a square is rotated 45 degrees (top row of figure 5.2), it is generally perceived as an upright diamond rather than as a tilted square. Now, if perceived shape equivalence were perfect over rotational transformations, these two figures would be seen as orientational variants of the same shape because they are, in fact, rigid rotations of each other. Their shapes are often *not* seen as the same, however, at least not in the same sense that, say, upright and 45-degree tilted "R"s are spontaneously seen as the same shape in different orientations (bottom row of Fig. 5.2).

The fact that the perceived shape of the square/diamond depends on its orientation indicates that shape equivalence is a bit trickier than it seemed at first. It is difficult to see how this anomalous case might be accounted for if shape perception is based on rotationally invariant features because these are, by definition, independent of orientation. One

FIGURE 5.2. An example of failure to detect shape equivalence over a 45-degree rotation (the square and diamond in the top row) and of success (the upright and tilted Rs in the bottom row).

can only conjecture that sometimes, under conditions as yet to be determined, rotationally variant features somehow "leak" into the shape representation and cause errors. This is not a very satisfying explanation, however, and its inelegance has led several theorists toward alternative accounts in terms of perceptual reference frames (e.g., Marr & Nishihara, 1978; Palmer, 1975; Rock, 1973).

Perceptual Reference Frames

The reference frame hypothesis makes use of the same underlying transformations—the Euclidean similarity group—in a somewhat different way. Rather than ignoring properties that vary over the transformations of the similarity group, it assumes that the effects of transformations are removed by imposing an "intrinsic frame of reference" that effectively eliminates the transformation, thereby achieving shape equivalence. The proposal that perceptual reference frames are "intrinsic" simply means that the frame is chosen to correspond to the figure's structure rather than being imposed arbitrarily by the environment's structure (e.g., gravity) or the observer's structure (e.g., head orientation).

To see how intrinsic reference frames can allow the detection of shape equivalence, consider an analogy to the use of coordinate systems in analytic geometry. Fig. 5.3A shows three circles, *a, b,* and *c,* that have the same "shape," but differ in size, position, or both. Each circle can be described by an equation within a single extrinsic reference frame, in this case a standard Cartesian coordinate system. As shown in Fig. 5.3A, the three circles have different descriptions because *a* and *b* differ in size, *a* and *c* in position, and *b* and *c* in both size and position. However, their equations differ because they are specified relative to the same reference frame. Suppose that *different frames* were used to describe each circle, ones that were somehow matched to the intrinsic structure of each circle to give the "simplest" description possible. This situation is depicted in Fig. 5.3B. Now the equations are the same for all three circles. The reason is that the origin of the reference frame for each circle has been placed at its center and the unit size has been made to correspond to its radius. By choosing *intrinsic reference frames* that are matched to these two fundamental parameters of each circle, the variations due to size and position can be eliminated from its description relative to the frame. They are, in effect, absorbed by the parameters of the frame itself, leaving the shape description (here, represented by the equations) invariant within the frame.

Intrinsic reference frames can compensate for differences in orientation and sense, as well as in size and position. This cannot be demon-

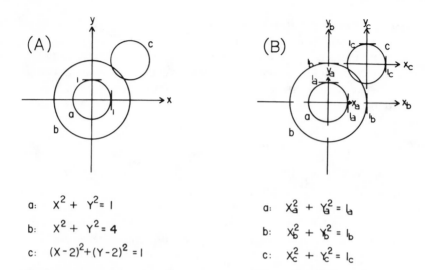

a: $X^2 + Y^2 = 1$

b: $X^2 + Y^2 = 4$

c: $(X-2)^2 + (Y-2)^2 = 1$

a: $X_a^2 + Y_a^2 = l_a$

b: $X_b^2 + Y_b^2 = l_b$

c: $X_c^2 + Y_c^2 = l_c$

FIGURE 5.3. Extrinsic (A) versus intrinsic (B) descriptions of circles in different reference frames. Equations for circles *a*, *b*, and *c* are given either relative to the same coordinate system (A) or different coordinate systems (B) selected to produce the "simplest" description.

strated for circles because they are both rotationally and reflectionally symmetric. For asymmetric figures, however, differences in orientation can be compensated by rotating the frame about its origin, and differences in sense by reflecting it about its major axis. The net result is that appropriately chosen intrinsic frames can compensate for any transformations induced by the similarity group: translations, rotations, dilations, reflections, and their composites. This means that if the same intrinsic frame were always chosen for the same figure, shape equivalence would be perfect over the entire similarity group, because all figural properties would then be invariant with respect to the selected frame. The difficulty, of course, is how the visual system could manage to choose the same frame each time. Part of the answer is that it does not, as we already saw in the case of the square/diamond.

It is important to realize that both theories of shape equivalence represent shape in terms of invariant properties over the similarity group, assuming that the appropriate frame is always chosen in the reference frame scheme. The difference lies in which properties are available for use and how they are detected. The reference frame scheme allows virtually any property to be made invariant simple by relating it to the appropriate intrinsic frame. The frame effectively absorbs all variation due to similarity transformations. For example, whereas line orientation varies when a figure is rotated, line orientation *relative to an intrinsic frame* (that rotates with the figure) does not. The same is true of information about location, size, and sense; each can be made transformationally invariant by selecting the same frame relative to the corresponding intrinsic properties of the figure. There is no magic in this. Whereas orientation, position, size, and sense vary over the similarity transformations, *relative* orientation, *relative* position, *relative* size, and *relative* sense are all invariant with respect to an appropriately chosen frame. The only problem is how to extract this information. The reference frame hypothesis suggests that it is done by imposing a structured set of relationships on the figure in the form of a "frame" that establishes privileged reference standards relative to which information is coded. The invariant features hypothesis is applied without using such reference standards, thereby reducing the set of invariant features potentially available.

Accounting for Anomalies in Perceived Shape Equivalence

I implied earlier that the reference frame hypothesis provided a plausible explanation for the anomaly in perceived shape equivalence that is evident in the perception of the ambiguous square/diamond. The nature of this explanation now needs to be stated explicitly. This helps to demonstrate some features of the reference frame hypothesis in action.

The analysis is based on three central assumptions. First, we suppose that shape is perceived relative to a reference-frame-like structure in which the orientation of the axes is taken as the descriptive standard (e.g., Rock, 1973). This is the most basic assumption of the RF hypothesis. Second, we assume that the perceptual system has some *heuristics* for assigning an "intrinsic" reference frame to an object such that the orientation of the frame relative to the object will be constant over different orientations. This allows detection of shape equivalence in the vast majority of cases because the description of the shape will then be identical even in quite different orientations. Because heuristics are imperfect rules of thumb, however, the first two assumptions together imply that there will be certain circumstances in which the wrong orientational assignment will be made. In such cases, the same object will receive different shape descriptions in different orientations, causing anomalies in perceived shape equivalence. Third, we assume that there are biases toward picking other salient orientations as the reference orientation, especially gravitational vertical or the top–bottom axis of the retina. Together with the first two assumptions, this implies that the perceived reference orientation for a given figure will be a joint function of both its intrinsic structure and its orientation relative to the observer and the environment. For instance, if a figure has two equally good axes for the reference orientation, and one of them happens to be aligned with gravitational vertical, that one will be chosen and it will produce some particular shape description. If the figure is then rotated so that the other good axis aligns with vertical, it will then be chosen as the reference orientation, producing a shape description *different* from the first. In fact, this is what is proposed to happen in the case of the ambiguous square/ diamond: It can receive two different shape descriptions, depending on which salient structure is aligned with environmental horizontal and vertical—its *sides* or its *angle bisectors*. When the sides align with horizontal and vertical, people perceive the "square" description, and when the angle bisectors are aligned with horizontal and vertical, they perceive the "diamond" description.

Hinton (1979) has made some closely related observations about reference frames based on experimental evidence using mental images of three-dimensional cubes. He asked his subjects to imagine a cube siting flat on a table (Fig. 5.4A), and then asked them to imagine rotating this cube so that two opposite vertices were vertically aligned (Fig. 5.4B). Once they had accomplished this transformation, he asked them to point to the additional vertices. Nearly everyone pointed to four coplanar vertices of a square on a horizontal plane bisecting the line between the opposite vertices. In fact, this does not define a cube, but quite a different shape (Fig. 5.4C). The correct answer is much more complicated: There are actually six vertices that lie alternately on two parallel planes connected by edges that go back and forth between them (see Fig. 5.4B). Hinton (1979) has several other nice demonstrations of this sort. They all suggest that a cube, like a square, has more than one structural organization, depending on the orientation taken as the principal axis of its reference frame. Each description makes different geometrical relations clear, and people are not at all facile at moving back and forth between them. The two descriptions are so different that they seem to be two different objects.

What I believe emerges from this type of analysis is that the ultimate effect of selecting a perceptual reference frame is to afford the observer different sets of geometrical relations contained in the structure of the figure. Because it would be impossible to extract all the possible relations in the figure—there being infinitely many,—and because many of them are highly redundant, the system needs to encode only a small subset of them. Ideally, it will pick the most stable and useful set it can find. It is this set of transformational relations that I believe constitutes the structure of a perceptual reference frame.

It may seem unreasonable to make such a fuss over these few oddities of shape perception, but Rock (1973) has shown them to be far more

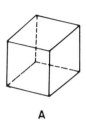
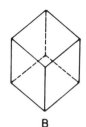
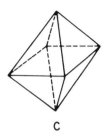

A   B   C

FIGURE 5.4. Three-dimensional shapes used by Hinton (1979). When subjects imagined rotating a standard cube (A) into an unfamiliar orientation (B), they made systematic errors in describing its shape as depicted in C.

pervasive than one might have guessed from everyday experience. The importance of these problematic cases lies in their implication that reference frames are routinely involved in detecting shape equivalence. As is often pointed out, the failures of a system sometimes turn out to be more illuminating about how it works than its successes. Still, we should not lose sight of the fact that correctly detecting shape equivalence is the rule, and failure is the exception. In terms of the reference frame hypothesis, this means that the frame is usually established in the same orientation relative to the object; only rarely is it misaligned.

Testing the Reference Frame Hypothesis

Irvin Rock (1973) was the pioneer in studying how shape and orientation might be perceived relative to a reference frame. He showed that when certain kinds of novel shapes are presented in one orientation and tested for recognition memory in another (see Figure 5.5A), people are far less likely to recognize them than if they were tested in the same orientation at which they were presented. This performance decrement indicates failure to detect shape equivalence. Rock further showed in many clever studies that the primary factors in determining the reference orientation are environmental and/or gravitational rather than retinal. When observers changed their head orientation by 90 degrees between presentation and test, recognition performance was not disrupted nearly as much as when the orientation of the figures was changed by 90 degrees. Rock took these and related results as evidence that shape is perceived relative to an environmental frame of reference in which gravity defines the reference orientation. If the orientation of the figure changes from presentation to testing relative to the environmental reference frame, the description of the figure at testing will not match the description stored in memory, and the observer will therefore fail to detect shape equivalence.

Wiser (1981) reported results that have extended and refined Rock's analysis in important ways. She has shown that Rock's results do not hold when the stimulus has a well-defined "intrinsic axis". Such figures are recognized as well when they are tested in different orientations as when they are tested in the same orientation. Under otherwise identical conditions, she (a) replicated Rock's results using figures that, like Rock's, lacked a good intrinsic axis (Fig. 5.5A), and (b) failed to replicate it using figures that possessed a good intrinsic axis (Fig. 5.5B). These results are actually quite consistent with Rock's (1973) theoretical analysis, although he was more interested in explaining the failures to detect shape equivalence than the successes.

In further experiments, Wiser showed that when an intrinsically structured figure is presented so that its axis is *not* aligned with vertical, subsequent recognition is fastest when the figure is tested in its *vertical* orientation. She interprets this result to mean that the shape is stored in memory as though it were upright, relative to its own intrinsic reference frame. This result is inconsistent with the simple hypothesis that shape recognition is "best" when figures are presented and tested in the same orientation. It is still consistent with an account in terms of reference frames, however. One merely needs to assume that the figures' intrinsic frame of reference is established by its own internal structure when that

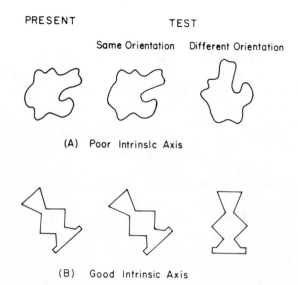

FIGURE 5.5. Comparisons between figures with poor (A) versus good (B) intrinsic axes in a memory task for figures presented in different orientations.

structure is sufficiently strong. Wiser's results then imply that the process of recognition operates most efficiently and effectively when the intrinsic frame of the figure is properly aligned with the extrinsic gravitational frame of its environment. The important point is that the shape of a figure is perceived relative to its own intrinsic frame of reference when it has the type of structure that clearly defines one, and relative to an extrinsic frame when it does not.

Notice that Wiser's results are consistent with detecting shape equivalence. The figure is recognized best in a different orientation because it is perceived as having the same shape. Note also that this only happens when the figure has a good intrinsic axis that "drives" the reference orientation to the same axis both times. If the figure has more than one good axis—or lacks any, as Rock's stimuli typically do—shape equivalence can fail to be detected when different axes align with a salient extrinsic orientation at presentation and at testing. Thus, the results of both Rock's and Wiser's experiments provide strong support for the reference frame hypothesis.

Other failures of shape equivalence have been reported when relatively amorphous three-dimensional objects have undergone an orientational change about a vertical axis (Rock, DiVita, & Barbeito, 1981). However, it is still the case that all failures discovered thus far result from changes in orientation of some sort. Rock and DiVita (1987) have recently reported poor detection of shape equivalence when an object's position is changed, but they also showed that this decrement was due to covarying orientational changes rather than to positional changes per se. The fact that all failures to detect shape equivalence over the transformations of the Euclidean similarity group seem to be due to changes in orientation poses something of a problem for the reference frame hypothesis. If perceptual reference frames are truly analogous to coordinate systems in analytic geometry, they also should contain information about size (unit distance), position (origin), and direction (sense), as well as orientation (axis), and these should likewise produce failures to detect shape equivalence.

There are at least three explanations that can be offered for the absence of failures due to differences in these other dimensions. The most obvious is that all shape properties are truly invariant over position, size, and sense. In this case, reference frame effects will never be found for these variables, because reference frames are simply not used for them. A second possibility is that psychologists have not yet looked in the appropriate places with sensitive enough measures. Or perhaps such effects are known, but their connection with reference frames has not been realized. A third explanation is that the stimulus variables that control the establishment of the position and size of the frame may be so unambiguous that the frame is inexorably attracted to the same values for the same shape. After all, the best reason to believe the reference frame hypothesis in the first place is that sometimes it *fails* for orientational changes. If it were *fail-safe* for these other dimensions, then one would never observe any failures, even though reference frames were constantly being used.

If the last possibility is true, however, it suggests that subtler effects of perceptual reference frames may still be observable. For example, if the process of compensating for a transformational difference takes an amount of time that varies systematically with the magnitude of the transformation, then we may be able to get evidence of the frame adjustment process from chronometric measures of perceptual processing. This kind of process may be what Shepard, Cooper, and their associates have studied in their well-known work on mental rotation (see Shepard & Cooper, 1982; Hinton & Parsons, 1981). Similar results have now been reported that strongly suggests the use of dilational transformations to compensate for differences in size. Bundesen and Larsen (1975) had subjects perform a same/different shape discrimination task using figures that varied in overall size. They found that subjects matched figures most rapidly when they had the same size, and took increasingly longer to match them as the size difference increased. This suggests that observers had to transform one of the figures to match the other in size before they could determine whether or not they had the same shape. This account is consistent with what would be expected from the reference frame hypothesis. Given these results, it is perhaps surprising that no evidence has yet been reported to support corresponding operations that compensate for differences in position. If such results were forthcoming, it would add significantly to the already strong case that shape equivalence is detected by using perceptual reference frames.

EXPERIMENTS ON FRAME SELECTION

The foregoing discussion concerned the theoretical rationale for perceptual reference frames and evidence supporting their use in perception and memory. The question I now address concerns how intrinsic reference frames are selected: What is it about the spatial structure of a figure that causes the visual system to choose one orientation as the intrinsic reference standard rather than another?

I have been studying this question for several years, using an experimental paradigm based on a phenomenon known as "perceived pointing of ambiguous triangles" (Bucher & Palmer, 1980, 1985; Palmer, 1980, 1985, in preparation; Palmer & Bucher, 1981, 1982; Palmer,

Simone, & Kube, in press). The phenomenon concerns the fact that equaliteral triangles are perceptually ambiguous in the sense that they can be perceived to point in any of three directions, but only one of them at once (Attneave, 1968). Thus, the triangle in Fig. 5.6A can be seen to point toward either 3, 7, or 11 o'clock and can sometimes be perceived to flip back and forth among these alternatives. Figure 5.6B shows that a random arrangement of such triangles all point in the same direction at once and that they all change direction at the same time. The phenomenon that is most intriguing, however, is a Gestalt-like configural effect that results when several triangles are placed in well-structured configurations. As shown in Fig. 5.6C, when several triangles are aligned along one of their axes of symmetry, perception is strongly biased toward seeing them point in a direction that coincides with the configural line. When they are aligned along one of their sides (Fig. 5.6D), they are seen to point in a direction perpendicular to the config-

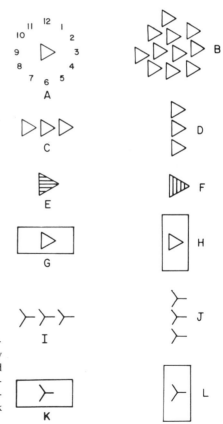

FIGURE 5.6. Ambiguous triangles (and Ys) in orientationally neutral conditions (A and B) and in contextual conditions that systematically bias perceived direction of pointing toward 3 o'clock (C–L).

ural line. Both of these effects have been verified experimentally using both self-report measures (Palmer, 1980) and perceptual performance techniques (Palmer & Bucher, 1981).

In a series of further experiments, we have shown that qualitatively similar bias effects can be produced by placing textural stripes inside a single triangle (Figs. 5.6E and 5.6F). Again, stripes parallel to an axis of symmetry bias perceived pointing in that direction, and stripes parallel to a side bias it in a perpendicular direction (Palmer & Bucher, 1982). It turns out that stripes on the perceptual ground produce similar, but weaker, effects. Another structural factor that produces this type of effect is the presence of a rectangular frame that surrounds a triangle (Figs. 5.6G and 5.6H). Again, perception of the triangle is biased toward pointing along the long axis of the rectangle when it is aligned with one of the triangle's axes and perpendicular to the long axis when it is parallel to one of the triangle's sides (Palmer, in preparation).

The Elongation Theory of Frame Selection

In trying for this diversity of effects, I was at first drawn to the elongation of the stimuli as the spatial structure that might have produced these biases. Others have had similar ideas (e.g., Humphreys, 1983; Marr & Nishihara, 1978; Wiser, 1981). It is not entirely clear, however, why an elongated stimulus should produce a bias along a direction *perpendicular* to its axis of elongation, especially one that seems to be every bit as strong as the bias *parallel* to its axis. Still, one can account for this sort of perpendicular effect by postulating some internal, mediating mechanism such as mutual facilitation between perpendicular orientations (e.g., Janez, 1983; Palmer, 1980; Palmer & Bucher, 1981). The idea of a Cartesian-like reference frame is particularly appropriate in this regard because it is defined by two perpendicular axes. Thus, if we assume that elongation in a given direction drives the frame selection process toward any frame that includes an axis along that line, both the parallel and perpendicular effects would be easily explained.

Testing the Elongation Theory

I set out to test the elongation theory using the same methods we had developed previously to study other contextual effects on perception of ambiguous triangles (e.g., Palmer & Bucher, 1981). In our paradigm, subjects are asked to perceive a particular one among the three possible pointings for each triangle, usually the one along a salient extrinsic orientation such as gravitational horizontal or vertical. For instance, they would be asked to see the triangle in Fig. 5.6A point directly to the right (toward 3 o'clock) rather than obliquely (toward 7 or 11 o'clock). The amount of time subjects take to achieve this percept is measured by requiring them to make a simple directional response as soon as they can determine in which of the designated directions the presented triangle points. Response time (RT) is taken as the primary measure of the difficulty in achieving the required percept for different stimulus conditions. Error rate is also measured, but its correlation with RT is usually so positive that it provides no additional information.

All of the studies about to be presented are based on the following rationale: If the target triangle is presented inside a frame whose orientation biases perception of pointing in a direction *consistent* with the required directional response—toward 3 o'clock in Figs. 5.7A and 5.7D—then RT's will be faster than if the same triangle is presented inside a frame whose orientation biases a direction *inconsistent* with the required response—toward 11 o'clock in Figs. 5.7B and 5.7E or 7 o'clock in Figs. 5.7C and 5.7F. The magnitude of the perceptual bias introduced by a given type of contextual frame can then be computed as the signed difference between the response times in corresponding inconsistent and consistent conditions. Reliable differences of this sort have consistently been obtained in previous experiments using this paradigm with configural and textural stimuli (Palmer & Bucher, 1981, 1982). The present "interference paradigm" was chosen over a more direct methodology in which subjects merely indicate the direction in which they first see the triangle point (Palmer, 1980), because it is less subject to alternative interpretations in terms of "demand characteristics" or other "optional perceptual processes" that might contaminate the results.

Experiment 1: Frame Elongation. There is an obvious way to test the elongation theory using rectangular frames: examine the effect of changing the aspect ratio (length-to-width ratio). If the elongation hypothesis is correct, there should be no bias effects for square frames, because they are not globally elongated. Moreover, the magnitude of the bias effect should increase monotonically as the aspect ratio increases. The perpendicular structure of the hypothesized Cartesian frame further predicts that the effects of elongation will be equal for axis- and base-aligned frames.

The stimuli for this experiment consisted of single equilateral triangles surrounded by frames of constant width and varying aspect ratios: 1:1 (squares), 1.5:1, 2:1, and 3:1 (see Fig. 5.7). The triangles were oriented so that each one could be seen pointing either directly left (toward 9 o'clock), or directly right (toward 3 o'clock). Subjects were instructed

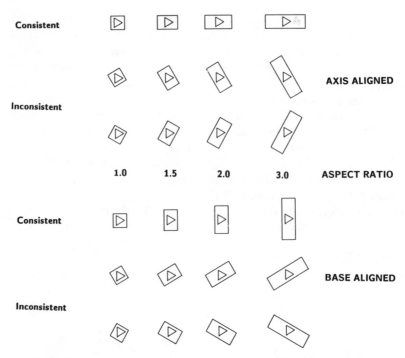

FIGURE 5.7. Stimuli in Experiment 1 (Frame Elongation). Axis- and base-aligned rectangular frames with aspect ratios of 1.0, 1.5, 2.0, and 3.0 were presented at orientations either consistent or inconsistent with the required response. All right-pointing conditions are shown; mirror-image left-pointing conditions were also included.

to discriminate between these two cases as quickly and accurately as possible by pressing the rightmost response with their right hand for the right-pointing triangles and the leftmost response key with their left hand for the left-pointing triangles. On one-third of the trials, the frame orientation was *consistent* with the required percept. In the axis-aligned consistent condition (Fig. 5.7A), the long axis of the frame coincided with the axis of symmetry that bisected the right- or left-pointing angle of the triangle. In the base-aligned consistent condition (Fig. 5.7D), the long axis of the frame was parallel to the side of the triangle opposite the right-or left-pointing angle. Reaction times to these trials should be fast and accurate, when the frame has a large aspect ratio. On the other two-thirds of the trials, the frame orientation was *inconsistent* with the required percept. For each of the other two possible directions of pointing there were both axis- and base-aligned inconsistent frames defined in analogous ways for the other two angles as shown in Figs. 5.7B, 5.7C, 5.7E, and 5.7F. Reaction times for these trials should be slower and/or less accurate to a degree that depends on the aspect ratio. In the square frames with aspect ratio of 1.0, of course, the axis- and base-aligned conditions are identical, and the elongation theory predicts no difference between consistent and inconsistent frame orientations.

Mean RTs are shown in Fig. 5.8 for consistent and inconsistent conditions as a function of frame elongation (aspect ratio). It is immediately apparent that the two critical predictions of the elongation hypothesis were not confirmed. Contrary to the prediction of no bias effect for square frames, these non-elongated frames produced a highly reliable bias effect: Responses to inconsistent orientations of the frame took nearly 150 msec. longer than consistent ones. Concerning the prediction of a monotonic increase in bias effects for increasingly elongated frames, there does seem to be a slight trend toward higher RTs for the longer frames, especially for the base-aligned frames, but even the difference between the most extreme aspect-ratio conditions fails to reach statistical significance. It seems safe to say that the measured variation in the amount of interference (inconsistent RT minus consistent RT) due to differences in frame elongation are quite unimpressive relative to the amount of interference that is present for the unelongated square frame. We conclude, therefore, that global elongation is unlikely to be a viable theory of these kinds of contextual effects.

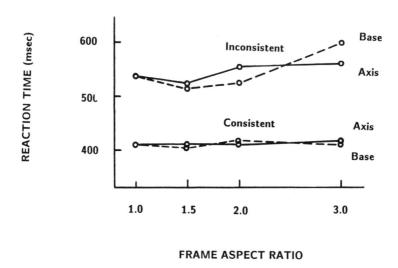

FIGURE 5.8. Results of Experiment 1 (Frame Elongation). Mean RTs are plotted for axis- and base-aligned frames in consistent and inconsistent orientations as a function of aspect ratio.

The Symmetry Theory of Frame Selection

A second possible theory to account for contextual effects on perceived pointing of ambiguous triangles can be formulated in terms of symmetry (Palmer, 1983, 1985; Palmer & Bucher, 1982). The proposal is that, roughly speaking, the visual system uses symmetry rather than elongation as the principal type of spatial structure used to select the orientation of its reference frame.[1] In this case, however, the theory is a bit more elaborate and elegant, and it makes some obvious predictions that turn out to be true. The following is a brief description of a qualitative theory that tries to account for how several contextual phenomena arise from symmetry structure, and how they are related to each other.

As with all reference frame accounts, we begin by assuming that people perceive the *shape* of an equilateral triangle relative to an intrinsic, oriented reference frame, and its *orientation* by the relation of this frame to a larger environmental reference frame. We further assume that the visual system has a powerful tendency to establish the orientation of a reference frame along an axis of reflectional symmetry, if one exists. Equilateral triangles have three such axes in their symmetry subgroup, the dihedral group D3 (Weyl, 1952). In this way, the theory accounts for the fact that equilateral triangles are three-ways ambiguous in perceived orientation and direction of pointing; the percept depends on which axis of symmetry is selected for the orientation of the frame (see Fig. 5.9). The triangle's *shape* is not correspondingly ambiguous, because all of its geometrical properties are invariant over the transformations that relate the alternative frames (i.e., rotations through an angle of 120 degrees and its integer multiples).

When additional elements are added to the display, their symmetries may or may not align with those of the original triangle. In the present

---

[1]One obvious objection to the symmetry hypothesis is that it applies only to geometrically symmetrical stimuli, and this is a very restricted set. However, the symmetry hypothesis concerns the *visual coding* of symmetry which, I argue, should be viewed as an analog dimension rather than a binary attribute. Geometrically speaking, a figure either is symmetrical about a given line or it is not. Perceptually speaking, however, there are undoubtedly degrees of symmetry. In fact, few things that we consider symmetrical—such as faces—are truly symmetrical in the strict geometrical sense. I presume that the perceptual system computes symmetry by a procedure that provides a continuous variable (or an approximation thereof) as output. When explicit judgments about symmetry are called for, this variable can then be thresholded at various criterial levels to determine binary outputs. However, I suspect that if the mechanism of reference frame selection used symmetry as a basis, it works with the continuous representation of "degree of symmetry" rather than the binary representation one would report in a forced-choice task. However, the precise quantitative nature of such an analog symmetry theory has not yet been formulated.

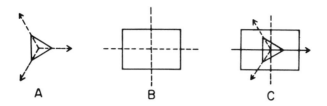

FIGURE 5.9.   A symmetry analysis of bias effects in perceived pointing of an ambiguous triangle.

cases—configural lines, textural stripes, and rectangular frames—the biasing factors all have a two-fold symmetry subgroup (the dihedral group D2) as illustrated in Fig. 5.9B. The intersection of these two sets of transformations is the symmetry subgroup of the resulting composite display. Because of the structure of the two component groups, D2 and D3, their intersection can contain, at most, one transformation, and this is reflection about a global axis of symmetry. Now, the theory assumes that the reference orientation is established along an axis of symmetry, if one exists. The reference orientation established for the whole display, then, will coincide with its global axis of symmetry, if one exists (Fig. 5.9C). The two merely local axes of symmetry of the triangle will therefore be less likely to be selected, and the triangle will tend to be seen pointing along the line of global reflectional symmetry. Note that this analysis holds equally for all three types of bias—due to configurations, textual stripes, and rectangular frames—and for both the axis-aligned and base-aligned versions of each. No further assumptions about interactions among perpendicular orientations are required for the cases we have considered.

This theory has the virtue of being easily extended to other cases, because it appeals only to the symmetry structure of the component stimuli. Therefore, it should apply equally to any other composite display whose components have the same symmetry subgroups, D3 and D2. Figs. 5.6I through 5.6L show one such extension to Y-shaped figures (symmetry group D3) positioned in configural lines or inside rectangular frames (symmetry group D2). These Ys, like equilateral triangles, are ambiguous in that they seem to "point" in one of three directions. They also can be biased toward pointing along axes of global symmetry within linear configurations and rectangular frames.

A second advantage of the present account is that it can be extended to other, analogous symmetry structures. In fact, we have already discussed one important example: the square/diamond figure. The ambiguity in shape of the square/diamond is analyzed as follows. This figure has four-fold symmetry (the dihedral group D4), and so its principal reference axes can be chosen in any of four ways. However, there are only two possible shape descriptions of the figure within these possible reference frames. The geometrical properties of this figure are the same for frames that share the same axes—because squares are rotationally symmetric about a 90–degree angle and its integer multiples—so there are really only two sets of frames that matter: the side-bisector frames and the angle-bisector frames. However, the properties of the figure *do* differ between these two sets of frames, and so the shape of the figure is two-ways ambiguous. As mentioned earlier, the side-bisector frames produce a shape description in which the sides are parallel and perpendicular to the frame axes, and so selecting one of them results in the perception of a "square" shape. The angle-bisector frames produce a shape description in which the sides are oblique relative to the frame axes, and so selecting one of them results in the perception of a "diamond" shape.

The symmetry theory further predicts that adding contextual figures with symmetry axes that align with one set of frames or the other should selectively bias one of these two different shape percepts. Indeed, this is the case, as illustrated in Figs. 5.10A through 5.10F. Squares aligned along a 45-degree diagonal (Fig. 5.10C) are generally seen as a tilted column of diamonds, and diamonds aligned along a 45-degree diagonal (Fig. 5.10D) are generally seen as a tilted column of squares (Attneave, 1968; Palmer, 1985). Similar effects due to rectangular frames Figs. 5.10E and 5.10F) were demonstrated many years ago by the Gesalt psychologist Kopfermann (1930). The present explanation in terms of symmetry further predicts that analogous effects should result for other figures whose symmetry subgroup is the same as for the ambiguous square/diamond. It can be readily observed in Figs. 5.10G and 5.10H that a " + " and an "x" are ambiguous alternative shapes of the same figure. They too can be biased by being aligned in a configural line along the 45–degree diagonal or enclosed in rectangles tilted by 45 degrees (Palmer, 1985). Thus, the symmetry theory seems to be supported by several extensions that turn out to be valid. In the next section, I describe some as yet unpublished research that we have recently completed to test the symmetry theory more explicitly.

Testing the Symmetry Theory

The obvious strategy for testing a theory based on symmetry is to do experiments in which symmetries are systemically broken. If symmetry is the key factor, then configural bias effects should disappear, or at least be significantly reduced, when one destroys a symmetry axis to which

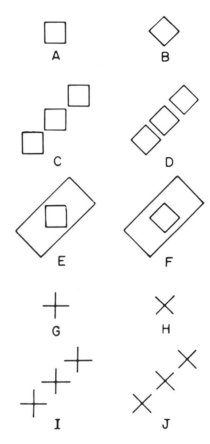

FIGURE 5.10. The ambiguous square/diamond (and +/x) in contextual conditions that bias their perceived shape.

the process of reference frame selection is supposedly drawn. The following experiments do this in a number of different ways to provide several independent tests of the theory.

Experiment 2: Frame Orientation.   The second experiment breaks the symmetry of framed triangles simply by varying the orientation of the frame. It examines the bias effect on perceived pointing of ambiguous triangles as the orientation of a surrounding rectangular frame is changed in 15–degree steps. The symmetry theory predicts that the orientation of the frame should affect perceived pointing in very systematic and predictable ways. For cases in which either of the two symmetry axes of the frame coincide with the relevant symmetry axis of the triangle—the "consistent" conditions—RTs to see the triangle point in the required direction should be short, because this will tend to draw the frame to the correct orientation for the task. For cases in which the reference frame axes coincide with either of the other two symmetry axes of the triangle—the "inconsistent" conditions—RTs should be long, because this will draw the reference frame to the wrong orientation for the task. When the frame axes are intermediate between these orientations, global symmetry has been broken, and RTs should be intermediate between the consistent and inconsistent conditions.

The 12 stimuli for the right-pointing triangle conditions are shown across the bottom of Fig. 5.11. The experiment also included 12 corresponding stimuli with left-pointing triangles that were just the mirror reversals of the stimuli shown here. Each of these 24 stimuli was presented 10 times to each of 13 subjects in a single session, and their RTs to discriminate triangles pointing directly left (9 o'clock) from those pointing directly right (3 o'clock) were measured.

The resulting RTs, averaged over replications and subjects, are presented in the graph directly above the corresponding stimuli. There is a large and systematic effect of orientation, quite similar to the predictions of the symmetry theory. Both the consistent axis-aligned frames (at 0 degrees) and the consistent base-aligned frames (at 90 degrees) are significantly faster than the corresponding inconsistent frames (at 60 and 120 degrees from axis-aligned frames and at 30 and 150 degrees for

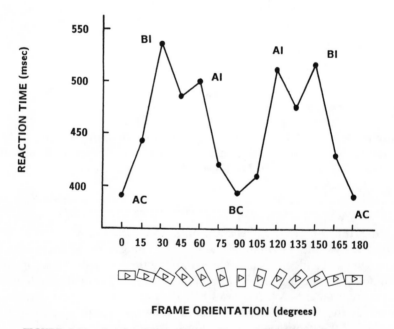

FIGURE 5.11.   Results of Experiment 2 (Frame Orientation). Mean RT is shown as a function of frame orientation (AC = axis-consistent; BC = base-consistent; AI = axis-inconsistent; BI = base-inconsistent).

base-aligned frames). The intermediate orientation in which symmetry is broken generally produce intermediate RTs, as predicted. However, there seems to be a substantial assimilation effect: The asymmetric configurations near one of the consistent orientations are reliably faster than those between the two inconsistent conditions. The symmetry theory does not explain why this should be so, but its major predictions are well supported by the data.

Experiment 3: Curved Frames.   Another way to break the symmetry of a rectangular frame is to bend it along its long axis. This has the effect of breaking the axis-aligned symmetry (the one along the long axis) while preserving the base-aligned symmetry (the one along the short axis). This makes a very interesting prediction: namely, that "straight" frames should have approximately equal biasing effects on an interior triangle in their axis-aligned and base-aligned orientations, but curved base-aligned frames should have a much bigger biasing effect than curved axis-aligned frames. The reason is simply that the base-aligned symmetry axis is intact after bending the frame, whereas the axis-aligned symmetry axis is broken. Because no previous experiments using the perceived pointing task have showed large differences between axis- and base-aligned effects, this is a strong prediction.

Examples of the stimuli are shown in Fig. 5.12. All frames were constructed with rounded ends to minimize orientational differences between the straight and curved frames at the short ends. The long sides of the curved frames were constructed using concentric circles whose radii differed by the same amount as the perpendicular distance between the sides of the straight frames. The stimulus design consisted of the orthogonal combination of four factors: frame alignment (axis- or base-aligned), frame bias (consistent or two inconsistent orientations), frame curvature (straight or two types of curved frames), and direction of triangle pointing (left or right). Each of 17 subjects saw six replications of each stimulus type.

The pattern of results shows reliable main effects, two-way interactions, and a three-way interaction among the factors of frame alignment, bias and curvature, as shown in Fig. 5.13. The straight frame conditions replicate the results usually found with standard rectangular frames: Consistent frames (dark bars) are reliably faster than inconsistent frames (light bars) by 120–150 msec., and the size of this frame effect is about the same for the axis- and base-aligned conditions. In contrast, the curved frames in the axis-aligned conditions fail to produce a reliable frame effect (less than 20 msec.), whereas the curved frames in the base-aligned conditions produce a frame effect as large as for the

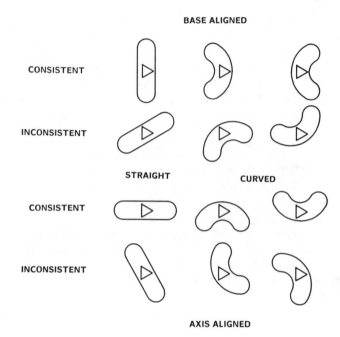

FIGURE 5.12. Example stimuli from Experiment 3 (Curved Frames). Bending the frame along its long axis preserves the symmetry of base-aligned conditions but breaks the symmetry of axis-aligned conditions.

straight, base-aligned frames (almost 150 msec.). This is precisely the form of the three-way interaction predicted by the symmetry theory.

Experiment 4: Line Position   The next experiment testing the symmetry hypothesis employed a single line as the contextual elements. We know from a previous (unpublished) study that a sufficiently long line segment aligned with or perpendicular to an axis of symmetry biases perceived pointing in much the same way as a rectangular frame around it. The single line context affords a particularly simple way of selectively breaking symmetries: namely, by varying the lateral displacement of the line relative to the triangle (see Fig. 5.14). When the line is axis-aligned, displacing it sideways (perpendicular to its length) breaks the global symmetry of the configuration, whereas when the line is base-aligned, displacing it sideways preserves global symmetry. Thus, the symmetry hypothesis predicts that the bias effect for axis-aligned lines will be close to zero for all positions except the central one—which will be large,— whereas that for base-aligned lines will be uniformly strong across a broad range of positions.

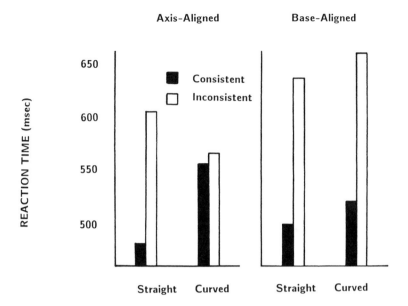

FIGURE 5.13.   Results of Experiment 3 (Curved Frames). Bending the axis-aligned frames eliminates the bias effect, whereas bending the base-aligned frames does not, as predicted by symmetry theory.

The present experiment examined bias effects for axis- and base-aligned lines at seven different positions (as shown in Fig. 5.14) for left- and right-pointing triangles. Eighteen subjects saw four replications of this factorial design under conditions quite similar to those of previous experiments.

The main results conform rather well to the predictions of the symmetry hypothesis (see Fig. 5.15). For the central position (0) there is a reliable bias effect for both axis-aligned stimuli (about 100 msec.) and base-aligned stimuli (about 70 msec.). For the axis-aligned lines, the bias effect drops dramatically when the position of the line is displaced just ¼ side length from the symmetry axis. For base-aligned conditions, however, the bias effect remains nearly constant across most of the range of displacements. Only when the line is outside the triangle toward the side it parallels does the bias effect diminish reliably. It is possible that this happens because the contextual line seems to form a larger triangle with the other two (nonparallel) sides. Despite this complication, the main pattern of results is quite clear and conforms rather well

AXIS ALIGNED

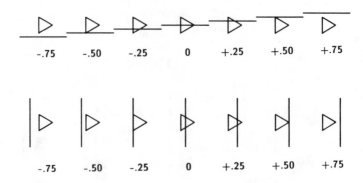

BASE ALIGNED

FIGURE 5.14.   Example stimuli from Experiment 4 (Line Position). Lateral displacement of a line segment preserves symmetry in the base-aligned
conditions, but breaks symmetry in axis-aligned conditions.

v /th the predictions of the symmetry theory: The bias effect is large
when the position of the line preserves global symmetry in the configuration, and small or nonexistent otherwise.

Experiment 5: Parts of a Frame.   The next experiment was actually un-
dertaken for a slightly different purpose, but it turns out to provide a
challenging test for the symmetry hypothesis. The idea was to study the
compositionality of the frame effect by measuring the bias effects produced by its individual sides and all possible combinations of them:
pairs, triples, and the complete square frame (see Fig. 5.16). The initial
question of interest was whether one could predict the effect of composing the piecewise parts of a frame by composing the bias effects produced by these same parts. The set of stimuli thus defined has the property of systemically breaking symmetries of the frame in certain cases
and preserving them in other cases. The unadorned symmetry hypothesis predicts that the symmetrical cases will produce reliable bias effects,
whereas the asymmetrical cases will not.

The experimental design consisted of the 16 configural conditions
shown in Fig. 5.16 in consistent and inconsistent orientations for both
left- and right-pointing triangles. Each of 16 subjects was shown each

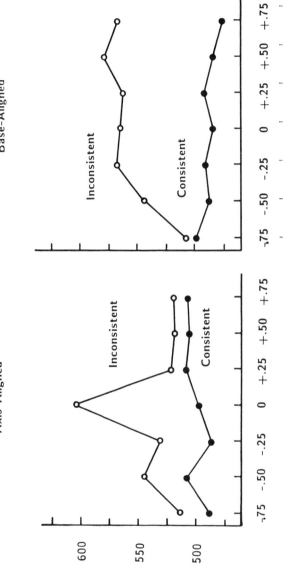

FIGURE 5.15. Results of Experiment 4 (Line Position). Displacing the line segment even slightly from a central position reduces the bias effect for axis-aligned conditions, whereas comparable displacements scarcely change the bias effect for base-aligned conditions.

condition three times, and RTs to discriminate left- from right-pointing triangles were measured.

The results in terms of interference RT (equals inconsistent RT minus consistent RT) are shown below each stimulus. For the symmetry hypothesis, there is some good news and some bad news. The good news is that the conditions in which the largest bias effects were found systematically came from symmetrical configurations: Six of the seven symmetrical stimuli produced the six highest bias scores. The bad news comes in two parts. First, all except one of the asymmetrical configurations produced statistically reliable amounts of bias. Second, and most problematic, the configuration that produced the *least* bias of all was, in fact, a symmetrical one.

There are various ways in which one could try to explain this pattern of results by modifying the symmetry hypothesis. For example, the one case in which a symmetrical configuration produces no measurable effect might well be due to the fact that it looks, at first glance, pretty much like a bigger triangle. (Recall that a similar effect was noted in the previous experiment.) Perhaps the initial processing of the figures takes place on spatial structure at a low resolution—such as in low spatial

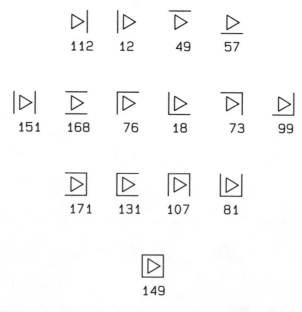

FIGURE 5.16. Example stimuli and results of Experiment 5 (Parts of a Frame). All possible combinations of sides of a square frame were measured for the amount of interference they produced. Numbers below each stimulus show the results: inconsistent RT − consistent RT = interference (in msec.)

frequencies—so that this particular stimulus would indeed be processed essentially as a bigger triangle. Then the symmetry hypothesis might still be viable, but only after the stimulus had been low-pass filtered.

Unfortunately, this "low resolution conjecture" does not seem also to explain the often-substantial effects of the asymmeric configurations. I do not spend any more time trying to account for these effects by further modifications of the symmetry hypothesis, however, because a reasonably good fit to these complex data is provided by an entirely different theory, the "low spatial frequency theory", to which I now turn.

The Low Spatial Frequency Theory of Frame Selection

A third theory to account for reference frame selection has been proposed by Luis Jañez of the University of Madrid (1983). His theory is based on a bold proposal originally made by Ginsberg (1971, 1986): namely, that Gestalt phenomena—such as the contextual effects I have been studying—can be explained in terms of the content of images at low spatial frequencies. Ginsberg's theory rests on the assumption that early stages in the human visual system perform spatial filtering operations at various spatial frequencies and orientations. There is now massive evidence, from both psychophysics and physiology, supporting this spatial filtering hypothesis (cf. DeValois & DeValois, 1980). Ginsberg has gone beyond this evidence to propose that Gestalt configural effects correspond to the pattern of output in visual channels selectively tuned to *low spatial frequencies*. As evidence, Ginsburg has shown that when images are low-pass filtered, so that only power at low spatial frequencies remains, the "emergent" properties to which the Gestalt theorists referred are often explicitly present in the filtered images. Thus, he argued, Gestalt properties correspond to information present in low spatial frequency channels.

Jañez (1983) has developed a precise mathematical formulation of Ginsberg's low spatial frequency hypothesis and has applied it to quantitative data from some of our early triangle experiments. He hypothesized that these Gestalt effects arose through differential activation in orientation channels at low spatial frequencies. Jañez's theory proposes that RFs are selected by a process that depends on the *dominance* of low frequency power at certain orientations relative to others. He formalizes this concept in terms of a *dominance ratio, D,* whose denominator represents the activity in low spatial frequency channels at orientations parallel or perpendicular to the required response, and whose numerator represents the activity in corresponding channels at orientations parallel or perpendicular to other possible directions of pointing. Thus, the higher the value of the ratio, the more activity there is in the irrelevant orientational channels, and the higher the RT is expected to be. (A mathematical description of Jañez's model is presented in the Appendix at the end of this chapter.)

To aid in understanding Jañez's theory, consider the middle row of Fig. 5.17 that shows the power spectra of Fourier transforms corresponding to the images in the upper row.[2] Notice that the circular configuration of triangles has a relatively isotropic power spectrum (i.e., uniform over orientation) in the low-frequency region. This configuration fails to produce systematic bias effects. When several triangles are aligned along their sides, however, the low frequency spectrum becomes markedly anisotropic, with most of the power in the orientation perpendicular to the configural line. These are configurations that produce marked biases in perceptual pointing. If effect, Jañez's dominance ratio formalizes these intuitive observations in that it reflects both the *degree* of anisotropy in the low frequency power spectrum and the *directional consistency* of that anisotropy with the required directional percept. The images in the bottom row of Fig. 5.17 show the spatial structures to which these low frequency power spectra correspond. They are low-pass filtered images of the triangle stimuli constructed by masking out all but the low frequency power inside the dashed circle of the middle-row Fourier transforms (including frequencies from 0 to the fundamental of a single triangle) and then resynthesizing images by the inverse Fourier transform. Notice that, as Ginsburg claimed, the emergent "Gestalts" of the configurations seem to be explicitly present in these low-pass filtered images.

Testing the Low Spatial Frequency Model

Jañez applied his model to the results of several of our early published experiments on perceived pointing of ambiguous triangles (Palmer & Bucher, 1981, 1982) and perceived shape of the ambiguous square/ diamond (Palmer, 1985), and he had notable success. We have replicated his results in an independent computer simulation of his theory, obtaining correlation coefficients generally in excess of .90 for the data

---

[2]Figure 5.17 displays power spectra as follows: The brightness of each point represents the amount of power present at the orientation and spatial frequency indicated by the direction and distance of that point from the center. Low spatial frequencies are near the center and high frequencies are far from the center. Orientations are displayed so that vertical gratings produce bright spots along the horizontal axis, and horizontal gratings produce bright spots along the vertical axis.

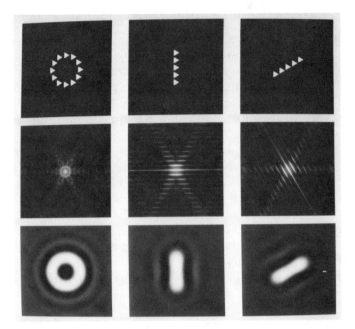

FIGURE 5.17. Examples of a low spatial frequency analysis for configurations of triangles. The left column shows a configuration that does not bias perceived pointing; the center and right columns show ones that do. The middle row shows the Fourier power spectra of the corresponding images in the top row. There are marked anisotropies in the low frequency spectra of the images that produce bias effects, but none for those that do not. The bottom row shows inverse Fourier transforms of just the low frequency portion of the spectrum.

he reported. We have now begun to explore his model's predictions for some of our later experiments more systematically, and some initial results are quite promising.

In further explorations, however, we have found some puzzling discrepancies between our data and Jañez's theory that need to be resolved. For instance, although some experimental results were well predicted, others were not. To find out why, we computed his dominance ratio separately for the different spatial frequency channels he proposed (.25, .50, 1.0, and 2.0 cycles/side-length), for several different experiments. It turns out that dominance predicts well the results of some experiments only in the low spatial frequency channels, others well only in the high frequency channels, and still others well only with a combination of channels. Figure 5.18 shows the correlation coefficients between the data and predictions based on Jañez's dominance ratio separately for each channel in three different experiments. The open symbols between .25 and .50 channels represent correlations with the predictions of Jañez's original formulation (because it is based just on the channels at .25 and .50 cycles/side), and those at the far right represent the correlation with predictions based on an optimal linear combination of the dominance ratio in all four channels. The curve labeled "Number" shows the fit for an experiment in which we varied the number of triangles in a configural line (Palmer & Bucher, 1981, Exp. 2.). Here, the best fit is approximated by Jañez's original formulation, with only the low frequency channels (at .25 and .50 cycles/side) providing good fits to the data. The curve labeled "Length" shows the fit for the experiment described earlier in this chapter in which we varied the aspect ratio (length-to-width ratio) of rectangular frames (Exp. 1). Here, Jañez's original model fares much worse, and the best fit is systematically obtained in the high frequency channels (1.0 and 2.0 cycles/side). This is not surprising because elongation has a big effect on isotropy in the low spatial frequencies, yet it had almost no effect on the magnitude of the bias effect. Finally, the curve labeled "Parts" shows the fit for the "parts of a frame" experiment described earlier (Exp. 5). Here, Janez's low-frequency model does quite poorly, and the predictions from the high frequency channels are only slightly better. However, it turns out that a linear combination of all four channels produces a correlation of .87 with the results. This strikes me as encouragingly high for such a complex and non-intuitive data set. Still, the differences across experiments are perplexing. One obvious possibility to account for the discrepancies is that the success of the dominance ratio in different channels might be related to its magnitude in those channels or even the total amount of spectral power they carry. We are in the process of examining possibilities of this sort.

Results such as those just reported suggest to us that Jañez's dominance ratio theory, and spatial frequency theories in general, deserve serious attention as possible explanations for the configural orientation effects we have been studying. We have therefore begun to conduct some experiments designed specifically to test them.

Experiment 6: Modelling Multiple Context Effects.   Both Janez's and our own simulations of the low spatial frequency theory have used data from experiments in which a single kind of stimulus structure has been used: for example, linear configurations of triangles that differ only in the number of triangles in the line (Palmer & Bucher, 1981, Exp. 2), or triangles with internal stripes that differ only in the fundamental spatial frequency of the stripes (Palmer & Bucher, 1982, Exp. 2). In order to provide an adequate account of this kind of Gestalt effect, however, the model has to work uniformly well on *all* of the different kinds of stimulus structure that produce the effect. Therefore, the model would be

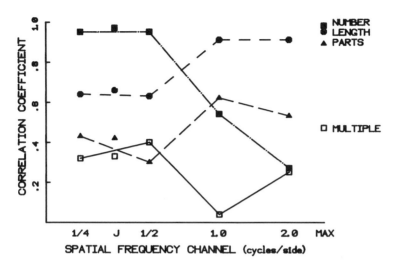

FIGURE 5.18. Fits of Jañez's dominance ratio model to the results of four experiments. Correlations between measured interference scores and the dominance ratio are plotted for individual spatial frequency channels (filled circles), Jañez's original formulation, including just the .25 and .50 cycles/side channels (open triangles), and the optimal linear combination of dominance ratios over all channels.

more rigorously tested by examining the effects of many qualitatively different kinds of contexts (e.g., configural lines, textural stripes, surrounding frames, and others). Although we have in fact used many different kinds of structure in our experiments over the years, they have been studied using different subjects in different experiments. This makes it impossible to test the model adequately against existing data. In the present experiment, therefore, we obtained data on many diverse kinds of contextual structure from a single group of subjects in the same experimental session.

The 16 stimuli for the experiment are shown in Fig. 5.19. Some of them were chosen from stimuli that we had used in previous experiments, and some of them were new, constructed on a purely intuitive basis. Consistent and inconsistent versions were shown to 12 subjects with six repetitions of each over the course of the experiment. We then computed the average bias effect over subjects, which is shown below the corresponding stimulus in Fig. 5.19. These data were then fitted to the dominance ratio predictions as described previously. The results are shown in Fig. 5.18 as the curve labeled "Multiple". Here, the fit of the model is quite poor in all channels, and the maximal linear combination produces a correlation of only .49, which is just barely above the value needed to achieve signifance at the .05 level. It is clear from these results that the simple model is not very robust in the face of stimuli as varied and complex as these. Still, there may be some more sophisticated form of this type of basic spatial frequency model—such as one weighting contributions from different channels by their overall activity level—that might perform much better. Therefore, we decided to test a prediction of a more general form of the theory.

Experiment 7: Symmetry versus Spectral Power.   One way in which spatial frequency theories can be tested experimentally against the symmetry hypothesis is by examining the contextual effects of single versus double sine-wave gratings (Palmer, Kube & Kruschke, in preparation). Both theories agree that if a single triangle is placed on a single sinusoidal grating oriented as in Fig. 5.20A, its perceived pointing will be biased perpendicular to the orientation of the stripes, as shown by the arrow. Given that the observer's task is to see the triangle point directly right (versus directly left), this stimulus is *inconsistent* with the required response, and should lead to long reaction times and/or relatively many errors. Analogous statements are true for the inconsistent stimulus shown if Fig. 5.20B; however, when the two inconsistent gratings are superimposed to form a double grating (Fig. 5.20C), the predictions of the two theories diverge.

Spatial frequency theories based on the orientational distribution of

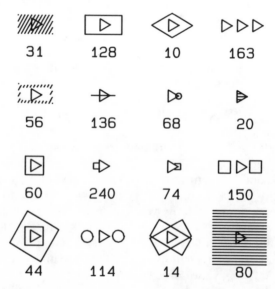

FIGURE 5.19.   Example stimuli and results of Experiment 6 (Multiple Contexts). Sixteen patterns were measured for the amount of interference they produced. Numbers below each stimulus indicate interference (in msec.) = inconsistent RT − consistent RT.

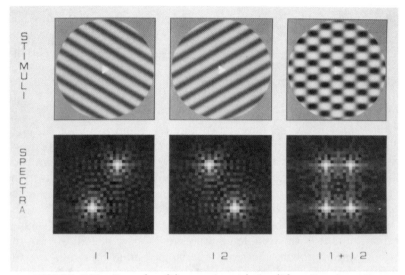

FIGURE 5.20. Examples of the experimental stimuli from Experiment 7. (Symmetry vs. Spectral Power). Two inconsistent single gratings are shown on the left and the double grating that results from adding them together is shown at right. Below each image is shown an enlarged image of the low-frequency region of it amplitude spectrum.

spectral power predict that the double grating will lead to performance at least as poor as for either inconsistent single grating alone, because the double grating's power is still concentrated at orientations inconsistent with the required percept. However, the symmetry theory predicts that the double grating will lead to much *better* performance than for either single grating alone, because the combination produces an *emergent axis of symmetry* that is consistent with the required response. The following experiment was performed to decide between these two theories in light of their different predictions for the double grating stimuli.

Subjects were shown a sequence of slides taken of computer-generated images, each of which contained one solid white equilateral triangle on a background that was either a single or double sinusoidal grating as shown in Fig. 5.20. The triangle was positioned at the center of the field at maximum (100%) contrast and one side subtended about 0.55 degrees of visual angle from the subject's viewing position. The single gratings had a spatial frequency of f/2 (1.1 cycles/degree of visu–l angle) and a contrast of 40%. The double gratings were created by adding together two such single gratings (with resulting contrast of 80%).

The orientation of the single gratings was consistent with the required direction of pointing on ⅓ of the trials (C), inconsistent at 120 degrees clockwise from the required direction on ⅓ of the trials (I1), and inconsistent at 120 degrees counterclockwise from the required direction on the remaining ⅓ of the trials (I2). The double gratings were constructed by adding together all non-identical pairs of single gratings (i.e., C+I1, C+I2, I1+I2). On half of the trials the triangle could be seen pointing directly rightward, and on the other half it could be seen pointing directly leftward. Each of 14 subjects saw each stimulus eight times during the experiment.

Mean response times for each condition are shown in Fig. 5.21. As predicted by both theories, responses to the single C gratings were much faster than those to the two single I gratings that did not differ from each other. The results for the double gratings conform well to the predictions of the symmetry theory and are incompatible with the spatial frequency account: The I1+I2 combination produced faster responses than the C+I1 and C+I2 combinations, which did not differ from each other. Response times to the double gratings were longer overall than to the single gratings, probably because the triangle had lower contrast to the brightest parts of the double gratings (100% vs. 80%) than to the brightest parts of the single gratings (100% vs. 40%), but the size of the bias effect in the double gratings is about the same as for the single gratings.

Thus, the results strongly disconfirm most models based on the low spatial frequency hypothesis, and are at least consistent with the predictions of the symmetry hypothesis. Although they do not categorically rule out all accounts in terms of spatial frequency channels, they do make them highly implausible. One could argue, for instance, that if the channels were very broadly tuned in orientation—with a half-amplitude bandwidth of *more* than 60 degrees—the I1+I2 double grating could produce more activation in a central channel at the consistent orientation than in either single channel at the inconsistent orientations of the two component gratings. Even if channels were tuned this broadly, such a model would predict a large reduction in the size of the double-grating effect. The reason is that even though the double grating would activate the central channel most strongly, it would also produce large amounts of activation in the channels of the two individual components, so that the dominance ratios in Jañez-type models would be much less extreme than for single gratings. In fact, however, the magnitude of the effect for double gratings is not significantly different from that for single gratings.

Still, it would be preferable to have a test that did not depend on such quantitative assumptions at all. We are therefore undertaking some further experiments that should allow a fairly general test of the relationship between the bias effects we have been studying and the power in spatial frequency channels. This work is currently in progress, so I can only present stimuli without results.

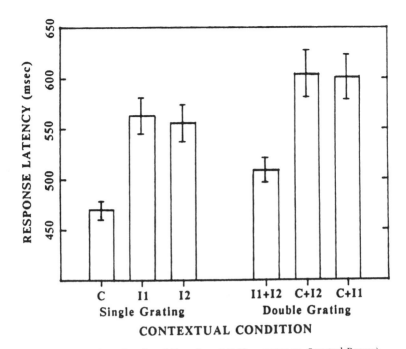

FIGURE 5.21. Results of Experiment 7 (Symmetry vs. Spectral Power). Mean RTs for single and double gratings indicate that double gratings produce the pattern of results predicted by the symmetry analysis and not by the spatial frequency analysis.

Experiment 8: Low-pass Filtered Stimuli. If the low spatial frequency channels are indeed responsible for Gestalt effects, then it should be possible to eliminate or greatly reduce our configural orientation effect simply by high-pass filtering the stimuli to take out the power in specified low frequency bands. We can then use our behavioral techniques to compare these filtered stimuli with their unfiltered counterparts in order to determine experimentally whether any configural effects remain after filtering and, if so, how much.

We plan to use a series of different cutoffs for the high-pass filtering operation: 0 (no filtering), ¼, ½, 1, 2, and 4 cycles per side. It seems intuitively clear that some configural bias effect is still present in these stimuli, even with 4 cycles/side as the cutoff frequency (see Fig. 5.22). Intuitions can be deceiving, however, and our experimental techniques will allow us to measure the effects of filtering precisely. We will be able to find out whether there is a reliable drop in the bias effect when low spatial frequencies are removed and, if so, at what cutoff frequencies the change begins and ends. If the bias effects are not measurably affected by filtering, however, it would constitute strong evidence that dominence in the low spatial frequency channels is not *necessary* for this Gestalt effect to occur, although it still might be *sufficient*. Further experiments are needed to test the sufficiency hypothesis.

Future Theoretical Directions

It is becoming clear that spatial frequency models of the sort we have tested are not strong candidates for explaining the kind of Gestalt contextual effects we have examined carefully in our experiments. Although the symmetry theory has nontrivial support from several experiments and seems to do better than spatial frequency models on several scores, it alone does not seem to be adequate to the job either. We are not in the somewhat embarrassing position of having disconfirmed all the presently available models. The next step, therefore, must be to develop new theories.

Perhaps the most promising direction for new theoretical developments is "connectionism" or "parallel distributed processing (PDP)" models (McClelland & Rumelhart, 1986; Rumelhart & McClelland,

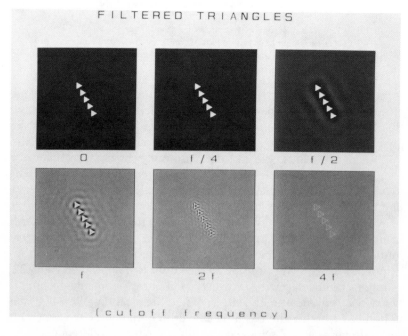

FIGURE 5.22. Examples of low-pass filtered configurations of triangles. All spatial frequencies below the specified cutoff frequency (in cycles/side) have been removed from the spectrum before resynthesizing these images.

1986). These models are based on the assumption that information is represented by patterns of activation over neuron-like *units* that are linked together by synapse-like *connections* that can be either excitatory or inhibitory. Certain units—called *input units*—are excited directly by structure in the enviroment, and other units—called *output units*—directly represent responses of the system. In between, there may be various levels of *hidden units* that perform the information processing required to map from input units to output units. Feedback loops among the units cause such systems to exhibit dynamic behavior in which the system "settles" into the pattern of activity that is most compatible with the connections among units.

Within this framework, we hope to model reference frames as patterns of excitatory and inhibitory interconnections among hidden units and code relations between the output of other units. If one assumes that frames are defined by certain relations that tend to co-occur in figures—so that relations (hidden units) within the same frame will tend to excite each other and those in different frames tend to inhibit each other—I suspect that many basic phenomena from our experiments can be modelled by the dynamic settling properties of these networks. In fact, this line of thinking is very similar to some of my own earliest ideas about reference frame selection (Palmer, 1981). The dynamic properties of networks during the process of "settling" into a state of "minimum energy" are very suggestive of some crucial phenomena—for example, the fact that ambiguous triangles are multistable to begin with, and the ways in which contextual structure seems to influence this multistability. The properties of these densely connected parallel neural networks are hauntingly similar to the ideas advanced many years ago by Gestalt theorists in their "field theories" of perceptual phenomena, and they are of considerable interest on these grounds alone.

Naturally, I do not yet know how successful such connectionist theories might be at accounting for the many facts we now know about the connfigural orientation effect—or even exactly how we will be able to test them if they are—but I see them as a promising line for future work in this area. Moreover, the plethora of data we have accumulated on these phenomena should prove a good testing ground for connectionistic theories of Gestalt interactions or any other theory that might emerge in the meantime.

ACKNOWLEDGMENTS

This research was supported in part by National Science Foundation Grants BNS-83-19630 and 87-19934 to the author and by an Alfred P. Sloan Foundation Grant to the Institute of Cognitive Studies at the University of California, Berkeley. I wish to thank Nancy Bucher, John Kruschke, and Paul Kube for their numerous intellectual contributions to the research project described in this chapter, and Jack Gallant, Susan Van Eyck, Cassandra Moore, and Gail Musen for their help in collecting and analyzing some of the data reported here. Ephram Cohen and Jack Gallant provided valuable programming assistance for the experiments, and Paul Kube single-handedly wrote all of the software to do Fourier analysis and synthesis of images, including the simulation of Jañez's low spatial frequency model.

REFERENCES

Attneave, F. (1968). Triangles as ambiguous figures. *American Journal of Psychology, 81*, 447–453.

Bucher, N.M, & Palmer, S.E. (1985). Effects of motion on the perceived pointing of ambiguous triangles. *Perception and Psychophysics, 38, 227–236.*

Bundesen, C., & Larsen, A. (1975). Visual transformation of size. *Journal of Experimental Psychology: Human Perception and Performance, 1, 214–220.*

Campbell, F.W., & Robson, J.G. (1968). Application of Fourier analysis to the visibility of gratings. *Journal of Physiology, 197, 551–556.*

DeValois, R.L., & DeValois, K.K. (1980). Spatial vision. *American Review of Psychology, 31*, 309–341.

DeValois, R.L., Yund, E.W., & Hepler, N. (1982). The orientation and direction selectivity of cells in macaque visual cortex. *Vision Research, 22, 531–544.*

Ginsberg, A. (1971). *Psychological correlates of a model of the human visual system.* Unpublished master's thesis, Air Force Institute of Technology, Wright-Pallerson AFB, Ohio

Ginsberg, A. (1986). Spatial filtering and visual form perception. In K.R. Boff, L. Kaufman, & J.P. Thomas (Eds.), *Handbook of perception and human performance, volume II: Cognitive processes and performance* (pp. 34-1–34-41). New York: John Wiley & Sons.

Hinton, G.E. (1979). Some demonstrations of the effects of structural descriptions in mental imagery. *Cognitive Science, 3, 231–250.*

Hinton, G.E., & Parsons, L.M. (1981). Frames of reference and mental imagery. In A. Baddeley, & J. Long (Eds.), *Attention and performance: IX, (pp.).* Hillside, NJ: Lawrence Erlbaum Associates.

Humphreys, G.W. (1983). Reference frames and shape perception. *Cognitive Psychology, 15, 309–341.*

Jañez, L. (1983). Stimulus control of the visual reference frame: Quantitative theory. *Informes de Psychologia, 2, 133–147.*

Kopfermann, H. (1930). Psychologische Untersuchungen uber die Wirkung zweidimensionaler korperlicher Gebilde, *Psychologische Forschung, 13, 293–364.*

Mach, E. (1959). *The analysis of sensations.* (Translatd from the German edition, 1897) New York: Dover.

Marr, D. (1982). *Vision.* San Francisco: W.H. Freeman.

Marr, D., & Nishihara, H.K. (1978). Representation and recognition of the spatial organization of three dimensional shapes. *Proceedings of the Royal Society of London, 207*, 187–217.

McClelland, J.L., & Rumelhart, D.E. (1986). *Parallel distributed processing: Explorations in the microstructure of cognition, V. 2: Psychological and biological models.* Cambridge, MA: MIT Press/Bradford Books.

Palmer, S.E. (1975) Visual perception and world knowledge: Notes on a model of sensory-cognitive interaction. In D.A. Norman & D.E. Rumelhart (Eds.), *Explorations in cognition* (pp. 279–307). San Francisco: Freeman.

Palmer, S.E. (1980). What makes triangles point: Local and global effects in configurations of ambiguous triangles. *Cognitive Psychology, 12,* 285–305.

Palmer, S.E. (1981). Transformational structure and perceptual organization. *Proceedings of the Third Annual Cognitive Science Conference,* (pp. 41–49). Berkeley, CA.

Palmer, S.E. (1982). Symmetry, transformation, and the structure of perceptual systems. In J. Beck (Ed.), *Representation and organization in perception.* (pp. 95–144). Hillsdale, NJ: Lawrence Erlbaum Associates.

Palmer, S.E. (1983). The psychology of perceptual organization: A transformational approach. In J. Beck, B. Hope, & A. Rosenfeld (Eds.), *Human and Machine vision,* (pp. 269–339). New York: Academic Press.

Palmer, S.E. (1985). The role of symmetry in shape perception. *Acta Psychologica, 59,* 67–90.

Palmer, S.E. (in preparation). Frame effects in perceived pointing of ambiguous triangles.

Palmer, S.E., & Bucher, N.M. (1981). Configural effects in perceived pointing of ambiguous triangles. *Journal of Experimental Psychology: Human Perception and Performance, 7,* 88–114.

Palmer, S.E., & Bucher, N.M. (1982). Textural effects in perceived pointing of ambiguous triangles. *Journal of Experimental Psychology: Human Perception and Performance, 8,* 693–708.

Palmer, S.E., Kube, P., & Kruschke, J. (in preparation). A test between two theories of a gestalt effect: Symmetry versus low spatial frequency channels.

Palmer, S.E., Simone, E.J., & Kube, P. (in press). Reference frame effects on shape perception in two versus three dimensions. *Perception.*

Rock, I. (1973). *Orientation and form.* New York: Academic Press.

Rock, I., & DiVita, J. (1987). A case of viewer-centered object perception. *Cognitive Psychology, 19,* 280–293.

Rock, I., DiVita, J., & Barbeito, R. (1981). The effect on form perception of change of orientation in the third dimension. *Journal of Experimental Psychology: Human Perception and Performance, 7,* 719–732.

Rumelhart, D.E., & McClelland, J.L. (1986). *Parallel distributed processing: Explorations in the microstructure of cognition, V. 1: Foundations.* Cambridge, MA: MIT Press/Bradford Books.

Selfridge, O.G., & Neisser, U. (1963). Pattern recognition by machine. In E.A. Feigenbaum & J. Feldman (Eds.), *Computers and thought.* New York: McGraw-Hill.

Shepard, R.N., & Cooper, L.A. (1982), *Mental images and their transformations.* Cambridge, MA: MIT Press/Bradford Books.

Weyl, H. (1952) *Symmetry.* Princeton, NJ: Princeton University Press.

Wiser, M. (1981, August). *The role of intrinsic axes in shape recognition.* Paper presented at the Third Annual Conference of Cognitive Science, Berkeley, CA.

APPENDIX

This appendix describes the Jañez tuned-channel model of reference frame effects.

The Fourier plane response (modulation transfer function) of a Jañez tuned channel centered at frequency ω and orientation θ is

$$F_{\omega,\theta}(u,\ v)\ =\ C(\omega,\ \theta)\ \exp\left[-\frac{\log 2}{\omega^2\tan^2 30^\circ}\ (u\ \sin\theta + v\ \cos\theta)^2\right]$$
$$\left\{\exp\left[-\frac{9\log 2}{\omega^2}\ (u\ \cos\theta - v\ \sin\theta + \omega)^2\right]\right.$$
$$\left.+\ \exp\left[-\frac{9\log 2}{\omega^2}\ (u\ \cos\theta - v\ \sin\theta - \omega)^2\right]\right\}$$

(Here, C is a psychophysically determined contrast sensitivity function; cf. Campbell & Robson [1968].) These channels have half-amplitude bandwidths of one octave in frequency and 30 degrees in orientation, values that are close to the average found in macaque cortex by DeValois et al. (1982). The corresponding spatial response (point spread function) of a channel is a cosine wave of frequency ω and orientation θ modulated by a two-dimensional Gaussian; that is, it is a two-dimensional Gabor function.

If a stimulus S has Fourier transform $F_s(u,\ v)$, the stimulus energy "seen" by a channel centered at ω, θ is given by

$$A_S(\omega,\ \theta)\ =\ \int_{-\infty}^{\infty}\int_{-\infty}^{\infty}\ \mid F_S(u,\ v)\ F_{\omega,\theta}(u,\ v)\mid^2\ du\ dv.$$

$A_s(\omega,\ \theta)$ is then the *activation* in the channel at ω, θ in response to S. The *total activation* at orientation θ in this formulation is

$$TA_S(\theta)\ =\ \sum_{\omega\in W}A_S(\omega,\ \theta)$$

where W is a set of admissible channel frequencies. Only relative low spatial frequencies were admitted in Jañez' original model (Jañez, 1983); there, W includes two frequencies ω_1, ω_2 such that $\omega_2 = 2\omega_1$ and $\omega_0/4 \leqslant \omega_1 < \omega_2 < \omega_0$, where ω_0 is the fundamental frequency of the target figure in S (i.e., the figure has spatial extent $1/\omega_0$). As discussed in the chapter, we have also considered variants of the model in which W contains a single frequency $\omega = k\omega_0$ for some factor k.

A measure of *dominance* is defined between sets of orientations. Given sets of orientations Θ_1 and Θ_2, the dominance of Θ_1 over Θ_2 is

$$D_S(\Theta_1,\ \Theta_2)\ =\ \frac{\max\limits_{\theta\in\Theta_1}TA_S\ (\theta)}{\max\limits_{\theta\in\Theta_2}TA_S\ (\theta)}$$

The model takes the dominance D_S as a predictor of reaction times in a perceptual reference frame task when Θ_2 is the set of orientations *con-*

sistent with the task, and Θ_1 is the set of *inconsistent* orientations. If the experimental task is to determine whether the target figure is an (upright) square or an (upright) diamond, 0 and 90 degrees are consistent orientations, because energy at these orientations should facilitate the selection of an "upright" reference frame in terms of which to describe the shape of the figure. Orientations of 45 or 135 degrees, however, are inconsistent, because energy at these orientations should facilitate the selection of a diagonal reference frame, which would lead to the description of an upright square as a (tilted) diamond, and an upright diamond as a (tilted) square. Thus, where $\Theta_1 = \{45, 135\}$ and $\Theta_2 = \{0, 90\}$, the model predicts that $D_S(\Theta_1, \Theta_2)$ should be positively correlated with reaction times in the experiments reported in this chapter.

6 GESTALTS AND THEIR COMPONENTS: NATURE OF INFORMATION-PRECEDENCE

Maria I. Lasaga
University of Virginia

INTRODUCTION

The General Question Then: Nature of Wholistic Perceptual Dominance

In the early 1900s, the Gestalt psychologists proposed that a perceived whole was different from the sum of its components (e.g., Koffka, 1935; Kohler, 1929; Wertheimer, 1923). Within shape perception, specifically, strong support for this notion was provided by demonstrations of perceptual inclusiveness (Vernon, 1937): Certain perceived shapes (e.g., see Fig. 6.1) absorbed their components to the point of making them no longer recognizable (Wertheimer, 1923; Kohler, 1925, 1929). It was argued that these demonstrations of perceptual inclusiveness supported the well-known Gestalt tenet in the following manner: Any perceived whole that cannot be perceptually analyzed into its components is not the sum of those components; just as a cement wall, which cannot be easily decomposed into lime, clay, and water, is not simply the sum of those elements.

In their investigations of shape perception, as with most of their investigations, the Gestalt psychologists employed the method of phenomenology. They introspected while perceiving in order to provide a description of their direct experience (Koffka, 1935). Evident in the nature of this methodology, the Gestalt psychologists were primarily concerned with the relationship between the whole and its components in

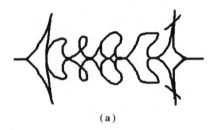

(a)

FIGURE 6.1. Examples of perceptual inclusiveness, in which
the perceived whole absorbs the
components to the point of making them no longer recognizable;
in (a), the word "heart" and its
reflection are unrecognizable, and
in (b), the initials M and W are
unrecognizable in the perceived
whole. Adapted from Wertheimer
(1923) and Kohler (1925, 1929).

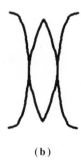

(b)

the percept itself. They aimed to specify the wholistic properties of the percept (e.g., good continuation, closure, etc.) that obscured the components of a stimulus (Koffka, 1935; Vernon, 1937; Wertheimer, 1923).
Thus, the Gestalt investigations addressed the nature of wholistic perceptual dominance.

The General Question Now:
Issue of Local/Global Precedence

Recently, studies of object perception have become concerned with the
properties that are *extracted* from the distal stimulation in the formation
of the percept. That is, current interest has focused on the microgenesis
of the perceived whole rather than on the nature of perceptual dominance. The Gestalt demonstrations that certain components become
perceptually imbedded in the perceived whole do not preclude the possibility that these components have been used to *generate* the perceived
whole. In other words, although certain components of the distal stimulus may become unrecognizable in the final percept, they could have
contributed information to the processes that generated that final percept nonetheless. Given this possibility, current studies have attempted
to specify the information that is extracted earlier from the distal stimu-

lus, information about the whole or about the components. The stimulus whole has been referred to as the global unit, the stimulus components as the local units, and the question as the issue of *local/global precedence.*

Precedence. Information about a set of stimulus properties is said to have precedence if it is available earlier than other information in the generation of a percept. Such *information-precedence* occurs if: (a) the set of properties is processed prior to another; or (b) the set of properties is processed simultaneously with another set but at a faster rate (see Ward, 1983). In the first case, which can be considered as *information-precedence in sequential processing* (e.g., see Fig. 6.2), the local/global properties are processed in a temporal order, with one set of properties (such as the global ones) being processed before another (such as the local ones). The processes themselves are temporarily ordered, and, therefore, so are their outputs. The assumption is often made that if the processes are sequential then the later (set of) process(es) must employ the information that is generated by the earlier (set of) process(es). In

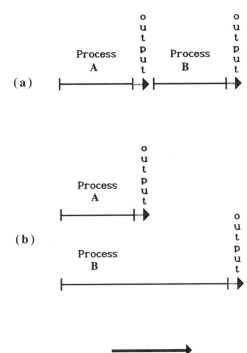

FIGURE 6.2. (a) Information-precedence of property A within sequential processes; (b) information-precedence of property A within parallel processes.

TIME

the second case, which can be considered as *information-precedence in parallel processing* (e.g., see Fig. 6.2), the local and global processes occur in parallel, but one set is completed prior to the other. (For similar distinctions, see Miller, 1981; Posner, 1978; Sebrechts & Fragala, 1985; Ward, 1983). It is, of course, possible to further distinguish between parallel processes that have identical onset times from those that have nonidentical onset times; or between interactive versus noninteractive parallel processes. These latter distinctions are important ones, but they are secondary to an initial determination of whether local/global processes are sequential or parallel in nature. Accordingly, current research has examined whether local versus global information-precedence occurs and whether the processes are sequential or parallel.

Outline of Present Chapter

In this chapter, I provide a simple framework for the discussion of current studies on the issue of local/global precedence, based on a distinction between two types of visual stimulus. Then, current studies on local/global precedence are examined within the framework that is provided. This discussion reveals two important methodological considerations for further studies of local/global precedence. Finally, I discuss some studies that have already addressed one or both of these issues.

BASIC FRAMEWORK FOR STUDIES ON THE ISSUE OF LOCAL/GLOBAL PRECEDENCE

Stimulus Structure and Configuration

Classification of Configurations. Pomerantz (1981, 1983) has distinguished between two types of *perceived wholes* based on the nature of the local information that is used to process the global unit. In *Type-P* configurations, only information about the *position* of the local units contributes to the identification of the perceived whole (e.g., a word derived from an arrangement of pebbles, for which the particular shapes and sizes of the pebbles do not matter but their position does). In *Type-N* configurations, the specific *nature* of the local elements, in addition to their position, matters for the identity of the perceived whole (e.g., the letter "T" derived from two perpendicular rectangular stones, which would be a letter "i" if the top rectangular stone were replaced with a round one). This distinction between configurations seems important for a resolution of the issue of local/global precedence. It suggests that different results will be obtained with different types of stimuli.

Types of Configuration and Local/Global Precedence.   Because information about location *and* nature of the local units is required for Type-N configurations as defined, the global properties of these configurations should require information about local properties in order to be perceived. Thus, Type-N configurations can be considered to involve sequential local/global processing with local precedence. On the other hand, because identity of the local properties is not necessary for a Type-P configuration, the global properties can be processed independently of the local ones (and vice versa); and precedence should depend on the set of properties (i.e., local or global) that is available first in the system, if any. (Note: The positions of the local units in a Type-P configuration do contribute to the processing of the global unit as defined, but the local and global properties themselves can be processed independently. Some minimal positional information about local units does seem necessary to define global properties, otherwise the global properties would have no physical basis.)

Types of Configuration and Stimulus Structure.   In essence, Pomerantz (1981, 1983) has provided us with a classification of configurations according to the type of information-precedence and processing they involve: configurations that arise when the global properties depend on the prior identity of the local properties (i.e., Type-N configurations); and those that arise from parallel global and local processes (i.e., Type-P configurations). These are not the only conceivable combinations of information-precedence and processing. In other words, Pomerantz' (1981, 1983) classification scheme does not include all possible combinations of type of information-precedence (i.e., local or global) with nature of processing (i.e., sequential or parallel). For example, one could consider a configuration in which the local units required information about the position and nature of the global unit in order to be processed. However, a Type-N configuration seems to be the most likely candidate for information-precedence with sequential processes, because of the logical relationship between parts and wholes: A whole is composed of parts, but not vice versa; a whole does not exist without parts, but not vice versa. To say that the whole, therefore, requires information about the nature and position of the parts seems more logically plausible than to say the opposite. And, a Type-P configuration is the most likely candidate for information-precedence with parallel processes for a similar reason: Because a whole is composed of parts, some minimal local information needs to be used for global properties, or they become nonexistent. Positional information is the least elaborate, but the rest could proceed in parallel. Thus, Pomerantz' classification scheme provides us with the most logical types of configuration based on information-processing and precedence. The type of local information that contributes to the whole in Type-N and Type-P configurations distinguishes between them (Pomerantz, 1981, 1983), and suggests the nature of the stimulus structure that may underly their respective types of information-processing and precedence.

Mapping of Stimuli Onto Configurations. If a distal stimulus consists of physically connected local units (hereafter referred to as *Type-C* stimuli), then the wholistic properties of the percept should require information about both the position of those local units and their nature (e.g., the nature of the local units will affect the contour of the perceived whole). On the other hand, if a distal stimulus consists of physically disconnected local units (hereafter referred to as *Type-D* stimuli), then positional information about the local units can suffice to uniquely generate most of the global properties of these percepts. Thus, Type-C stimuli are potential Type-N configurations, and Type-D stimuli are potential Type-P configurations, although this mapping is not critical as discussed in the previous section. For the present examination of the issue of local/global precedence, current studies are organized according to the type of stimulus that they've used, and stimuli are defined by the (dis)connectedness of their local units. In this manner, we can examine the type of precedence that different types of stimulus do produce, and under what conditions. It is shown that different factors do affect the two types of stimulus during the microgenesis of the perceived whole; and that the type of stimulus has influenced the methodology chosen to examine the issue of local/global precedence.

LOCAL/GLOBAL PRECEDENCE
WITH TYPE-D STIMULI

Studies that have used Type-D stimuli to examine the issue of local/global precedence have generally used one particular kind of Type-D stimulus: compound letters, which are large letters composed of smaller letters (e.g., see Fig. 6.3). Most of these studies have compared the *speed* with which the local and global units are identified (Grice, Canham, & Boroughs, 1983; Kinchla & Wolfe, 1979; Martin, 1979; Miller, 1981; Navon, 1977; Navon & Norman, 1983; Pomerantz, 1983, Experiments 1 & 2; Ward, 1982). Other paradigms that have been used with Type-D stimuli have also compared response times, but the task has varied:

Navon (1983) employed a same/different paradigm, in which reaction times (RTs) to detect local versus global differences were compared; Pomerantz and Sager (1975) used a speeded-classification task and compared the speed of local and global classification; and Hoffman (1980) used a memory-scanning paradigm, in which RTs to search for global and local targets were compared. These studies have usually found that global information is processed prior to local information (Kinchla, 1977; Miller, 1981; Navon, 1977, 1983; Navon & Norman, 1983; Ward, 1982). However, several studies have found evidence that various experimental variables can affect the type of information-precedence, local or global, that is obtained (Grice et al., 1983; Hoffman, 1980; Kinchla & Wolfe, 1979; Martin, 1979; Navon, 1983; Navon & Norman, 1983; Vurpillot, Ruel & Castrec, 1976–1977; Ward, 1982).

Factors That Influence Local/Global Precedence With Type-D Stimuli

Several studies with Type-D stimuli have found evidence for both local and global precedence, each under different experimental conditions. These findings reveal several factors that influence the type of precedence obtained with Type-D stimuli.

Size of Visual Angle. Kinchla and Wolfe (1979) varied the visual angle of compound letters and found that information-precedence depended on the size of the visual angle subtended by the stimuli. At large visual angles, local precedence was obtained and at small visual angles, global precedence was obtained. Vurpillot et al. (1976–1977) obtained similar results with infants. However, Navon and Norman (1983) controlled for a factor that they argued was confounded with precedence in Kinchla and Wolfe's study: eccentricity—that is, distance from the fovea. In typical compound letters, the global unit has greater eccentricity than many of the local units. Thus, Navon and Norman used C's and circles so that

```
S    S
S    S
S S S S
S    S
S    S
```

FIGURE 6.3. Sample compound letter (Type-D stimulus).

all of the local units of each stimulus were located along the perimeter of the global pattern. Global precedence was obtained at both a large and a small visual angle. Thus, Navon and Norman's study suggests that, if eccentricity is controlled by using special stimuli, then global precedence will be obtained, regardless of the size of the visual angle. But Kinchla and Wolfe's (1979) and Vurpillot et al.'s (1976–1977) studies suggest that if eccentricity is not controlled, as within typical Type-D stimuli, the size of the visual angle will affect the type of precedence, local or global, that is obtained.

Sparsity.   Martin (1979) examined the role of sparsity (i.e., the spacing between local units) in local/global precedence by varying the number of elements in compound letters. The global pattern of these compound letters subtended the same visual angle, regardless of sparsity. With many-element stimuli, global information was processed more quickly; and with few-element stimuli, local information was. However, Navon (1983) found that the number of elements was not as important as was the actual pattern produced by the elements. He used triangular and rectangular patterns made up of smaller, triangular and rectangular patterns that were, in turn, composed of circles. Consistent with Martin's results, the sparse stimuli tended to produce local precedence (i.e., the local information was processed more quickly than the global information). But inconsistent with her results, some of the triangular patterns produced global precedence even with as few local units as four. Navon could offer no overarching scheme for which patterns would produce which type of information-precedence. Yet, Navon and Martin's results, taken together, suggest that unless the global unit has exceptionally salient properties, sparsity will produce local precedence and density will produce global precedence.

Location of Stimulus Presentation.   Grice et al. (1983) presented compound letters in a fixed (central) location or in uncertain (peripheral) location within the visual field. With fixed (central) location, Grice et al. obtained neither local nor global precedence. With uncertain (peripheral) location, they obtained evidence for global precedence.

Stimulus Quality.   Hoffman (1980) used compound letters in a memory-scanning task, and found that when he distorted the letters at one of the two levels, information-precedence would be demonstrated for the other level.

Level of Prior Attentional Allocation.   Ward (1982) examined how prior allocation of attention to local or global properties can affect the speed

with which a current stimulus is processed. He required subjects to identify the local or global unit(s) of pluses or X's made of pluses or X's. The
stimuli were presented sequentially in pairs, and, prior to each pair, subjects were told the unit(s), local or global, that they were to identify for
each stimulus. Ward's results revealed that identifications were faster for
a given level, local or global, if that same level had just been processed
for the preceding stimulus.

Information-precedence in Parallel Processing of Type-D Stimuli?

The evidence that various factors (e.g., sparsity, visual angle, etc.) affect
the type of information-precedence that is obtained with Type-D stimuli
indicates that the local and global properties are not processed in a sequential fashion. Local and global information-precedence are obtained
with the same type of stimulus under different conditions. Because the
factors described previously do affect the relative availability of local and
global information, they reveal parallel local/global processes at play.

Relative Response Speed As Indication of Precedence: A Caveat

Because different types of information have precedence under different
conditions of sparsity, size of visual angle, eccentricity, location of stimulus presentation, stimulus quality, and level of prior attentional allocation, it was concluded that local and global properties of Type-D stimuli
are not processed in any necessary sequential fashion. However, these
findings also indicate that care should be taken in the interpretation of
relative response speed as indication of precedence. They demonstrate
that relatively large differences between the local and global units (e.g.,
size, eccentricity, sparsity) of Type-D stimuli, which are normally inherent to these levels, can produce information-precedence because of
these differences and not because of the difference in level of complexity, per se. The results might not be reflecting any type of processing sequence based on the level of complexity, but, rather differential
discriminabilities of the two levels (Garner, 1983; Lasaga, in preparation; Pomerantz, 1983). That is, because the smaller local units of
Type-D stimuli *are* smaller—or less eccentric at large visual angles, or
less sparse—they are harder to discriminate from each other. Because
relative discriminability is reflected in absolute RTs, and the local and
global units of Type-D stimuli typically vary in relative discriminability,
then the differences in discriminability either need to be controlled or

varied. In other words, if relative speed of performance with local and global units is compared, and relative discriminability is not controlled or varied, then the type of information-precedence that is obtained in an experiment could reflect sequential *or* parallel processes. Conclusions can describe the type of information-precedence obtained but not the nature of the local and global processes. Unfortunately, because of the logical relationship between parts and wholes, control over relative discriminabilities at these two levels of complexity can be difficult. However, other, less common, methodologies have been used that allow a distinction between parallel and sequential local/global processes without needing to vary the relative discriminabilities of the units.

Methodologies That Don't Require Interpretation of Relative Response Speeds

One simple general logic for methodologies that do not compare speeded performance at the local and global levels has been as follows: A property at one level, local or global, is varied in a way that is known to differentially affect speed of processing *at that level*, and the effect of this variation on judgments about properties at the other level is examined. For example, a task is constructed so that the levels of a local property, a and b, map onto the responses, R1 and R2, but the levels of the global property do not (see Figure 6.4, depiction of Task 1). Further, the global property is chosen so that its levels, A and B, are known to be processed at different speeds in and of themselves (e.g., A is a good property and B is a poor one). If speed or accuracy of judgments about the local elements differs according to the (response-irrelevant) global property, then the global property must have been processed prior to the local. The same experimental situation can also be arranged to examine for effects of local properties on processing of global units. In this condition, the local elements are varied in a response-irrelevant fashion, and only judgments about the global units are required of subjects (see Figure 6.4, depiction of Task 2).

Within such a paradigm, the nature of the underlying local/global processes (i.e., parallel or sequential) is indicated by the absence or presence of *differential* performance produced by the response-irrelevant property. That is, if the response-irrelevant property affected performance *based on the ease or difficulty with which that property's levels are processed*, then the underlying local/global processes must be sequential in nature. If such differential effects are not obtained, then support for parallel processing is obtained. Note that the overall speed of task performance can be affected by the variation of the response-irrelevant prop-

STIMULUS PROPERTIES

Levels of Global Property: **A & B**
Levels of Local Property: **a & b**

EXPERIMENTAL CONDITIONS

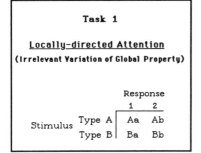
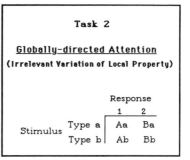

FIGURE 6.4.   Schematic representation of general logic used in methodologies that don't require interpretation of relative response speeds.

erty, regardless of the nature of processing (e.g., due to difficulty of attentional allocation). The comparison of interest is that between performance at the different levels of the response-irrelevant property. Thus, the confounding between relative discriminability and precedence that potentially arises when response speeds of local and global judgments are compared to each other is circumvented with these alternative methodologies by requiring only judgments at one level under response-irrelevant variation of the other level and examining relative speed of performance according to this latter variation.

Examples of Studies Using Alternative Methodologies

Kinchla's (1977) Study.   Kinchla's (1977) study on the role of structural redundancy in object perception is an example of the use of logic similar to that just described. Kinchla varied the probability with which local targets would occur in different Type-D stimuli. The stimuli were two mixed compound letters (T and L) of the type shown in Fig. 6.5. They were presented individually for 10 msec. on each trial. Kinchla manipulated the probabilities that each large letter would contain a local target; that is, the degree of local/global redundancy: The target letter was twice as likely in one of the large letters (i.e., high structural redundancy) as it was in the other (i.e., low structural redundancy). Subjects simply had to indicate whether the local target occurred in the stimulus or not. Kinchla found that subjects were highly influenced by the degree of structural redundancy. The presence or absence of a target in the compound letter that was more likely to contain the target produced a higher hit rate. His results suggest that, even with such briefly presented stimuli and a global property that was not structurally contained by the stimulus, the global unit was being processed prior to the local units.

Lasaga and Llaneras' (in preparation) Study. Lasaga and Llaneras (in preparation) examined the contribution of a global property to the processing of local units in Type-D stimuli using a different paradigm from Kinchla's, but similar logic. The experiment employed a cued-location paradigm: A stimulus matrix was presented to the subject for a duration that maintained a pre-specified accuracy rate, followed by a brief mask, and then a cue that indicated the location of the local element that the subject was to report. The stimuli consisted of two colored letters arranged vertically, horizontally, and obliquely. These orientations have been found to vary in pattern goodness (e.g., Lasaga & Garner, 1983). The evidence that good patterns are encoded faster than poor patterns in other information-processing tasks (e.g., Bell & Handel, 1976; Checkosky & Whitlock, 1973; Garner & Sutliff, 1974; Sebrechts & Garner, 1981), and the evidence that vertically and horizontally aligned stimuli are encoded faster than obliquely aligned stimuli (e.g., Attneave & Olson, 1967; Lasaga & Garner, 1983), would lead one to predict that a vertical or horizontal global unit should be processed faster than an oblique global unit. Thus, it was predicted that the local conjunctions of color and form would be more accurate in the vertical/horizontal global patterns than in the oblique patterns *if global properties are processed prior to local properties.* This conclusion was based on the assumption that, with limited time to process the matrix, more time is left on trials with good global patterns to extract the necessary response information.

The correct conjunctions of local color and form showed a sensitivity

	H	S J N G F
	X	H
	B	X
FIGURE 6.5. Stimuli adapted	R	B
from Kinchla (1977).	**S J N G F**	R

to axis of orientation: 38% of the conjunctions were correct for vertically and horizontally aligned stimuli, and 43% were correct for diagonally aligned stimuli. Surprisingly, items located along vertical and horizontal axes were correctly conjoined less often than items along the diagonal axes. This finding is actually a reversal of the oblique effect, and contrary to the predicted results. Goodness of global pattern was certainly affecting local proccessing. But a simple sequence of global-then-local processing should have produced the opposite pattern, as indicated previously. The correct conjunction of local color and form was affected by the orientation of the global pattern, with vertical and horizontal patterns producing fewer correct conjunctions than oblique ones. The results from this study suggest that good global properties interfere with the processing of the local units of Type-D stimuli. The findings suggest a more complicated pattern of the microgenesis of the perceived whole than has yet been considered in this chapter: that good global properties are more salient than bad global properties, detract attention from the local units, and delay local processing. The next study has led to similar and stronger conclusions.

Sebrechts and Fragala's (1985) Study. Sebrechts and Fragala (1985) used a same–different paradigm. Pattern goodness was varied at both the global and local levels (see Fig. 6.6 for sample stimuli). The patterns, local or global, were defined as good if they were symmetrical about their vertical, horizontal, and diagonal axes, and as poor if they were not. Within two of their experimental conditions, "same" or "different" judgments were required of patterns at *one level*, local or global, while goodness varied irrelevantly at the other level. These two conditions are of particular interest to the present discussion. In one condition, Sebrechts and Fragala required subjects to respond "same" only if the global patterns of the target and probe (presented sequentially) were identical. In the other condition, subjects responded "same" only if the local patterns of the target and probe were identical. Pattern goodness was varied at the response-irrelevant level in both of these conditions. Thus, we can examine the effect of varying pattern goodness at one level—in a response-irrelevant fashion—on performance with units at the other level, without confounding level of complexity with relative discriminabilities.

Goodness of the unattended level did, indeed, affect RTs to units at the attended level. When subjects were responding "same" or "different" to the local units only, they were slower when the patterns at the global level were both good than when those patterns were both poor. The same was true when subjects were attending to the global patterns only: Response times were slower when the local units were good than

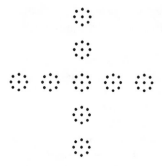

LOCALLY AND GLOBALLY GOOD

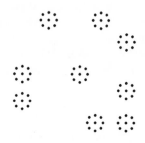

FIGURE 6.6. Stimuli adapted from Sebrechts and Fragala (1985).

LOCALLY GOOD AND GLOBALLY POOR

when they were poor. These results strongly suggest that a good pattern at either level detracts attention from the other level and interferes with processing at that other level. Given that responses were slower when good patterns occurred at the response-irrelevant level, processing at the other level seems to have been postponed. These results are consistent with the findings of Lasaga and Llaneras (in preparation), and the two studies support the conclusion of sequential local/global processing of Type-D stimuli. However, the order of these processes, and therefore the nature of information-precedence, seems to depend on the relative salience (i.e., pattern goodness and not discriminability) of the two levels.

LOCAL/GLOBAL PRECEDENCE
USING TYPE-C STIMULI

Other investigations of the issue of local/global precedence have examined performance with lines presented in a connected context (i.e., Type-C stimuli) and lines presented in isolation. An example of each of these is presented in Fig. 6.7. These studies (e.g., Earhard, 1980;

Earhard & Armitage, 1980; Enns & Prinzmetal, 1984; Klein, 1978; McClelland, 1978; McClelland & Miller, 1979; Schendel & Shaw, 1976; Weisstein & Harris, 1974; Williams & Weisstein, 1978) have usually involved brief stimulus presentation and have compared the accuracy of identifying lines with or without contexts. Two other studies examined speed of response to the lines in different contexts (Pomerantz, 1983, Exp. 5) and to lines in isolation versus in a context (Pomerantz, Sager, & Stoever, 1977).

The results from studies using Type-C stimuli have shown (a) that the identification of lines in context is usually more accurate than the identification of these lines in isolation, although such a result depends on several factors (Earhard, 1980; Earhard & Armitage, 1980; Enns & Prinzmetal, 1984; Klein, 1978; McClelland, 1978; McClelland & Miller, 1979; Pomerantz et al., 1977; Schendel & Shaw, 1976; Williams & Weisstein, 1978), and (b) that the identification of lines in contexts that produce coherent, three-dimensional configurations is better than that of lines in contexts producing flat, disconnected configurations, again, depending on several factors (Earhard, 1980; Earhard & Armitage, 1980; Enns & Prinzmetal, 1984; Klein, 1978; McClelland & Miller, 1979; Weisstein & Harris, 1974; Williams & Weisstein, 1978). In studies with Type-C stimuli, the effect of global information-precedence (i.e., the finding that performance with lines in context is better than performance with lines in isolation) has usually been termed the "object-superiority effect." Hereafter, I continue using the term *global information-precedence*, because the results have been attributed to properties of the global, or "object," level.

Factors that Influence Local/Global Precedence With Type-C Stimuli

As mentioned earlier, several factors have been found to influence local/global precedence when comparing performance between lines in isolation and lines in context.

Three-dimensionality. Weisstein and Harris (1974) and Williams and Weisstein (1978) found that subjects were able to identify lines in context (i.e., produce a unique response for each different line, regardless of

FIGURE 6.7. Sample line-in-isolation and line-in-context (Type-C stimulus).

context) more accurately when the context produced a unitary and three-dimensional configuration with the target line than when the result was less coherent and flat.

Location of Fixation Point.   Earhard (1980) illustrated that coherence and three-dimensionality are neither necessary nor sufficient conditions for global precedence. Rather, Earhard's results show that global precedence was affected by the location of the fixation point: Locating the fixation point at the intersection of stimulus line segments produced no precedence, whereas locating the fixation point in an open area of the stimulus did produce global precedence. Earhard and Armitage (1980) explored the factor of the location of the fixation point in more detail. Their results are consistent with Earhard's (1980) findings.

Type of Stimulus Mask.   Klein (1978) and McClelland (1978) found that the advantage of coherent, three-dimensional configurations over flat, less coherent configurations was eliminated with a masking stimulus that was composed of random lines or random dots. McClelland also found that an "object" mask that contained coherent, three-dimensional objects, similar to those in the stimuli, produced local precedence (i.e., lines in isolation were identified more accurately than lines in context).

Redundancy.   Enns and Prinzmetal (1984) found that global precedence depends on the redundancy between the lines in isolation and the configurations produced by these lines in context. That is, if a particular line occurs only in a particular configuration within the stimulus set, performance is facilitated more than when it is only partially correlated or not at all.

Similarity of Configurations.   Enns and Prinzmetal (1984) also illustrated that global precedence depends on the dissimilarity of the configurations that are produced by the lines in context. The more dissimilar the configurations, the more likely it is that global precedence will be obtained.

Global Precedence in Sequential
Processing With Type-C Stimuli?

The studies just described indicate that the most influential factors in determining local/global precedence when identifying lines in context versus lines in isolation are (a) the nature of the context (i.e., produces flat versus coherent configurations, similar versus dissimilar configurations, etc.), (b) location of fixation; and (c) nature of stimulus mask. Conclusions regarding precedence have been based on a comparison between performance with single lines and performance with the lines in (different) contexts. If performance with the lines is facilitated by the presence of the context, it is assumed that global properties are being processed prior to the local ones and serve as the basis for performance. To sum up the findings, with coherent three-dimensional contexts, global precedence has usually been obtained; and with flat disconnected contexts, no precedence has usually been obtained (e.g., Enns & Prinzmetal, 1984; Weisstein & Harris, 1974; Williams & Weisstein, 1978). However, if the fixation point is located at the intersection of line segments, no precedence is produced, regardless of the dimensionality of the contexts (Earhard, 1980). And if a masking stimulus is used that is composed of random lines or dots, then, again, no precedence is obtained (Klein, 1978; McClelland, 1978). These studies suggest that global precedence is being produced by sequential processes when and if the configuration is processed, because the addition of contexts either facilitates performance or has no effect on it.

To the author's knowledge, only three studies to date have shown evidence for local precedence with Type-C stimuli. McClelland (1978) found that an "object" mask that contained coherent, three-dimensional objects, similar to those in the stimuli, produced local precedence (i.e., the lines in isolation were identified more accurately than the lines in context). Unfortunately, the object mask may also have changed the nature of processing Type-C stimuli by effectively interfering with the global level, even though global precedence would otherwise be obtained with these stimuli. Enns and Prinzmetal (1984) also obtained local precedence when single lines and the same lines with ten different contexts were all presented within the same block of trials. In this experimental condition, however, only two different local units (a right and left diagonal) mapped onto two responses, whereas 22 global units (each of ten contexts and no-context combined with each line) mapped onto the responses. Even if global precedence was occurring, the unmanageable number of global units could be more effectively handled if the identity of the global unit was ignored and the local level processed; in which case, the no-context stimuli would be processed with the greatest ease, as was found. Finally, McClelland and Miller (1979) compared performance with single lines to that with the same lines when they were structurally irrelevant within the provided contexts (e.g., the target line appeared to lean against the inside of one of two squares but had no structural relevance to the global unit). They found that performance with single lines was better than performance with the stimuli that contained structurally irrelevant target lines. However, the predominant global properties of the stimuli with structurally irrelevant target lines were not easily discriminable; unique identity of each stimulus critically depended on the identity of the target line, regardless of the global properties. Thus, these three studies leave open the question of whether local precedence is truly possible with Type-C stimuli when the normal course of processing is unchanged and both local and global units provide equivalent amounts of response information.

Accuracy, Speed, and Relative Discriminability.   When accuracy or speed of performance with local and global units of Type-C stimuli is compared, the effects of level of complexity can also be confounded with those of relative discriminability. Studies using Type-C stimuli have tended to use accuracy of identification as the dependent variable, rather than speed of identification, probably because the local units (i.e., line segments) in Type-C stimuli do not often have the same identity as the global units. However, in order to compare accuracy rates, Type-C stimuli are presented for very brief exposures that are set to maintain some pre-specified overall accuracy rate. By making the exposure time brief, subjects have only so much time to extract information. If differential discriminability of local/global units exists in a stimulus set, it will influence accuracy of performance with local and global units. The more discriminable units (local or global) will require less time for discrimination, and therefore, with brief exposure, be correctly identified more often than the less discriminable units. No studies to date, and to the author's knowledge, have varied the discriminability of units at both the local and global levels of Type-C stimuli (a challenge, indeed). *Thus, the question remains as to whether the global information-precedence that has been obtained with Type-C stimuli is due to sequential processing or to parallel processing of properties with differential discriminabilities.*

Attempts to Circumvent Problem of Relative Discriminability.   The problem of confounding level of complexity with relative discriminability can be addressed by using the same general logic as described in the section on Type-D stimuli. In fact, several studies with these type of stimuli have indeed shown that variations of the global property affect accuracy or speed of local identifications (e.g., Earhard, 1980; Earhard & Armitage, 1980; Enns & Prinzmetal, 1984; Klein, 1978; McClelland & Miller, 1979; Weisstein & Harris, 1974; Williams & Weissten, 1978). As mentioned earlier, these studies compared identification of line segments in contexts that produce coherent, three-dimensional configurations to identification of the same line segments in contexts that produce flat, disconnected configurations. The variation of the global property of two- versus three-dimensionality affected the accuracy with which the local identifications were made. However, the variation of the global properties could have produced response-relevant information in these studies (i.e., discrimination of stimuli was not made according to the line orientation but according to properties of the global unit). Changes in the local elements will change the global properties because the local elements are connected, producing global units in these studies that do map onto responses based on their orientation. Studies are also needed, within this paradigm, that compare global responses under response-irrelevant variation of local elements in order to fully determine whether this precedence involves sequential or parallel processes. But again, given the nature of Type-C stimuli, such variations of local elements cannot be made without affecting global properties.

Problem of Identification of Context.   As mentioned earlier, the nature of the context that is added to a line has been shown to affect whether or not global or no precedence is obtained. However, with the various Type-C stimuli that have been used in these studies, it is not clear whether the entire context is affecting performance, or whether the context is allowing some intermediate level of complexity, between the local and global levels, to facilitate performance. Thus, an additional problem arises: the isolation of the actual global level of complexity that enhances processing of the lines within context over single lines.

"Contexts" Contain Several Levels of Complexity

Although most studies on the processing of wholes and their components have examined performance with a set of global and a set of local properties, the local elements of most visual stimuli can be said to occur at different levels of complexity. Every stimulus potentially has several levels of complexity, and not all components are structurally equivalent. For example, a square is composed of lines; these, in turn, compose angles; and these, in turn compose the overall configuration of square. The description of the various structural levels of complexity within any given stimulus, and their hierarchy, depends on the logical structure of that stimulus. (See also Palmer, 1977; Fu, 1974; Kinchla, 1977; for a similar definition.) That is to say, if certain parts of a stimulus (such as the lines in the preceding example) combine to form another structural unit in the same stimulus (such as an angle), then the former are contained by the latter and represent a lower level of complexity (see Lasaga, in preparation).

A METHODOLOGY TO EXAMINE LOWER-LEVEL
PROCESSING OF COMPLEX TYPE-C
AND TYPE-D STIMULI

Given that various levels of complexity are contained by most Type-C stimuli that have been used in studies of local/global precedence, and that independent variations of the units at different levels of complexity have been difficult to produce, Lasaga (in preparation) used an alternative methodology that allowed the examination of performance with information from various levels of complexity. Subjects simply classified the stimuli into groups according to different rules. This methodology was also easy to employ with Type-D stimuli, and so performance with both Type-C and Type-D stimuli were examined within the same paradigm.

In the design used by Lasaga (in preparation), *patterns* of performance with stimulus sets of successively greater complexity were compared, and not just absolute RTs. The pattern of performance with a simple stimulus set was first obtained. Then, these stimuli were combined to form more complex stimuli, and the pattern of performance was examined for the presence of that found with the earlier (simpler) stimulus set; the data were also examined for any new patterns that would be due to the additional level of complexity now present in the more complex stimulus set. If a lower level of complexity is the only contributor to performance, then that lower level of complexity should contribute to the *relative* speed of performance in the same way as when the lower-level units were presented individually. By comparing patterns of performance across experiments, we can determine whether properties from the highest level of complexity are the sum of properties from the lower levels.

The nature of the local/global processing, sequential versus parallel, was examined within each experiment by comparing absolute RTs. If information-precedence occurs within a given set of stimuli due to sequential processing of properties, then only the properties of the level with precedence should predominate given the nature of the tasks; they are the properties that are available first, regardless of discriminability. If information-precedence occurs within a given set of stimuli due to parallel processing of properties, then the properties at both levels should affect the ability to distinguish between stimuli. This logic is discussed in more detail after the general methodology is described.

General Methodology

Tasks. Subjects performed 13 different tasks in each experiment of Lasaga's (in preparation) study. In each task, the subject was instructed to assign each stimulus to one of two groups. Subjects grouped the stimuli by pressing a lever in one of two directions at each presentation of a stimulus. Either two or four alternative stimuli were used in each task from a total set of four different stimuli for each experiment.

Description of Task Types Used.   The 13 tasks in each experiment were of three types: classification, focusing, and discrimination. In describing these task types, the letters A, B, C, and D are used to represent any four stimuli. The groupings in each task are indicated by parentheses; for example, (A B)(C D) indicates that the stimuli A and B are assigned one response and the stimuli C and D are assigned the other response. In the classification tasks, all four possible stimuli were used, and two of the stimuli were assigned to each of the two responses (see Fig. 6.8). In the focusing tasks, all four stimuli were used again, but one stimulus was assigned to one response, whereas the other three were assigned to the other response (see Fig. 6.8). And in the discrimination tasks, only two stimuli were used, and these two stimuli were assigned to different responses (see Fig. 6.8).

Purpose of These Task Types.   These three types of task allow us to examine a total stimulus set for two types of properties: interstimulus and stimulus-specific properties. In any task involving more than one stimulus, the processing of any given individual stimulus can be influenced by its similarity relationships to other stimuli. Such interstimulus properties need to be distinguished from stimulus-specific properties, which are

Classification Tasks
———————————
(AB)(CD)
(AC)(BD)
(AD)(BC)

Focusing Tasks
———————————
(A)(BCD)
(B)(ACD)
(C)(ABD)
(D)(ABC)

Discrimination Tasks
———————————
(A)(B)
(A)(C)
(A)(D)
(B)(C)
(B)(D)
(C)(D)

FIGURE 6.8.   General paradigm used in Lasaga and Garner's (1983) study and in first three experiments of Lasaga's (in preparation) study, with response groups for each task indicated by parentheses.

the *particular* properties of the individual stimuli, independent of their relationship to other stimuli in the task (e.g., see Sebrechts & Garner, 1981).

The classification tasks tells us which grouping of the four stimuli maximizes the perceived differences between groups and minimizes the differences within groups of stimuli. Lockhead (chapter 9) introduces these notions in great detail, and describes some interesting results on the effects of varying within and between category variability. The notions as used here are similar, except that the total set is kept constant, and pairings of stimuli are imposed on the subjects. If small within-group variability and large between-group variability exist, then the classification task should be easy. This variability could be interstimulus or stimulus-specific.

The discrimination tasks reveal relative degrees of interstimulus similarity between each stimulus and each of the others in the set. If a pair of stimuli are perceived as very similar, then discriminating between them will be very difficult.

The focusing tasks reveal any differences in the properties of the individual stimuli (e.g., ease of encoding, ease of maintenance in memory) independent of their relationship to other stimuli in the task. If a focusing stimulus has good stimulus-specific properties, then that task should be an easy one. These focusing tasks exploit the specific properties of individual stimuli by placing each stimulus in a class by itself.

General Logic of the Design Across Experiments

Because each successive experiment involves an additional level of complexity, the pattern of results is compared with the pattern obtained in the preceding experiment (which contained one level of complexity less). The purpose of the comparison is to determine whether processing (dis)advantages from lower levels still express themselves in stimuli of greater complexity, or whether processing (dis)advantages at the additional higher level influence the pattern of results. Further, because the tasks require classification according to different properties of the stimuli, the ease with which each task can be performed will allow us to examine for effects of parallel versus sequential processing.

Stimulus–Response Mappings. The discrimination and classification tasks are similar in that they involve response groups of equal size (i.e., one stimulus per group in the discrimination tasks and two stimuli per group in the classification tasks). For our purposes, the interesting difference between these tasks involves the stimulus–response mappings of the different stimulus properties. The classification tasks allow a 1:1 stimulus–response mapping if a property can be used to distinguish between the two response groups (e.g., if stimuli in one group share a value of that property and stimuli in the other group share another). If no property distinguishes between response groups, then the stimulus-response ratio becomes 2:1. The stimuli need to be uniquely identified in order to be classified. With the present stimulus sets, sometimes a classification task will allow grouping according to a property at one level with 1:1 mapping and according to another level with 2:1 mapping. That is, a property at one of the levels allows distinction between the groups $(A_1A_1)(A_2A_2)$, but a property at another level does not, $(B_1B_2)(B_1B_2)$. In these cases even if sequential processing occurs with level B as the earlier process, task difficulty might encourage continuation of processing to the property that allows the 1:1 mapping.

The discrimination tasks, as mentioned, allow a 1:1 mapping when a property can be used, for example, $(A_1)(A_2)$. But when a property at a given level cannot be used, information about it is response-irrelevant, for example, $(A_1)(A_1)$. In this latter case, only the property that *allows* discrimination between the stimuli (e.g., B property) can be used.

Specific Task Comparisons. If local/global processes are *sequential*, then *discrimination between stimuli that share a property at the level of precedence should always be more difficult than a discrimination between stimuli that do not share a property at that level*; and if identity of the units at the level of precedence do not suffice, for example, as in $(A_1)(A_1)$, then another set of properties would need to be processed. On the other hand, if local/ global processes are *parallel*, then the *similarity of units at all levels should affect performance*. A task that involves discrimination between stimuli that do not share properties at any level should be easier than a task that involves discrimination between the most discriminable properties, which, in turn, should be easier than discrimination between stimuli that share less-discriminable properties. Given the nature of these tasks, ease of performance now reflects either (a) the ability of the subject to use prior information from sequential processes, or (b) the inability to disrupt parallel processing, and therefore, the influence of response-irrelevant information on classification.

Levels of Complexity Examined

A Low Level of Visual Complexity. One of the smallest units of complexity in a visual stimulus is that of a line, and many studies (e.g., Attneave & Olson, 1967; Campbell & Maffei, 1970; and Essock, 1980) have examined how we process single lines. Even with such simple visual stimuli as these, there already exist differences in speed and accuracy of performance depending on line orientation. As numerous as the studies on line orientation are, all of them produce a similar result: the oblique effect.

The Oblique Effect.   The oblique effect is the finding that performance with oblique lines (i.e., lines that are not vertically or horizontally aligned) is poorer than that with vertical and horizontal lines. Lasaga and Garner (1983) examined the bases for the oblique effect with suprathreshold stimuli in information-processing tasks. In their first experiment, they used classification, focusing, and discrimination tasks. A vertical (V), a horizontal (H), and two diagonal lines—45 deg. counterclockwise (L, for left diagonal) and 45 deg. clockwise from the vertical (R, for right diagonal)—served as the four stimuli. The results from the classification tasks (see bottom of Table 6.1) showed that the task that involved grouping the vertical and horizontal lines together and the two diagonals together was faster then either of the other two ways of grouping the stimuli. The focusing tasks (see middle of Table 6.1) revealed that the vertical and horizontal lines served as better focusing stimuli, that is, had better stimulus-specific properties, than either of the two diagonals. And the discrimination tasks (see top of Table 6.1) showed that the two diagonals were more confusable with each other than any other pair of stimuli, and the other pairs of stimuli did not differ in the confusability of their members. These results led to the conclusion that two factors were producing an oblique effect with suprathreshold stimuli in information-processing tasks: The two diagonal lines were the most confusable (an interstimulus factor), and the vertical and horizontal lines were more easily encoded and held in memory (a stimulus-specific factor).

The Oblique Effect and the Local/Global Issue.   For our purposes, the oblique effect presents an ideal characteristic of processing at a lower level of complexity because it can be reflected in differential pattern of performance within a given level of complexity. The pattern of performance at higher levels of complexity with stimuli composed of vertical, horizontal, and diagonal lines can now be analyzed.

Higher Levels of Visual Complexity.   In order to compare the pattern of results produced by units at a lower level of complexity with the pattern obtained when that level is subsumed in more complex stimuli, it was important to combine only *similar* lower-level units into more complex stimuli. That is, lower-level units that were easily grouped together and

TABLE 6.1
Mean Correct Reaction Times (in msec.) per Task
in Lasaga & Garner's (1983) Study

Discrimination Task				Task Mean	
(V)(H)				415	
(V)(R)				414	
(V)(L)				415	
(H)(R)				410	
(H)(L)				407	
(R)(L)				432	

	Stimulus				
Focusing Task	V	H	R	L	Task Mean[1]
(V)(HRL)	394	480	469	463	432
(H)(VRL)	469	403	447	460	430
(R)(VHL)	508	494	456	567	490
(L)(VHR)	496	499	534	434	472

Classification Task				Task Mean	
(VH)(RL)				469	
(VR)(HL)				561	
(HR)(VL)				568	

[1]Focusing task means were weighted.

appear similar when presented as units were combined together in subsequent stimulus sets, but not those that did not share similar properties at the lower level (Lasaga, in preparation). The groupings of the stimuli that produced the fastest classification task provided the basis for the combination of lower-level units into stimuli with higher levels of visual complexity (e.g., vertical and horizontal lines were combined to form one stimulus and diagonal lines another, for stimuli with two levels of complexity).

Results from Lasaga's Study

Experiment 1. The first experiment involved four right angles (see Fig. 6.9), which contained properties at two levels of complexity: orientation of lines; and direction of pointing or figural stability (i.e., corner vs. arrow configuration) of angles. If you consider each task as a classification according to line orientation (see Table 6.2), the pattern of results obtained with the present stimulus set is not similar to that obtained when the lines were presented singly (see Table 6.1). Such a finding suggests that the higher level of complexity was not simply the

FIGURE 6.9. Stimulus set used in Lasaga's (in preparation) Experiment 1. From left-to-right: U-arrow (up arrow), D-arrow (down arrow), U-corner (upper corner), and L-corner (lower corner).

sum of units at the lower level of lines. This conclusion is supported by several findings: First, the two most difficult classification tasks, each of which involved the same mixture of units at the level of lines, differed in difficulty from each other. In addition, all of the stimuli seemed to serve equally well as focus stimuli, unlike when the single lines were used. And, finally, the discrimination between angles that were composed of oblique lines was actually easier than discrimination between angles that were composed of vertical and horizontal lines.

Given the pattern of results just described, we can rule out local information-precedence of any kind. The effects of parallel versus sequential processes with global precedence can now be examined from comparisons of task difficulty.

If parallel processes are occurring, the easiest discrimination tasks should that involve discrimination between angles that do not share any global or local properties (i.e., up-arrow vs. down-corner and down-arrow vs. up-corner). These should be followed by tasks with stimuli that share properties at only level or both levels (i.e., up-arrow vs. up-corner, down-arrow vs. down-corner, up-arrow vs. down-arrow, and up-corner vs. down-corner). This pattern was clearly not obtained. (*Sealed* parallel processing is assumed to be empirically indistinguishable from sequential).

If sequential processing is occurring, the tasks that involve discrimination between stimuli that do not share a property at the global level should always be easier than the tasks with stimuli that do share a property at that level, even if the latter stimuli share a property at the lower level of complexity. However, two global properties were available for classification of these stimuli, that is, direction of pointing and figural instability. And all of the discrimination tasks allowed discrimination according to one of these two global properties. Further, line orientation was structurally confounded with stability of angle in the present stimulus set. Thus, the desired comparisons cannot be made. Regardless, the finding that the (U-corner)(D-corner) task was harder than the

FIGURE 6.10. Stimulus set used in Lasaga's (in preparation) Experiment 2. From left to right: square, diamond, plus, and "X."

TABLE 6.2

Mean Correct Reaction Times (in msec.) per Task in Lasaga's (in preparation) Study, Experiment 1

Discrimination Tasks	Task Mean
(U-arrow) (D-arrow)	419
(U-arrow) (U-corner)	433
(U-arrow) (D-corner)	415
(D-arrow) (U-corner)	430
(D-arrow) (D-corner)	459
(U-corner) (D-corner)	450

Focusing Task	Stimulus				
	U-arrow	D-arrow	U-corner	D-corner	Task Mean[1]
(U-arrow) (D-arrow U-corner D-corner)	441	510	471	457	460
(D-arrow) (U-arrow U-corner D-corner)	472	423	436	469	441
(U-corner) (U-arrow D-arrow D-corner)	453	451	424	478	442
(D-corner) (U-arrow D-arrow U-corner)	446	446	479	414	436

Classification Task	Task Mean
(U-arrow D-arrow) (U-corner D-corner)	462
(U-arrow U-corner) (D-arrow D-corner)	520
(U-arrow D-corner) (D-arrow U-corner)	602

[1]Focusing task means were weighted.

(U-arrow)(D-arrow) task weakly suggests that sequential processing with global precedence is occurring. The former task involves discrimination of lines that are vertical and horizontal, differing simply in relative location; the latter task, discrimination of oblique lines. Yet this local information did not make performance easier in the former task. When this result is considered together with the evidence against parallel processing of the current stimuli, performance in the discrimination tasks weakly indicates that sequential processing is occurring that provides global information-precedence.

In all four focusing tasks (see Table 6.2), the nonfocus stimulus that was the hardest to reject was the stimulus that shared the property of line orientation *or* figural stability (i.e., if the focus was an arrow, then the other arrow was hardest to reject, and if corner then corner). We cannot distinguish between which of these properties was being used.

The easiest classification task (see Table 6.2) was easier than the task that allowed classification according to the global property of direction of pointing. This finding could indicate that the two properties of the highest structural level are being used but differ in their discriminability (i.e., figural stability and direction of pointing); or that both levels are contributing to performance, with the easiest task being performed according to line orientation and/or figural stability, and the task of medium difficulty being performed according to direction of pointing.

The results from Experiment 1 (Lasaga, in preparation) indicated unequivocally that the highest level of complexity is not simply the sum of the lower level of lines and that sequential local precedence was not occurring. However, the global property of figural stability was structurally confounded with the local property of line orientation. Thus, it is not clear whether global information-precedence was provided by parallel or serial processing. In Experiment 2, therefore, stimuli were constructed that were not structurally confounded. Because we do know the pattern of performance obtained with the set of angles used in Experiment 1, regardless of the nature of processing, we can now examine its contribution to performance with more complex stimuli.

Experiment 2. The second experiment used a square, a diamond, a plus, and an "X" (see Fig. 6.10). These stimuli contained a level of lines, a level of angles, and a level of overall closure/nonclosure. If you consider each task as a classification according to line orientation (see Table 6.3), the pattern of results obtained with the present stimulus set is not similar to that obtained when the lines were presented singly (Lasaga & Garner, 1983). If you consider each task as a classification according to angle properties, the present pattern also does not resemble the pattern obtained in Experiment 1. Such findings suggest that, again, the highest level of complexity was not simply the sum of units at either of the lower levels; and that sequential local precedence of either level was not occurring. This conclusion is supported by the finding that the two most difficult classification tasks, each of which involved the same mixture of units at the level of lines and at the level of angles, differed in difficulty from each other. In addition, the square served as a better focus than any other stimulus; and the nonfocusing stimulus that was hardest to reject in all tasks was the one that shared the property of closure/nonclosure. Finally, the discrimination between stimuli composed of oblique lines and arrow angles, (Diamond)("X"), was one of the easiest tasks (unlike the pattern obtained with single lines) and as easy as the discrimination of stimuli composed of vertical/horizontal lines and corner angles (unlike the pattern obtained with angle stimuli).

If sequential global precedence is occurring, then the tasks involving discrimination between stimuli that share a property at that level (i.e., square vs. diamond and plus vs. "X") should be the hardest tasks, even though neither pair of stimuli share a property at the lower level (i.e., in both tasks, the discrimination at the lower level is an easy one). Further, the easiest tasks should be the ones that involve discrimination between

TABLE 6.3
Mean Correct Reaction Times (in msec.) per Task
in Lasaga's (in preparation) Study, Experiment 2

Discrimination Tasks	Task Mean			
(Square) (Diamond)	426			
(Square) (Plus)	385			
(Square) ("X")	384			
(Diamond) (Plus)	390			
(Diamond) ("X")	386			
(Plus) ("X")	443			

	Stimulus				
Focusing Task	Square	Diamond	Plus	"X"	Task Mean[1]
(Square) (Diamond Plus "X")	401	495	416	418	422
(Diamond) (Square Plus "X")	484	437	429	441	444
(Plus) (Square Diamond "X")	422	420	433	489	438
("X") (Square Diamond Plus)	414	437	515	450	453

Classification Task	Task Mean
(Square Diamond) (Plus "X")	398
(Square Plus) (Diamond "X")	513
(Square "X") (Diamond Plus)	576

[1]Focusing task means were weighted.

stimuli that do not share any global properties (i.e., closure or nonclosure), regardless of the properties of the lower-level units. If global precedence in parallel processing affects performance, then the discrimination between stimuli that do not share properties at any level should be the easiest (i.e., square vs. "X" and diamond vs. plus). The discrimination between stimuli that share a property at one level should be the next easiest (i.e., the rest of the tasks). These latter tasks could differ in difficulty, reflecting relative discriminabilities of the different properties, but the crucial patterns that distinguish between sequential versus parallel processing is that discriminations between closure and nonclosure should be equally difficult with sequential processing, but with parallel processing discrimination should be harder if the stimuli share a lower-level property. The results support a conclusion of sequential global precedence. Only the square vs. diamond and the plus vs. "X" were more and equally difficult than the rest.

The results from the focusing tasks (see Table 6.3) reveal performance according to the highest level property only. The square was the best focusing stimulus, and the only nonfocus stimulus that was difficult to reject was the one that shared the highest-level property of closure/ nonclosure with the focus stimulus. This pattern again suggests that parallel processes are not operating, because similarity at the level of lines or angles did not make a stimulus difficult to reject.

The classification data (see Table 6.3) revealed that the easiest task allowed classification according to the highest-level property of closure/ nonclosure. The two more difficult tasks also differed in difficulty from each other. Given that the discrimination and focusing data indicate that sequential processes are at play, this pattern suggests that subjects continued to a lower level of processing in the (Square Plus)(Diamond "X") task for a lower stimulus–response ratio. This is an interesting finding. It indicates that when the stimulus–response ratio drops from an earlier stage of processing to a later one, it seems easier to continue to the later stage than to use a higher stimulus response ratio available for earlier information.

The results from the second experiment (Lasaga, in preparation) suggest strongly that global precedence in sequential processing is occurring with these Type-C stimuli. The results also suggest that, even though a level may be processed with precedence, if a subsequent level allows a decrease in stimulus–response ratio, processing will continue to the subsequent level. Finally, because the pattern of processing with single lines and single angles is known, the findings with this stimulus set were not due to properties that are intermediate between the lines and the highest level—that is, the level of angle.

Experiment 3.   The third experiment consisted of Type-D stimuli: a large square, a large diamond, a large plus, and a large "X," which were composed of small pluses, small diamonds, small squares, and small X's, respectively (see Fig. 6.11). These stimuli contained six levels of complexity (with two levels of lines, small and large; and two levels of angles, small and large).

If you consider each task as a classification of line orientation or angle, the pattern of results obtained with the present stimulus set does not resemble that obtained when the lines, angles, or geometric figures, are presented singly. (See Table 6.4.) In fact, this is true whether the properties of line orientation or of angle are examined at the lower (i.e., Type-C) or at the higher (i.e., Type-D) levels of complexity. Such findings suggest that the highest level of complexity is not simply the sum of units at any of these lower levels and that none of these lower levels are processed first in a sequence.

None of the discrimination tasks were more difficult than any other (see Table 6.4). Such a result, albeit null, supports a conclusion that sequential processing is not occurring.

The focusing tasks (see Table 6.4) revealed that no stimulus served as a better focus. (Note that two stimuli were redundant at the third and

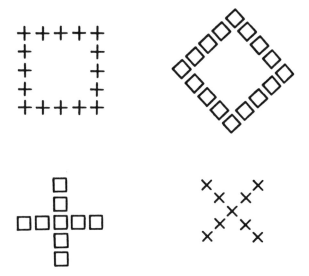

FIGURE 6.11.   Stimulus set used in Lasaga's (in preparation) Experiment 3. Large Square composed of small pluses, large Diamond composed of small diamonds, large Plus composed of small squares, and large "X" composed of small x's.

TABLE 6.4
Mean Correct Reaction Times (in msec.) per Task
in Lasaga's (in preparation) Study, Experiment 3

Discrimination Tasks	Task Mean
(SQUARE) (DIAMOND)	394
(SQUARE) (PLUS)	386
(SQUARE) ("X")	378
(DIAMOND) (PLUS)	376
(DIAMOND) ("X")	370
(PLUS) ("X")	398

| Focusing Task | Stimulus | | | | |
	Square	Diamond	Plus	"X"	Task Mean[1]
(SQUARE) (DIAMOND PLUS "X")	409	465	427	414	422
(DIAMOND) (SQUARE PLUS "X")	433	400	427	407	411
(PLUS) (SQUARE DIAMOND "X")	397	414	486	439	401
("X") (SQUARE DIAMOND PLUS)	405	399	391	383	391

Classification Task	Task Mean
(SQUARE DIAMOND) (PLUS "X")	412
(SQUARE PLUS) (DIAMOND "X")	476
(SQUARE "X") (DIAMOND PLUS)	439

[1]Focusing task means were weighted.

sixth levels, yet this structural redundancy did not produce better stimulus-specific properties.) However, the stimuli that were more difficult to reject were the ones that shared the property of closure/nonclosure at one or both levels with this property, that is, the third and sixth levels. This finding suggests that the properties of these two levels are processed in parallel and are equally discriminable within the present stimulus set.

Finally, the results from the classification tasks (see Table 6.4) support the conclusion that closure/nonclosure at the third and highest levels is processed in parallel. The tasks did not differ in difficulty based on information from any one level of complexity, regardless of possible reduction in the stimulus–response ratio. The two easiest tasks were equivalent in ease, suggesting that the properties used in these tasks (i.e., closure/nonclosure at the third and highest level) were equally discriminable and neither was processed with sequential precedence.

Conclusions from Lasaga's Study. The results from these three experiments led to the conclusions that, for these geometric forms, (a) lower-level properties were dominated by higher-level ones, and (b) lower-level properties could be made as easily available as higher-level ones if the units at that lower level were disconnected from each other. These experiments with both Type-C and Type-D stimuli suggest that only sequential global precedence was occurring with the Type-C stimuli; whereas, with Type-D stimuli, *disconnected* lower units were processed in parallel with those of the highest level.

CONCLUSIONS FROM STUDIES WITH TYPE-D AND WITH TYPE-C STIMULI

The studies with Type-D stimuli and the studies with Type-C stimuli that varied properties at one level while requiring responses to the other level have brought us to different conclusions. With Type-D stimuli, the local and global properties seem to be processed in parallel with information-precedence dictated by relative discriminability of the properties within a stimulus. In addition, Lasaga and Llaneras (in preparation) and Sebrechts and Fragala (1985) found evidence that an unattended (response-irrelevant) property interfered with processing of an attended (response-relevant) property when the former property was good rather than bad. Salience at one level can detract attention from another.

With Type-C stimuli, comparison between performance with line segments in three-dimensional configurations and performance with line segments in flat configurations suggested that the global property of two- versus three-dimensionality affected the accuracy with which the local identifications were made. However, the variation of the global properties were correlated with response information. That is, the global properties alone, or some intermediate level of complexity, could have been used for the tasks. In which case, the problem of relative discriminability would arise. Regardless of this qualification, no evidence for local precedence has been obtained in such studies.

Lasaga (in preparation) examined performance with several levels of structural complexity. Her results indicate that lower-level properties are processed after the highest-level ones in Type-C stimuli, but can be as salient as the highest-level ones with Type-D stimuli.

MAPPING OF STIMULUS TYPES ONTO CONFIGURATION TYPES RECONSIDERED

The various studies on factors affecting local/global precedence with Type-D and Type-C have indicated that different factors affect the microgenesis of their perceived whole. For Type-D stimuli, size of visual

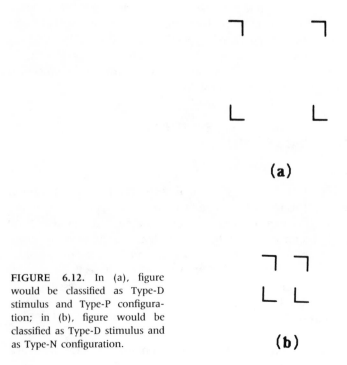

FIGURE 6.12. In (a), figure would be classified as Type-D stimulus and Type-P configuration; in (b), figure would be classified as Type-D stimulus and as Type-N configuration.

angle, sparsity, location of stimulus presentation, stimulus quality, and level of prior attentional allocation have been shown to affect the type of precedence that is obtained. For Type-C stimuli, three-dimensionality of context, location of fixation point, type of stimulus mask, local/global redundancy, and similarity of configurations have influenced information-precedence.

In our examination of methodologies for Type-D stimuli in which processing of only one level was required for response, we found that local/global redundancy (Kinchla, 1977) also affected precedence with Type-C stimuli; and that the goodness of the pattern at the local (Sebrechts & Fragala, 1985) or at the global level (Lasaga & Llaneras, in preparation; Sebrechts & Fragala, 1985) affected performance with units at the other level. Although not reported in this chapter, Lasaga (in preparation) also examined whether variations of visual angle affected performance with Type-C stimuli, and no effect was found.

At the moment, it appears that precedence with Type-C and Type-D stimuli is affected by different factors. However, more studies are needed to further substantiate this distinction. For example, studies are needed that examine the effects of similarity of configurations, three-dimensionality, location of fixation point, and type of stimulus mask on precedence with Type-D stimuli. Or, with Type-C stimuli, given that local information precedence has not been obtained without changing the nature of processing or the stimulus–response ratio, an examination of the effects of level of prior attentional allocation on precedence could be important. Unfortunately, given the nature of Type-C stimuli, the effects of varying sparsity and stimulus quality (i.e., at local and global levels independently) cannot be examined. The difference in the logical nature of the two types of stimuli, and the difference in the types of precedence obtained with them, support the distinction made between them theoretically in this chapter.

The question remains as to whether the mapping of Type-D and Type-C stimuli onto the Type-P and Type-N configurations is appropriate. The precedence that should be revealed by each of the two types of configuration was discussed earlier. With Type-P configurations as defined, evidence for parallel local or global precedence should be obtained. Studies using Type-D stimuli revealed such evidence. With Type-N configurations as defined, sequential local precedence should always be obtained because the nature and the position of the local units are required for the identity of the global properties. Unfortunately, our examination of studies that have used Type-C stimuli have revealed that, if any precedence is obtained, it is global precedence, and Lasaga's (in preparation) study has suggested that such precedence involves sequential processes.

Figure 6.12 illustrates two Type-D stimuli. Figure 6.12a presents a configuration that has been classified as Type-P by Pomerantz (1981), and Fig. 6.12b presents a configuration that has been classified as Type-N (Pomerantz, 1981). Because visual angle (and therefore relative size of local and global units [Navon & Norman, 1983]) has been found to affect the type of information-precedence obtained with Type-D stimuli, it is not surprising that the properties of the local units are more salient with the stimulus in Fig. 6.12 than with the stimulus in Fig. 6.12. These figures can be seen as illustrating the effect of relative discriminability with Type-D stimuli.

Given that different factors affect the microgenesis of the perceived whole with Type-C and Type-D stimuli, and that the two stimulus structures differ in the degree to which change at one level affects the nature of units at the other, the distinction seems to be a useful one for further investigations of local/global precedence. However, it has become clearer through this examination of studies with Type-C and Type-D stimuli that performance with Type-C stimuli is still poorly understood.

GENERAL CONCLUSIONS

The issue of global/local precedence was a challenging issue for Gestalt psychology, and it remains one today. The logical relationship between wholes and parts, that the latter are contained by the former by definition, has produced many of the methodological problems that have been encountered by investigators today. In addition, different types of stimulus seem to produce different types of perceived whole. The relationship between local and global processes with one type of stimulus, Type-C, is still quite poorly understood. The factors affecting relative discriminability of local/global levels with Type-D stimuli also need further investigation.

This chapter has been an attempt to present some methodological considerations within a theoretical framework for the study of local/global precedence. Although the studies on the local/global issue have been numerous, the present examination of those studies has revealed many remaining gaps in our understanding of the microgenesis of the perceived whole.

ACKNOWLEDGMENTS

The author thanks Stephen Palmer for engaging in a helpful discussion on some of the ideas that were presented at the symposium on object perception that was held in Madrid. This discussion helped to highlight some points that needed further clarification (and hopefully received clarification in this chapter). The author also thanks James Pomerantz for various detailed and insightful comments on an earlier version of this chapter.

REFERENCES

Attneave, F., & Olson, R.K. (1967). Discriminability of stimuli varying in physical and retinal orientation. *Journal of Experimental Psychology, 74*, 149–157.
Bell, H.H., & Handel, S. (1976). The role of pattern goodness in the reproduction of backward masked patterns. *Journal of Experimental Psychology; Human Perception and Performance, 2*, 139–150.
Campbell, F.W., & Maffei, L. (1970). Electrophysiological evidence for the existence of orientation and size detectors in the human visual system. *Journal of Physiology, 207*, 635–652.
Checkosky, S.F., & Whitlock, D. (1973).The effects of pattern goodness on recognition time in a memory search task. *Journal of Experimental Psychology, 100*, 341–348.
Earhard, B. (1980). The line-in-object superiority effect in perception: It depends on where you fix your eyes and what is located at the point of fixation. *Perception & Psychophysics, 28*, 9–18.

Earhard, B., & Armitage, R. (1980). From an object-superiority effect to an object-inferiority effect with movement of the fixation point. *Perception & Psychophysics, 28,* 369–376.

Enns, J.T., & Prinzmetal, W. (1984). The role of redundancy in the object–line effect. *Perception & Psychophysics, 35,* 22–32.

Essock, E.A. (1980). The oblique effects of stimulus identification considered with respect to two classes of oblique effects. *Perception, 9,* 37–46.

Fu, K.S. (1974). *Syntactic methods in pattern recognition.* New York: Academic Press.

Garner, W.R. (1983). Asymmetric interactions of stimulus dimensions in perceptual information processing. In T.J. Tighe & B.E. Shepp (Eds.), *Perception, cognition and development: Interactional analyses* (pp.   ). Hillsdale, NJ: Lawrence Erlbaum Associates.

Garner, W.R., & Sutliff, D. (1974). The effect of goodness on encoding time in visual pattern discrimination. *Perception & Psychophysics, 16,* 426–430.

Grice, G.R., Canham, L. & Boroughs, J.M. (1983). Forest before trees? It depends on where you look. *Perception & Psychophysics, 33,* 121–128.

Hoffman, J.E. (1980). Interaction between global and local levels of a form. *Journal of Experimental Psychology; Human Perception and Performance, 6,* 222–234.

Kinchla, R.A. (1977). The role of structural redundancy in the perception of visual targets. *Perception & Psychophysics, 22,* 19–30.

Kinchla, R.A., & Wolfe, J.M. (1979). The order of visual processing: "Top-down," "bottom-up," or "middle-out." *Perception & Psychophysics, 25,* 225–231.

Klein, R. (1978). Visual detection of line segments: Two exceptions to the object superiority effect. *Perception & Psychophysics, 24,* 237–242.

Koffka, K. (1935). *Principles of Gestalt psychology.* New York: Harcourt, Brace, & World, Inc.

Kohler, W. (1925). An aspect of Gestalt psychology. In C. Murchison, (Ed.), *Psychologies of 1925* (pp. 163–198). Worcester, MA: Clark University Press.

Kohler, W. (1929). *Gestalt psychology.* New York: Liveright.

Lasaga, M.I. (in preparation). Classification of stimulus sets with successively greater degrees of structural complexity.

Lasaga, M.I., & Llaneras, R.E. (in preparation). *Conjunctions of color and form in vertically, horizontally, and diagonally aligned stimuli.*

Lasaga, M.I., & Garner, W.R. (1983). The effect of line orientation on various information-processing tasks. *Journal of Experimental Psychology, Human Perception and Performance, 9,* 215–225.

McClelland, J.L. (1978). Perception and masking of wholes and parts. *Journal of Experimental Psychology, Human Perception and Performance, 4,* 210–223.

McClelland, J.L., & Miller, J. (1979). Structural factors in figure perception. *Perception & Psychophysics, 26,* 221–229.

Martin, M. (1979). Local and global processing: The role of sparsity. *Memory & Cognition, 7,* 476–484.

Miller, J. (1981). Global precedence in attention and decision. *Journal of Experimental Psychology: Human Perception and Performance, 7,* 1161–1174.

Navon, D. (1977). Forest before trees: The precedence of global features in visual perception. *Cognitive Psychology, 9,* 353–383.

Navon, D. (1983). How many trees does it take to make a forest? *Perception 12,* 739–254.

Navon, D., & Norman, J. (1983). Does global precedence really depend on visual angle? *Journal of Experimental Psychology: Human Perception and Performance, 9,* 955–965.

Palmer, S.E. (1977). Hierarchical structure in perceptual representation. *Cognitive Psychology, 9,* 441–474.

Pomerantz, J.R. (1981) Perceptual organization in information processing. In M. Kubovy

& J.R. Pomerantz (Eds.), *Perceptual organization*. (pp. 141–179). Hillsdale, N.J.: Lawrence Erlbaum Associates.

Pomerantz, J.R. (1983). Global and local precedence: Selective attention in form and motion perception. *Journal of Experimental Psychology: General, 112*, 516–540.

Pomerantz, J.R., & Sager, L.C. (1975). Asymmetric integrality with dimensions of visual pattern. *Perception & Psychophysics, 18*, 460–466.

Pomerantz, J.R., Sager, L.C., & Stoever, R.J. (1977). Perception of wholes and of their component parts: Some configural superiority effects. *Journal of Experimental Psychology: Human Perception and Performance, 3*, 422–433.

Posner, M.I. (1978). *Chronometric explorations of mind*. Hillsdale, N.J.: Lawrence Erlbaum Associates.

Schendel, J.D., & Shaw, P. (1976). A test of the generality of the word-context effect. *Perception & Psychophysics, 19*, 383–393.

Sebrechts, M.M., & Fragala, J.J. (1985). Variations on parts and wholes: Information precedence vs. global precedence. In *Proceedings of the Seventh Annual Conference of the Cognitive Science Society*, 11–18.

Sebrechts, M.M., & Garner, W.R. (1981). Stimulus-specific processing consequences of pattern goodness. *Memory & Cognition, 9*, 41–49.

Vernon, M.D. (1937). *Visual perception*. London: Cambridge University Press.

Vurpillot, E., Ruel, J., & Castrec, A. (1976-1977). L'organisation perceptive chez le nourrison: Response au tout ou a ses elements. *Bulletin de Psychologie, 327*, 396–405.

Ward, L.M. (1982). Determinants of attention to local and global features of visual forms. *Journal of Experimental Psychology: Human Perception and Performance, 8*, 562–581.

Ward, L.M. (1983). On processing dominance: Comment on Pomerantz. *Journal of Experimental Psychology: General, 112*, 541–546.

Weisstein, N., & Harris, C.S. (1974). Visual detection of line segments: An object-superiority effect. *Science, 186*, 752–755.

Wertheimer, M. (1923). Untersuchungen zur Lehre von der Gestalt. II.. *Psychologischen Forschung, 4*, 301–350.

Williams, A., & Weisstein, N. (1978). Line segments are perceived better in a coherent context than alone: An object-line effect in visual perception. *Memory & Cognition, 6*, 85–90.

7 ON PERCEIVING OBJECTS: HOLISTIC VERSUS FEATURAL PROPERTIES

Bryan E. Shepp
Brown University

INTRODUCTION

Psychologists, and philosophers before them, have recognized that objects can be characterized by either holistic or featural properties. Indeed, a long-standing debate concerns which set of properties takes precedence over the other in perception. Although the debate persists in contemporary theory (e.g., Lockhead, 1972, 1979; Treisman & Gelade, 1980), there is little doubt that the adult perceiver gains easy access to either property in many sets of multidimensional objects.

Child perceivers, on the other hand, do not have easy access to either property, and developmental theorists have traditionally claimed that object perception is dominated by holistic or global properties in the young child and by analytical or featural properties in the older child and adult. This view is not very old (e.g., Gibson, 1969) and the evidence for it has not been very compelling, often taking the form that the young child shows few or no signs of using featural or dimensional information, whereas the older child and adult show obvious sensitivity to features and dimensions.

During the last ten years or so, however, a view has emerged that offers a specific and precise formulation of the holistic to featural trend in perceptual development (e.g., Shepp & Swartz, 1976; Smith & Kemler, 1977). This view, based on distinctions made by Garner (1974, 1976) and Lockhead (1966a,b, 1972) between integral and separable stimuli, claims that objects that are perceived by the older child and

203

adult as features on separable dimensions are perceived by the young child as integral wholes.

Integral stimuli differ markedly from separable stimuli. Phenomenologically, integral stimuli (e.g., chroma and value of a Munsell chip) are seen as wholes, whereas separable stimuli, (e.g., size and brightness of a square) are seen as specific features. Integral stimuli also differ operationally from separable ones. Columns 1 and 2 of Table 7.1 summarize the differences between the two kinds of stimuli across a variety of converging tasks, and for unspeeded tasks, at least, there are consistent differences between the stimuli.

There is also strong converging evidence that object perception becomes more separable with increasing age, a view that Shepp (1978) has dubbed the *separability hypothesis*. In speeded sorting, for example, the younger child shows a redundancy gain with correlated values and interference with orthogonal values in a selective attention task— performances that are typical for integral stimuli. But with the same stimulus sets, older children and adults exhibit no redundancy gain and no interference effect—performances that are permitted by separable stimuli (Shepp & Swartz, 1976; Smith & Kemler, 1978). Analogously, in restricted classification tasks, younger children classify by the similarity structure that characterizes integral stimuli, whereas older children and adults classify the same stimuli by the dimensional structure so characteristic of separable stimuli (Shepp, Burns, & McDonough, 1980; Smith & Kemler, 1977; Ward, 1980).

Generally speaking, these results clarify or extend several lines of argument in perceptual and cognitive development. First, this work makes clear that object perception in the young child is not unstructured, and that holistic perception is not simply the absence of dimensional perception. Rather, wholes have specific properties that lead to performance consequences that are very different from those of dimensional properties. Second, the work illustrates the importance of separating different aspects of perceptual and cognitive development. Younger children are often said to perceive objects holistically and to fail in tasks that require selective attention. But if young children perceive objects as integral stimuli, then their failure to attend selectively is no different from that of adults when confronted with integral stimuli in a task that requires selective attention. In this case, the failure to attend cannot be attributed to a lack of resource control. Moreover, a claim that the young child cannot allocate attention must clearly be accompanied by the demonstration that the sources of information are independent.

Finally, the separability hypothesis, or the revised differentiation hypothesis, as Kemler (1983a) has called it, has illuminated the analysis of several traditional developmental issues, such as classification (L. Smith,

1979, 1981, 1983), conservation (Kemler, 1983a), and concept learning (Kemler Nelson, 1984; Ward & Scott, 1987), and has yielded important insights into these aspects of cognitive development.

Despite what can be considered substantial success of this view of perceptual development, there are several basic issues that are unresolved. Some investigators still view the concept of holistic organizations as incompatible with a dimensional organization (Aschkenasy & Odom, 1982), despite the fact that there is no inherent incompatibility (see Kemler, 1983b). Moreover, the architects of the initial separability hypothesis have begun to stake out formulations that are distinctive from one another (see, for example, chapters 11 and 12), and the performance domains to which each can effectively speak may differ greatly.

During the past several years, the research in my laboratory has focused on the multiple representations of objects, the kinds of constraints on representations that are imposed by different kinds of stimuli, the types of cognitive operations that give access to particular representations, and the role of such factors in the development of perceived structure. This chapter first describes differences between integral, separable, and separate stimuli, and the perceptual and processing consequences of each in the adult perceiver. Next, comparisons between separable and separate stimuli are described that differentiate clearly between the development of perceived structure and the development of attention. Finally, we consider the relation between the type of prime and the accessing of holistic and featural representations.

INTEGRAL, SEPARABLE, AND SEPARATE DIMENSIONS

Garner (1970, 1974) asserts that two dimensions are integral if the existence of one requires the existence of the second; dimensions are separable if there are no constraints on their existence. Prototypic integral dimensions are chroma and value of a Munsell chip, but the definition applies equally well to other properties of objects, for example, color, shape, and size. Prototypic separable dimensions are size of circle and angle of a radial line or other features that are spatially separated, for example, chroma and value presented in different spatial locations. These are statements about stimulus concepts, and provided that these concepts had mapped consistently to converging tasks, the relations between stimuli and percepts would have been simple indeed.

Unfortunately, some stimuli are well behaved, whereas others are not. Variations of value and chroma on a single Munsell chip yield performances that consistently meet the operational criteria of integral stimuli, whereas the spatial separation of value and chroma yield performances that are invariably separable (e.g., Garner, 1974, Garner & Felfoldy, 1970). But the majority of object properties (e.g., combinations of color, shape, and size) misbehave, sometimes giving the appearance of integral stimuli (e.g., Biederman & Checkosky, 1970: Garner, 1977; Gottwald & Garner, 1972), but other times giving the appearance of separable stimuli (e.g., Handel & Imai, 1972; Smith & Kemler, 1978).

This wide range of results has led to the view that there is a continuum of integrality rather than a simple dichotomy between integral and separable dimensions (e.g., Garner, 1974). Stimuli generated by such combinations as chroma and value would anchor one end of the continuum, whereas stimuli composed of combinations like spatially separated chroma and value would exist at the other end. According to this view, movement along the continuum would lead to a reversal of the primary and secondary perceptual processes evoked by the stimuli. The primary process of value and chroma of a Munsell chip is a holistic similarity structure; perceived dimensional structure is secondary and derived. In contrast, the primary structure for spatially separated value and chroma is dimensional; similarity is secondary and derived. The fundamental change in the primary process that would occur with shifts along the continuum would, of course, have considerable consequences on performance in a variety of tasks.

There is another view of the integrality continuum, however, that leads to different conclusions about perception and has different consequences for information processing. Suppose that the continuum exists only for physically integral stimuli and is defined by the degree of analyzability of the stimuli. One end of the continuum is anchored by difficult-to-analyze stimuli, such as the value and chroma of a Munsell chip, whereas the other end is anchored by easy-to-analyze stimuli, such as color and form or size and brightness.

For all stimuli on the continuum, a holistic organization is primary; these are Lockhead's (1972) "blobs." The dimensional features in these stimuli become available only when the stimulus is analyzed. But, importantly, the dimensional structure is assumed to be more accessible at the easily analyzed end of the continuum. Indeed, the mature observer might gain equal access to either the holistic or featural representation, and might select the representation that permits the optimal performance of the task.

Although physically integral stimuli can be analyzed into their constituent features, the analysis of wholes into constituent features does not mean that the features have all of the properties of psychologically separable dimensions. In particular, the coexistence of integral features means that if one is processed, so too is the other. The consequence of processing both features is that selective attention may fail when an irrelevant feature gives rise to response competition or the relevant feature is extracted after processing of an irrelevant feature is completed. We return to this issue later in this chapter.

Consider now spatially separated dimensions, which we call separate rather than separable. These stimuli are invariably perceived according to their dimensional structure, and the structure is perceived automatically, without effort, regardless of task demand or age of the observer. Moreover, I know of no convincing evidence that separate stimuli can be perceived as wholes. In Lockhead's terms (1972), a combination of two separate dimensions is seen as two blobs, and attention can be directed to one without interference from the other.

Although the distinctions that I have drawn between integral, separable, and separate dimensions are not widely recognized, there is ample evidence (which is summarized in Table 7.1) that supports the distinctions. The first four rows summarize the evidence from tasks that are unspeeded, whereas the last five rows give the evidence for speeded

TABLE 7.1

Three Types of Dimensional Combinations and Their Consequences
in Different Perceptual Tasks

Perceptual Task	Type of Dimensional Combination		
	Integral	Separable	Separate
Basis of Similarity Scaling?	Euclidean Metric	City Block Metric	City Block Metric
Additive Difference Model Independence?	No	Yes	Yes
Basis of Classification?	Overall Similarities	Dimensional Similarities	Dimensional Similarities
Dimensional Preferences in Classification?	No	Yes	Yes
Selective Readout:			
Facilitation with correlated dimensions?	Yes	Yes	No
Interference with orthogonal dimensions?	Yes	Yes	No
Reaction Time:			
Facilitation with correlated dimensions?	Yes	Yes/No	No
Selective attention with orthogonal dimensions?	No	No/Yes	Yes
Successful divided attention to conjunctions?	Yes	Yes	No

tasks. Notice that in unspeeded tasks, the performances with separable and separate stimuli are very similar to each other, but different from integral stimuli. In contrast, the performances in speeded tasks indicate that integral and separable stimuli are frequently alike and different from separate stimuli.

Evidence from Unspeeded Tasks

Consider first the tasks in which similarity is judged directly. One of the earliest distinctions between integral and separable stimuli holds that the former are described by a Euclidean metric, whereas the latter are fitted by a city block metric (e.g., Attneave, 1950; Shepard, 1964; Torgerson, 1958).

Garner (1970, 1974) argues that such results reflect two properties that affect perceived structure. Integral stimuli are organized by a similarity or distance (Euclidean) structure; they are not perceived as dimensions, but as unitary stimuli. In contrast, separable stimuli are governed by a dimensional structure; perceived dimensional relations dominate, and similarity or distance does not exist for such stimuli.

An alternative way of describing the results of similarity judgment tasks has been suggested by Burns, Shepp, McDonough, and Wiener-Ehrlich (1978) and Burns and Shepp (1988). These investigators argue that integral stimuli do not meet the formal criteria for subjective dimensions, whereas separable stimuli do. The criteria that define the subjectively independent dimensions are given by an additive difference model (e.g., Krantz & Tversky, 1975; Tversky & Krantz, 1970), and these criteria are consistently violated by integral stimuli but are upheld for separable stimuli.

A comparison between the two interpretations favors the additive difference view. The Euclidean and city block metrics are really special cases of additive difference metrics, and a satisfactory test of either requires the prior fulfillment of the criteria of independence. Integral stimuli usually do not do so (see Burns & Shepp, 1988). Moreover, recent evidence suggests that while both separate (e.g., size of circle vs. angle of a radial line) and separable (size vs. brightness) dimensions meet the criteria of subjective independence, they do not conform to either a Euclidean of a city block metric (Burns et al., 1978; Dunn, 1983; Ronacher & Bautz, 1985).

Although there is disagreement about the kinds of metrics that optimally characterize similarity judgments, the disagreement should not obscure two fundamental points. By either view, integral stimuli should not be perceived as subjective dimensions, whereas separable and separate stimuli should be so perceived. Second, the data, on balance, indicate that integral stimuli are not seen as dimensions, whereas both separable and separate stimuli are so perceived.

Classification tasks are especially sensitive to the similarity and dimensional structure of objects. In free classification, for example, subjects are presented with subsets of stimuli and are told to "put together the ones that go best together". Consider the following triad of stimuli that provides either a similarity or a dimensional classification. Stimulus A (X_1Y_1) and B (X_1Y_6) share an identical value on one dimension (X) but differ considerably on the second (Y); the classification of A and B together is based on a dimensional relation. Stimulus B (X_1Y_6) and C (X_2Y_5) share no value on either dimension but are highly similar on both; the classification of B and C together honors a similarity structure. The classification of A and C together is not based on any systematic relation, and is considered haphazard.

The evidence from the classification task is extremely clear. Subjects invariably classify integral stimuli by putting B and C together, but classify both separable and separate stimuli by putting A and B together (Burns et al., 1978; Handel & Imai, 1972). Other details of classification are considered in chapters 8, 11, and 12.

The classification task has also been used to demonstrate dimensional preferences. Consider the four stimuli large/light, large/dark, small/light, and small/dark. If subjects are asked to classify the stimuli into two classes of two stimuli, some subjects will classify on the basis of size and some on the basis of brightness. The selected dimension may be the preferred dimension and continue to serve as the basis for classification even though the values on the nonpreferred dimension are made more discriminable. Experiments conducted with the classification task have shown that both separable and separate dimensions show dimensional preferences that are impervious to variations in discriminability. Integral stimuli, however, do not show dimensional preferences, and classifications of them are easily changed by varying the discriminability of the stimuli (Garner, 1970, 1974; Burns et al., 1978).

Evidence from Speeded Tasks

In many speeded tasks, subjects are instructed to classify or identify the features of one dimension while the features of a second either are correlated with those of the first or varied orthogonally to them. If the stimuli are integral, variation on one dimension affects perception of the second. Thus, correlated values are more distinctive and are classified more quickly than are control values. Orthogonal values yield twice the num-

ber of stimuli and are classified more slowly than the controls. If, on the
other hand, the stimuli are separate, variation of the values on one dimension should not affect perception of the other. As a consequence,
neither correlated or orthogonal values should affect performance. Separable stimuli, of course, give mixed results.

Recently, Burns (Burns, 1987; Burns & Hopkins, 1987), following
earlier arguments by Burns et al. (1978) and Shepp (1983), has hypothesized that features of integral stimuli are combined early in visual processing, whereas those of separate stimuli are segregated early. To test
this hypothesis, she used a Sperling partial report procedure in which
subjects were either cued to report the stimuli in a particular row of a
3x3 matrix or were instructed to give a whole report of the matrix. The
stimuli that were displayed in the matrix included two sets of integral
stimuli (height and width of rectangles; size and brightness of square)
and one set of separate stimuli (size of circle and angle of a radial line).
On any particular trial, the subject was instructed to report the values of
only one dimension while the values of the second dimension were held
constant, were correlated, or were orthogonal.

Although height and width are perceived holistically and size and
brightness are perceived by dimensional relations in unspeeded tasks,
Burns has argued that both sets of stimuli should be perceived as wholes
at early stages of perception. Accordingly, partial report accuracy for
both combinations should be improved by correlated values and impaired with orthogonal values relative to the control condition. In contrast, separate stimuli should already be segregated at early perceptual
stages, and relative to the control condition, neither correlated nor orthogonal values should affect partial report accuracy. The results of the
experiments confirmed all predictions.

The results of speeded classification also support the claim that dimensional combinations like size and brightness, like those of value and
chroma, also have holistic properties. Beiderman and Checkosky (1970)
have reported facilitation with correlated values, and Garner (1977) has
shown interference with orthogonal values. But some claim that the effects are small (e.g., Garner, 1977), and sometimes the effects do not
appear at all (e.g., Smith & Kemler, 1978).

The elusive nature of holistic effects with easy-to-analyze stimuli
have led some (Smith & Kemler Nelson, 1984; Ward, 1983) to use special conditions such as an additional task or instructions to give first impressions in order to observe the effects of holistic properties. Such experiments have been generally successful in showing these easy-to-
analyze stimuli do exhibit holistic properties. It should be noted,
however, that this elusiveness may be due to the automatic accessibility
of dimensional relations in such stimuli and the general insensitivity of

the tasks to tap into early perceptual organization.

That holistic properties are easily accessible in all integral stimuli has been shown by Shepp (1983). A task that combines aspects of both priming and matching to sample was used. Each trial presented two consecutive stimuli. The first, or prime, informed the subject as to which specific feature(s) to look for in the second, or target array. Typically, the duration of the prime was 500 msec. The target array followed the termination of the prime and was visible until the subject responded. Reaction time was the primary dependent measure.

In one set of experiments, subjects were instructed to look for the features on either of two dimensions or the conjunction of features displayed by the prime. The searches for the features of single dimensions and the searches for conjunctions occurred in different blocks of trials. Two sets of integral stimuli, hue versus brightness and size versus brightness, and one set of separate stimuli, size of circle versus angle of a radial line, were used.

If stimuli are perceived holistically, the reaction time to find a conjunction should be no slower that the appropriate control. If, on the other hand, the stimuli are perceived as features on dimensions, the reaction time to find the conjunction should be slower than the appropriate control according to either a parallel or a serial process.

The results of these experiments showed that the reaction times to find the conjunction were equal to the controls when the stimuli were either of the integral sets, but the reaction times to find the conjunction were slower than the controls when the stimuli were separate.

Taken together, the results from both unspeeded and speeded tasks support the distinction between integral, separable, and separate stimuli. The misbehavior of separable stimuli in some speeded tasks is troublesome and disrupts an otherwise clear account. I believe that at least one variable that contributes to this misbehavior has been identified and it is considered in a later section of this chapter.

THE DEVELOPMENT OF PERCEIVED STRUCTURE

The investigation of the development of perceived structure has been pursued, with few exceptions, by a single strategy: the demonstration that stimuli that are perceived by the older child and adult as separable are perceived by the young child as integral. The theoretical nature of this developmental trend can obviously take more than one direction (see, for example, chapters 11 and 12), and the adoption of a particular point of view depends on how the evidence that distinguishes between integral and separable stimuli is interpreted.

In the preceding section of this chapter, a distinction was drawn between physically integral stimuli that were easy to analyze and those that were difficult to analyze. The former stimuli, which include many properties of common objects (e.g., shape, color, and size), are psychologically separable in unspeeded tasks. But there is evidence from speeded tasks that these stimuli are first perceived holistically and only subsequently as features on dimensions. This characterization is, of course, Lockhead's "blob" model. But whereas Lockhead (1972) assumed that blobs are analyzed into features only if required by the task, it appears that such analysis may become increasingly automatic during the course of development. The automatic accessibility of features makes the model of Smith and Evans (chap. 11) all the more appealing.

In my view, however, highly analyzable stimuli are represented either as wholes, which come first, or as features on dimensions, which come later. The young child and the adult both perceive these stimuli holistically. What develops is the child's ability to access featural and dimensional information and the child's control over attentional resources. Perceptual learning in Gibson's sense (1969) probably improves both the access to features and dimensions and the control of attention, but as I have suggested earlier (Shepp, 1978) the child may also acquire the skill of directing attention to the internal representation of either holistic or featural properties.

Difficult-to-analyze stimuli like the dimensions of the Munsell system are, for all intents and purposes, seen as wholes by children and adults alike. Under some circumstances, adults can extract featural information from such stimuli, but not spontaneously; even with instructions to use dimensional relations accuracy is poor (Burns & Shepp, in press; Foard & Kemler Nelson, 1984; Shepp, 1983). Moreover, there is no convincing evidence that selective attention to such stimuli is ever possible. Thus, although the performances with these difficult-to-analyze stimuli provide a standard against which to evaluate developmental changes in perceived structure when they do occur, such stimuli do not themselves permit the study of any interesting developmental changes in perceived structure.

Just as integral stimuli are perceived as holistic throughout development, so too are separate stimuli seen as features on dimensions, at least from kindergarten onward (Shepp, Barrett, & Kolbet, 1987). Given that these stimuli are seen only as features, they also provide a standard for two kinds of developmental studies. Firstly, the development of selective attention can be directly assessed with separate stimuli. Secondly, by comparing the performances with separate and separable stimuli at different ages, it becomes possible to detect the child's skill in accessing holistic or featural information, as well as the limits of attention that particular perceived structures permit. Several recent studies in my laboratory have used this strategy.

Multiple Trends in Perceptual Development.   The separability hypothesis claims that developmental differences in perceived structure must be distinguished from developmental differences in attention, and that the failure to do so misleads the theoretical analysis of perceptual and cognitive development. To illustrate, there is a well-established trend in the literature that indicates that older children perform more effectively than younger ones in tasks where success depends on ignoring irrelevant information. Such performance differences have been observed in speeded classification (e.g., Pick & Frankel, 1973), incidental learning and memory (e.g., Kemler, Shepp, and Foote, 1976; Hagen & Hale, 1973), and unspeeded classification (e.g., Bruner, Olver, & Greenfield, 1966; Wohlwill, 1962).

This developmental trend can be interpreted in either of two ways. The first asserts that the differences in performance are due to differences in attention. Accordingly, the younger child is believed to focus attention less well than the older. The younger child may have difficulty in focusing on the relevant aspects of a task or in the filtering of irrelevant information, or possibly both. By this view, the child, with increasing age and experience, is assumed to gain increasing command over attentional resources (e.g., Pick & Frankel, 1973; Hagen & Hale, 1973).

Alternatively, this performance trend may be due to developmental differences in perceived structure as well as attention. If young children perceive objects as integral stimuli, selective attention is not a possibility. For some stimuli (e.g., hue vs. brightness) the holistic structure remains dominant throughout development, but for many stimuli (e.g., color vs. form) the holistic perception of the young child gradually yields to a featural organization. The ability of the child to access features can result in the improvement of performance if the child is also capable of controlling attention. For still other stimuli (e.g., spatially separated dimensions) the dominant perceptual organization may be featural at all developmental levels, and the limitations on performance should be directly determined by the child's command of attention.

Recently, Shepp et al. (1987) have addressed the second and third alternatives by having kindergarten, second-, and fifth-grade children perform a speeded sorting task with either the integral or spatially separated stimuli. The stimuli are illustrated in Fig. 7.1. The stimuli have three dimensions: the number of lines in the outer ring (10 vs. 15), the orientation of the pointer (330 vs. 30 degrees), and the color of the inner configuration (red vs. red-orange). The separate stimuli were composed of the number of lines versus the color of the inner disk (the

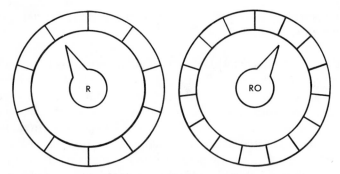

FIGURE 7.1.   An illustration of the stimuli used by Shepp et al. (1987). See text for explanation.

pointer was removed), whereas the integral stimuli were composed of orientation of the pointer versus color of the configuration (the lines were removed). Separate groups of children were run with each type of stimulus and all children sorted three types of decks: control, correlated, and orthogonal.

The experiment tested two hypotheses. The first concerned perceived structure. Color and orientation should be integral stimuli, but with increasing age, the features of these dimensions should become increasingly accessible. But number of lines and color should be separate. A comparison of the sorting times on correlated condition relative to the control supported the hypothesis. With the integral stimuli, the kindergarten children showed a redundancy gain, but neither of the older groups of children did so. With separate stimuli, on the other hand, comparison of the correlated and control conditions showed that there was no redundancy gain at any developmental level.

The second hypothesis concerned the development of attention. Attention to integral stimuli is not possible, and, as expected, the sorting times in the orthogonal condition were slower than the control. But the inference due to orthogonal dimensions is not the result of the same perceptual organization at all ages. Kindergarten children perceive these stimuli holistically; the slower sorting times in the orthogonal condition relative to the control may be due either to the added time to decompose the whole into its features or because the child performs the task by mapping two stimuli onto each response. But the older children perceived these stimuli according to their constituent features. Attentional interference must be due to response competition. Response competition is assumed to occur because both relevant and irrelevant features are attended on a given stimulus card. When the subject begins to sort the next card, there are occasions when the irrelevant feature will be processed first, and will mislead, at least temporarily, the response. In this connection, it is important to note the interference can be asymmetric. In this study, the interference occurred with both dimensions for second graders. However, it was asymmetric for fifth graders—orthogonal variations in color interfered with the classification of orientation, but irrelevant variations in orientation did not interfere with the classification of color.

The development of attention is much easier to discern with separate stimuli that are seen as independent features by even very young children. Interference does occur with orthogonal dimensions relative to the control, and the amount of interference decreases with age.

The results of Shepp et al. (1987) show clearly that there are multiple trends in perceptual development. Many objects are perceived holistically by young children and only gradually do the features of many of these objects become readily accessible during the course of development. But when the aspects of a stimulus are separate, featural perception is invariant throughout development.

The nature of attentional development clearly depends on the perceptual organization. When perception is holistic, selective attention is not a logical possibility: There is only one thing. But even when the features of some integral stimuli—for example, color versus form—become readily accessible, they are still parts of the same perceptual unit that commands attention and, under some conditions, can produce a failure of selective attention. When features are spatially separated, the selection of specific features does become possible with age, and irrelevant sources of information no longer interfere with performance.

The Analyzability of Separable Stimuli. The shift from a holistic to a featural organization of separable stimuli during the course of development is frequently signaled by the presence or absence of facilitation in speeded sorting with correlated values: Young children show redundancy gains, whereas older children do not. This performance trend indicates that the analysis of wholes into features improves with age.

Another operation that reflects the relative accessibility of wholes and features is the variation of irrelevant stimuli. In most selective attention tasks, the subject attends to the features on a relevant dimension while the features on an irrelevant dimension are permitted to vary orthogonally. If the relevant and irrelevant stimuli are physically integral, they are perceived as wholes, and orthogonal variation from trial to trial leads to distinctive wholes that subjects must classify. If, on the other hand, the relevant and irrelevant dimensions are separate, the stimuli are perceived as features, and orthogonal variation can only interfere with attention.

Barrett and Shepp (in press) have recently observed the effects of irrelevant stimuli on both perceived structure and attention and how such effects change during development. They used a discrete trial task that combines aspects of delayed-matching-to-sample and priming. On each trial, two stimuli are presented consecutively. The first, or prime, is a single stimulus, whereas the second, the target array, contains a pair of stimuli. The subject is instructed to find the feature in one of the stimuli of the target array that matches a designated feature in the prime, and to press the response button underneath the stimulus that contains the correct feature. Reaction time is the primary dependent measure.

The stimulus sets vary on two dimensions and, in a given block of trials, subjects are told to attend to one dimension and to ignore the other. So, for example, with the stimuli presented in Fig. 7.2, subjects might be instructed to find the stimulus in the target array that has the same color as the external square of the prime and to ignore the internal shape. The perceptual and attentional consequences of priming are evaluated by varying the relation between the irrelevant feature in the prime and the irrelevant feature that appears in the correct stimulus of the target array. When the correct stimulus of the array matches the prime on both the relevant and irrelevant dimensions, the array is designated *same irrelevant* (SI). When the correct stimulus matches on the relevant dimension but differs from the prime on the irrelevant dimension, the array is designated *different irrelevant* (DI). Within a target array, either the features on the irrelevant dimension are held constant (the control conditions) or they are varied (the experimental conditions). Both control and experimental conditions contain SI and DI arrays.

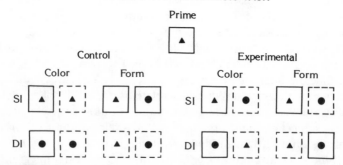

FIGURE 7.2. A schematic of the selective attention task used by Barrett and Shepp (in press). The task is illustrated with spatially separated color-form stimuli. Color differences were displayed on the contour of the external square. In the figure, red squares are depicted with a continuous line and green squares are depicted with a broken line. Form differences were displayed internally as black triangles and circles. See text for additional explanation.

The relation between the irrelevant cue in the prime and its subsequent pairing with either the target or the distractor in the target array permits inferences about the nature of perceived structure as well as selective attention. Consider first the pattern of results that would occur if the objects were perceived holistically. In this case, responses to the SI pairs in either the control or experimental conditions should be fast, because the same object is present in both the prime and the target array. Both DI pairs, however, pose a problem for the subject because the correct member of the target array is a completely different object from that presented in the prime. A correct decision on these DI trials, then, involves picking the stimulus that is closer to the prime in terms of overall similarity, or executing an additional stage of stimulus analysis. By either alternative, response times for both DI arrays would be longer than for the corresponding SI arrays.

If observers encode each feature independently and are able to focus attention only on the targeted dimension, then variations on the irrelevant dimension should not affect performance. In this case, equivalent reaction time should be obtained for the control and experimental conditions, and there should be no difference between SI and DI arrays.

Finally, consider what should happen if subjects perceive the feature separately but are not able to attend selectively. Under these conditions, both features in the prime are attended. In the control condition, the subject matches on the relevant dimension, and because the irrelevant feature offers no conflicting information, the reaction times on SI and DI arrays should be equivalent. In the experimental condition, subjects should also respond quickly on SI trials, because the irrelevant features in these arrays are identical to the irrelevant feature in the prime. On DI trials, however, the irrelevant cue of the prime is presented with the incorrect feature on the target dimension. On at least some trials, the irrelevant feature would be processed more quickly than the relevant one, and the resulting response competition would slow down reaction times.

In a recent experiment, Barrett and Shepp (in press), used this version of a selective-attention task to examine the development of perceived structure and attention in groups of second- and fifth-grade children and adults. Separate groups of subjects performed the selective attention task with either integral color-form stimuli or spatially separated color-form stimuli such as those shown in Fig. 7.2. With the latter stimuli, we expected no differences between SI and DI arrays in the control condition on the grounds that the spatially separated stimuli would be perceived according to features. With integral color-form stimuli, however, we expected to see a difference in the control condition between SI and DI arrays with younger children, but not with adults. But given that selective attention to the features of even highly analyzable stimuli is not possible, we expected that reaction times to SI arrays would be faster than reaction times to DI arrays in the experimental condition at all age levels.

Before describing the results, let me give a few procedural details. The stimuli were relatively large (approximately 5°) and were separated by about 10° of visual angle from center to center. The prime was presented about 8° above the target array and centered relative to the pair of stimuli in the target array. The prime was presented for 750 msec. and was immediately followed by the target array. The target array remained on until the subject responded. Subjects were run for two days, but only the data of the second day were analyzed.

Error rates were small (5%) and were not analyzed. But it is important to note that more errors occurred in the more difficult conditions, so there does not appear to be a speed–accuracy trade off. The results for the spatially separated dimensions are shown in Table 7.2. The performances of our subjects are easy to characterize. There are no differences between SI and DI arrays in the control condition at any age level. Thus, these stimuli appear to be perceived as separate features. In contrast, DI arrays give significantly slower reaction times than SI arrays in the experimental condition for both second- and fifth-grade subjects, but for the adults there is no difference between the two types of arrays.

The results for integral color-form stimuli show a very different pattern and are shown in Table 7.3. In the control conditions, the reaction times to SI arrays are significantly faster for both second- and fifth-grade children than on DI arrays, indicating that the stimuli are first perceived holistically. But the two types of arrays do not differ in the performances by adults. In the experimental conditions, the SI arrays yield significantly faster reaction times than DI arrays at all age levels.

The results of Barrett and Shepp are consistent with those of Shepp et

TABLE 7.2
Median Reaction Time (msec.) for Spatially
Separated Dimensions

Age	Type of Irrelevant Stimulus	Control	Experimental
2nd Gr	Same (SI)	542.4	547.5
	Different (DI)	554.2	607.8
5th Gr	Same (SI)	406.6	395.6
	Different (DI)	401.8	420.9
Adult	Same (SI)	389.4	393.8
	Different (DI)	392.5	397.4

TABLE 7.3
Median Reaction Time (msec.) for Spatially
Integrated Dimensions

Age	Type of Irrelevant Stimulus	Control	Experimental
2nd Gr	Same (SI)	533.5	537.8
	Different (DI)	574.1	691.7
5th Gr	Same (SI)	422.8	424.8
	Different (DI)	441.4	488.9
Adult	Same (SI)	355.4	353.2
	Different (DI)	350.2	384.0

al. (1987). When stimuli are spatially separated, featural perception seems to be the rule at all developmental levels. There was no hint of a difference between SI and DI arrays in the control conditions. But it is also clear that with spatially separated stimuli, there is a developmental difference in the degree to which children can control their attentional resources and thus perform the task successfully. The degree of interference shown by second graders is somewhat greater than that shown by fifth graders, but both age levels do show a failure to attend selectively. Adults, of course, show no such deficit.

Integral stimuli appear to be initially perceived as holistic by both second- and fifth-grade children, but adults appear to extract the featural information from these stimuli effortlessly. The interpretation of performance differences between SI and DI arrays in the experimental condition is related to the nature of such differences in the control condition. In the case of both second- and fifth-grade children, the evidence from the control condition indicates holistic perception. Thus, the difference between SI and DI arrays in the experimental condition is attributable, at least in part, to the time required to decompose the integral whole into its constituent features. Given that there are no differences between SI and DI arrays in the control condtion for the adult, however, the difference between SI and DI arrays in the experimental condition is most likely attributable to response competition.

The results with integral stimuli do indicate that these stimuli are perceived holistically by second- and fifth-grade children, even though the stimuli may be subsequently decomposed into constituent features. The effect is clearly weaker in the older children than in the younger ones, and the effect is missing altogether in the performances of adults. It is, of course, possible that the duration of the prime has contributed to this particular pattern of results. We have argued that subjects become more skilled with increasing age in the extraction of featural information from multidimensional stimuli, and it is also the case that the selective attention task is a task that stresses stimulus analysis. It may simply be the case that the prime in this experiment was sufficiently long that both fifth-grade and adult subjects had nearly or completely finished the perceptual analysis before the target display appeared.

Accessing Holistic and Featural Information.   We have made two claims about separable stimuli. Firstly, such stimuli have both holistic and featural properties; holistic properties are perceived first, whereas featural properties are the result of analysis. Secondly, children become increasingly proficient in the accessing of features during the course of perceptual development. Taken together, these claims suggest that with increasing age children should gain easy access to either holistic or featural properties, and should, as a result, perform tasks that call for either type of property with increasing proficiency.

Recently, Shepp and Barrett (1986) have reported the results of two sets of experiments that support these claims. The subjects were asked to perform either divided-attention or selective-attention tasks to assess the operation of holistic or featural properties respectively. The stimuli, shown in Fig. 7.3, were combinations of size and form, and were presented either as integral or as spatially separate dimensions.

Consider first the experiments on divided attention. Our subjects were asked to search for conjunctions of features using a variation of the task used by Shepp (1983) and illustrated in Table 7.4. This is a discrete trial task that presents two consecutive stimuli on each trial. The first, or prime, is a single stimulus, whereas the second, or target array, is a pair of stimuli. The prime instructs the subject about the feature(s) to look for in the target array. The subject presses a response button under the stimulus in the array that contains the correct feature(s). The primary dependent measure is reaction time. In the control condition, the subject looks for a feature on just one dimension (size or form), but in the experimental condition, the subject looks for the conjunction of features.

INTEGRAL STIMULI

FIGURE 7.3.   An illustration of integral and spatially separated size and form stimuli used by Shepp and Barrett (1986).

SEPARATE STIMULI

TABLE 7.4
An Illustration of a Divided Attention Task

		Prime		
		S_1F_1		
		Target Arrays		
		Conditions		

Control				Experimental
Size	Form			Size and Form
S_1F_1 S_2F_1	S_1F_1 S_1F_2			S_1F_1 S_2F_1
				S_1F_1 S_1F_2

Note: S and F refer to Size and Form, respectively. The numbers 1 and 2 refer to specific values on a dimension. Note that only half of the lateral positions are shown.

The subject can perform the divided attention task by responding to either the holistic or the featural properties of stimuli. When the task is performed on the basis of holistic properties, the reaction time to find the conjunction should be no slower than the controls, but when the task is performed analytically (either in parallel or serially), the reaction time to find the conjunction is slower than the controls.

The integral size-form stimuli, by hypothesis, are first perceived holistically at all developmental levels, and the reaction times to find the conjunctions should be no slower than the controls for children and adults alike. The spatially separated size-form stimuli, on the other hand, are perceived as separate features at all developmental levels. Thus, the reaction time to find the conjunctions should be slower than the controls for children and adults alike.

Different groups of kindergarten, second-grade children, and adults performed the task with the integral and the spatially separated stimuli. The results are summarized for the integral stimuli in Fig. 7.4, and for the separate stimuli in Fig. 7.5.

An inspection of Fig. 7.4 shows that there are substantial differences in the reaction times across age; these differences were highly reliable. There were no differences between the reaction times to size and form. Importantly, there were no differences between the control and experimental conditions. The reaction times to find the conjunctions were no slower than the controls, indicating that the task was performed on the basis of holistic properties.

An inspection of Fig. 7.5 shows a markedly different pattern of results. Again there were substantial differences in the reaction times across ages and no differences in reaction time to dimensions. There were, however, highly reliable differences between the reaction times to

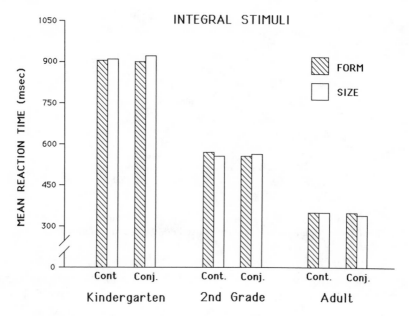

FIGURE 7.4. Mean reaction times to integral size-form stimuli in a divided attention task for kindergarten, 2nd-grade, and adult subjects.

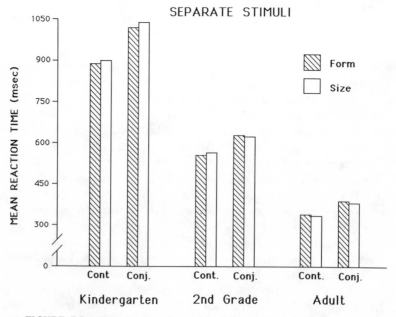

FIGURE 7.5. Mean reaction times to spatially separated size-form stimuli in a divided attention task for kindergarten, 2nd-grade, and adult subjects.

find the conjunctions and the control. The reaction times to the conjunctions were slower than the controls, indicating that subjects of all ages were searching for conjunctions of features in these stimuli, rather than holistic properties.

Consider now the selective attention experiments. They were run using a discrete trial classification. The subject was presented with one stimulus on each trial, and, by pressing a left or right response button, classified it appropriately. In control tasks the stimuli varied on only one dimension (size or form). In the orthogonal-dimensions tasks, both dimensions varied; one was relevant, the other irrelevant.

Although the integral size-form stimuli are initially perceived as holistic, featural information can be accessed, and the ease with which features are accessed should improve with increasing age. As a consequence, selective attention should improve with increasing age, and in adult performance the asymmetry between size and form reported by Shepp (1983) could be expected to appear. The spatially separate size-form stimuli should be perceived as features at all ages, and performance differences should reflect developmental differences in selective attention. Thus, interference effects should vary inversely with age.

Different groups of kindergarten, second-grade children, and adults performed the task with the integral and spatially separated stimulus sets. The results for the integral stimuli are summarized in Fig. 7.6. An analysis revealed reliable differences between ages, but no differences occurred between dimensions. As expected, reaction times were longer for the orthogonal dimensions conditions than the controls, and there was also an interaction of Age x Condition x Dimension. The interaction is easily observed in Fig. 7.6. The interference in the performance of kindergarten and second graders occurred with either dimension as target. The interference for adults, however, was asymmetric: Orthogonal variation in size had no effect on the classification of form, but orthogonal variations in shape interfered with the classification of size.

The results for the spatially separate stimuli are shown in Fig. 7.7. Again, there are large age differences in reaction time, but there are no effects due to dimensions. As expected, there are substantial interference effects in the performance of the orthogonal-dimensions task, and the amount of interference decreases with age. Indeed, adults show no interference effects.

Taken together, the results provide strong support for our claims. Integral, but highly analyzable, stimuli are perceived initially as wholes. Such holistic organization characterizes the perception of children and adults alike, and the only performance differences in divided attention tasks searching for conjunctions were due to age. That these stimuli can be analyzed, however, has been shown by Shepp (1983), and is further

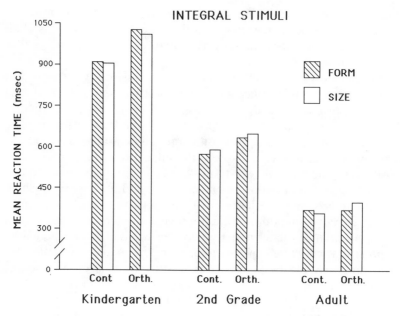

FIGURE 7.6. Mean reaction times to integral size-form stimuli in a selective attention task for kindergarten, 2nd-grade, and adult subjects.

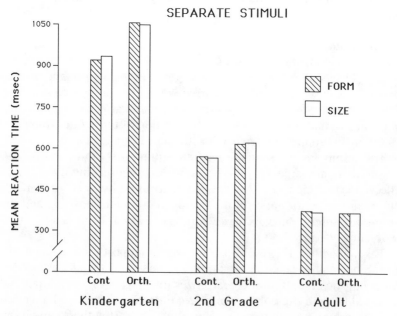

FIGURE 7.7. Mean reaction times to spatially separated size-form stimuli in a selective attention task for kindergarten, 2nd-grade, and adult subjects.

supported by the performances of the adults in the present selective-attention tasks. The asymmetric interference effects in the orthogonal tasks show a separation of size and form. Such results also show the presence of selective attention, but the operation of attention is clearly constrained by the internal relations of size and form. Size and form can exist at different levels (Garner, 1983), but it seems more likely with these kinds of stimuli that the features are extracted in parallel and that the asymmetry is due to differences in the rate of extraction. Form information is extracted more quickly than size, Thus, form interferes with the classification of size, but size does not interfere with the classification of form. By this interpretation, the principal developmental achievements are the rapid analysis of holistic stimuli into their constituent features and the adoption of strategies that minimize response competition.

The performances with separate stimuli, of course, provide a very different picture. The evidence from both divided and selective attention tasks indicate that subjects at all ages see these stimuli according to their separate features. Thus, the search for conjunctions is achieved analytically, and, with increasing age, attention becomes sufficiently focused to avoid the consequences of response competition.

Spatially separated stimuli have been used in the experiments of this chapter to provide separate features in perception at all developmental levels and to provide features to which, in principle, selective attention could be directed. These goals have been accomplished in the present experiments. But spatial separation does not guarantee either featural independence or selective attention. Sometimes, spatially separated features yield emergent properties, and the resulting configural stimuli are very different from features (see, for example, Pomerantz & Schwaitzberg, 1975). Kahneman (1973) also reports experiments in which spatially related items form a perceptual unit, and attention is distributed equally to all members of the unit. Such results mean that not all spatially separated stimuli yield separate features, and other than suggesting that differences in color, form, and position contribute to separate dimensions (see Shepp, et al., 1987), there can be little confidence that *a priori* arrangements will yield such stimuli.

VISUAL VERSUS NAME COMPARISONS IN ACCESSING HOLISTIC AND FEATURAL PROPERTIES

Two fundamental techniques have been used to study divided attention to conjunctions of features. One of them, used by Shepp (1983), presents a visual prime followed by a target array. The subject is required to identify the stimulus in the target array that contains the target feature(s). Under these conditions, the conjunction can be identified by matching two visual inputs—one in memory and one visible. This kind of comparison permits reaction times to identify the conjunctions that are as fast as the controls. The fact that conjunctions are found so quickly undoubtedly reflects the subjects' use of identity matches, which are known to be very fast (see Nickerson, 1972).

But not all identity matches are equally fast. Only when subjects search for physically integral stimuli are reaction times to conjunctions as fast as the controls. When the dimensions are spatially separated, the reactions times to identify conjunctions are slower than the controls. This pattern of results indicates that the conjunctions of integral stimuli are identified by holistic properties, whereas conjunctions of spatially separated stimuli are identified by a search for separate features.

The search for conjunctions of easy-to-analyze integral stimuli sometimes, of course, produces reaction times that are much slower than the controls. One of the clearest examples comes from the work of Treisman (e.g., Treisman & Gelade, 1980), in which the subjects' search for conjunctions of features (e.g., green T) typically shows RTs that are longer than the controls. Although there are many differences between Treisman's procedure and those that we have used, one difference seems to be especially significant, namely the way the subjects are instructed.

Instead of presenting a visual prime, Treisman gives the instruction to find the green T for specific block of trials. Because the temporal constraints of the task make it unlikely that the subjects generate a visual image to direct the search, the alternative that the names of the features are held in memory to direct the search gains force. I believe that these procedural differences reflect two fundamental kinds of comparisons. The priming procedure involves a visual-visual comparison that mimics the kinds of comparisons that are ordinarily used in searching among objects in the real world. The Treisman procedure involves a comparison between names and visual stimuli that mimics the kinds of comparisons that are generated by verbally initiated searches among objects in the real world.

The possibility that both visual and name matches can affect performance suggests that objects not only initiate holistic and featural percepts, they also may activate names and other representations that organize cognition. The view that the physical stimulus undergoes a series of transformations, with deeper levels of processing becoming more conceptual in nature, is due to Posner and his associates (e.g., Posner, 1969, 1978; Posner & Mitchell, 1967). Much of the evidence for their view has come from a letter-matching task in which pairs of letters are presented to the subject who is instructed to respond "same" or "different" as quickly as possible. The criterion for same can be a physical match (A,A), a name match (A,a), or a rule such as vowels (A,E). The reaction times to the physical matches are faster than name matches, which, in turn, are faster than rule matches. Such results have led Posner to concluded that different levels are involved in producing different reaction times. Physical identity is encoded first, followed by name and rule identities, and the differences in levels yield differences in reaction times.

It is plausible that either holistic or featural properties can activate names and other representations, and that any of these properties can initiate a visual search, a memory search, and a variety of comparisons, A direct implication of these assumptions is that the names of features are separate, and that visual searches initiated by a conjunction of features should give the result for separate features, namely that the reaction time to find a conjunction should be slower than the controls. Such a result should obtain for either easy-or hard-to-analyze integral stimuli.

We have recently conducted a series of experiments to test these predictions. The task was the priming task that was described earlier, in which each trial presented two consecutive stimuli, a prime and target array. The target array presented two stimuli, and subjects were instructed to press the button under the stimulus that contained the conjunction (the experimental condition) or a target feature (the control conditions). The dimensions were color (red vs. green) and form (rectangle vs. triangle).

Three conditions were run with adult subjects. In the Visual condition, the prime was a visual pattern, whereas in the Name condition, the prime was a visually presented name. On each trial, control and experimental alike, two features (e.g., red triangle) were displayed. The subjects were instructed to attend to just one feature in the control conditions, but to attend to the conjunction in the experimental condition. In the Auditory condition, the subject was told the target feature(s) by the experimenter at the beginning of a block of trials.

The Visual condition permits a visual-visual comparison, and the search can be conducted for a conjunction of features using the holistic properties of the color-form stimuli. Thus, the reaction times to find conjunctions should be no slower than the respective control. In the Name and Auditory conditions, however, a name-visual comparison is required. The names of features are separate, and the search for the conjunctions must be carried out in an analytical rather that a holistic mode. The features should be extracted in parallel, and RTs to conjunctions should be slower than the controls.

The results, summarized in Table 7.5, clearly support an analysis based on different types of comparisons. Color was an easier dimension than form and the Visual condition was faster than either of the other conditions. Most important theoretically, however, are the comparisons between the control and experimental conditions. In the Visual condition, the RTs to find the conjunction did not differ from the controls. But the search for conjunctions in both the Name and Auditory conditions took significantly longer than the controls. The RTs to find the conjunctions were also longer in the Name than in the Auditory condition, possibly reflecting greater demands on short-term store in the former condition.

This set of experiments demonstrates conclusively that some integral stimuli have holistic properties that facilitate some comparisons, but that can be decomposed when attention is initiated by visually or auditorily presented names. Space permitting, experiments demonstrating related effects for tasks that require selective attention could be presented. In both cases, substantial differences in performance can be understood by identifying the nature of the internal representation that determines the nature of the comparison with external objects in the execution of the task.

CONCLUSIONS

I have argued in this chapter that a meaningful distinction can be drawn between integral, separable, and separate stimuli, and that the evidence from a variety of converging tasks supports the distinction. Integral and separable stimuli anchor opposite ends of a continuum of physically integral stimuli that vary in their degree of analyzability. They are initially perceived as unitary wholes but can be analyzed into their constituent

TABLE 7.5
Mean Reaction Times to Color-Form Stimuli
in a Divided Attention Task with Different
Types of Primes

	Condition			
	Control Dimension		Experimental Dimension	
Type of Prime	Color	Form	Color	Form
Visual	317	351	321	349
Visual Name	347	392	428	474
Auditory Name	357	389	398	419

features. Separable stimuli are easy to analyze, but integral stimuli are not. Separate stimuli are generated by combining spatially separated dimensions; they are automatically perceived as separate features.

In unspeeded tasks, separable and separate stimuli yield similar performances that indicate a perceptual organization based on dimensional relations. In speeded tasks, on the other hand, integral and separable stimuli frequently yield similar performances that indicate a holistic or similarity organization. Taken together, the results indicate that integral stimuli are perceived as wholes, whereas separate stimuli are perceived as specific features. Separable stimuli have both holistic and featural properties that can be readily accessed.

The experiments reported in this chapter compared performances in divided and selective attention tasks with separable and separate stimuli. The experiments had two goals. Firstly, they were designed to speak to the accessibility of holistic and featural properties of separable stimuli in adult perception. Secondly, they attempted to illuminate further the development of perceived structure and attention.

Consider the accessibility of holistic and featural properties. By hypothesis, separate stimuli are seen only as features: Selective attention should succeed, but divided attention to a conjunction of features should fail; that is, the RT to conjunctions should be slower than the controls. Separable stimuli, on the other hand, may be perceived holistically or analyzed according to features. Holistic perception permits divided attention to conjunctions of features to occur successfully, meaning that the RT to conjunctions should be as fast as the controls. Featural perception improves performance on selective attention tasks, relative to performance on such tasks that require responses to holistic stimuli (Shepp, 1983), but response competition does interfere with response selection. The results of several experiments support the hypothesis.

An important finding of our work is that the access to holistic and featural properties of separable stimuli is affected by the nature of the internal representation that initiates a visual search. When the search for a conjunction of features is initiated by a visual prime, the search is based on holistic properties, but when the search for a conjunction is initiated by name primes, either visual or auditory, the search is based on features. Such results indicate that the interpretation of visual stimuli does not depend on perceived structure in a simple way, but depends on the relation between perceived structure and higher order representation in memory.

Our results also indicate that both perceived structure and attention change during the course of perceptual development. When children are confronted with spatially separated stimuli, separate features are perceived. Thus, children, like adults, search for conjunctions of features in an analytical mode. But in the selective task, children do have difficulty, unlike adults, in focusing attention.

When children are confronted with separable stimuli, their perceptual organization, with one exception, is qualitatively very similar to that of adults, The perception of such stimuli is initially holistic, and children are able to search for conjunctions of features as integral wholes. Separable stimuli are analyzable by children, and although featural perception may improve their performance on a selective attention task, the performance, like that of the adult, is limited by response competition. The exception to an otherwise similar pattern of perceptual organization is the younger child's lesser skill in extracting featural information from separable stimuli. Even with instructions to analyze the stimulus, the younger child's initial perception is still holistic, and the access to features requires more time for the younger than the older child.

ACKNOWLEDGMENTS

I am indebted to Peter Eimas for a critical reading of this paper. The experiments were made possible by the exceptional cooperation of the administration, principals, and teachers of the East Providence Schools.

REFERENCES

Aschkensay, J.R., & Odom, R.D. (1982). Classification and perceptual development: Exploring issues about integrality and differential sensitivity. *Journal of Experimental Child Psychology, 34,* 435–448.

Attneave, F. (1950). Dimensions of similarity. *American Journal of Psychology, 63,* 516–556.

Barrett, S.E., & Shepp, B.E. (in press). Developmental changes in attentional skills: The effect of irrelevant variations on encoding and response selection. *Journal of Experimental Child Psychology, ,* – .

Biederman, I., & Checkosky, S.F. (1970). Processing redundant information. *Journal of Experimental Psychology, 83,* 486–490.

Bruner, J.S., Olver, R.R., & Greenfield, P.M. (1966). *Studies in cognitive growth.* New York: Wiley.

Burns, B. (1987). Is stimulus structure in the mind's eye? An examination of dimensional structure in iconic memory. *The Quarterly Journal of Experimental Psychology, 39a,* 385–408.

Burns, B., & Hopkins, A. (1987). Integral and separable stimulus structure in iconic memory: A replication and extension of Burns. *Perceptual and Motor Skills, 64,* 263–270.

Burns, B., & Shepp, B.E. (1988). Dimensional interactions and the structure of psychological space: Are hue, saturation, and brightness uniformly represented as integral dimensions? *Perception and Psychophysics, 43,* 494–507.

Burns, B., Shepp, B.E., McDonough, D., & Weiner-Ehrich, W.K. (1978). The relation between stimulus analyzability and perceived dimensional structure. In G.H. Bower (Ed.), *The psychology of learning and motivation: Advances in research and theory, vol. 12* c(pp. 77–115). New York: Academic Press.

Dunn, J.C. (1983). Spatial metrics of integral and separable dimensions. *Journal of Experimental Psychology: Human Perception and Performance, 9*, 242–257.

Foard, C.F., & Kemler Nelson, D.G. (1984). Holistic and analytic modrimental Psychology: The multiple determinants of perceptual analysis. *Journal of Expeon speeded General, 113*, 94–111.

Garner, W.R., (1970). The stimulus in information processing. *Amerurnal of Experimental Child 350–358.*

Garner, W.R., (1974). *The processing of information and structure + 40).* Minneapolis, MN: Erlbaum.

Garner, W.R., (1976). Interaction of stimulus dimensions in concept and unanalyzable stimcesses. *Cognitive Psychology, 8*, 98–123.

Garner, W.R., (1977). The effect of absolute size on the separability of the dimensions of size and brightness. *Bulletin of the Psychonomic Society, 9*, 380–382.

Garner, W.R. (1983). Asymmetric interactions of stimulus dimensions in perceptural information processing. In T.J. Tighe & B.E. Shepp (Eds.), *Perception, cognition, and development: Interactional analyses* (pp. 1–38), Hillsdale, NJ: Lawrence Erlbaum Associates.

Garner, W.R., & Felfoldy, G.L. (1970). Integrality of stimulus dimensions in various types of information processing. *Cognitive Psychology, 1*, 225–241.

Gibson, E.J. (1969) *Principles of perceptual learning and development.* New York: Academic Press.

Gottwald, R.L., & Garner, W.R. (1972). Effects of focusing strategy on speeded classification with grouping, filtering, and condensation tasks. *Perception and Psychophysics, 11*, 179–182.

Hagen, J.W., & Hale, G.H. (1973). The development of attention of children. In A.D. Pick (Ed.), *Minnesota symposia on child psychology, Vol 7* (pp. 117–140). Minneapolis, MN: University of Minnesota Press.

Handel, S., & Imai, S. (1972). The free classification of analyzable and unanalyzable stimuli. *Perception and Psychophysics, 12*, 108–116.

Kahneman, D. (1973). *Attention and effort.* Englewood Cliff, NJ: Prentice-Hall.

Kemler, D.G. (1983a). Holistic and analytic modes in perceptual and cognitive development. In T.J. Tighe & B.E. Shepp (Eds.), *Perception, cognition, and development; Interactional analyses.* (pp. 77–102). Hillsdale, NJ: Lawrence Erlbaum Associates.

Kemler, D.G. (1983b). Exploring and reexploring issues of integrality, perceptual sensitivity, and dimensional salience. *Journal of Experimental Child Psychology, 36*, 365–379.

Kemler Nelson, D.G. (1984). The effect of intention on what concepts are acquired. *Journal of Verbal Learning and Verbal Behavior, 23*, 734–759.

Kemler, D.G., Shepp, B.E., & Foote, K.E. (1976). The sources of developmental differences in children's incidental processing during discrimination trials. *Journal of Experimental Child Psychology, 21*, 226–240.

Krantz, D.H., & Tversky, A. (1975). Similarity of rectangles: An analysis of subjective dimensions. *Journal of Mathematical Psychology, 12*, 4–34.

Lockhead, G.R. (1966a). Effects of dimensional redundancy on visual discrimination. *Journal of Experimental Psychology, 72*, 95–104.

Lockhead, G.R. (1966b). Visual discrimination and methods of presenting redundant stimuli. *Proceeding of the 74th Annual Convention of the American Psychological Association, 1*, 67–68.

232   SHEPP

Lockhead, G.R. (1972). Processing dimensional stimuli: A note. *Psychological Review, 79,* 5, 410–419.

Lockhead, G.R. (1979). Holistic versus analytic process models: A reply. *Journal of Experimental Psychology: Human Perception and Performance, 79,* 746–755.

Nickerson, R.S. (1972). Binary-classification reaction time: A review of some studies of human information-processing capabilities. *Psychonomic Monograph Supplements, 4,* 275–317.

Pick, A.D., & Frankel, G.W. (1973). A study of strategies of visual attention in children. *Developmental Psychology, 9,* 348–358.

Pomerantz, J.R., & Schwaitzberg, S.D. (1975). Grouping by proximity: Selective attention measures. *Perception & Psychophysics, 18,* 355–361.

Posner, M.I. (1969). Abstraction and the process of recognition. In G.H. Bower (Ed.), *The psychology of learning and motivation: Advances in learning, vol 3* (pp. 44–100). New York: Academic Press.

Posner, M.I. (1978). *Chronometric explorations of mind.* Hillsdale, NJ: Lawrence Erlbaum Associates.

Posner, M.I., & Mitchell, R.F. (1967). Chronometric analysis of classification. *Psychological Review, 74,* 392–409.

Ronacher, B., & Bautz, W. (1985). Human pattern recognition: Individually different strategies in analyzing complex stimuli. *Biological Cybernetics, 51,* 249–261.

Shepard, R.N. (1964). Attention of the metric structure of the stimulus space. *Journal of Mathematical Psychology, 1,* 54–87.

Shepp, B.E. (1978). From perceived similarity to dimensional structure: A new hypothesis about perceptual development. In E. Rosch & B.B. Lloyd (Eds.), *Cognition and Categorization* (pp. 135–167). Hillsdale, NJ: Lawrence Erlbaum.

Shepp, B.E. (1983). The analyzability of multidimensional stimuli: Some constraints on perceived structure and attention. In T.J. Tighe & B.E. Shepp (Eds.), *Perception, cognition and development: Interaction analyses* (pp. 39–75). Hillsdale, NJ: Lawrence Erlbaum Associates.

Shepp, B.E., & Barrett, S.E. (1986). *Some observations on wholistic and analytical views of perceptual development: Converging evidence from selective and divided attention tasks.* Paper presented at regional meeting of the Society for Research in Child Development, Nashville, TN.

Shepp, B.E., Barrett, S.E., & Kolbet, L.L. (1987). The development of selective attention: Holistic perception vs. resource allocation. *Journal of Experimental Child Psychology, 43,* 159–180.

Shepp, B.E., Burns, B., & McDonough, D. (1980). The relation of stimulus structure to perceptual and cognitive development: Further tests of a separability hypothesis. In J.Becker & F. Wilkening (Eds.), *The integration of information by children* (pp. 113–146). Hillsdale, NJ: Lawrence Erlbaum Associates.

Shepp, B.E., Swartz, K.B. (1976). Selective attention and the processing of integral and nonintegral dimensions: A developmental study. *Journal of Experimental Child Psychology, 22,* 73–85.

Smith, J.D., & Kemler Nelson, D.G. (1984). Overall similarity in adults' and children's classifications: The child in all of us. *Journal of Experimental Psychology: General, 113,* 137–159.

Smith, L.B. (1979). Perceptual development and category generalization. *Child Development, 50,* 705–715.

Smith, L.B. (1981). The importance of the overall similarity of objects for adults' and children's classifications. *Journal of Experimental Child Psychology: Human Perception and Performances, 1,* 811–824.

Smith, L.B. (1983). Development of classification: The use of similarity and dimensional relations. *Journal of Experimental Child Psychology, 36,* 150–178.

Smith, L.B., & Kemler, D.G. (1977). Developmental trends in free classification: Evidence for a new conceptualization of perceptual development. *Journal of Experimental Child Psychology, 24,* 279–298.

Smith, L.B., & Kemler, D.G. (1978). Levels of experienced dimensionality in children and adults. *Cognitive Psychology, 10,* 502–532.

Torgerson, W.S. (1958). *Theory and method of scaling.* New York: Wiley.

Treisman, A., & Gelade, G. (1980). Feature-integration theory of attention. *Cognitive Psychology, 12,* 97–136.

Tversky, A., & Krantz, D.H. (1970). The dimensional representation and the metric structure of similarity data. *Journal of Mathematical Psychology, 7,* 572–596.

Ward, T.B. (1980). Separable and integral responding by children and adults to the dimensions of length and density. *Child Development, 51,* 676–684.

Ward, T.B. (1983). Response tempo and separable-integral responding: Evidence for an integral-to-separable processing sequence in visual perception. *Journal of Experimental Psychology: Human Perception and Performance, 9,* 103–112.

Ward, T.B., & Scott, J.G. (1987). Analytic and holistic modes of learning family-resemblance concepts. *Memory and Cognition, 15,* 42–54.

Wohlwill, J. (1962). From perception to inference: A dimension of cognitive development. *Monographs of the Society for Research in Child Development, 72,* 87–107.

8 SOME DETERMINANTS OF PERCEIVED STRUCTURE: EFFECTS OF STIMULUS AND TASKS

Soledad Ballesteros
Universidad Nacional de Educacion a Distancia

INTRODUCTION

The real world is made up of objects that make an impression on our senses and produce an organized and significant perceptual experience. The identification of objects constitutes one of the most important activities in human cognition. One object may be perceived in a global way, whereas another is perceived in an analytic way. Furthermore, the same object can be perceived analytically in some cases and yet globally in others. What factors influence these differences and changes in the mode of processing? In addition, individual differences have been found in the perception of multidimensional stimuli. Whereas some subjects process information in an analytic manner, others process the same information in a holistic manner (Cooper, 1982). For some time, several investigators have dedicated their research programs to the study of the mental representation of stimuli, and nowadays this is a research subject that attracts a good number of investigators (Cooper & Shepard, 1973; Cooper, Mumaw, & Morrow, 1984; Garner, 1974; Krantz & Tversky, 1975; Palmer, 1977, 1978; Pomerantz, 1981; Shepp, 1983).

One way of trying to explain the phenomenon of perception consists in studying the nature of the stimuli that shape the world of our perceptual experience in order to describe it in an appropriate way and see how it affects the mode of processing.

In this chapter, we consider the manner in which certain stimulus and task variables affect perceived structure.

Distinctions Between Stimuli:
Integral versus Separable Dimensions

Concepts such as *stimulus* and *stimulus dimension* are very important for information processing theories. However, these concepts have hardly been studied in a systematic manner. As Shepp (1983) has pointed out, the investigator usually adopts some physical description of the stimulus and assumes that this description can characterize the stimulus relations perceived by the observer in a fairly effective manner. However, this is not always the case; the simple physical description of the stimulus may not correspond with the subject's perception.

The nature of the perceptual stimulus and the relations produced among different classes of stimuli have been the main subject of study by Garner (1974, 1976, 1983, 1986), and his work has not only ended the lack of systematic research that previously existed in this field, it has also inspired the work of many others.

Many investigators following Garner's lead now defend the importance of stimulus properties and emphasize the need to take into account the interactions occurring among stimuli, organisms, and experimental tasks, in order to explain processing (Foard & Kemler Nelson,1984; Ward, 1985; Ward, Foley & Cole, 1986; Ward & Vela, 1986)

A very useful conceptualization to explain perceived structure produced by multidimensional stimuli has been the distinction between *integral* and *separable* dimensions. This distinction was originally proposed by Lockhead (1966) and Garner (1970, 1974), using previous contributions by Attneave (1950), Torgerson (1958), and Shepard (1964).

Garner (1974, 1976) has shown that when different stimulus dimensions are combined, they yield multidimensional stimuli that produce different perceptual interactions in the observer; the most interesting and best studied are integral and separable interactions. Garner (Garner & Felfoldy, 1970) has identified a series of converging operations that make it possible to differentiate these two kinds of interactions.

The holistic and analytic modes of processing are characteristic of *integral* and *separable* dimensions, respectively. The most up-to-date formulation of the old "parts" and "whole" issue, makes use of the integral-separable distinction in such a way that the perception of separable dimensions has been related to analytic perception, whereas the processing of integral dimensions has been related to holistic perception.

Lockhead (1972, 1979) has proposed a processing model that assumes that objects are first perceived as holistic. Accordingly, objects are initially represented as "blobs", or points in a multidimensional subjective space, and then, if necessary, are analyzed according to dimensions.

A stimulus that is generated by combining integral dimensions is perceived as a single blob, but a stimulus that is created by combining separable dimensions is seen as two or more blobs. Lockhead's model can successfully claim much of the converging evidence that differentiates between the two types of dimensions.

There are several converging operations that make it possible to differentiate integral from separable dimensions. One of these operations is the type of metric that best describes the results from similarity scaling experiments. When the dimensions from which the stimuli have been generated are integral, the Euclidean metric provides the best description of the relationship of perceived distance, but when the dimensions are separable, the observed results are best described by the "city-block metric" (Attneave, 1950; Garner, 1974; Shepard, 1964; Handel & Imai, 1972; Handel, Imai, & Spottswood, 1980; Tversky & Gati, 1982; Burns, Shepp, McDonough, & Weiner-Ehrlich, 1978; Weiner-Ehrlich, 1978; Dunn, 1983).

Tversky & Gati (1982) found considerable differences between integral and separable dimensions in two specific aspects: (a) the triangle inequality and, (b) the index estimation in the power model. Strong confirmation of the triangle inequality has been found with integral dimensions (i.e., hue and chroma) and strong violation of this principle with separable dimensions (i.e., plants varying in elongation of the leaves and the form of the pot). The direct path between two points a–c should not be longer than the indirect path through b, $D(a,b) + D(b,c) \geqslant D(a,c)$. In relation to the estimates of the appropriate index that best describes the judgments of similarity between stimuli, it has been found that the "city-block" metric (exponent 1) is the most appropriate to judge separable materials, whereas the Euclidean metric (exponent 2) is the more appropriate for integral materials. Tversky & Gati's results are compatible with the statement that separable stimuli do not fit the Euclidean model, but it seems that neither do they entirely fit the "city-block" model, because the estimates of r are lower than unity.

Restricted classification tasks (Garner, 1974: Burns et al. 1978; Shepp, Burns, & McDonough, 1980), in which triads of stimuli similar to those shown in Fig. 8.1 are presented, require the subjects to group the stimuli that they think go best together. Generally, the classifications made are a function of the types of materials used. If the stimuli are produced by integral dimensions, the dominant classifications are those of *global similarity* (i.e., stimuli B and C are grouped together), whereas if they have been generated from separable dimensions, the classifications tend to be based on *dimensional similarity* (i.e., stimuli A and B are grouped together).

In *speeded classification tasks*, it has been found that if the stimuli were

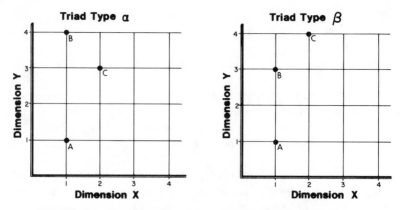

FIGURE 8.1. Representation of the two types of triads chosen from the possible combination of four levels on dimension X and four levels on dimension Y.

generated from *integral dimensions*, then, relative to a control task, correlated tasks are facilitated and interference is produced in orthogonal tasks. In contrast, if the stimuli have been generated from *separable dimensions*, correlated tasks are not facilitated, nor is interference produced in orthogonal tasks. Such results indicate that when the dimensions are integral, the subject perceives the stimuli holistically. However, when they are separable, he perceives them as independent dimensions (Garner & Felfoldy, 1970).

In addition to these criteria, the notion of privileged axes should be considered (Smith & Kemler, 1978). When the dimensions are separable, ruled by the "city-block" metric, it is not possible to change the axes of the dimensions without altering the way the stimuli are perceived. The axes have psychological privilege. In the case of integral dimensions, however, ruled by the Euclidean metric, the change of the dimensional axes does not alter the perceived distance between stimuli—axes are arbitrary, and one set is as good as any other.

To summarize, *integral dimensions* are those that show an increase in the speed of processing when the two dimensions are correlated, and interference when they are orthogonal; selective attention to a dimension is not possible (perception is dominated by the overall similarity structure); in similarity judgment tasks the results fit better into the Euclidean metric; they do not have privileged axes. On the other hand, *separable dimensions* are those that do not show any improvement in the speed of processing when the dimensions are correlated, nor interference when they vary orthogonally; the metric that best describes the distance relationships is the "city-block"; perception of separable dimensions is dominated by dimensional structure; they have privileged axes and require focalized attention.

Although the converging operations treat integral and separable dimensions as categories, experimental results have shown that there is a continuum of analyzability in which the two extremes are the integral and separable poles. The dimensions located close to the separable end of the continuum are easy to analyze and are processed in an analytic manner, whereas those near the integral end are processed holistically (Garner, 1974; Foard & Kemler Nelson, 1984; Smith, 1980). Burns et at. (1978) have distinguished three types of dimensions that can be situated along this continuum: (a) *separate* dimensions, such as size of the circle and inclination of the radius, which are separated without any cognitive effort and perceived automatically; (b) *separable* dimensions, such as saturation and size of the square, which can be separated by analyzing the stimulus; and (c) *integral* dimensions, such as hue and saturation, which are perceived globally.

Determinants of Perceived Structure: Background

Stimulus Effects.   In recent years, an interesting debate has developed about the role of the stimulus structure in perceived experience. According to Garner, the concepts of integrality and separability are stimulus concepts; the structure is in the stimulus. If the stimulus processed by the organism is formed from integral dimensions, the perceiver will not be able to direct his selective attention toward one dimension when a second dimension varies concurrently with the first. On the other hand, if the stimuli are formed from separable dimensions, facilitation will not occur when the two dimensions are correlated, nor will interference occur in the orthogonal condition. According to Garner, this clearly demonstrates that the type of process does not depend on the perceiver; otherwise, he would be able to integrate the information provided by separable dimensions and to attend selectively to one dimension when classifying stimuli formed from integral dimensions. Despite these claims, Garner also distinguishes between a primary and a secondary or derived process: for integral stimuli, a similarity structure is primary and a dimensional structure is derived; for separable stimuli, the reverse is true. What is not yet clear are those conditions that control the occurrence of a secondary process.

A stimulus factor that influences dimensional analysis is the degree of discriminability. It has been shown that great interstimulus differences favor analytic behavior, whereas reduced discriminability can even alter the type of dimensional interaction. When discriminability is low the level of interference found has been more than twice the normal in the orthogonal condition compared with the control condition in speeded classification tasks using saturation and brightness (Garner & Felfoldy, 1970, Exp. 5: Callaghan, 1984).

These effects have also been found with the separable dimensions, form and size (Ballesteros, Gonzalez Labra, & Fernández Trespalacios, 1986, Exp. 2). A small variation in the levels of a dimension (1 or 2 mm. in size) changed the pattern of the interactions. With the less discriminable stimuli, a clear interference in the orthogonal condition and a facilitation in the correlated condition compared with the control were observed. This pattern of results is typical of integral dimensions. So it would seem that with either integral or separable dimensions, the degree of discriminability affects performance in a way that modifies conclusions about the nature of dimensional interactions.

Dimensional complexity is another factor that reduces analytic processing of the subject. When stimuli consisting of four dimensions were presented to adults, they tended to produce classifications based on overall similarity, but when stimuli consisted only of two dimensions, they were classified by their dimensional structure. Each separate pair of dimensions functioned as separable, but the four dimensions together acted like integral dimensions (Smith, 1981).

Tasks Effects.   Santee and Egeth (1980) have claimed that the distinction between integral and separable dimensions could depend to a certain extent on the type of experimental task used in the research. These authors used stimuli generated from the dimensions of form and size and form and shading. The first experiment included a speeded classification task similar to that used by Garner; orthogonal interference did not occur, and these dimensions appeared to be separable. However, these same dimensions produced interference in the second and third experiments, in which a simultaneous and successive comparison task were used, respectively. Santee and Egeth concluded that the capacity to attend selectively to one stimulus dimension seemed to depend not only on the type of stimulus dimensions used, but also on task demands.

In view of these results, we tried to check in our laboratory (Ballesteros, Gonzalez Labra, & Fernández Trespalacios, 1985) whether the dimensions of form and size acted in the same manner when a speeded classification task and a simultaneous comparison task were used using similar stimuli. For this purpose, both types of tasks were combined in the same experiment, and no differences either between the type of task or between the subtasks were found. This indicated that the subjects were able to filter irrelevant information and attend to the relevant dimension (selective attention was possible on form or size, depending on the experimental condition) in either type of task. These results were replicated in another study (Ballesteros et al., 1986, Exp. 1). In view of the discrepancies between these results and those of Santee and Egeth, a firm decision about the nature of the interactions between task and stimulus structure must be suspended.

Recent studies have shown that there are some task factors that can affect the way visual stimuli are processed. Ward (1983), using the dimensions of length and density of lines of dots (moderately separable dimensions) to generate stimulus triads for a restricted classification task, found that when adults were asked to answer quickly they produced more classification based on global similarity and fewer on dimensional identity than when they were told to answer slowly. Smith & Kemler Nelson (1984) obtained similar results using triads that varied in size and brightness. When subjects were asked to answer on the basis of their first impression, they produced more overall similarity classifications and fewer dimensional classifications. But these same subjects, when asked to give carefully considered judgments, produced more dimensional classifications and fewer similarity classifications. In another experiment, subjects also modified the type of classification when they were obliged to carry out an additional cognitive task. In this case, the number of similarity classifications increased, and there were fewer dimensional classifications.

Ward et al. (1986) have found that the classification of certain types of materials showed strong individual differences related to the "response tempo", whether controlled by the observer or imposed by the investigator. Answering slowly produced more dimensional classification, although not with all types of material. For example, brightness and saturation, height and width of rectangles, and other aspects of configural and prototypical form were not influenced by response time.

Subjects Effects. In addition to the effects of stimulus and tasks factors, there are processing factors within the subject. Many authors, without denying the importance of the stimulus, prefer to stress the importance of the perceiver. Extensive literature exists that supports developmental effects. Shepp and Swartz (1976) proposed the *separability hypothesis* for the first time, and formulated it in the following way: "dimensional combinations which are perceived as separable by the older child and the adult, are perceived as integral by the young child" (p. 75). The first results favoring this hypothesis were presented by Shepp and Swartz using a speeded classification task. Children in first and fourth grade classified cards displaying hue and brightness or color and form. As expected, there were no differences between the two groups with the integral dimensions of hue and brightness. However, an interaction was found with color and form materials: The children in fourth grade perceived these stimuli according to their specific dimensions and were able to use selective attention so that the classification time in the three conditions (control, correlated, and orthogonal) were similar, whereas the children in first grade perceived these stimuli as integral; a facilitation appeared in the correlated task and an interference in the orthogonal task compared with control tasks. Smith and Kemler (1978) found a similar pattern of results using stimuli consisting of saturation and brightness, and size of the square and tone of gray. At present, there are a large number of experimental results favoring this hypothesis (Shepp, 1978; Shepp et al., 1980; Smith & Kemler, 1977; Smith, 1980, 1981; Kemler, 1982a, 1982b; Ward, 1980, 1983).

But not only children classify multidimensional stimuli according to overall similarity. Smith & Kemler Nelson (1984) have shown that with certain experimental manipulations, young children and adults classify in a similar way. That is, adults can change their usual dimensional classification to overall similarity classification when speed is emphasized, when a concurrent cognitive task is given to them or when they allow themselves to be guided by their first impressions. The authors interpret their results to mean that an asymmetry exists: Separable dimensions allow adults two forms of classifications, but integral dimensions only allow one.

Determinants of Perceived Structure: Some New Experiments

In the first of the following experiments, we examine the relation between the perceived structure (dimensional or overall similarity) of three sets of materials generated from two dimensions with four levels each (Exp. 1). In two other experiments, we try to find out whether this relation could be modified by experimental manipulations of the task instructions (Exp. 2), or by controlling the stimulus exposure time, in addition to instructions affecting the perceptual processing. We believe that the effect, if it exists, will not be uniform among the three sets of stimulus materials. According to the existing literature, it seems that the stimulus properties preferentially mark the limits of the perceiver's action. Whereas the integral dimensions appear to limit processing capacity in a fairly precise way, producing an overall similarity processing in children and adults, it seems that separable dimensions, or those located at an intermediate level in the integrality-separability continuum, give the perceiver more freedom to respond easily to the demands.

The experimental procedure that we use enables us to measure the type of classification and RTs. We believe the RTs could be shorter in either of the two types of classifications (dimensional or similarity), depending on the type of stimulus dimensions from which the stimuli have been constructed. In the sets generated from separable dimensions, dimensional classifications would be faster, whereas in those constructed from integral dimensions, similarity classifications would be faster. In other words, each type of material will show an optimum response time according to its dominant stimulus structure. Furthermore, the structure of the triad (type alpha or type beta) could affect the classification behavior.

As it can be seen in Fig. 8.1, the distance between stimuli B and C is the same in both types of triads. These stimuli differ at one level in dimension X and at another level in dimension Y. The distance between the two other possible pairs of stimuli vary from one triad to the other. With regard to stimuli A and B (classification according to dimension identity), it can be seen that in the alpha triad, both stimuli share a value in one dimension (dimension X in this example), but differ in the distance in the second dimension. This distance is greater in type alpha triad than in type beta triad.

Should the structure of the triads influence classification, one would expect classification by overall similarity to be similar in both types of triads; however, this structure ought to affect the number of dimensional and haphazard classifications. Type beta triads should produce more dimensional classifications and fewer haphazard classifications than type alpha triads.

General Procedures

We now describe those aspects that are common to all three experiments, such as the types of stimuli from which the triads were constructed, the experimental task, and the description of the laboratory equipment.

The three pairs of dimensions used in this study were: (a) form and size, (b) saturation and brightness, and (c) inclination and length of a straight line. In previous studies (Ballesteros et al., 1985, 1986), form and size acted as separable dimensions. We try in these experiments to verify whether in a restricted classification task these dimensions also act as separable dimensions, which would extend the generalization of previous results to a wider set of experimental tasks.

Saturation and brightness (chroma and value in the Munsell terminology) were also used. These dimensions have proved to be the best examples of integral dimensions in a wide range of tasks and perceivers.

The third pair of dimensions used are inclination and length of a straight line. These dimensions have not been studied in depth, but there are some data that appear to indicate that the dimensions of line location and orientation are integral (Redding & Tharp, 1981; Dunn, 1983), or at least, produce intermediate results (Smith & Kilroy, 1979; Smith, 1980).

The three sets of stimulus materials were constructed from two dimensions with four levels each, giving a total of 16 stimuli. The form and size set contained four geometric shapes: triangle, square, hexagon, and circle, and each form varied in four sizes that had previously proved easily distinguishable. The sides of the triangles measured 8, 10, 13, and 15 mm.; the sides of the square measured 6, 8, 10, and 12 mm.; the hexagons measured 7, 8.5, 10.5, and 13 mm. from one side to the opposite side. Finally the circles measured 8, 10, 12. and 14 mm. along the radius.

The second pair of dimensions used was saturation and brightness (chroma and value). Levels 2, 4, 6, and 8 of chroma and levels 3, 4, 5, and 6 of value were used. The hue was held constant at 5PB (purple-blue) on the Munsell Scale. All the stimuli were prepared on 11 mm. squares of matte Munsell paper.

The third stimulus set was formed from the dimensions of inclination and length. The levels of the inclination dimension were 45, 90, 135, and 180 degrees. The four values of the length dimension were 0.62, 0.81, 1.05, and 1.37 cm.

From each pair of dimensions, 12 different triads were constructed, 6 type alpha and 6 type beta triads. Half of these shared a level on one dimension and the other half shared a level on the other dimension.

From each of these original triads, 6 triads were prepared varying the position of the three stimuli on the tachistoscope card. With these 6 triads it would be possible to give 12 answers, as there were 2 possibilities of response on each trial. Out of these 12 possibilities, 4 referred to dimensional, 4 to similarity, and 4 to haphazard answers. The number of triads for each stimulus set was 72, so the total number of triads were 216. Each triad was centered on a tachistoscope card and the stimuli occupied between 2 and 2.5 degrees of visual angle.

The task used was a modification of the **restricted classification task**. This task has been widely used with children and adults in perception and cognition research because it is the most suitable to evaluate the perceived structure (Burns et al. 1978; Garner, 1974). This task consisted of presenting a triad of stimuli and asking the subject to choose two out of the three that go best together. No reference about dimensional identity was made, nor was the word "similarity" mentioned.

The two types of triads used in these experiments are shown in Fig. 8.1. They were all constructed in such a way to allow two types of systematic classification, one based on dimensional structure and the other based on overall similarity structure. If A and B were grouped together, it is a dimensional classification; the perceiver is able to discover the shared dimensional relation. If B and C were chosen, it is an overall similarity classification; the perceiver only takes into account the distances between stimuli. If A and C were classified together, it is an haphazard classification, because these two stimuli offer no basis for systematic classification.

The variation introduced into this task relates to the way in which the triads were presented, the instructions given to the participants, and the type of response. The presentation of the triads was made using a three-field tachistoscope fitted with an automatic card changer. With this type of presentation, the exposure time, the illumination, and the subjects' reaction time to each triad could be controlled. The illumination was kept constant at 1.5 lux. The procedure was completed with a manual response key with two buttons. When one of these buttons was pressed, a light appeared on a device located opposite the experimenter and was used to verify the type of classification given by the subject. The instructions were as follows: "Looking at the visual field, you will see three stimuli located as if they were the three vertices of a triangle. You have to observe these three stimuli and put together those you think go best together. You will respond by pressing one of the two buttons on the manual response key. If you think the stimulus at the top goes better with the stimulus on the right-hand side, you will press the right hand button, if you think it goes better with the left-hand one, you will press the button on the left. Answer as quickly and accurately as possible. There are not right or wrong answers in this task, it all depends on how you carry out the classification".

EXPERIMENT 1

The main goal of this experiment was to determine the perceived structure of the three sets of stimuli used: form-size, saturation-brightness and inclination-length.

Method

Subjects. Twelve undergraduate psychology students at the UNED (Universidad Nacional de Educacion a Distancia) took part in this experiment. They all participated voluntarily and had normal or corrected to normal vision and normal color vision.

BALLESTEROS

Design. A 3 x 2 x 2 within-subjects factorial design was employed. The factors were stimulus sets (form-size, saturation-brightness, and inclination-length), types of triad (type A and B), and shared dimension (the dimension that shared a value in the trial). Types of classification and RTs were the dependent variables.

Procedure. The subjects were tested individually. The order of the triads in each material set was established at random, and the order of presentation of the material sets was counterbalanced so that each of the three stimulus sets appeared with the same frequency in the first, second, and third place. The experimental session started with ten practice trials. Half of the subjects started with the right hand and half started with the left hand. Every 36 trials, half-way through each block, they were allowed to rest while the experimenter fit a new pack of cards into the automatic changer. When restarting the experiment, the subject was asked to change hands.

Results and Discussion

Dimensional, similarity, and haphazard responses given to each type of stimulus material in each experimental condition were analyzed separately.

Table 8.1 shows the mean number of dimensional, similarity, and haphazard responses given to each stimulus dimension according to the type of triad and to the dimension that shared a value in the triad.

A within-subjects analysis of variance was carried out on the number of *dimensional* responses given to the three stimulus sets, the type of

TABLE 8.1
Mean Number of Dimensional (D), Similarity (S), and Haphazard (H)
Classifications for Each Component Dimension of the Three Stimuli Sets
in Each Type of Triad

	Materials/Component Dimension											
	Form-Size				Chroma-Value				Inclination-Length			
Type of Triad	Alpha		Beta		Alpha		Beta		Alpha		Beta	
	F	S	F	S	C	V	C	V	I	L	I	L
D	9.0	6.0	11.0	9.0	4.4	1.1	6.8	5.8	7.4	9.3	6.0	10.2
S	6.8	6.4	5.9	8.2	9.0	10.0	9.2	10.4	7.6	4.4	9.0	4.2
H	2.2	5.6	1.1	0.8	4.6	6.9	2.0	1.8	3.0	4.3	2.5	3.6

Note: The maximum value in any cell is 12.

triad, and the shared dimension as factors. This analysis showed that stimulus set was significant, $F (2, 22) = 60.26, p < .01$.

The number of dimensional responses given to form and size and inclination and length was significantly greater than that given to chroma and value, as can be seen in Fig. 8.2. The type of triad was also significant, $F(1, 11) = 37.10, p < .01$. Type beta triads produced a greater number of dimensional classifications. In addition to these main effects, the interaction between type of triad and type of stimulus set was significant, $F(2, 22) = 10.66, p < .01$.

As can be seen in Fig. 8.3, there were more dimensional classifications for form-size and chroma-value in type beta triads, but there was almost no difference between types of triads in the inclination-length set. The interaction between the shared dimension and stimulus set was also significant, $F(2, 22) = 25.52, p < .01$. There were more dimensional classifications when the triads shared a value in form, chroma, or length than when they shared a value in size, value, or inclination.

The ANOVA of the *similarity* responses produced a pattern of results that complemented the aforementioned. The effect of stimulus set was significant, $F(2, 22) = 20.27, p < .01$. The number of overall similarity classifications to chroma-value was greater than that given to the other two sets (See Table 8.1). The interaction between stimulus set and shared dimension was also significant, $F(2, 22) = 15.92, p < .01$. There were more responses based on overall similarity when the shared di-

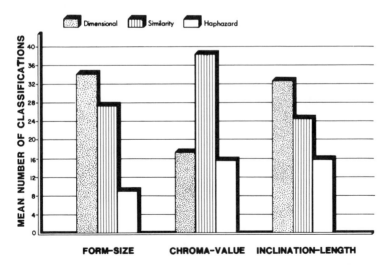

FIGURE 8.2.   Mean number of the dimensional, similarity, and haphazard classifications made with form and size, chroma and value, and inclination and length dimensions in Experiment 1.

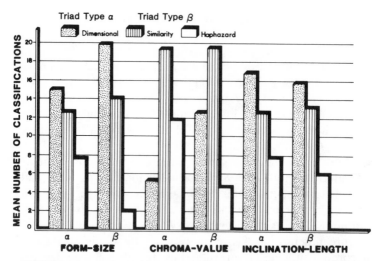

FIGURE 8.3. Mean number of the dimensional, similarity, and haphazard classifications made with the type alpha and type beta triads in the three
sets of materials used in Experiment 1 averaged over dimension that shared
a value in the triad.

mension was inclination than when it was length, but there were no
differences with the other two sets of materials.

Although *haphazard* classifications are not usually analyzed, we did
so because their number was greater than usually found in the standard
procedure. The ANOVA performed with haphazard classifications
showed that stimulus set was significant, $F(2, 22) = 10.94$, $p < .01$.
There were more haphazard classifications given to chroma-value and
inclination-length than to form-size. The type of triad was also
significant, $F(1, 11) = 113.39$, $p < .01$. Type alpha triads produced more
haphazard responses than type beta triads. The dimension that shared a
level in the triad produced a significant effect, $F(1, 11) = 15.12$, $p < .01$.
There were more haphazard classifications with triads that shared a
value in the dimensions of size, value, and length than when the value
shared was in the dimensions of form, chroma, and inclination. There
was a significant interaction due to stimulus set by type of triad, $F(2, 22)$
$= 5.23$, $p < .05$. Although the type of triad had almost no influence in
triads formed from inclination-length, its influence was significant in
the other stimulus sets.

Table 8.2a shows RTs corresponding to dimensional, similarity, and
haphazard classifications, taking into account the dimension that shared
a value in the triad; Table 8.2b shows RTs for the two types of triads.

Using RTs for *dimensionsl* classifications, an ANOVA for stimulus set
by type of triad was performed. Main effects for stimulus set, $F(2, 22) =$

TABLE 8.2a

Mean Reaction Times in Milliseconds of Dimensional and Similarity
Classifications for Each Type of Material in Each Component Dimension

| | Materials/Component Dimension | | | | | |
| | Form-Size | | Chroma-Value | | Inclination-Length | |
	F	S	C	V	I	L
Dimensional	905	1129	1192	1148	1128	1153
Similarity	1119	1155	933	954	1201	1403

TABLE 8.2b

Mean Reaction Times for Each Type of Material in Both Types of Triads

Type of Triad	Alpha	Beta	Alpha	Beta	Alpha	Beta
Dimensional	1028	981	1305	1108	1161	1123
Similarity	1128	1127	935	952	1242	1337

9.24, $p <.01$, and type of triad, $F(1, 11) = 7.65, p <.05$, were reliable.
The dimensional responses to form-size were faster than those to the
other two sets. In addition, the type beta triads produced faster responses than type alpha triads.

Figure 8.4 shows the average time (in milliseconds) for the dimensional and overall similarity responses depending on the stimulus set
and on the dimension that shared a value in the triad.

The mean RTs corresponding to the similarity classifications were
submitted to an ANOVA for repeated measures with stimulus set and
type of triad as factors. The only significant main effect was stimulus set,
$F(2, 22) = 10.51, p <.01$. The similarity responses to color stimuli were
faster than the same kind of responses to the other sets. No other effect
was significant.

A greater number of dimensional classifications were obtained when
chroma was the shared dimension than when it was value, but there
were more similarity responses to value than to chroma. Although both
dimensions are integral, there are differences between them. Furthermore, the type of triad also influenced the analyzability of color stimuli.
There were more dimensional responses to the beta triads than to the
alpha triads. These results are similar to those presented by Shepp
(1983, Table 2.2) in his findings on the restricted classification task with
Type I and Type II triads, which are fairly similar to type beta and alpha
in this experiment.

The results of the first experiment show that the objects constructed
from color dimensions are classified preferentially by their overall similarity relations, whereas those constructed from form-size and inclina-

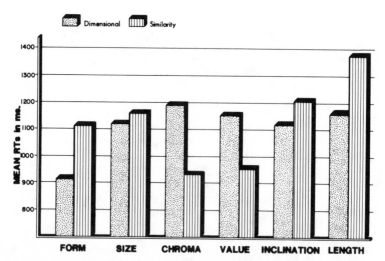

FIGURE 8.4. Mean reaction times in milliseconds corresponding to the dimensional, similarity, and haphazard classifications in the form and size, chroma and value, and inclination and length dimensions.

tion-length dimensions are preferentially classified by their dimensional structure. This latter set seems to occupy an intermediate position on the analyzability continuum. When the effect of the dimension that shared a value in the triad was analyzed, it was found that form and size interact in an asymmetric way. When the shared dimension was form, the number of dimensional classifications was larger than when it was size. Similar effects were found by Shepp (chapter 7, this book), using a selective attention task. Adults' performance showed that orthogonal variations of size do not affect the classifications of shape, but orthogonal variations of shape interfere with the classification of size. The same happened with length and inclination. The number of dimensional classifications was larger when the shared dimension was length than when it was inclination.

With regard to the RTs, the dimensional classifications with the more separable dimensions (form-size materials) were faster than the classifications with the rest of the materials. In addition, type beta triads produced shorter RTs. The RTs of similarity classifications were shorter with chroma-value materials, and the type of triad had no effect. Overall similarity classifications to color stimuli were faster than dimensional classifications and the overall similarity classifications to the other sets.

These results are consistent with the previous results reported by other investigators. The type of dimensions from which the stimuli are formed influences the way in which the perceiver processes these stimuli. When the stimuli are integral, the perceiver cannot direct his or her selective attention to the dimensional values, and he or she classifies by overall similarity. On the other hand, when the dimensions are separable, the perceiver can analyze the dimensional structure easily, and classify according to the dimension that shares a value in the triad.

In the second and third experiments, we investigate whether the mode of processing the stimulus structure can be modified under the influence of certain task variables, such as type of instruction and control of the stimulus exposure time.

EXPERIMENT 2

Previous research has shown that certain task demands can influence the number of dimensional or similarity classifications. Ward (1983) found that adults made more dimensional classifications with stimuli generated from lines of points that varied in length and density when they were asked to respond slowly than when they were asked to respond quickly. The opposite occurred with overall similarity classifications.

Smith and Kemler Nelson (1984) also found that adults produced more overall similarity classifications with size and brightness dimensions when they were told to respond on the basis of their first impression than when asked to be meticulous in their judgments. Whereas the instruction to be careful produced a proportion of similarity classifications of .20, the instruction to classify on the first impression produced a proportion of .70. The influence of type of instruction was also reflected in the time taken for the task. The careful group was almost four times slower than the first-impression group (218 seconds vs. 56 seconds).

Ward et al. (1986, Exp. 3) tried to find out whether the subjects could alter voluntarily their styles of classifications. One group of subjects classified triads of stimuli constructed from saturation and brightness and another group classified triads constructed from circles that varied in area and radius orientation. Each group carried out the task under two different conditions: "first impression" and "careful comparison". The results indicated that task instructions influenced both the number of similarity classifications made with the circle material (4.94 careful comparison vs. 8.14 first impression) and the number of dimensional classifications (17.97 vs. 13.19). Furthermore, the task instructions affected the time taken for the classification: The first impression instruction took far less time than with careful instruction (77.5 sec. vs. 136 sec., respectively). Nevertheless, the classification of the stimuli generated from the integral dimensions saturation and brightness were not altered with the type of instruction received, although the instruction did influence the time taken for the classification (66 sec. vs. 136 sec.). From these results, they deduced that integral materials could not be influenced by task instructions.

The second experiment was designed to test whether the simple change in the instructions could influence classification behavior enough to alter the perceived stimuli structure, and whether these results could be extended to other stimulus dimensions.

Method

Subjects.   Twelve subjects, students in the UNED and Complutense University of Madrid, participated in this experiment. They all took part voluntarily, had normal or corrected to normal vision, and were not color blind.

Stimuli and Procedure.   The stimuli, task, and equipment were the same as those in Experiment 1. The subjects were assigned at random to one of two groups with six participants each. The general instructions were the same as those given in the previous experiment. The "first impression group" received the additional instruction to allow themselves to be guided by their first impression in their answers, without thinking too much about it. The "precise group" was reminded before starting each block of trials to be careful in their responses and to think before responding.

Results and Discussion

The dimensional, similarity, and haphazard responses given by each group to each of the three sets of materials according to the type of triad and the dimension that shared a value in the triad are shown in Table 8.3.

The *dimensional* classifications were submitted to an analysis of variance for a mixed factorial design having type of instruction as a between-subject factor and stimulus set, type of triad, and shared dimension as within-subject factors. The analysis showed that the type of instruction was not significant, $F(1, 10) = .19, p > .05$. There were significant effects of stimulus set, $F(2, 20) = 48.51, p < .01$, and type of triad, $F(1,10) = 33.18, p < .01$. The number of dimensional classifications given to form-size and inclination-length was significantly greater than the number given to chroma-value. Type beta triads produced more dimensional classifications than type alpha triads. The following interactions were also significant: type of instruction by type of triad, $F(1, 10) = 6.82, p < .01$; stimulus set by shared dimension, $F(2, 10) =$

TABLE 8.3
Mean Number of Dimensional (D), Similarity (S), and Haphazard (H)
Classifications of Precision and First Impression Groups

	Materials/Component Dimension											
	Form-Size				Chroma-Value				Inclination-Length			
Type of Triad	Alpha		Beta		Alpha		Beta		Alpha		Beta	
	F	S	F	S	C	V	C	V	I	L	I	L
Precision												
D	11.5	4.0	11.3	8.7	3.2	2.4	7.4	6.7	4.5	9.0	8.5	11.0
S	5.3	8.2	6.5	8.1	10.2	10.3	9.0	8.9	9.0	4.2	8.8	3.8
H	1.2	5.8	0.2	1.2	4.6	5.3	1.6	2.5	4.5	4.8	0.7	3.2
First Impression												
D	9.8	5.7	9.8	8.5	4.4	2.4	6.3	6.0	9.7	7.1	7.9	7.9
S	5.8	6.3	7.2	8.2	8.3	9.3	8.5	9.2	6.2	4.4	7.5	5.1
H	2.3	6.0	1.0	1.3	5.3	6.3	3.1	2.8	2.1	6.5	2.6	5.0

Note: The maximum value in any cell is 12.

13.92, P <.01, and type of triad by shared dimension, $F(2, 10) = 7.79$, p < .01.

Figure 8.5 shows the interaction between type of instruction and type of triad. Although the "first impression" group made more dimensional classifications than the "precise" group in type alpha triads, the opposite results occurred in type beta triads.

When the shared dimension was form, there were more dimensional classifications than when it was size, but there were no differences in the number of dimensional classifications between triads with the other sets.

In the ANOVA performed on the *similarity* classifications, the only significant main effect was stimulus set, $F(2, 20) = 20.39, p < .01$. This pattern of results was complementary to that obtained with the dimensional classifications. There were also three significant interactions: type of instruction by type of triad, $F(1, 10) = 6.91, p < .05$; stimulus set by type of triad, $F(2, 20) = 4.98, p < .05$; and stimulus set by shared dimension, $F(2, 20) = 10.88, p < .01$. The "first impression" group made fewer similarity classifications in type alpha triads than in type beta triads, whereas the "precise" group made approximately the same number in each type of triad. On the other hand, type alpha triads produced more similarity classifications with color stimuli, whereas in the other two stimulus sets there were more similarity classifications with type

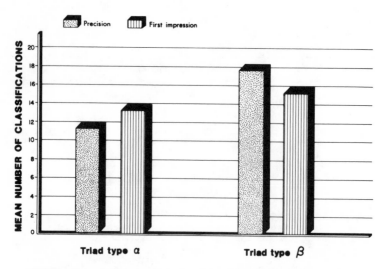

FIGURE 8.5. Interaction between type of instruction and type of triad found in the dimensional classification. The "First impression" group made more dimensional classifications than the "Precision" group in the type alpha triads, but the opposite occurred in the type beta triads.

beta triads. Fewer similarity classifications were obtained when form or length were the shared dimensions than when they were size or inclination.

As shown in Table 8.3, the stimuli generated from form and size produced fewer haphazard classifications than the group that responded according to their first impression.

The ANOVA performed on haphazard classifications showed that there was a significant effect in stimulus set $F(2, 20) = 19.44, p < .01$. There were fewer haphazard classifications with form-size dimensions than from the other two sets. In addition, there were more haphazard classifications with type alpha triads than with type beta triads, $F(1, 10) = 81.97, p < .01$.

To summarize, the "precise" group showed a trend to make fewer haphazard classifications within the three sets than the "first impression" group, although this tendency was not statistically significant. Furthermore, chroma and value stimuli and type alpha triads produce more classifications of this type.

These results differ from those studies that have found that type of instruction produces a change in subjects processing. This change has been interpreted to mean that subjects, when asked to be more careful, produce more dimensional responses, which proves that they process the stimuli in an analytical way. However, when they are told to respond on the basis of their first impressions, they produce more responses based on overall similarity, showing a more holistic type of processing. As a whole, the analysis of the type of response did not indicate this effect. Nevertheless, the type of instruction did influence the number of haphazard classifications. Subjects who were told to be precise tended to make fewer haphazard classifications in the three sets of materials than those who were told to be guided by their first impressions.

As in Experiment 1, the stimulus set was significant. The results seemed to show that the types of dimensions from which the stimuli were generated influenced the type of perceived structure more than the kind of instruction given to the participants. But looking at Table 8.3, it can be seen that the precise group produced more dimensional classifications with the triads that shared a value in the dimensions form and length than the "first impression" group. A new mixed factorial analysis of variance was conducted with *dimensional* classifications having type of instruction as between-subject factor and stimulus set and type of triad as within-subject factors, but only with the classification from form, chroma, and length. There was a main effect of type of instruction, $F(2, 20) = 36.12$, $p < .01$. The number of dimensional classifications given to the triads constructed from form and length was significantly greater than that given to the triads constructed from chroma.

The ANOVA performed with the *similarity* classifications given to the same dimensions showed that the only main effect was stimulus set, not type of instructions.

These results show that type of instruction influences the number of dimensional classifications made with stimuli formed from very separable stimulus dimensions, but does not affect the classifications of other dimensions. Furthermore, it would seem that the instruction to respond on the basis of the first impression does not increase the number of similarity classifications.

Table 8.4 shows the mean reaction times of dimensional and similarity classifications in the two groups.

An ANOVA for type of instruction by stimulus set by shared dimension performed on the mean reaction times of *dimensional* responses showed that type of instruction was significant, $F(1, 10) = 11.87$, $p < .01$. The "precise" group took almost twice as long to perform the task as the "first impression" group. The stimulus set was also significant, $F(2, 20) = 10.50$, $p < .01$. The responses to the form-size were very fast, followed by the responses to inclination-length, the slowest being those to chroma-value. No other effect was significant.

A similar analysis conducted with the mean reaction times of *similarity* responses showed that, as in the case of dimensional classifications, the "precise" group was slower than the "first impression" group. No other effect was significant.

TABLE 8.4a
Mean Reaction Times in Milliseconds of Dimensional and Similarity
Classifications for Each Type of Material in Each Component Dimension
for the Precision and First Impression Groups

| | Materials/Component Dimension | | | | | |
| | Form-Size | | Chroma-Value | | Inclination-Length | |
Precision	F	S	C	V	I	L
Dimensional	1023	1698	1669	1725	1467	1548
Similarity	1650	1563	1469	1385	1579	1664
First Impression						
Dimensional	701	812	928	960	918	955
Similarity	878	788	854	871	952	1055

TABLE 8.4b
Mean Reaction Times for Each Type of Material in Both Types
of Triads in Each Group

Type of Triad	Alpha	Beta	Alpha	Beta	Alpha	Beta
Precision						
Dimensional	1303	1246	1964	1642	1551	1451
Similarity	1617	1572	1370	1484	1627	1616
First Impression						
Dimensional	743	771	987	916	927	933
Similarity	844	822	896	826	1039	972

These analyses show that the type of instruction had a significant effect on both the RTs of dimensional and similarity classifications. Although the type of instruction had no effect on the type of classifications made by the subjects, the instruction did influence the number of dimensional classifications given to form and length. The "precise" group took longer and made fewer haphazard classifications, whereas the group working on their "first impression" took less time and made more haphazard classifications.

The results of Experiment 2 are in line with those of Ward et al. (1986), and they show that the effects of task instructions appear to be limited by the nature of the stimulus dimensions. The results show that totally integral dimensions, such as value and chroma, are perceived on basis of their overall similarity, and subjects do not analyze the values of their component dimensions even when asked to be meticulous in their judgments. Nevertheless, the effect of instruction influenced the RTs and the number of haphazard classifications, which would appear to indicate that the perceiver tried to fulfill the task demands imposed by the researcher.

On the other hand, it has been observed that type of instruction can affect the number of dimensional classifications made with stimuli from clearly separable dimensions such as form and length.

EXPERIMENT 3

The aim of Experiment 3 was to see whether the manipulation of the exposure time influenced the way multidimensional stimuli were processed, and if so, whether these effects could be observed throughout the entire analyzability continuum.

Ward (1983), working with moderately separable dimensions (length and density of dots lines) demonstrated that when the subjects were asked to respond in less than 2 seconds, they made more similarity classifications than when they were asked to take at least 5 seconds to respond. Furthermore, Ward et at. (1986), using triads of stimuli generated from two stimulus sets, one physically separable and the other integral, found that experimental manipulation (2 sec. vs. 5 sec.) produced significant effects in dimensional and similarity classifications given to stimuli formed from physically separable dimensions, but did not affect classifications to stimuli formed from integral dimensions. Experiment 3 was designed to study the influence of exposure time over the type of classification.

Experiment 3 was designed to test whether the time allowed to process the stimuli has some influence over mode of processing in two specific exposure time conditions.

Method

Subjects. Twelve psychology students from the Complutense University of Madrid took part in this experiment. All participants had normal or corrected vision and normal color vision.

Stimuli. The participants were assigned at random in two experimental groups of six each. One group was assigned to the 500 milliseconds and the other to the 5-seconds exposure condition. The stimuli and design of the experiment were similar to those of Experiment 2. In addition to the explanation of the task, the following instructions were read to the 500 ms. group: "In each trial, the stimuli will be exposed for a short period of time. You must put together as quickly as possible those you think go best together, avoiding random answers". The following complementary instructions were read to the 5 sec. group: "Put together what you think goes best together, but do not decide until the stimuli disappear. It is very important that you observe the stimuli attentively and are sure before responding". It was subsequently proved that this instruction was scrupulously attended, as only one subject out of six answered twice over 216 trials in less than 5 seconds.

Results and Discussion

Table 8.5 shows the average number of dimensional, similarity, and haphazard classifications given by the two groups to the three stimulus sets.

An ANOVA was performed for a mixed factorial design in which the between-factor was groups and the within-factors were material sets, type of triad, and dimension that shared a level. There were significant main effects of stimulus set, $F(2, 20) = 86.40, p < .01$; type of triad, $F(1, 10) = 134.61, p < .01$; and dimension that shared a value, $F(1, 10) = 21.21, p < .01$.

Figure 8.6 shows the mean dimensional and similarity classifications made by the two experimental groups in the three stimulus sets. As in Experiments 1 and 2, the number of dimensional classifications made with the form-size and inclination-length stimuli were significantly greater than those made with chroma-value; type beta triads produced

TABLE 8.5

Mean Number of Dimensional (D), Similarity (S), and Haphazard (H)
Classifications For Each Component Dimension for the Three Stimuli Sets
in Each Type of Triad in the Two Exposition Time Conditions

	Materials/Component Dimension											
	Form-Size				Chroma-Value				Inclination-Length			
Type of Triad	Alpha		Beta		Alpha		Beta		Alpha		Beta	
500 msec.	F	S	F	S	C	V	C	V	I	L	I	L
D	11.0	4.0	11.3	8.7	3.0	1.8	7.2	7.0	8.5	6.8	9.4	8.0
S	4.5	7.0	5.2	8.6	9.5	9.7	8.8	9.4	7.5	4.6	7.3	4.7
H	2.5	7.0	1.5	0.7	5.5	6.5	2.0	2.6	2.0	6.6	1.3	5.3
5 sec												
D	11.7	4.2	11.5	8.7	1.5	1.4	7.5	6.1	9.5	9.2	10.5	11.5
S	5.5	6.8	6.0	8.7	10.7	10.8	10.2	11.2	6.7	3.5	7.2	4.2
H	0.8	7.0	0.5	0.6	5.8	5.8	0.3	0.7	1.8	5.3	0.3	2.3

Note: The maximum value in any cell is 12.

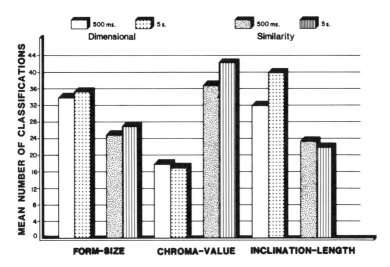

FIGURE 8.6. Mean number of the dimensional and similarity classifications given by the "500 msec." and the "5 sec." exposure time groups. Data collapsed over type of triad.

more dimensional classifications than type alpha triads, and when the shared dimension was form, chroma, or inclination, more dimensional classifications were produced than when the other dimensions shared a value.

The following interactions were also significant: exposure time by stimulus set, $F(2, 20) = 5.9, p < .01$, see Fig. 8.7; stimulus set by type of triad, $F(2, 20) = 11.22, p < .01$; stimulus set by shared dimension, $F(2, 20) = 8.06, p < .01$; and type of triad by shared dimension, $F(1, 20) = 8.37, p < .01$.

The 5 sec. group made more dimensional classifications than the 500 msec. group, but only with the inclination-length stimuli. Although beta triads produced more dimensional classifications than alpha triads in chroma-value and form-size sets, there were no differences in the inclination-length set. More dimensional classifications were obtained on form-size sets when the shared dimension was form than when it was size, but no differences occurred on the other two sets. Type alpha triads produced more dimensional classifications when the shared dimensions were form, value, or inclination than when they were size, chroma, or length. No differences appeared on type beta triads.

The ANOVA performed with *similarity* classifications showed that exposure time was not significant, but the interaction between exposure time and set of material was reliable, $F(2, 20) = 4.54, p < .05$. With the chroma-value stimuli, the longer exposure condition produced more similarity responses than the shorter one. Stimulus set proved to be

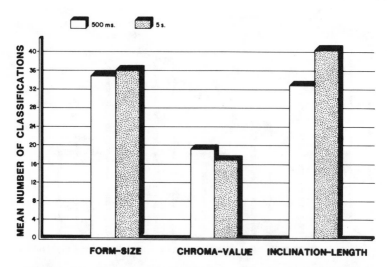

FIGURE 8.7. Interaction obtained between the exposure time and the material sets in the dimensional classifications. Although there was no difference between the two experimental conditions in form-and-size and chroma-and-value materials, there was a reliable difference in inclination and length.

highly significant, $F(2, 20) = 86.81$, $p < .01$. The similarity classifications made with chroma-value were significantly higher than made with the other two sets. As expected, the type of triad was not significant. The interaction between stimulus set and shared dimension was significant, $F(1, 10) = 7.42$, $p < .05$. Although a larger number of similarity classifications were found on form-size when the shared dimension was size than when it was form, and on inclination-length when the shared dimension was inclination than when it was length, no differences appeared on value-chroma set.

The number of haphazard classifications was greater in the 500 msec. condition than in the 5 sec. condition. There were also other significant effects. Type alpha triads produced a greater number of haphazard classifications than type beta triads,. $F(1, 10) = 205$, $p < .01$,; the dimension that shared a value was significant, $F(1, 10) = 162.88$, $p < .01$. When this dimension was size or length, there were more haphazard classifications than when it was form or inclination.

Taken as a whole, the results of this experiment show that the effects of manipulating the exposure time are limited by the nature of the stimulus dimensions used. The exposure time influenced the number of dimensional classifications given to stimuli generated from inclination and ngth, but did not influence the other materials. With form and size there was a similar trend, but the differences were not significant. With the chroma and value there was no increase in the number of dimensional classifications with the longer exposure time, although the number of similarity classifications did increase. It seems that the longer the time the perceiver had to analyze the stimuli, the less he analyzed them. Adults are unable to separate these dimensions. The pattern of results obtained with chroma-value is fairly similar to that obtained in Experiment 2, wherein the instruction to be "precise" increased the number of similarity classifications but did not affect dimensional classifications.

GENERAL DISCUSSION

The results obtained in these three experiments clearly show the influence of stimulus dimensions on the type of perceived structure. When the multidimensional objects shown were generated from integral dimensions—that is, saturation and brightness,—the predominant type of classification was overall similarity, regardless of the type of instructions used in the task and the exposure time allowed to the subject. These results agree with those of other authors who have worked with these types of stimulus dimensions (Garner, 1974; Shepp, 1983; Ward, 1983; Ward et al. 1986, etc.).

It seems that it is easier to analyze the features of certain objects but not others, and as Garner has argued, the stimulus structure limits the subject's processing options. There are some changes, of course, in perceived structure that occur during development. Stimuli that are perceived by the older child and adult as separable are perceived by the young child as integral. However, the perception of objects formed from integral dimensions would not appear to vary in the course of development (Ballesteros & Gonzalez Labra, 1987a, 1987b; Shepp & Swartz, 1976; Shepp et al., 1980; Smith, 1980; Ward et al., 1986).

Other dimensions close to the separable end of the analyzable-integral continuum are more flexible and can be influenced to some extent by task demands such as type of instructions or exposure time. Experiment 2 has shown that the instruction "to be precise" or "be guided by your first impression" affects the number of dimensional classifications made with triads of stimuli that share a value in form or length of a straight line. Experiment 3 showed that an increase in the exposure time only produced significant results favoring greater dimensional analysis with the stimuli formed from inclination and length.

Smith and Kemler Nelson (1984), have stated that adults can classify separable dimensions in two ways (one analytical and the other wholistic), but they can only classify integral dimensions on the basis of overall similarity. The dimensions used in this study located towards the separable end of the continuum of analyzability were organized according to their dimensional structure. Under the right conditions, the subject can act in an even more analytical manner and increase the number of dimensional classifications. We cannot say, however, that the classifications based on similarity vary with experimental manipulation. Under circumstances favoring analytical processing, the perceiver behaves in this manner, not at the expense of the number of similarity classifications but at the expense of haphazard classifications. Although analysis occurs with separable dimensions, integral stimuli are not perceived as dimensions. Dimensions may exist for the investigator, but do not affect the perceptual experience of the subject, who classifies the stimuli according to their similarity structure.

The results of these experiments suggest, however, that saturation and brightness have some psychological status as dimensions. Although the dominant type of classification with color stimuli was based on similarity, the number of dimensional classifications made with the type beta triads in our experiments was significantly greater than that made with type alpha triads, whereas the number of classifications based on similarity was the same in both types of triad. In parallel, the number of haphazard classifications decreased with type beta triads. The way that elements within the triad were arranged affected the number of dimensional and haphazard classifications made by the perceivers. In Experiments 2 and 3, this effect can be observed in the two experimental conditions. These results are consistent with those reported by Smith and Kemler Nelson (1984).

Shepp (1983) has presented similar results with materials formed from hue, saturation, and brightness. When the subjects were instructed to choose the stimuli that shared a value on a dimension, there were fewer similarity classifications and more dimensional classifications. However, the subjects were not very accurate. The results were not much better when they worked with a specialized population of students at the Rhode Island School of Design. Color Stimuli were as difficult for them to analyze into their constituent dimensions as for everyone else. Ward et al. (1986) and Foard and Kemler Nelson (1984) made the same point when they stated that in the case of color stimuli, the subjects classified by similarity independently of the time allowed or the task instructions. We can say that Garner's assertion that it is the nature of the stimuli that establishes the limits of the subject's ability to process the information appears to be correct.

On the other hand, the results of these experiments seem to point towards the existence of a continuum of analyzability along which the stimulus dimensions are situated in the way suggested by Smith and Kilroy (1979). They found that adults made dimensional classifications faster with stimuli consisting of the separable dimensions size and brightness, but with the integral dimensions saturation and brightness the similarity classifications were faster than the dimensional ones. The third stimulus set formed from length and inclination produced intermediate results. The results obtained in Experiment 1 were fairly consistent with those of Smith and Kilroy. The adult subjects classified the integral stimuli more rapidly on the basis of holistic similarity (940 msec.), whereas the dimensional classifications of the separable stimuli formed from form and size were faster (1017 msec.) than those based on similarity. In the third set formed by straight lines, dimensional classifications were slightly faster than those based on similarity. This pattern of results was repeated in Experiment 2, both in the "first impression" group and in the "precise" group. In line with these results, the three stimulus sets used in this study can be ranked from most integral to most separable, inclination-length occupying an intermediate position closer to the separable end. This ranking is apparent both in the RTs and in the types of classifications made with the different materials.

In conclusion, it can be said that the perception of separable stimuli is dominated by their dimensional structure; objects are compared and classified by the values they share. The objects formed from integral dimensions, however, are perceived holistically and are compared and classified by their overall similarity. Nevertheless, the interactions found between stimulus set and task demands complicate the existing panorama and require that the preceding claims be adequately qualified.

ACKNOWLEDGMENTS

The laboratory equipment used in this research was purchased with funds from the CAICYT. The author thanks the MEPSA staff for technical assistance, Dr. Dionisio Manga, who provided part of the subjects, and Dr. Marìa Josè Gonzàlez Labra for her collaboration in various aspects of this work. The author also expresses appreciation to Bryan E. Shepp for his helpful comments on earlier drafts of this paper.

REFERENCES

Attneave, F. (1950). Dimensions of similarity. *American Journal of Psychology, 63,* 516–556.

Ballesteros, S., & Gonzalez Labra, M.J. (1987a, August). *Are children more holistic than adults in the perception of color dimensions?.* Paper presented at the Fourth International Conference on Event Perception and Action, Trieste, Italy.

Ballesteros, S., & Gonzalez Labra, M.J. (1987b, September). *Stimulus and observer determinants in the holistic and analytic processing.* Poster presented at the Second European Conference for Research on Learning and Instruction, Tubingen, F.R. of Germany.

Ballesteros, S., Gonzalez Labra, M.J., & Fernández Trespalacios, J.L. (1985). Integralidad o separabilidad de las dimensiones forma y tamaño como concepto del estímulo, de la tarea o del organismo. *Revista de Psicología General y Aplicada, 40,* 2, 183–207.

Ballesteros, S., Gonzalez Labra, M.J., & Fernández Trespalacios, J.L. (1986). Influencia de las dimensiones forma y tamaño en el procesamiento de la informacio'aan visual. *Revista de Psicología General y Aplicada, 41,* 1, 25–42.

Burns, B., Shepp, B.E., McDonough, D., & Weiner-Ehrlich, W. (1978). The relation between stimulus analyzability and perceived dimensional structure. In G.H. Bower (Ed.), *The psychology of learning and motivation: Advances in research and theory,* Vol 12 (pp. 77–115). New York: Academic Press.

Callaghan, T. (1984). Dimensional interactin of hue and brightness in preattentive field segregation. *Perception & Psychophysics, 36,* 1, 25–34.

Cooper, L.A. (1982). Strategies for visual comparison and representation: Individual differences. In R.J. Sternberg (Ed.), *Advances in the psychology of human intelligence* vol 1 (pp. 77–123). Cambridge, MA: Cambridge University Press.

Cooper, L.A., Shepard, R.N. (1973). Chronometric studies of the rotation of mental images. In W.G. Chase (Ed.), *Visual information processing* (pp. 75–177). New York: Academic Press.

Cooper, L.A., Mumaw, R.J., & Morrow, L. (1984, November). *Probing the nature of mental representation of visual objects.* Paper presented at the 25th annual meeting of Psychonomic Society, San Antonio, TX.

Dunn, J.C. (1983). Spatial metrics of integral and separable dimensions. *Journal of Experimental Psychology: Human Perception and Performance, 9,* 2, 242–257.

Foard, C.F., & Kemler Nelson, D.G. (1984). Holistic and analytic modes of processing: The multiple determinants of perceptual analysis. *Journal of Experimental Psychology: General. 113,* 94–111.

Garner, W.R. (1970). The stimulus in information processing. *American Psychologist, 25,* 350–358.

Garner, W.R. (1974). *The processing of information and structure.,* Hillsdale, NJ: Lawrence Erlbaum Associates.

Garner, W.R. (1976). Interaction of stimulus dimensions in concept and choice processes. *Cognitive Psychology, 8,* 98–123.

Garner, W.R. (1983). Asymmetric interactions of stimulus dimensions in perceptual information processing. In T.J. Tighe & B.E. Shepp (Eds.), *Perception, cognition and development: Interactional analysis* (pp. 1–38). Hillsdale, NJ: Lawrence Erlbaum Associates.

Garner, W.R. (1986). Interactions of stimulus and organism in perception. In S.H. Hulse & B.F. Green (Eds.), *One hundred years of psychological research in America: G. Stanley Hall and the Johns Hopkins tradition* (pp. 199–240). Baltimore, MD: The Johns Hopkins University Press.

Garner, W.R., & Felfoldy, G.L. (1970). Integrality of stimulus dimensions in various types of information processing. *Cognitive Psychology, 1,* 225–241.

Handel, S., & Imai, S. (1972). The classification of analyzable and unanalyzable stimuli. *Perception & Psychophysics, 12,* 108–116.

Handel, S., Imai, S., & Spottswood, P. (1980). Dimensional, similarity and configural classification of integral and separable stimuli. *Perception & Psychophysics, 28,* 3, 205–212.

Kemler, D.G. (1982a). Classification in young and retarded children: The primacy of overall similarity relations. *Child Development, 53,* 768–779.

Kemler, D.G. (1982b). The ability for dimensional analysis in preschool and retarded children: Evidence from comparison, conservation and prediction tasks. *Journal of Experimental Child Psychology, 34,* 469–489.

Krantz, D.H., & Tversky, A. (1975). Similarity of rectagles: An analysis of subjective dimensions. *Mathematical Psychology, 12*, 4–34.

Lockhead, G.R. (1966). Effects of dimensional redundancy on visual discrimination. *Journal of Experimental Psychology, 72*, 95–104.

Lockhead, G.R. (1972). Processing dimensional stimuli: A note. *Psychological Review, 79*, 410–419.

Lockhead, G.R. (1979). Holistic versus analytic process models: A reply. *Journal of Experimental Psychology: Human Perception and Performance, 5*, 746–755.

Palmer, S.E. (1977). Hierarchical structure in perceptual representation. *Cognitive Psychology, 9*, 441–474.

Palmer, S.E. (1978). Fundamental aspects of cognitive representation. In E. Rosch & B. Lloyd (Eds.), *Cognition and categorization* (pp. 262–304). Hillsdale, NJ: Lawrence Erlbaum Associates.

Pomerantz, J.R. (1981). Perceptual organization in informatin processing. In M. Kubovy & J.R. Pomerantz (Eds.), *Perceptual organization* (pp. 141–180). Hillsdale, NJ: Lawrence Erlbaum Associates.

Redding, G.M., & Tharp, D.A. (1981). Processing line location and orientation. *Journal of Experimental Psychology: Human Perception and Performance, 7*, 1, 115–129.

Santee, J.L., & Egeth, H.E. (1980). Selective attention in speeded classification and comparison of multidimensional stimuli. *Perception & Psychophysics, 28*, 3, 191–204.

Shepard, R.N. (1964). Attention and the metric structure of the stimulus space. *Journal of Mathematical Psychology, 1*, 54–89.

Shepp, B.E. (1978). From perceived similarity to dimensional structure: A new hypothesis about perceptual development. In E. Rosch & B. Lloyd (Eds.), *Cognition and Categorization* (pp. 140–169). Hillsdale, NJ: Lawrence Erlbaum Associates.

Shepp, B.E. (1983). The analyzability of multidimensional objects: Some constraints on perceived structure, the development of perceived structure, and attention. In T. Tighe & B.E. Shepp (Eds.), *Perception, Cognition and Development: Interactional Analysis* (pp. 39–75). Hillsdale, NJ: Lawrence Erlbaum Associates.

Shepp, B.E., Burns, B., & McDonough, D. (1980). The relation of stimulus structure to perceptual and congitive development. Further tests of a separability hypothesis. In J. Becker & F. Wilkening (Eds.), *The integration of information by children* (pp. 113–145). Hillsdale, NJ: Lawrence Erlbaum Associates.

Shepp, B.E., & Swartz, K.B. (1976). Selective attention and the processing of integral and nonintegral dimensions: A developmental study. *Journal of Experimental Child Psychology, 22*, 73–85.

Smith, L.B. (1980). Development and the continuum of dimensional separability. *Perception & Psychophysics, 28*, 164–172.

Smith, L.B. (1981). Importance of overall similarity of objects for adults' and children's classifications. *Journal of Experimental Psychology: Human Perception and Performance, 7*, 811–824.

Smith, L.B., & Kemler, D.G. (1977). Developmental trends in free classification: Evidence for a new conceptualization of perceptual development. *Journal of Experimental Child Psychology, 24*, 279–298.

Smith, L.B., & Kemler, D.G. (1978). Levels of experienced dimensionality in children and adults. *Cognitive Psychology, 10*, 502–532.

Smith, L.B., & Kilroy, M.C. (1979). A continuum of dimensional separability. *Perception & Psychophysics, 25*, 285–291.

Smith, J.D., & Kemler Nelson, D.G. (1984). Overall similarity in adult's classification: The child in all of us. *Journal of Experimental Psychology: General, 113*, 137–159.

Torgerson, W.S. (1958). *Theory and methods of scaling.* New York: Wiley.

Tversky, A. & Gati, I. (1982). Similarity, separability and the triangle inequality. *Psychological Review, 89,* 2, 123–154.

Ward, T.B. (1980). Separable and integral responding by children and adults to the dimensions of length and density. *Child Development, 51,* 676–684.

Ward, T.B. (1983). Response tempo and separable–integral responding: Evidence for an integral-to-separable processing sequence in visual perception. *Journal of Experimental Psychology: Human Perception and Performance, 9,* 103–112.

Ward, T.B. (1985). Individual differences in processing stimulus dimensions: Relation to selective processing abilities. *Perception & Psychophysics, 37,* 471–482.

Ward, T.B., & Vela E. (1986). Classifying color materials: Children are less holistic than adults. *Journal of Experimental Child Psychology, 42,* 273–302.

Ward, T., Foley, C.M. & Cole, J. (1986). Classifying multidimensional stimuli: Stimulus, task and observer factors. *Journal of Experimental Psychology: Human Perception and Performance, 12,* 2, 211–225.

Weiner-Ehrlich, W.K. (1978). Dimensional and metric structures in multidimensional stimuli. *Perception and Psychophysics, 24,* 5, 399–414.

9 CATEGORY BOUNDS AND STIMULUS VARIABILITY

Gregory R. Lockhead
Duke University

INTRODUCTION

This chapter examines the boundaries that separate categories. The goals of the research are to better predict what stimuli are naturally classified by people into one or another category and to better predict identification and classification performance in a variety of tasks. More particularly, the research asks what it is about the stimulus set that determines the classification of individual stimuli.

For this purpose, the data from various classification studies were examined for regularities across tasks and stimulus domains. The considered tasks were the method of just noticeable boundaries (JNB), absolute identifications (AI), and speeded sortings. The considered stimulus domains included intervals in time and space, loudnesses of tones, sizes of rectangles, and animal names. To anticipate the primary result, in every data set the variability of each dependent measure was directly proportional to the variability of the stimulus set.

Because not all category situations are addressed in this chapter, it is necessary first to limit this discussion. A category is a division in some classification scheme. In some schemes categories are not structured, whereas in others they are structured. In addition, categories may or may not be related to one another. As described hereafter, this chapter only considers situations having relations between categories.

Logical Categories. The Aristotelian definition of categories is a logical one. According to this view, categories are either–or structures whose memberships depend on criterial attributes. An object having the criterial attribute(s) is a member of the category and has equivalent category membership with all objects having that attribute(s).

In *Categories*, Aristotle defined that all things may be said to "be" in ten different ways. One way was specific thinghood (ousia). His most quoted example is that the substance "man" may be variously predicated without changing its basic "thingness." "Substance," he reasoned, "does not admit of more or less . . . if this substance is a man, it will not be more a man or less a man either than itself or than another man" (Ackrill, 963, 3^{b}33). For Aristotle, there was some essential quality that makes a man a man.

Aristotle did not identify that quality and did not enumerate specific defining attributes for category membership. Thus, he did not answer questions like: Is a man without arms still a man? Is one who lacks 46 chromosomes or the ability to reason still a man? More generally, he did not answer the question: If the object of interest is lacking one of the defining features of X, is it still an X? By this formulation, there is no measure or importance of variability between members within a category and there is no consideration of relations between categories.

In their influential book *A Study of Thinking*, Bruner, Goodnow, and Austin (1956) demonstrated the enduring quality of Aristotle's view by continuing his essential thesis 2300 years later. Consistent with that instant classic, Bourne (1968) said that "A concept exists whenever two or more distinguishable objects or events have been grouped or classified together and set apart from other objects on the basis of some common feature or property characteristic of each" (p. 26). All dogs, Bourne explained, have certain features in common and these serve as a basis for a conceptual grouping.

However, concepts such as dogs have not often been studied by researchers taking this view. More commonly, they have studied geometric designs that vary discretely on defined dimensions, like color (red, green, blue), form (triangle, square), or size (large, small). The subject's task was usually to learn which stimuli were and were not predetermined by the experimenter to be members of the category.

Fortunately, the categories were not predetermined in all category studies. For example, Wing (1969) taught people to discriminate Poggles from non-Poggles. These were flower-like drawings with wide or narrow leaves and short or long stems combined according to logical rules. Following training with subsets of these stimuli, people were asked to choose Poggles from the full range of varying leaf widths and stem heights. An important feature of this study was that the stimulus dimensions were not binary. Instead, there were several levels on each dimension and the amount of each attribute was important.

Two of the findings are of interest here. First, as revealed in a generalization test, the number of leaf-width and stem-height categories into which the subjects thought the continuum had been divided was greater when that dimension was more relevant. This mirrors the observation by anthropologists that the number of classifications for a substance increases with its increasing importance to the classifier. Eskimos have more words for snow than do most Spaniards. Second, when the combination rule for determining whether or not a stimulus was a Poggle was more complex, it was generalized across more levels of each dimension. This is consistent with a conclusion made in this chapter: Increased stimulus variability results in wider and more variable category boundaries.

Structured Categories.   Category membership in Wing's results was determined partly by importance and partly by stimulus variability. Membership was not determined completely by attributes. If it had been, then any particular item would always have been, or would always have not been, a category member. This was not the case. This suggests that although an Aristotelean view might describe some categories, it is not a correct description of all categories. Category membership can depend on factors other than defining attributes.

Over the past two decades, several such factors have been shown to be important. These include context, expertise of the judge, whether the category is functional, relational, or descriptive, whether it is derived or direct, whether relevant attributes are continuous or discrete, whether attributes or dimensions interact, and more.

Berlin and Kay (1969) provided an important empirical beginning to this line of research that also provided the further conclusion that some categories are internally structured. They examined color naming across cultures. They found that if a culture had only two color names, then those names corresponded to light and dark. If a culture had three color names, those corresponded to light, dark, and red. A culture with four color names added green or yellow to these three; a five-name culture added the other, yellow or green. The sixth term added was usually blue, the seventh, brown. Purple, pink, orange, and grey then proliferated; if there was a term for one of the last four colors, then there was a term for all of them.

As well as color names, color perceptions are also structured across cultures. Some patches of color are "good" and others are "poor." There are a few good reds and many poor reds. Apparently, the decision to call some color "good" depends jointly on physiologically given preferences and culture. All normal people, independent of culture, treat good colors in the same way, but the boundaries separating color categories are less well defined in cultures having a more impoverished naming structure.

Color names and good colors or natural prototypes (the items chosen by Berlin and Kay's respondents), as well as perceptions of colored patches, are also related across cultures. Patches selected as "good" colors are the ones that best exemplify color names. Furthermore, colors similar to a prototype are easier to learn than are other colors (Rosch, 1973). Because of such findings, the prototype is often thought of as a center of a structured category.

Posner suggested that this center results from an averaging process. Using dot patterns as stimuli, Posner and Keele (1970) showed that more variable categories are harder to learn than are less variable categories. When subjects were shown various stimuli and later asked if new stimuli were members of the previously learned set, more stimuli were responded to as being members when the learned set was more variable.

Mapping Tasks. In 1:1 mapping tasks, each stimulus is assigned a separate category. Absolute identification is a 1:1 mapping or categorization task. In many:1 mapping tasks, several different stimuli belong in the same category. Separately classifying animals and vegetables is a many:1 sorting or categorization task. In either case, categories may or may not be related. If they are not related, as in paired associates learning, then the situation is not relevant to this chapter. If they are related, as with 1:1 mappings of tones that vary in loudness or many:1 mappings of animals as large or small, then the task is relevant here.

In general, this chapter considers how stimulus variability between and within classes affects categorization performance.

VARIABILITY OF CATEGORY BOUNDARIES

This section considers two types of experiments, absolute identification (AI) and the production of just noticeable category boundaries (JNB). In AI studies, the subjects attempt to categorize each stimulus as prescribed by the experimenter. In JNB studies, the subjects create boundaries to separate stimuli into categories.

Absolute Identifications   are 1:1 mappings where each stimulus is assigned a unique category. An example is when a sequence of ten loudnesses is labeled 1, 2, 3, . . . 10. The subjects' task is to assign the correct label to each randomly presented stimulus.

Pollack (1953) compared AI performance on 10 uniformly spaced auditory frequencies with performance on two widely separated groups of five tones each. The separations between successive stimuli within the five-tone groups was the same as that in the 10-tone group. When either five-tone group was tested separately, performance was essentially perfect. When these two groups were randomly intermixed so that all ten tones had to be identified, the subjects made many errors.

The important observation for this chapter is that identification precision was worse with 10 tones separated into two groups than with 10 uniformly separated tones. The total stimulus variability was greater in the two-groups condition, resulting in a broader distribution of responses to each stimulus.

This spread-scale effect is robust and general. It occurs whether many stimuli (Pollack's studies) or only three stimuli (Gravetter & Lockhead, 1973) are used, indicating that the number of stimuli is not an explanation. Therefore, channel capacity ideas concerning the number of stimuli or responses do not account for the results. It also occurs whether the stimulus dimension is loudness (Lockhead & Hinson, 1986), flicker rate (Hinson & Lockhead, 1986), or pitch (Pollack, 1953), indicating that stimulus domain is not important to the explanation. The result also occurs whether birds (Hinson & Lockhead, 1986) or people (Lockhead, & Hinson, 1986) are the subjects, indicating that complex mental processes are not an explanation. *In general, increasing the physical differences between stimulus members results in less precise identification of individual stimuli.*

This result has variously been called a range-effect, a spread-scale effect, and a variability effect. Because performance differs when range is fixed while variability between items within that range is varied (Gaylord & Lockhead, 1987), the result is treated as a variability effect in this chapter.

Just Noticeable Category Boundaries. In AI studies, the experimenter decides what stimuli belong to what categories. In just noticeable boundary (JNB) studies, the subject decides what stimuli belong to what categories.

The JNB procedure was introduced by Gaylord and Lockhead (1987) to examine the formation of natural categories. The procedure was adapted from the method of just noticeable differences that was used by Weber to investigate differential sensitivity (Fechner, 1966). For that JND technique, a stimulus is adjusted to the point where it is *just* discriminated from another stimulus. Use of that procedure resulted in Weber's Law: The amount by which an intensity has to be changed, in order for the original intensity and the new intensity to be just noticeably different, is proportional to the average of those intensities. Furthermore, this proportionality is a constant for each stimulus domain and is usually a different constant for different domains.

For the JNB technique, a stimulus is adjusted to the point where it is perceived as *just not* grouped with other stimuli. The experimental question concerns how such category boundaries relate to features of the stimulus set and to classification.

One report of the JNB method measured the spatial position at which a dot was perceived as *just grouped* with another dot (Gaylord & Lockhead, 1987). People were given a piece of paper with two dots separated by 5 cm. The instructions were: Imagine that there is a dot in the middle between the two dots above. Now, using your pencil, move the imaginary dot towards the left until you can just begin to feel that the two dots on the left belong together as a 'group' while the one on the right is by itself. Place the dot at this point.

To measure this grouping point, the distance between the subject-generated dot and the stimulus dot farthest from it was divided by the distance between the two original stimulus dots, 5 cm. These ratios from the 25 subjects ranged from 0.55 to 0.71, with a mean of 0.64 and a standard deviation of 0.046.

The opposite instruction was also given to 25 people: . . . move this imaginary dot towards the right until you can just begin to feel that it no longer appears 'grouped' with the one on the left. Place the new dot at this point. These 25 grouping ratios ranged from 0.49 to 0.64, with a mean of 0.57 and standard deviation of 0.044.

The mean of these measures, the just-outside boundary and the just-inside boundary, $[(0.57 + 0.64)/2] = 0.605$, estimates the position of the boundary separating these subjective categories. The difference between these two boundary measures, $0.64 - 0.57 = 0.07$, estimates the width of this boundary. This boundary width, 7% of the stimulus range, and the variances of the boundary judgments, 0.044 and 0.046, are numerically small.

JNB Variability and Stimulus Variability. AI data are more variable when the stimulus variability is larger. The similar result occurs for JNB data. This was shown in a JNB study using pairs of vertical lines of various heights as the stimuli (Gaylord & Lockhead, 1987). The individual stimulus lines ranged in height from 30 to 63 mm, and the two lines in a stimulus pair differed in height by either 0 (identical lines), 7, 13, or 20 mm. When the lines were of different heights, the left line and the right line were taller equally often.

Each stimulus was two vertical lines separated horizontally by 8 mm. and presented at the lower edge of a 17 cm. wide × 24 cm. high oscilloscope screen that was freely viewed from about 60 cm. The subjects manipulated a "joy stick" lever in the vertical direction in order to draw a third line, the response. This third line began 8 mm. to the right of the stimulus lines and at their baseline. Hence, the three lines were separated equally along the horizontal axis and began at the same position along the vertical axis.

For each stimulus, the subjects were instructed to draw the third line to be *just* tall enough to belong to a different category than the stimulus lines and thus to isolate them into their own, separate category based on their lesser heights.

Results. The boundary heights (the third line) were taller when the two stimulus lines were more different from one another. Configuration (left line taller, lt, or left line shorter, ls) also affected the boundary. The effect of height difference (intra-stimulus variability) on the subject-generated boundary was described by a linear equation for each configuration (*ps* < 0.02). In the form $y = mx + c$, these empirical equations are:

$$\text{for } lt: B = 1.65 (l - r) + h + 13.93,$$

$$\text{for } ls: B = 2.42 (l - r) + h + 13.86,$$

where B (Boundary) = height of subjects' response, $(l - r)$ = height difference in the stimulus, and h = height of the left line. The height of the subject-generated boundary increased linearly with increases in the difference between stimulus elements.

Response variability, measured by the standard deviation of all responses to each stimulus, also increased with stimulus variability (*ps* <0.01 according to ANOVA). Repeating the preceding analysis but with variability rather than mean category placements as the dependent variable provided the following equations:

$$\text{for } lt, v = .30 (l - r) + 4.03$$

$$\text{for } ls, v = .42 (l - r) + 3.66$$

where v = variability measured as standard deviation of responses.

The subjects had been instructed to make their decision reliably but quickly. These response times also increased linearly with stimulus variability. These equations were:

$$\text{for } lt, t = 0.034 (l - r) + 1.2$$

$$\text{for } ls, t = 0.042 (l - r) + 1.2$$

These decision times (t = response time in sec. minus an independent estimate of the time needed to draw a line of that height) ranged from 1.2 sec. (when the two stimulus lines were the same length) to 3 sec.

(when the stimulus lines were most different) for *lt* stimuli, and, respectively, from 1.2 to 3.6 sec. for *ls* stimuli.

In summary, *as the variability between lines within the stimulus increased: The boundary height increased, the variability of the boundary judgments increased, and decisions took longer.*

Relations Between Categories

The preceding JNB measures show that a category becomes wider and less well defined when the stimulus elements are made more different from one another. The summarized AI data show that the variability of category judgments increases when the stimulus range is increased. For both classes of experiments, response precision decreased when stimulus variability increased.

The following study examined whether the bounds of one category depend on the structure of another category. That is, are the boundaries that delimit a category due just to that category or are they determined by other categories? In the previous line-pair study, the subjects created the lower bound of the adjacent category. In this study, the subjects created the upper bound of that second category.

Each stimulus had three lines. These were each of the stimulus pairs in the previous study (the first category) plus the average subject-generated lower bound of the second category (the beginning of the sec-

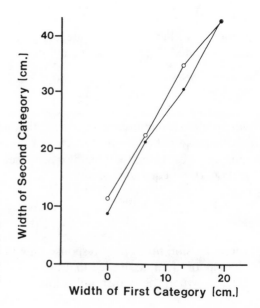

FIGURE 9.1. The width of the adjacent, second category as a function of the width of the initial category, when subjects categorized line heights by producing JNBs.

ond category) that was produced by that subject for that stimulus. The subjects drew a fourth line to represent the *upper* bound of the second category. The instruction was to make this line as tall as it could be and still belong to the second category.

The results averaged over subjects are shown in Fig. 9.1 for when the left line of the original category was shorter (filled circles) than the right line and when it was taller (open circles) than the right line. When the difference in length between the two lines in the first category increased, then the difference between the upper and lower bounds of the second category also increased. Both functions are essentially linear and both Pearson product-moment correlations are greater than 0.99.

According to these results, when the difference between the two stimulus lines in the initial category was greater, then the upper bound for the second category was greater and the difference between it and the lower bound for the second category was also greater. *When the first category is wide, the second category is also wide.*

We attempted to extend this observation to a third category; however, the oscilloscope was not tall enough and the subjects ran out of space when attempting to generate a fifth line. The absence of those data notwithstanding, it is interesting to speculate that additional categories might be added in the same way as was this second category. If so, then the structure of a third category would also depend proportionally on that of the first category. This might be the general case for natural categories of related stimuli. If these results were to so generalize, then the categories would be nested so that measures of one category would imply measures of all categories. One expectation of this outcome is that category memberships of new stimuli would seldom be confused.

Such speculation aside, it is appropriate to conclude for these stimuli that *the width of one category is directly proportional to the variation between members of the adjacent category.* This is consistent with the Gestalt principle of grouping. Whether particular items will be grouped together does not depend on attribute values or features; rather, it depends on relations with the other elements in the situation. These results suggests that those relations are lawful and might be measured by the JNB procedure.

JNBs AND THE STIMULUS DOMAIN

In AI data, the quality of identification performance is inversely proportional to stimulus range. This has been demonstrated for brightness, pitch, loudness, extent, numerosity, duration, area, and vibration. Thus, the result is independent of the continuous stimulus domain.

If JNBs and AIs reflect a common process, which is a thesis here, then JNB effects should also be independent of domain. The JNBs summarized previously were for groupings of dots and of lines. In this section, JNBs are reported for flicker rate, loudness, brightness, tone duration, time between tones, and, once more, dot separations. To anticipate, category boundaries were directly proportional to stimulus variability in each study. The effect appears to be independent of stimulus domain.

JNBs for Intervals

JNBs were examined for intervals of time and space. The spatial study repeated the previous dot study. This was to test reliability of those results and to allow comparison of performance on different tasks by the same subjects. The temporal study examined auditory beeps separated in time. Eight subjects performed each task. Four people did the tone tasks first and the other four people performed the dot tasks first.

Beeps in Time. Each tone was a 50-msec. duration, 1000 Hz sinewave at an intensity of about 60 dB. These brief tones were called beeps by the subjects. There were three conditions. In each condition, each trial consisted of three beeps. These were two experimenter determined tones that began and ended the trial and an intermediate tone at a position in time determined by the subject.

In one condition, the subjects placed the adjustable second beep, by manipulating a joy stick left–right, at that point in time when it was heard as *just* grouped with the first beep, leaving the third beep by itself. In the second condition, the subjects placed the second beep at that point in time when it was heard as just grouped with the last beep, leaving the first beep by itself. In the third condition, each subject adjusted the middle beep so that the three beeps were heard as equally spaced in time. For each condition, the three tones cycled, with 3 seconds between trials, until the subject indicated being satisfied with the position of the middle tone by pressing a key.

Each task was performed at two stimulus ranges. The outer beeps were separated by either 1 second or 2 seconds.

Dots in Space. For this dot study, the subjects performed the same three conditions as in the beep study, but with a spatial array of three dots presented on a computer screen, rather than a temporal array of three beeps presented over headphones. As in the beep study, there were two stimulus ranges. The outer dots were separated by either 3.5 cm. or 7 cm. The subject manipulated the joy stick to move the dot back and forth until satisfied with the position and then pressed the response key.

Results. The average points along the continuum at which grouping and bisection occurred, measured as proportions of the physical range between the experimenter's reference stimuli, are shown for both stimulus sets in Table 9.1.

According to a repeated measures analysis of variance, there was a numerically small but statistically significant ($p < 0.01$) difference between the grouping points of the temporal stimuli and the grouping points of the spatial stimuli. There was no reliable effect of stimulus range on any ratio. Overall, the grouping point for the tone beeps at both ranges was 0.58 (S.D. = 0.02) and the average grouping point for the dots in space was 0.63 (S.D. = 0.01).

Tone Durations

The beep and dot studies examined JNBs for empty intervals of space and time. This study examined JNBs for filled intervals. Four subjects grouped three 1000 Hz tones that varied in duration. There were three inter-tone (offset-onset) interval conditions, 0.25 0.5, and 1 second.

The conditions examined before with beeps and dots were also examined here. Subjects selected the duration of the second tone so that it was just grouped with the duration of the first tone or with that of the last tone and so that it was perceived to be the average of the first and third durations. Stimuli were presented in random order. Each subject

TABLE 9.1
The Mean Grouping Positions for Beeps and Dots at Each Stimulus Range.

		Responses as a Percentage of the Total Range			
Task	Stimulus Range	Grouped with First Beep or Dot	Midway	Grouped with Last Beep or Dot	Mean Ratio**
Tones	1000 msec	39(61)*	49	57	.59
in time	2000 msec	42(58)	49	57	.58
				Average Ratio = .58	
Dots	100 units	37(63)	51	64	.63
in space	200 units	38(62)	51	63	.62
				Average Ratio = .63	

*Numbers in parentheses are 100 minus this grouping for comparison with the "last beep" numbers.

**[(100 − first grouping point) + (last grouping point)/2]

made four responses per condition. The short duration tone was always presented first. The results are shown in Table 9.2.

No consistent differences in grouping ratio with varying range were detected according to a repeated measures analysis of variance (all $ps >$ 0.1). Overall, the grouping ratio was 0.64 (S.D. = 0.03). This number is similar to all other grouping ratios that have been measured. However, unlike most other studies, this 0.64 is an average of individual numbers that were very different from this value. The grouping numbers were different when the first two tones were grouped than they were when the last two tones were grouped. Because the short duration tone was always presented first, this might reflect a perceptual error associated with stimulus order. If so, the perceived ratios might have been identical for the two cases.

JNBs for Loudness: Actual and Estimated Grouping Points

Only one stimulus order was used in the preceding duration study, short followed by long. Here, with loudnesses of 1000 Hz tones as the stimulus domain, grouping points were examined both when the first tone was quiet and when the first tone was loud.

These first and third tones were 50 and 60 (or 60 and 50) dB in intensity. Using the joy stick control, the subjects could vary the middle tone continuously between 50 and 60 dB. They adjusted the middle tone until it was *just* quiet enough or *just* loud enough, depending on the condition, to appear grouped with the quieter end-tone or with the louder end-tone.

After each response, each subject estimated the percentage distance of his or her selected boundary tone from quiet to loud or from loud to quiet, depending on the particular JNB condition. For example, for the quiet to loud sequence, the instruction was to imagine that the tones were on a continuum with the quiet end-tone at 0% and the loud end-tone at 100%. The question was, "at what percentage along this continuum is your just-grouped tone?" The subjects typed their responses on a keyboard.

Results and Discussion. The averaged results are shown in Table 9.3. The dB scale is logarithmic in energy but is treated here as linear to better approximate discriminability differences. Using this scale, the mean ratio for the actual grouping point was 0.64. This average is similar to the results of the studies reported earlier. However, as was also the case for tone durations, this 0.64 is the average of very different numbers. When

TABLE 9.2
The Mean Responses When a Tone Duration Was Selected as Just-Grouped
With the Shorter or Longer Duration Tone, and When the Duration
Midpoint Was Estimated

Inter-Tone interval	Stimulus Range	Response as a Percentage of the Total Range			Mean Grouping Ratio
		Short	Midpoint	Long	
	700 msec.*	13(87)	32	43	.65
250 msec	(300–1000 msec.)	**	17	34	.62
	800 msec.	10(90)	17	34	.62
	(200–1000 msec				
	900 msec.	19(81)	27	41	.61
	(100–1000 msec.)				
500 msec	700 msec.	18(82)	32	55	.69
	800 msec.	21(79)	31	52	.66
	900 msec.	27(73)	36	49	.66
1000 msec	700 msec.	20(80)	39	44	.62
	800 msec.	25(75)	38	58	.67
	900 msec.	26(74)	32	48	.61
		Average ratio = .64			

*For this example: The first tone was sounded for 300 msec, then there was 250 msec of silence, then the adjustable tone was presented for the duration selected by the subject, then another 250 msec of silence, and then the third tone was sounded for 1000 msec. Following a 2 sec. interval during which the subject could move the joystick left or right to decrease or increase the duration of the second tone the sequence repeated. This cycle continued until the subject pressed the interrupt key to indicate the response.

**Numbers in parentheses are 100 minus this grouping for comparison with the long duration numbers.

the middle tone was grouped with the quiet one, the intensity percentage of the JNB was 34.8 if the quiet tone was first but was 24.8 if the quiet tone was last. When grouping was with the loud tone, these numbers were 50.9 and 62.9.

When the subjects estimated the two percentage distances, there was little if any effect of order. The average perceived ratio was 0.81 and all four judgments that produced this average were nearly identical. This 0.81 perception is in striking contrast to the physical average of 0.64.

These results suggest two factors. One factor is that configuration affects loudness, and boundary judgments are made in terms of perceived intensities (loudness) rather than actual intensities. This is indicated by the interaction between the grouping point and stimulus order. That is, stimulus order affects perceived loudness and grouping is in terms of the perception. The second factor suggested is that elements perceived as grouped are, additionally, perceived as overly similar. This is suggested by the subject's underestimation of physical differences between the

280

TABLE 9.3
Mean JNB Intensities, in dB, When the Middle Tone was Judged
as Grouped With the Quieter Tone, as Separated Equally Between
the Tones, or as Grouped With the Louder Tone (Top Panel), and
the Mean of the Subjects' Numerical Estimates of the Two
Grouping Proportions (Bottom Panel).

| SPL | Actual Percentage of Total Range | | | |
	Quiet	Medium	Loud	Mean
50–60	34.8 (65.2)*	53	62.9	.64
60–50	24.8 (75.2)	37.7	50.9	.63
				Mean = .64

| SPL | Estimated Percentage of Total Range | | |
	Quiet	Loud	Mean
50–60	17.8 (82.2)	78.0	.80
60–50	17.8 (82.2)	82.8	.82
			Mean = .81

*Numbers in parentheses are 100 minus this grouping for comparison with the loud grouping numbers.

grouped tones. This is the expected result if grouped elements assimilate toward one another.

Summary of the JNB Results

In each JNB study, subject-generated boundaries were directly proportional to stimulus variability. Although there are other effects, such as numerical differences associated with stimulus order and modality differences, the similarities between the several JNBs are much more striking than the differences. Also, when JNBs are averaged across stimulus orders, the observed proportions are impressively similar across the several studies. To better reveal this similarity, the JNBs that have been

TABLE 9.4
The Average JNB in Each Study.

First dot study	0.64
Beept in time	0.58
Dots in space	0.63
Tone durations	0.64
Loudness in time	0.64
Mean grouping point = 0.626	

measured to date are summarized in Table 9.4. The average of these ratios is 0.626. As discussed later, in the GENERAL DISCUSSION section, this ratio is numerically close to the golden section, 0.618.

MULTIDIMENSIONAL STIMULI AND CATEGORY BOUNDS

The JNB and AI studies discussed previously used stimuli that varied on a single physical dimension. In each univariate case, response precision decreased when stimulus variability increased. If this is a generalizable observation, then stimulus and response variabilities should also be related when multidimensional stimuli are examined. This section summarizes two classification studies using multidimensional stimuli and in which stimulus variability was manipulated between conditions. In one study, people classified rectangles that varied in height and width. In the other study, people classified names of animals that varied in similarity.

Classifying Rectangles

FORMATED-LINE/ This study was constructed to examine the classification of multidimensional patterns as a function of stimulus variability. The experiment was conducted by Paul Gruenewald (1978) and was partially reported by Gruenewald and Lockhead (1977).

The stimuli for the many:1 mapping tasks were selected from the 25 rectangular forms indicated in Fig. 9.2. There were six stimulus sets with four rectangles each. Three of the sets, labeled A, B, and C, are those rectangles shown with the member stimuli connected by solid lines in Fig. 9.2. These are called non-spread sets. The variability between stimuli within each of these sets is relatively small.

To increase the variability between stimuli within each category, spread sets were created by substituting two new rectangles for two of the original forms in each non-spread set. These spread sets are indicated by the dotted lines connecting the old (substituted-for) stimuli to the new (substituted-with) stimuli. These stimulus sets are identified as A', B', and C'. The variability between members within each of these sets is relatively large.

The different sets were sorted against each other in 12 tasks having various levels of between- and within-category variability. Using the notation AB to indicate that members of category A are sorted against members of category B, the 12 tasks examined were AB, AC, BC (non-spread sets); A'B', A'C', B'C' (spread sets); and A'B, A'C, AB', AC', B'C, BC' (mixed sets).

There were six subjects. Half did the 12 tasks in one order, the other

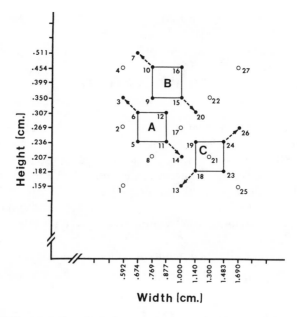

FIGURE 9.2. The physical parameter space for the rectangles in the speeded-classification task. Solid lines connect the four stimuli used in the non-spread groups, A, B, And C. Dashed lines indicate stimuli that replaced the connected ones in the spread groups, A', B', C'.

half did the 12 tasks in the reverse order. For each task, rectangles were presented one at a time on an oscilloscope screen. Following practice, the subjects responded to 120 random stimulus presentations for each condition. The instruction was to press the appropriate one of two buttons as quickly and accurately as possible.

Separately, each subject also gave similarity ratings to the 27 stimuli indicated in Fig. 9.2. All possible pairwise combinations of rectangles were presented and the subject rated the similarity between them by assigning a number from 1 to 7.

Results. The overall mean correct sorting times and error rates were 371 ms. and 13.6% of responses, respectively. Correct sorting times and errors were correlated, r = 0.79. According to a mixed factorial analysis of variance, there were significant main effects ($p < 0.01$) of variability within categories and of variability between categories.

The similarity data of the six subjects were submitted to an INDSCAL analysis using the ALSCAL similarity scaling program (Takane, Young, & de Leeuw, 1977). A two-dimensional solution provided a reasonable fit to the data and was used for all analyses.

The stimulus coordinates and subject weights from this scaling solution were used to compute mean values of d(B) and d(W) for each subject and task. The measure d(B) was calculated as the sum of all similarity distances between each item in one category and all items in the other category. This provides a measure of the difference or variability *B*etween categories for each task. For example, in comparing sets A, B, and C, d(B) was smallest for A versus B, next smallest for A versus C, and largest for B versus C.

To determine intra-category variabilities, the distance between members *W*ithin each set was calculated as the sum of the distances between each member and all other members of that set. This measure, called d(W), was larger for A', B', and C' respectively, than, for A, B, and C. This provided a measure of the variability of items within each category.

These measures were used to evaluate the thesis that performance is a joint function of stimulus variabilities between and within categories. Simple correlations between these measures across subjects and tasks revealed a negative correlation between d(B) and correct sorting times ($r = -0.44$) and a positive correlation between d(W) and correct sorting times ($r = 0.35$). The correlation between d(B) and d(W) was small ($r = -0.12$).

A Classification Model.   The total distance, d(T), between all stimuli in each rectangle sorting task can be defined as:

$$d(T) = d(B) + d(W).$$

Consistent with the empirical fact that response variability in 1:1 mapping tasks using unidimensional stimuli is directly proportional to stimulus variability, discriminability between stimulus sets is described here by the expression:

$$D(B) = d(B)/d(T)$$

and, for many:1 mapping tasks, this is extended to the expression:

$$D(B) = d(B)/[d(W) + d(B)]$$

where D(B) is the predicted discriminability between groups.

This model states that any increase in variability between stimuli within a category, d(W), that is not accompanied by a commensurate increase in the distance between categories, d(B), produces a decline in sorting performance (cf. Gruenewald, 1978, 104–109).

An analysis of the within subjects' variance, regressing correct sorting times on the independent measures d(B) and d(W), was calculated for each subject. The previous model provided the estimate that 44% of the within subject's variance in sorting time can be accounted for by d(B) and d(W). The actual and predicted sorting times are shown in Table 9.5; the correlation between these measures is r = 0.84.

Summary. Classification performance depends on these two variability measures: (a) when the categories is to be sorted separately are perceptually different from one another, d(B), then classification is fast and accurate; and (b) when members of the same category are perceptually different from one another, d(W), then classification is slow and imprecise. Furthermore, these effects can compensate one for the other. A performance improvement due to an increase in d(B) can be reduced or eliminated by a concomitant increase in d(W).

Categorizing Words.

An analogous result to this one with rectangles has been reported when words were the stimuli (King, Gruenewald, & Lockhead, 1978). The stimuli were 40 animal names that were scaled for similarity. Figure 9.3 shows the 40 names and their locations on dimensions 1 and 3 of the three-dimensional scaling solution that resulted when the similarity judgments were scaled using the ALSCAL program (Takane, Young, & deLeeuw, 1977). These displayed dimensions suggest that size and predacity are important underlying semantic dimensions (cf. Henley, 1969). Dimension 2 of the scaling solution separated smooth-skinned

TABLE 9.5
Mean Correct Sorting Times (RT), Predicted Sorting Times (RT'),
Average Distances Between, d(B), and Average Distances Within,
d(W), Sorted Sets in the Rectangle Classification Study.

Task*	RT	RT'	d(B)	d(W)
A'B'	434	456	2.00	1.44
A'C'	404	389	2.05	1.12
B'C'	378	370	2.26	1.23
A'B'	481	433	1.92	1.23
AC'	357	356	2.05	0.95
B'C'	306	319	2.35	1.04
AB'	422	329	1.98	1.27
A'C	369	382	1.89	0.92
BC'	292	308	2.38	1.02
AB	388	406	1.90	1.06
AC	348	352	1.90	0.76
BC	279	261	2.45	0.82

*Refer to Fig. 9.3 for stimulus set identifications.

FIGURE 9.3. The spatial representation of dimensions 1 (predacity) and 3 (size) from the three-dimensional scaling solution of the similarity judgments of the noted 40 words. Circles and squares denote animals classified as nice and nasty; filled and open figures denote animals classified as big and little, respectively. (From King et al., 1978, with permission).

animals from those with fur or feathers, suggesting skin characteristics as another important underlying dimension.

Different people than those who did the similarity scaling sorted the words in 12 conditions as described next. The 40 names were divided into the four groups of 10 names each that are indicated by the filled and open circles and squares in Fig. 9.3. This provided a 2 × 2 matrix having two levels of size (big and little) and two levels of predacity (nasty and nice). Hence, this is called the Big-Little-Nasty-Nice, or BLNN, study.

These assignments of animal names to cells of the 2 × 2 matrix were made by the experimenters before the similarity scaling had been done and do not precisely align with the similarity solution. Two obvious discrepancies are "turkey" and "bluejay." The experimenters classified turkey as large and bluejay as nasty. In the scaling solution, however, turkey is near small animals and bluejay is near nice animals. Perhaps these subjects grew up in cities.

The classifications shown by the open and filled squares and circles in Fig. 9.3 were used in the sorting tasks. The similarities as measured by the three-dimensional solution of the similarity judgments, two dimensions of which are shown in Fig. 9.3, were used to predict response times and error rates.

The 2 × 2 arrangement, BLNN, provided nine sorting tasks: four univariate, two correlated, two orthogonal, and one condensation. These tasks are defined as follows: In *univariate tasks*, stimuli differ on only one dimension. An example is when words labeled with filled dots (nice, big animals such as deer and flamingo) are sorted against words labeled with filled squares (nasty, big animals such as crocodile and vulture). These words differ only on the nasty–nice dimension. There are four such univariate tasks; these are each row and column of the 2 × 2 matrix. Thus, only two of the four cells in the matrix are involved in any univariate task.

Correlated tasks also use only two of the four cells. There are two correlated conditions, the major and minor diagonals of the matrix. Members of these categories differ from one another along two dimensions. Either nice-little animals are sorted against nasty-big ones (e.g., kitten vs. shark), or nice-big animals are contrasted with little-nasty ones (e.g., cow vs. eel).

Orthogonal tasks use all four cells of the matrix. There are two orthogonal conditions. In one, subjects classified animals as nice or nasty independent of size; in the other, subjects classified animals as large or small independent of precacity. This is frequently called a filtering task, a name that presumes—erroneously, I believe—a process of active rejection of an attribute.

Condensation tasks also use all four cells. Both large-nasty and small-nice animals belong to one category, and small-nasty and large-nice animals belong to the other category. For example, crocodile and robin are assigned one response, while collie and eel are assigned the other response.

Because some conditions use four cells whereas others use only two cells, there were different numbers of stimuli available for some tasks than others. In order to have the same number of words in all tasks, each cell of the 2 × 2 matrix was divided in two sets of five words. For the orthogonal and condensation tasks (four-cell conditions), each five-word set in one cell was paired with a five-word set in each other cell. This provided two different 10-item sets for the tasks using all four cells.

In order to use also all 40 words in all tasks, the orthogonal and condensation conditions were conducted twice, once with each subset of words.

These procedures resulted in 12 tasks having two sets of 10 words each. These were four univariate conditions, two correlated conditions, two sets of the two orthogonal conditions, and two sets of the two condensation conditions. Each of 12 paid observers served in each task according to a Latin square order. Prior to each task, the subject was given a card with the words to be classified arranged into two columns. The subject studied this list as long as desired before beginning the session, and the list was available throughout the session. When the study began, the stimulus words appeared one at a time in random order on an oscilloscope screen. The observer responded to each word by pressing one of two buttons as quickly and accurately as possible. There were 20 presentations of each of the 20 words to each subject in each condition.

Results. Distances between words in the three-dimensional similarity scaling solution were used as the measure of distances between stimuli. These measures were used to calculate d(W) for each sorted group and to calculate d(B) for each condition as described in the rectangle study. These results are shown in Table 9.6.

The d(B) measures were largest for the correlated tasks, smaller for the orthogonal tasks, still smaller for the univariate tasks, and smallest of all for the condensation tasks.

The d(W) measures were largest for the condensation sets and next largest for the orthogonal sets, and smallest for the correlated and univariate sets.

Sorting Times. Over the 12 tasks, the correlations between sorting times and d(B) and d(W) were −0.45 and 0.76, respectively. The correlation of d(B) with d(W) was 0.18. The multiple correlation between d(B), d(W), and sorting times was 0.99. With d(B) partialed out, the correlation of times with d(W) was 0.99; with d(W) partialed out, times and d(B) correlated −0.99.

Errors. The multiple correlation was 0.76. That with d(B) partialed out was 0.75; that with d(W) partialed out was −0.45.

Model Prediction. The multiple regression equations for d(B) and d(W) with response times and errors were calculated for six two-cell tasks, the univariate and correlated conditions. Predicted response times and errors for all 12 tasks were then calculated based on these equations.

TABLE 9.6

Measures of the Average Distance Between Groups, B, the Average
Distance Between Items Within Groups, W, Average Response Times in
msec., RT, Predicted Response Times, RT', Average Errors, E, and
Predicted Errors, E', in Each BLNN Task.

Task	B	W	RT	RT'	E	E'
Univariate						
nice vs. nasty big animals	2.51	1.53	299	301	4.92	4.28
nice vs. nasty little animals	2.36	1.46	297	300	3.58	4.14
big vs. little nice animals	2.11	1.29	295	294	4.75	4.92
big vs. little nasty animals	2.35	1.71	333	330	4.75	4.92
Correlated						
little-nice/big-nasty	2.99	1.39	263	260	3.42	3.58
big-nice/little-nasty	2.90	1.61	288	290	4.42	4.31
Orthogonal						
big vs. little (a)*	2.65	1.89	305	335	3.25	5.30
(b)	2.51	2.18	326	376	4.08	6.27
nice vs. nasty (a)	2.63	1.91	313	339	4.67	5.38
(b)	2.73	1.94	300	337	4.92	5.41
Condensation big-nice, little-nasty/ little-nice, big-nasty						
(a)	2.32	2.25	482	394	6.08	6.59
(b)	2.33	2.39	580	409	7.50	7.02

Note: RT' = 115.55W − 51.64B + 253.64; E' = 3.07W − 0.55B + 0.96. *(a)
and (b) denote one each of the two sets of words in these 4-cell tasks.

These predictions and the observed average response times and error
rates for each condition are shown in Table 9.6.

Discussion. When the similarity difference between sorted groups,
d(B), increased, performance improved. When the difference between
items within a group, d(W), increased, performance became worse.

It should be noted that this performance increase with d(B) does not
indicate that more precise judgments are made. This is because there are
only two categories in these studies and so there is no opportunity to
measure precision. Response precision can be measured in three category tasks. There, when one stimulus is made more different from the
other two, discriminability between the unchanged stimuli becomes
worse (Lockhead & Hinson, 1986). That is for 1:1 mappings. Such a
study has not been reported using many:1 mappings.

Performance on the different tasks in this study is consistent with the literature. Correlated sets are usually easiest, univariate sets next, then orthogonal tasks, and finally the condensation task (Garner, 1974, describes such results and some discrepancies from them). This performance pattern was again found here with ten stimuli per cell. Correlated tasks were performed fastest (275 msec. per response on average), the univariate tasks were next (306 msec.), then the orthogonal tasks (311 msec.), and finally the condensation task (531 msec.).

The predictions based on d(B) and d(W) reflect this pattern, the rank order in Table 9.6 is perfect. However, the numerical predictions are far from perfect. The linear model underestimated the actual sorting times in the condensation tasks by quite a lot. Either the model is wrong or the measures used are noisy or non-linearly related.

If this model is not fundamentally wrong, then similarity measures should account for the frequently observed order correlated-univariate-orthogonal-condensation. They apparently do. When such studies have been examined for similarity, the correlated stimuli were found more different from the univariate stimuli. This predicts that correlated tasks are easier than univariate tasks. Further, d(W) was zero in those univariate and correlated tasks. Because they used 1:1 mappings, there was only one stimulus per category. However, d(W) was real in the orthogonal and condensation tasks because then there were two stimuli per category. The preceding model predicts that these many:1 tasks (orthogonal and condensation) are more difficult than the 1:1 tasks (univariate and correlated).

Although similarity measures and sorting tasks have often been confounded in the literature, this is not necessary. There are studies where the stimuli for the 2 × 2 matrix were selected so that correlated stimuli were more similar than univariate stimuli. Then the correlated tasks were more difficult than the univariate tasks (Lockhead & King, 1977). This allows the conclusion that similarity, and not the logic of the task, predicts performance.

What makes stimuli perceptually similar or different, or why some elements of multi-dimensional stimuli configure differently than others which may be the same essential question, is an important but not understood problem. Whatever the reasons, similarity measures predict performance in all classification studies that have been so examined. No feature analysis or other approach suggested to date does this.

GENERAL DISCUSSION

Which stimuli will be categorized together or separately, and how readily this categorization is done, depends on stimulus variability. The judgment of what particular stimuli belong to which category was studied using the method of just noticeable boundaries. How readily a stimulus is assigned to a category was examined with speeded sorting tasks. In each case considered, performance was directly proportional to stimulus variability.

Just Noticeable Boundaries

When people generated boundaries to separate categories, the boundary selected was directly proportional to stimulus variability. More variable stimulus sets were assigned wider separations between the category bounds, and the variability of these judgments and the time to produce them increased. Furthermore, the width of an adjacent category also increased when the variability of its neighbor category was increased.

For simple JNB situations, these boundary placements were not just proportional to the stimulus measures. The same particular proportion was found in each study, approximately 0.63. This value is numerically similar to the golden section, 0.618. Rather than this being simply happenstance, these data might reflect the golden section. This is that unique number for which the ratio of the smaller section to the larger section equals the ratio of the larger section to the whole, $0.38196/0.61803 = 0.61803/1$.

If this proportional nesting of a category within its adjacent category really is a basis for boundary placements in JNB tasks, it could reflect a balance point to apportion categories. This would provide categories that are independent of scale and would allow the generation of new categories such that each category stands in a fixed proportion to the other. In that case, the number of categories could change without affecting any of the relations between them.

Independent of this or any other inferences concerning the golden section (see Gaylord & Lockhead, 1987), the JNB data clearly show that more variable stimulus sets are further separated from one another than are less variable sets. The data further show that this increase in category width is consistently accompanied by an increase in the variability of the boundary judgments. This proportional relation between category boundaries and stimulus variability is consistent with Weber's law, except for categories rather than individual stimuli.

Categorization Tasks

In absolute identification tasks, and in speeded sorting tasks, unlike JNB tasks, the subjects cannot choose what category an element belongs to and cannot decide where category boundaries should be placed along stimulus continua. Those are determined by the experimenter or by the environment. In addition, there are often several categories in such tasks so that any reference the subject may use in judging can change from trial to trial. Such complications make it difficult at best to demonstrate a dependence on the golden section in these tasks, even if there is a dependence.

The golden section is a particular proportion that, even if it is relevant to category judgments, is masked by these complexities. It is difficult to support the idea of a particular proportion when categories have been fixed by the experimenter. However, such judgments could still be proportional, with the particular proportion depending on particulars of the stimulus set. JNB data collected when one category was determined by the experimenter are consistent with this suggestion. With the first category given by the experimenter, the subject-generated boundaries for the category were directly proportional to the variability of the first category, with the particular proportionality depending on the condition. For example, the proportionality constant in the linear equation describing boundary positions was different for tall-short lines than for short-tall lines, and was again different for other tasks (cf. Gaylord & Lockhead, 1987). Yet, in each instance, response variability was some direct proportion of stimulus variability.

The same result was found in AI data and sorting data. Response variability was again directly proportional to stimulus variability. In AI tasks (1:1 mappings), increased stimulus variability resulted in poorer discriminability of fixed stimuli in the set. In sorting tasks (1:1 and many:1 mappings), increasing the stimulus range, as when shifting from univariate to orthogonal tasks, again resulted in poorer performance in classifying a stimulus element.

In general, if the perceived structure of the stimuli is defined (definition of the physical domain is often not sufficient; Monahan & Lockhead, 1977), it appears possible to predict performance in mapping tasks.

This framework is applicable to several experimental problems. For example, Dixon and Just (1978) showed that the ability of people to judge whether pairs of ellipses are the same or different width is a function of the variation in ellipse height. If the ellipses vary over a large range of heights, then the task is difficult. In another same–different task, Crist (1981) showed that the ability to report that two letters are physically identical or, in other conditions, belong to the same category, again depends on $d(B)$.

Comparative judgments have also been reported in which people indicate the ordering of stimulus pairs according to some attribute of the stimulus set. With stimuli varying in size, and subjects instructed to indicate which of two stimuli appears larger, Moyer (1973) showed that comparison judgments are more difficult when the stimuli are perceived as near each other along the perceptual continuum. He attributed this to an "internal psychophysical" representation of the sizes of real objects. We measure this as d(B).

For complex stimuli as well, the difficulty of comparison judgments is related to the range of the comparison dimension(s). Comparisons are easier in the context of a small range than that of a large range. Similarly, "anchor" effects due to the relative discriminability of items along a continuum (Murdock, 1960) are also found in comparative judgment tasks.

When the range of the comparison dimension is held constant, variations in an irrelevant dimension (orthogonal vs. univariate sorting tasks) increase d(W). This results in more difficult judgments because the variations along the second dimension increase total range and thus decrease relative discriminability between members of the stimulus set. This is consistent with many sorting tasks using geometric stimuli (Garner, 1974) and with the BLNN data summarized here.

That predictions based on d(B) and d(W) may apply to more complex tasks is suggested by the pervasiveness of range or variance effects in many judgment situations (Parducci, 1963, 1983; Eiser and Stroebe, 1972). However, extension of the model to very complex domains, such as verbal sentences or social situations, is not without difficulty. An important reason is that, at least to date, the model is a response-response model, and similarity measures are needed. There is a question as to whether similarity judgments of complex stimuli reflect a multidimensional representation of stimuli (Krumhansl, 1978) or if they reflect differences between stimuli on heterogeneous collections of features conditional on the particular stimulus pair presented (Tversky and Gati, 1983; Sjoberg and Thorslund, 1979). Although the former position is conveniently compatible with the needs of the model, the latter is not.

The conditions of a feature model, however, do not eliminate the possibility for dimensional variation among complex stimuli. That a mouse and an elephant differ by the presence or absence of a trunk, among other features, does not preclude the evident possibility that they may still be scaled according to their sizes. Complex stimuli are complex because, among other reasons, both features and dimensions are involved in their representation (Garner, 1978). Further, it is clear from extensive scalings of complex terms that general dimensions do emerge in geometrical representations of similarity of verbal items (see particularly Fillenbaum & Rapoport, 1971; Henley, 1969; Smith, Shoben, & Rips, 1974; Rumelhart & Abrahamson, 1973). These general dimensions would appear to represent aspects of the stimulus set common to most of the scaled items.

This is consistent with the BLNN study, in which animal names were used in a speeded sorting task. Measures of d(B) and d(W) derived from similarity judgments accounted for much of the variance in the response times and errors in that study.

To summarize, the more stimuli differ from one another, the more difficult it is for people to precisely identify their magnitudes or to establish precise boundaries separating them. The JNB data demonstrate that the position of the subject created boundary, the variability of that judgment, and the time taken to make it, all increase in proportion to the variability among the stimuli being categorized. For simple, univariate stimuli, these JNB judgments produce categories that may reflect the golden section.

JNB data collected when a category is determined by the experimenter, absolute judgment data, and sorting data are also consistent with the preceding observation. In each case examined, response variability was directly proportional to stimulus variability, with the particular variability dependent on the stimulus set and the particular task. Taken together, the results suggest that a fundamental nature of the categorization of continuous or integral domains is one of proportionalities.

ACKNOWLEDGMENTS

Supported in part by AFOSR 84-0302. I thank Susan Gaylord and Paul Gruenewald for their many contributions.

REFERENCES

Ackrill, J.L. (1963). *Aristotle's Categories and De Interpretatione* (transl.) Oxford: Clarendon Press.
Berlin, B., & Kay, P. (1969). *Basic color terms: Their universality and evolution.* Berkeley, CA: University of California Press.
Bourne, L.E., Jr. (1968). *Human conceptual behavior.* Boston: Allyn and Bacon.
Bruner, J.S., Goodnow, J.J., & Austin, G.A. (1956). *A study of thinking.* New York: Wiley.
Crist, W.B. (1981). Matching performance and the similarity structure of the stimulus set. *Journal of Experimental Psychology: General, 110,* 269–296.
Dixon, P., & Just, M. (1978). Normalization of irrelevant dimensions in stimulus comparisons. *Journal of Experimental Psychology: Human Perception and Performance, 4,* 36–46.
Eiser, J., & Strobe, W. (1972). *Categorization and social judgment.* New York: Academic Press.

Fechner, G. (1966). *Elements of psychophysics*. Volume I. (H.E. Adler, Trans.). New York: Holt, Rinehart, and Winston, Inc.

Fillenbaum, S., & Rapoport, A. (1971). *Structures in the subjective lexicon*. New York: Academic Press.

Garner, W.R. (1974). *The processing of information and structure*. New York: Wiley.

Garner, W.R. (1978). Aspects of a stimulus: Features, dimensions and configurations. In E. Rosch & B.B. Lloyd (Eds.), *Cognition and categorization*. New York: Wiley.

Gaylord, S.A., & Lockhead, G.R. (1987). *On the formation of natural categories*. Unpublished manuscript.

Gravetter, F., & Lockhead, G.R. (1973). Criterial range as a frame of reference for stimulus judgment. *Psychological Review, 80*, 203–216.

Gruenewald, P.G. (1978). *The classification of multidimensional stimuli*. Unpublished doctoral dissertation, Duke University, Durham, NC.

Gruenewald, P.G., & Lockhead, G.R. (1977). *Sorting perceptual sets*. Bulletin of the Psychonomic Society, 258.

Henley, N.M. (1969). A psychological study of the semantics of animal terms. *Journal of Verbal Learning and Verbal Behavior, 8*, 176–184.

Hinson, J.M., & Lockhead, G.R. (1986). Range effects in successive discrimination. *Journal of Experimental Psychology: Animal Behavior Processes, 12*, 270–276.

King, M.C., Gruenewald, P., & Lockhead, G.R. (1978). Classifying related stimuli. *Journal of Experimental Psychology: Human Learning and Memory, 4*, 417–427.

Krumhansl, C.L. (1978). Concerning the applicability of geometric models to similarity data: The interrelationship between similarity and spatial density. *Psychological Review, 85*, 445–463.

Lockhead, G.R., & Hinson, J.M. (1986). Range and sequence effects in judgment. *Perception & Psychophysics, 40*, 53–61.

Lockhead, G.R., & King, M.C. (1977). Classifying integral stimuli. *Journal of Experimental Psychology: Human Perception and Performance, 3*, 436–443.

Monahan, J.S., & Lockhead, G.R. (1977). Identification of integral stimuli. *Journal of Experimental Psychology: General, 106*, 94–110.

Moyer, R.S. (1973). Comparing objects and memory: Evidence suggesting an internal psychophysics. *Perception & Psychophysics, 13*, 180–184.

Murdock, B.B., Jr. (1960). The distinctiveness of stimuli. *Psychological Review, 67*, 16–31.

Parducci, A. (1963). Range-frequency compromise in judgment. *Psychological Monographs, 7* (Whole No. 565).

Parducci, A. (1983). Category ratings and the relational character of judgment. In H-G Geissler & V. Sarris (Eds.), *Modern trends in perception*. Berlin: VEB Deutscher Verlag der Wissenschaften.

Pollack, I. (1953). The information in elementary auditory displays. *Journal of the Acoustical Society of America, 24*, 765–769.

Posner, M.I., & Keele, S.W. (1970). Retention of abstract ideas. *Journal of Experimental Psychology, 83*, 304–308.

Rosch, E. (1973). On the internal structure of perceptual and semantic categories. In T.E. Moore (Ed.), *Cognitive development and the acquisition of language* (pp. 111–144). New York, NY: Academic Press.

Rumelhart, D.E., and Abrahamson, A.A. (1973). A model for analogical reasoning. *Cognitive Psychology, 5*, 1–28.

Sjoberg, L., and Thorslund, C. (1979). A classificatory theory of similarity. *Psychological Research, 40*, 223–247.

Smith, E.E., Shoben, E.J., and Rips, L.J. (1974). Structure and process in semantic memory: A feature model for semantic decisions. *Psychological Review, 81*, 214–241.

Takane, Y., Young, F.W., and deLeeuw, J. (1977). Non-metric individual differences multidimensional scaling: An alternating least squares method with optimal scaling features. *Psychometrika, 42*, 7–67.

Tversky, A. (1977). Features of similarity. *Psychological Review, 84*, 327–352.

Tversky, A., and Gati, I. (1983). Similarity, separability, and the triangle inequality. *Psychological Review, 89*, 123–154.

Wing, H. (1969). *Conceptual learning and generalization.* Unpublished doctoral dissertation, The Johns Hopkins University, Baltimore, MD.

10 ANALYTIC AND HOLISTIC PROCESSES IN CATEGORIZATION

J. David Smith
New School for Social Research

ANALYTIC AND HOLISTIC PROCESSES IN CATEGORIZATION

A distinction between analytic and holistic cognitive processes has long concerned psychologists, and is now enjoying a productive revival. The conceptualization of analytic and holistic processing that guides much of this current work comes from a distinction in the perceptual literature between dimensional separability and integrality (Garner, 1974; Lockhead, 1972; Shepard, 1964). In brief, analytic processing involves treating the stimulus in terms of its constituent properties—comparing stimuli by their values on independent dimensions that may be selectively attended. Holistic processing, by contrast, implies treating the stimulus as an integral whole or "blob" (Lockhead, 1972)—comparing stimuli in terms of their overall similarity relations rather than according to their values on independent dimensions.

To gain some idea of holistic stimulus comparisons, consider why a brother and sister look alike. Often we have a holistic impression of "family resemblance", with little appreciation as to why. Even if we can later justify the impression (the eyes or mouth are similar), this justification seems less immediate, forced, and unsatisfying. This feeling of "I don't know why, they're just alike," captures the intuition that objects can be compared as unitary wholes.

The modal task to tap analytic and holistic processing is shown in Fig. 10.1. In this free classification task, the subject is presented with three

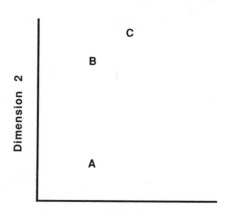

FIGURE 10.1. The structure of a free classification triad. Groupings A-B, B-C, and A-C represent dimensional, similarity, and haphazard classifications, respectively.

stimuli that vary along two dimensions, and is asked simply to put together the ones that go together. The stimuli are selected so that only one pair of stimuli (A & B) has an identical value on either dimension and a different pair (B & C) is the most similar overall in the triad of stimuli. Hence, analytic processing is revealed by a spontaneous A-B classification; holistic processing by a spontaneous B-C classification.

Studied through this and related tasks, the analytic/holistic distinction has proved useful in understanding an array of stimulus, task/set, and perceiver effects. For example, stimulus factors that govern analytic or holistic processing include stimulus integrality and complexity (both elicit holistic processing—Garner, 1974; Handel & Imai, 1972; L. Smith, 1981). Task/set factors include response speed, a concurrent cognitive load, and an impressionistic instruction set, all of which elicit more holistic processing (Smith & Kemler Nelson, 1984; Ward, 1983). Perceiver effects include developmental immaturity and impulsivity (Shepp & Swartz, 1976; L. Smith & Kemler, 1977; Smith & Kemler Nelson, 1988; Ward, 1983), both of which elicit more holistic processing.

An elegant simple principle summarizes much of this work. Holistic perceptual processing, a direct appreciation of overall similarity among objects, seems to emerge when higher, deliberate and intentional cognitive processes "let go", and a nonstrategic, fallback mode of cognition suffices instead (Kemler Nelson & Smith, in press; Smith & Kemler Nelson, in press.

In this paper, I consider analytic and holistic processes in categorization. In a categorization task, objects that vary in several attributes or dimensions (e.g., color and shape in Fig. 10.2) are grouped together as instances of Category A, Category B, and so forth. The grouping is by some similarity principle, so that objects are more like other members of their own category than like members of other categories (e.g., in Fig.

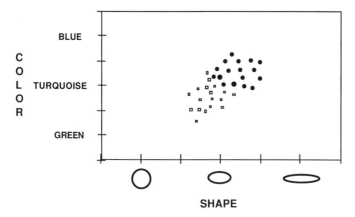

FIGURE 10.2. A hypothetical concept task, with two categories of objects varying in color and shape.

10.2, the cloud of greenish-roundish objects versus the cluster of bluish-ellipses). The learner sees these objects one at a time, and tries to use past experience with exemplars to classify new cases appropriately.

If perceptual processes are sometimes holistic, why mightn't categorization processes be? One direct link between the two domains is this: Categories are assemblages of similar objects. But they could relate by overall similarity, or by shared attributes that were quite separable and independent. Further, classifying new instances requires comparing a stimulus to some existing mental representation(s), and this process could involve either the analytic comparison of components, or a holistic judgment about overall similarity.

What might holistic categorization feel like? Most of us "know" on sight our spouse's handwriting. But we would be hard pressed to say what we know. Are there separable components to our knowledge, some weighted for selective attention but not others? It doesn't seem so—the process of recognition seems immediate, automatic, non-analytic.

In fact, we learn our spouse's handwriting *incidentally*, seeing it at 6:45 on the shaving mirror ("Pick up X at school"), on grocery lists, and so on, when our focal minds and attention are elsewhere, on the message's content. In this, we may be like children who acquire concepts like wildfire, but probably nonstrategically. Thus the following convergence with the perceptual literature might hold: that holistic concepts and categorization emerge when primitive, nonstrategic cognition holds sway during experience with the concept.

So the analytic/holistic distinction, so productive in describing perceptual processing, might also be useful in describing categorization. I evaluate that possibility from four perspectives. First, I consider several current senses of "holistic" categorization, which make weak holistic assumptions, or blend selective attention with interesting dimensional interactions, but do not describe holistic processing in any strong or pure sense. Second, I consider the common idea that less deliberate cognition elicits holistic processing. This principle, which seems general in many studies of perception, holds only selectively for categorization tasks. Third, I consider the possibility that current research underestimates the role of selective attention in categorization, and overestimates the importance of holistic nonindependence among attributes.

So with three strikes against holistic categorization, is it "out"? No, because the question outweighs the answer—the hypothesis is valuable for inviting a close analysis of the processes and representations underlying categorization and similarity calculations. In the fourth section, I consider some of these issues.

HOLISTIC CATEGORIZATION—
WHY THE VERY IDEA

Until recently, the whole idea of holistic categorization was wholly farfetched. Typical concept studies used simple stimuli, with analyzable components, some of which perfectly defined category membership. Subjects analyzed and tested hypotheses to derive a stateable classification rule (Bruner, Goodnow & Austin, 1956; Trabasso & Bower, 1968). As a result, the concept learning literature was a bastion of the analytic and abstractive thinking that long characterized cognitive psychology (Jacoby & Brooks, 1984, p. 19)—analytic for encouraging stimulus analysis; abstractive for encouraging a summary rule for a category. The focus on abstraction also tended to disallow holistic processing because abstraction processes first analyzed the stimuli of a class, then found the mean or mode of the exemplars for each dimension separately. So, all Category A colors in Figure 10.2 would yield a "greenish" average; the analyzed shapes would yield a "roundish" average. The prototype would concatenate unidimensional averages, and you can't get to holistic processing from there. But recently, four different perspectives have opened the possibility of holistic categorization.

Ill-defined Categories and Family Resemblance.   Rosch and Mervis (1975) argued that natural categories are not usually defined by a criterial attribute. Instead, they have a strong family-resemblance structure, with many attributes *usually* predicting category membership. Thus, category members share clusters of attributes, rendering them generally alike overall, but generally not like other objects. Certainly for categories with clearly defining features, selective attention and analytic processing would be especially adaptive. However, absent any defining features, it would be adaptive to smear attention broadly over many probabilistic features so as to capture the less good information each offered. It might be most adaptive, if possible, to directly apprehend overall similar objects and form them into categories, without analyzing the sources of similarity. Thus family resemblance encourages the intuition that categorization processes might be holistic (see also Kemler Nelson, 1984; Smith & Kemler Nelson, 1984).

Exemplars and Analogies.   Brooks (1978) described analytic categorization procedures by which subjects hypothesized about particular attributes and chose for full attention the most informative ones. He closely linked analysis and the abstraction of a general rule (as is usual), because the abstract rule represents special weight given to individual components.

By contrast, Brooks described nonanalytic procedures by which subjects retained specific concept instances and categorized new instances by analogy to the old. Brooks showed that exemplar memorizers classified successfully and acted just like category rules had been learned. And he specified conditions under which storing exemplars and classifying by analogy could be the learner's best bet (Brooks, 1978, 1983; Jacoby & Brooks, 1984; Reber & Allen, 1978).

The analogy strategy feels holistic in several senses. First, relaxing the abstraction assumption removes the necessity for analyzing stimuli so as to average them one dimension at a time. Second, specific cases retained in their own memory bins can retain their integrity (if not integrality) as unitary wholes, with category-relevant and category-irrelevant attributes encoded together. Finally, overall similarity by analogy seems diffusely attentive to all of the stimulus components, and contrasts with selective attention to particular attributes.

Thus, both family-resemblance and exemplar views of categorization emphasize overall similarity among stimuli, not attention to single properties. However, the underlying processes need not be considered holistic. Exemplars could be encoded as unitary wholes, and family resemblance calculated as on "integral" stimuli, with features not psychologically real or available. Or comparisons among stimuli could use independent properties serially and analytically, or in parallel but analytically.

Two different senses of holistic processing are at work here: (a) a global analysis sense, in which broad attention to many separable properties replaces selective attention to individual properties; and (b) an inte-

302   SMITH

gral sense, in which individual properties lose their immediate psychological status, and similarity is calculated among unitary wholes (see chapter 12; see also Kemler Nelson & Smith, in press; Smith & Kemler Nelson, 1988; and following). The first and weaker sense easily accounts for either family-resemblance or exemplar-based categorization. It requires stronger assumptions about the nature of exemplar storage and similarity calculations to approach more closely holistic ("integral") categorization.

Exemplars and the Context Model.   Medin and Schaffer's (1978) classification model also depended on exemplar storage and an analogy mechanism. To this exemplar/analogy frame was added a computation of similarity that is holistic, at least in assuming the nonindependence of attributes.

To see this, consider a set of stimuli varying along five equally salient binary dimensions (e.g., color—green/blue; shape—circular/elliptical; etc.). As stimuli are compared, let the output of unidimensional comparisons be 1.0 for an exact match (green-green); and .4 for a difference (circular, elliptical). How might overall similarity be computed from five of these comparisons?

Many categorization models, called independent cue models, would *add* the five results. So two stimuli having five to zero identical attributes would have overall similarities of 5, 4.4, 3.8, 3.2, 2.6, and 2.0 (Fig. 10.3 shows these similarities scaled by a factor of five for comparison's sake). Each dimensional comparison affects overall similarity independently of all others—the contextual pattern of other shared and different values does not enter the computation at all. And similarity falls off linearly as psychological distance increases. This additive similarity computation

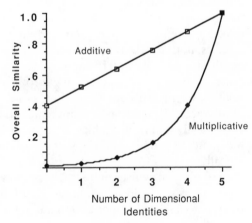

FIGURE 10.3. Overall similarity as an additive or multiplicative function of number of shared properties.

calls to mind the city-block metric that organizes distance relations among separable stimuli. Stimuli differing one step along 0–5 dimensions in a city-block space would have overall psychological distances of 0,1,2,3,4,5—unidimensional distances simply add (increase linearly).

Instead, Medin and Schaffer's context model computed the overall similarity between two stimuli by *multiplying* the results of the five dimensional comparisons. Thus, stimuli sharing five to zero attributes would have overall similarities of 1.0 (1x1x1x1x1), .4 (1x1x1x1x.4), .16, .064, .03, and .01 (see Fig. 10.3). Here, a shared value adds more overall similarity as the contextual pattern already contains more shared values between the stimuli. In this sense, similarity comparisons are holistic, because the whole context matters, the dimensions interact and are not independent. As a result, similarity, falls off exponentially as dimensional differences increase—this is the hallmark of the context model and related models (see following and Nosofsky, 1986, 1987). Identical stimuli find each other in memory with an explosive resonance of similarity that fades quite rapidly as stimulus differences accrue. Multiplicative similarity calls to mind the Euclidean metric that organizes distance relations among integral stimuli. Stimuli differing one step along 0–5 dimensions in a Euclidean space would have psychological distances of 0.0, 1.0, 1.41, 1.73, 2.00, and 2.24—the first unidimensional difference would increase psychological distance most; each successive difference less. Thus, in several senses, the context model suggests more holistic processing.

One prediction of a multiplicative rule is that an exemplar will be classified more efficiently if it is highly similar to one instance and dissimilar to a second than if it has medium similarity to two instances of a category. Analytic models of classification do not. (One can easily verify this using the two curves in Fig. 10.3).

Figure 10.4 shows the simplest concept tasks that systematically exploit such differential predictions (Kemler Nelson, 1984; Medin & Schwanenflugel, 1981). In Task A, the modal prototypes for Categories I and II are 0 0 0 and 1 1 1. If a subject accepted as category members any stimuli with two of three characteristic attributes, all exemplars would be successfully classified. Formally, these categories are linearly separable—it is possible to build a linear discriminant function that additively combines information from the three independent attributes and perfectly separates members of Category I and II.

In concept Task B, the modal prototypes are again 0 0 0 and 1 1 1. But here, a two-of-three rule will fail, because the outlier stimuli I-3 and II-3 actually share more attributes with the opposing category. In fact, the presence of complementary pairs of stimuli in Task B (stimuli I-2 and I-3; II-2 and II-3) guarantees that it is impossible to build a linear

Task A -- Categories Linearly Separable

Category I		Category II	
Structure	Stimuli	Structure	Stimuli
0 0 1	D A B	1 1 0	S E K
0 1 0	D E K	1 0 1	S A B
1 0 0	S A K	0 1 1	D E B

Sim. E_1E_1 1.67   Sim. E_2E_2 1.67

Sim. E_1E_2 1.33
Str. Ratio   1.25

Task B -- Categories Not Linearly Separable

Category I		Category II	
Structure	Stimuli	Structure	Stimuli
0 0 0	D A K	1 1 1	S E B
0 0 1	D A B	0 1 1	D E B
1 1 0	S E K	1 0 0	S A K

Sim. E_1E_1 1.67   Sim. E_2E_2 1.67

Sim. E_1E_2 1.33
Str. Ratio   1.25

FIGURE 10.4. A comparison of concept tasks built from categories that
are, or are not, linearly separable. Shown are the abstract structure of the
categories, sample nonsense-word stimuli, and the level of within-category
and between-category similarity.

discriminant function that will perfectly separate Categories I and II. To
see this, note that if one were to weight the three components of Stimulus I-3 so as to include it in Category I, the third attribute would need
heavy emphasis—so heavy in fact, that stimulus I-2 would perforce
than be judged a member of Category II.

These tasks are matched for (additive) within- and between-category
similarity. However, the NLS categories are somewhat better structured
according to multiplicative similarity, because the context model assumes that classification efficiency will be guided by the presence of
highly similar exemplars in a category. For the LS categories, there are
no within-category pairs sharing two common attributes, but six
between-category pairs do. For the NLS categories, there are two highly

similar within-category pairs, and only four between. So one might predict a performance advantage on the NLS categories. But certainly if subjects seek rules or prototypes derived from independent attributes, one would predict inefficient performance on the NLS task.

The independence assumption of many categorization models makes the outcome of experiments such as this important and surprising. Medin and Schwanenflugel (1981) reported several comparisons wherein LS categories never gave a performance advantage, and sometimes NLS categories produced superior learning. Kemler Nelson (1984) also found an NLS advantage.

Apparently, then, subjects are not always using rules and prototypes to categorize, but sometimes adopt exemplar storage and holistic/ nonindependent processing of dimensions.

The context model, though, is not strongly holistic—stimulus analysis and selective attention do have important roles. First, the stimulus properties involved are separable. Second, each unidimensional comparison is made independently. Third, these particular dimensions are obligatory, because other rotations of the axes in multidimensional space would change the result of the multiplicative similarity calculation. This is unlike the holistic processing of integral dimensions. In a Euclidean space, distances are preserved over any rigid rotation of axes—there is no priviledged set of axes (see Foard & Kemler Nelson, 1984; Kemler Nelson, 1984; L.B. Smith & Kemler, 1978). But dimensions retain their priviledged status in the context model.

Fourth, the context model relies on selective attention to weight different attributes during learning. Attention affects the unidimensional similarity when two stimuli differ. For complete nonattention, similarity is 1.0 whether or not the stimuli differ on a dimension, so that a difference will not lower overall similarity. For rapt attention, unidimensional similarity = 0 for a difference, so that overall similarity = 0 even if the stimuli differ only on that one dimension. This adjustment of weights for selective attention can even represent active, explicit hypothesis testing by the subject (e.g., Medin & Schaffer, 1978, p. 212).

Thus the context model involves separable dimensions, selective attention, active strategizing and hypothesizing, but nonetheless a dimensional interaction in which the unidimensional similarities bootstrap off each other. There is an interesting mixture of analytic and holistic processing, to which I return.

Exemplars and the Exponential Decay of Similarity. Nosofsky (1984, 1986, 1987) also used an exemplar/analogy mechanism to model performance in identification and categorization tasks. For Nosofsky, the exemplars to be categorized have prior perceptual representations in a multidimensional psychological space. In many concept tasks that use separable dimensions, psychological distances in that space will be governed by a city-block metric where unidimensional distances (d's) simply add to yield total psychological distance (D--see Medin & Schaffer, 1978; Nosofsky, 1984, 1986; Shepard, Hovland, & Jenkins, 1961).

In Nosofsky's model, overall similarity decays exponentially as distance increases. Within a scaling factor, overall similarity $= e^{-D}$; or, for separable dimensions, $e^{-\Sigma d}$. So, for two stimuli differing in 0 to 5 binary properties, total distances would be 0, 1, 2, 3, 4, and 5, respectively, and overall similarity would be $= 1.00(e^{-0})$, $.37(e^{-1})$, .14, .05, .02, and .007.

These predictions are practically identical to those of the multiplicative model in Fig. 10.3. In fact, if one sets the similarity parameter for a dimensional difference to e^{-1} (.3679), instead of .40 as in Fig. 10.3, the multiplicative calculation and an exponential decay calculation of similarity converge.

Thus, Nosofsky's model preserves a nonindependence of attributes identical to Medin's. The similarity calculation acts on the entire complex of similarities and dissimilarities simultaneously. It is essentially blind to how total distance was calculated (which metric), how many attributes were discrepant, by how much, and which differences were weighted by attention. Instead, the whole context determines the similarity contribution of any one property. Once again, very similar stimuli will resonate explosively (exponentially) with one another, to aid or confuse in classification or identification.

Despite this nonindependent/holistic flavor, selective attention is a critical feature of categorization. In fact, what sets categorization tasks apart from rote, paired-associate learning (as in identification paradigms) is the transmission of some higher level kind of information about which attributes are informative or not (see Shepard et al. 1961; Nosofsky, 1984, 1986, 1987; Medin & Schwanenflugel, 1981, pp. 361–362). Nosofsky models this transmission as an attentional shift that weights more heavily more informative dimensions in calculating psychological distance. At the extreme (e.g., Shepard et al., 1961, Task 1) subjects might weight one property absolutely, indicating complete attention to a single attribute, and be able to state their criterial-attribute rule.

Once again, selective attention mixes with a more holistic interaction among dimensions. I return to this holistic/analytic middle ground. First I consider holistic categorization from a second perspective, one that links it to a nonstrategic, fallback mode of cognition.

HOLISTIC CATEGORIZATION AND THE
FALLBACK MODE OF COGNITION

Several lines of evidence link holistic perception to a less deliberate and strategic fallback mode of cognition. By contrast, analytic perception is linked to deliberate cognitive effort (Kemler Nelson & Smith, in press; Smith & Kemler Nelson, 1988).

First, consider Smith and Kemler Nelson's (1984) studies of adult perceptual segregation. Enforced speed, a concurrent task, and an impressionistic instruction set resulted in the holistic classification of separable stimuli. All of these manipulations lead adults to give up their normally strategic, resource-intensive approach and fall back on impressionistic, nonstrategic cognition (see also Ward, 1983).

Second, young children spontaneously classify separable stimuli as though they were integral (Shepp, Burns, & McDonough, 1980; L.B. Smith & Kemler, 1977; Ward, 1980)—retardates do as well (Kemler, 1982, 1983). Some (e.g., Smith & Kemler Nelson, 1984) suggest a connection between this holistic processing and the impressionistic nonstrategic set often ascribed to children (Brown & DeLoache, 1978; Flavell, 1977).

Third, two-stage models of stimulus comparison frequently distinguish between a fast and preattentive comparator that operates on wholes and a slower, optional comparator that checks feature by feature (e.g., Bamber, 1969; Krueger, 1973). Again, less active perceptual processing is more holistic. Broadbent (1977) also distinguishes two processing systems. One is attuned to low spatial frequencies and provides global information about objects quickly and effortlessly. The other is tuned to high spatial frequencies and analyzes objects in detail, but slowly and effortfully.

Thus, the perceptual literature links holistic processing to impressionistic performance. What about categorization? Brooks (1978) linked incidental conditions to analogy strategies based on overall similarity to stored whole exemplars. He linked intentional learning to hypothesis-testing about components and analytic rules. In short, he distinguished "deliberate, verbal, analytic control processes and implicit, intuitive, nonanalytic processes"(p. 207).

Kemler Nelson (1984) contrasted explicit conditions (favoring analysis and criterial-attribute rules), and incidental conditions (favoring exemplar encoding and learning about holistic family resemblance). Figure 10.5 shows the logical structure of categorization tasks used to evaluate this contrast, along with corresponding stimuli from experiments we have run (Smith and Shapiro, in press).

Category I		Category II	
Structure	Stimuli	Structure	Stimuli
0 0 0 0	B U N O	1 1 1 1	K Y P A
1 0 0 0	K U N O	0 1 1 1	B Y P A
0 1 0 0	B Y N O	1 0 1 1	K U P A
0 0 0 1	B U N A	1 1 1 0	K Y P O

Sim. E_1E_1 2.87   Sim. E_2E_2 2.87

Sim. E_1E_2 1.12
Str. Ratio   2.56

Test Stimuli

1 1 0 1   K Y N A

0 0 1 0   B U P O

FIGURE 10.5.   A concept task learnable by either a criterial-attribute rule (N or P in the third position) or a (holistic) family-resemblance rule.

In this task, the third attribute is defining, because value 0 for that attribute occurs only and always in Category I and value 1 occurs only and always in Category II. The other attributes are characteristic; in the example, value 0 occurs more often in Category I and value 1 in Category II, but these associations are not certain.

The two test stimuli in the figure are selected to diagnose the kind of learning that occurs. Subjects who are classifying stimuli by the single, defining attribute will place the Test stimuli in Categories I and II, respectively. More holistic categorizers will respond to the cluster of attributes that will place the stimuli in Categories II and I.

Kemler Nelson's explicit learners more often discovered the analytic criterial-attribute rule. But subjects who experienced the exemplars incidentally, via a cover task, more often used the holistic family-resemblance solution.

Ward and Scott (1987) failed to replicate one of Kemler Nelson's three demonstrations of the incidental/holistic link. This has provoked some discussion (Kemler Nelson, 1988; Ward, 1988; chapter 13 of this volume). One possible explanation is that some incidental conditions encourage analytic processing so much that it is carried over to subsequent categorization tasks. This may be even more likely if the subject has learned little about the categories from the incidental exposure, and is struggling to construct a categorization rule at the time of transfer.

In any case, there is a more basic point. Even a strong incidental/holistic link need not imply that nonstrategic, fallback cognition generally elicits holistic categorization. In any incidental condition, subjects know nothing of the categories or the goal of classification—so it is not an impressionistic categorization task for them, but mere exemplar exposure. One does not know from this if intentional, but impulsive, lazy, or distracted category learning will also be holistic. In recent experiments we tested this hypothesis, by comparing incidental exposure, speeded category learning, and learning with a concurrent cognitive load (Smith & Shapiro, in press). These last two conditions were borrowed from Smith and Kemler Nelson (1984). In their perceptual segregation task, subjects under speed or a concurrent load did "let go" of analysis. Will they in categorization?

Subjects received categorization tasks just as in Figure 10.5, either with no constraints, or with only 1-second exposure to each training instance, or with the horiffic concurrent task to count backwards by sevens, or incidentally, using a speed-reading cover task. In all four conditions (unconstrained, speeded, concurrent task, and incidental) subjects learned the categories quite well (85%, 100%, 91%, and 71% of subjects reached the learning criterion). Figure 10.6 gives the total correct (of 30) for learners in each condition, their proportion of family-resemblance responses, and the proportion of subjects who showed a strong family-resemblance pattern to their learning.

Category learning under concurrent load or incidental conditions produced substantial family-resemblance learning. By never engaging categorization processes (incidental conditions) or by disallowing hypothesis testing (concurrent task conditions) one elicits holistic family-resemblance responses. But speeded categorization showed no holistic hint. Speeded subjects made significantly fewer family-resemblance responses than either concurrent task or incidental subjects, and were as analytic (concentrating on a single criterial attribute) as unconstrained subjects. Often, these speeded subjects chose a wrong attribute to treat as criterial. Nonetheless, something about speed concentrates the mind wonderfully.

These results inform in three ways the growing consensus that a fallback mode of cognition elicits holistic processing. First, incidental and speeded conditions produce different results, suggesting that not all operations to produce fallback cognition are equivalent. One may produce holistic processing by making analysis impossible (concurrent task); another by discouraging analysis (impressionistic instructions); another by deceiving subjects so that analysis is never initiated (incidental conditions). Most importantly, speed produces narrow attention in categorization. To the extent of such differences we must break up the

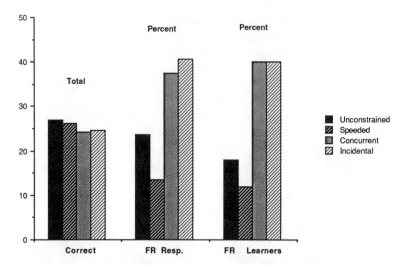

FIGURE 10.6. Total correct, percent family-resemblance responses, and percent family-resemblance learners under four conditions of category learning.

family of manipulations to produce impressionistic cognition and come to understand their different information processing implications.

Second, a current idea is that we learn many real-world categories (e.g., a spouse's handwriting) holistically, because we learn them impressionistically. Such impressionistic learning can occur in early (holistic) childhood (e.g., Anglin, 1977; Rescorla, 1981; Smith & Kemler Nelson, 1984), or when we acquire category knowledge secondarily to accomplishing other tasks and goals. Most demonstrations of holistic categorization use incidental conditions—instance memorization (Reber, 1976), paired-associate learning (Brooks, 1978), passive stimulus observation (Reber & Allen, 1978), or some cover task (Kemler Nelson, 1984). And if incidental exposure (absent knowledge that there are categories or any intent to learn them) is the appropriate model for everyday category learning, then real-world categorization may well be biased toward holistic similarity relations. But if speed/impulsivity is the best description of everyday category learning, then adults may know that there are categories to be learned, and useful criteria to be applied, but will lack time or resources to learn systematically. Like speeded subjects, they may satisfice with a hasty analytic rule.

Third, the results indicate only a partial convergence between the domains of perception and categorization. Whereas speed and a concurrent task commonly produce holistic responses in perceptual tasks, this is not true of categorization. Why so? In the typical categorization task, one stimulus appears on each trial, and the classification decision appeals to some internal criterion—the stimulus array alone does not specify a solution. Further, the internal criterion is stable over trials. I believe that something about maintaining a stable rule over trials creates a strong set for analysis and selective attention, even under conditions of speed. By contrast, in a triad classification task (Figure 10.1), each triad specifies by itself one or more grouping solutions (i.e., on one's first observed triad, one already has a basis for grouping; as is not the case in categorization). Further, the dimension of identify shifts over triads, so a stable criterion is more difficult to sustain. Under these circumstances, it seems that subjects can let go their analytic bias and form holistic perceptual groupings.

Kemler and L. Smith (1979) reached a similar conclusion. Their subjects learned to distinguish Type A and Type B stimulus pairs. In one condition, Type A and Type B pairs had a size identity and brightness identity, respectively. In another condition, Type A and B pairs were similar overall or not, respectively. Essentially, this is a categorization task, with single instances (pairs) placed according to a stable, subject-held rule. Kemler and L. Smith found that even with integral stimuli, subjects seemed to be searching for dimensional principles to guide classification. And, with separable dimensions, they found kindergartners and fifth graders equally likely to acquire the dimensional rule. Thus, triad classification of integral stimuli is holistic, but pairs categorization of integral dimension is analytic (or "tries" to be). Young children are holistic on the triad task; analytic on the pairs task. In my research, speeded triad classification is holistic, speeded categorization is not. Apparently, "in tasks that call for higher level accessing of principles (e.g., concept learning, scientific theory construction)—rather than simply obedience to them—humans have a bias to seek dimensionally-based principles" (Kemler and L. Smith, 1979, p. 148).

HOLISTIC CATEGORIZATION AND THE SIZE AND COHESIVENESS OF CATEGORIES

In fact some current research may overestimate for two reasons the importance of holistic dimensional interactions in categorization, because it relies on small exemplar sets, and extremely difficult categorization tasks which might encourage exemplar-based strategies and holistic representations. I consider those two factors in turn.

Small or Large Categories. A young child may see only the same few instances of the category dog. Holistic exemplar representation might be best in this case, for several reasons: (a) idiosyncratic exemplar information could be important (THIS ONE BITES); (b) memory capacity would be no problem; (c) the cognitive savings gained by abstracting a summary representation would be minimal; (d) abstraction would be difficult because the typical features (the signal) would only barely stand out from the irrelevant features (the noise); and (e) false abstraction could easily occur, where a "defining" attribute (can be petted) turned disastrously noncriterial at a new encounter. A conceptual system would sensibly stay exemplar-based during the early stages of exemplar experience (see also Brooks, 1978).

But with a large category (many exemplars), capacity might not allow the storage of all exemplars. So, storing a category rule (with footnotes about particulars) would produce cognitive savings. Such abstraction would be easy, because the characteristic attributes would stand out from the crowd. And there would be little chance of a false generalization. A conceptual system would sensibly become prototype-based after a great deal of exemplar experience.

Homa, Sterling, and Trepel (1981) found this transition. For small but not large categories, subjects generalized using similarity to training exemplars (suggesting exemplar storage). And only for large categories did the prototype (supposedly the ideal category member) have favored status in classification (suggesting abstraction). (This conclusion was tested and partially supported by Busemeyer, Dewey & Medin, 1984).

Arguing in parallel to Homa et al., one might link small categories, holistic representations, and *no* advantage of LS (linearly separable) categories over NLS categories (because no abstraction occurred). By contrast, one would link large categories, analytic representation of independent cues, and an advantage of LS categories as subjects abstracted a category generalization.

Medin and Schwanenflugel (1981; see also Medin, Dewey, & Murphy, 1983) were concerned that most tests of the context model had used very small categories. Perhaps subjects, with so few stimulus-category pairings to be learned, adopted something like a paired-associate learning strategy, wherein an LS advantage could not show. So they compared the learning of LS and NLS categories with large exemplar sets and found no LS advantage. However, in both cases, many subjects did not reach a preset learning criterion (in Medin et al., 1983, 72% did not). Hence, there is no large-category test of the context model where subjects learned much. This is not an ideal inferential state of affairs, because barely learnable category tasks might themselves especially elicit holistic exemplar strategies.

Structural Ratio.   There are well-defined concepts, ill-defined concepts, and really sickly-defined concepts. As two exemplar clouds are *each* tightly clustered, and far apart from each other, the two categories have high within-category similarity, low between-category similarity, and therefore a high structural ratio (the ratio of the two similarities). For the opposite case, the structural ratio approaches 1.0 (where the two exemplar clouds totally overlap each other).

Will well- or poorly-defined categories most elicit holistic categorization? One perspective (Medin & Schwanenflugel, 1981 is that abstraction (and the importance of linear separability) might only emerge with higher structural ratios than they employed. Smith and Medin (1981, pp. 171–172) also linked high within-category similarity to prototype abstraction.

The idea is that with poorly differentiated categories, any particular attribute chosen for hypothesis testing will only marginally favor one category decision over another. Thus frustration and failure could induce subjects to adopt an exemplar strategy instead. Brooks (1978, pp. 175–176) agrees that stimulus structures that thwart analysis will elicit holistic exemplar strategies, and Nosofsky (1987) also questioned the naturalness of his concept tasks (p. 103).

At the extreme, the so-called categorization task could degenerate into an identification paradigm, where the subject rotely memorized whole instances and their category labels, but had no feeling that there were two cohesive groupings. In fact, some cases of exemplar-based "category learning" are really just the result of rote instance memorization later applied to categorization decisions (Reber, 1976; Brooks, 1978). (Those interested in this paired-associate interpretation of categorization performance can follow this discussion in Medin & Schwanenflugel [1981], who argued against this interpretation of their results, and Nosofsky [1986, 1987] who finds a relation between rote stimulus identification and exemplar-based learning in simple concept tasks [through the intervening influence of selective attention—see also Shepard, Hovland, & Jenkins, 1961]).

There are two hints in the literature that structural ratio affects processing in a categorization task. First, Nosofsky (1987) gave subjects six different classification tasks. I used the average Euclidean distance between stimuli within each category, and between categories, to estimate each task's structural ratio. It varied from 1.17, essentially no category differentiation, to 2.39, enough category structure to float an armada. Nosofsky fit both an exemplar-based model (the context model), and a prototype-based model to subjects' classification performance. In Fig. 10.7, I plot the fit of both models against the structural ratio of each category task. Where categories are well-differentiated, prototype models capture the data extremely well, as well as the best exemplar-based model. For indistinct and unnatural categories, prototype models no longer suit at all.

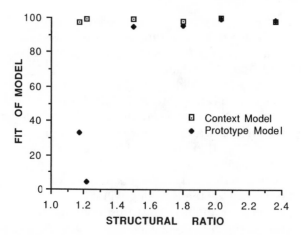

FIGURE 10.7. The fit of two categorization models to performance in tasks of different structure. (Tasks from Nosofsky, 1987).

Second, Medin and Schaffer (1978) and Medin and Smith (1981) used an independent cue model and the context model to predict the rank-order difficulty of items in a categorization task. The fit of each model could be estimated by a rank order correlation between the predicted and observed difficulty levels across items. Over five conditions in the two studies, the stimulus set had a structural ratio of 1.46. Another stimulus set had poorer category structure (structural ratio = 1.28. Figure 10.8 shows the relation between structural ratio and rank order cor-

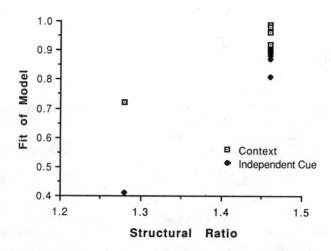

FIGURE 10.8. The fit of two categorization models to performance in tasks of different structure. (Tasks from Medin & Schaffer, 1978; Medin & Smith, 1981).

Task A -- Categories Linearly Separable

Category I		Category II	
Structure	Stimuli	Structure	Stimuli
0 0 0 0 0 0	G I R U P O	1 1 1 1 1 1	L E T A N Y
1 0 0 0 0 0	L I R U P O	1 1 0 1 1 1	L E R A N Y
0 1 0 0 0 0	G E R U P O	1 1 1 1 0 1	L E T A P Y
0 1 1 0 0 0	G E T U P O	0 1 1 1 1 0	G E T A N O
1 0 0 0 0 1	L I R U P Y	1 0 1 1 1 0	L I T A N O
0 0 1 0 1 0	G I T U N O	0 1 0 1 1 1	G E R A N Y
0 0 0 1 0 1	G I R A P Y	1 0 1 0 1 1	L I T U N Y

Sim. $E_1 E_1$ 3.88   Sim. $E_2 E_2$ 3.88

Sim. $E_1 E_2$ 2.12
Str. Ratio   1.83

Task B -- Categories Not Linearly Separable

Category I		Category II	
Structure	Stimuli	Structure	Stimuli
0 0 0 0 0 0	G I R U P O	1 1 1 1 1 1	L E T A N Y
1 0 0 0 0 0	L I R U P O	0 1 1 1 1 1	G E T A N Y
0 1 0 0 0 0	G E R U P O	1 0 1 1 1 1	L I T A N Y
0 0 1 0 0 0	G I T U P O	1 1 0 1 1 1	L E R A N Y
0 0 0 0 1 0	G I R U N O	1 1 1 0 1 1	L E T U N Y
0 0 0 0 0 1	G I R U P Y	1 1 1 1 1 0	L E T A N O
1 1 1 1 0 1	L E T A P Y	0 0 0 1 0 0	G I R A P O

Sim. $E_1 E_1$ 3.88   Sim. $E_2 E_2$ 3.88

Sim. $E_1 E_2$ 2.12
Str. Ratio   1.83

FIGURE 10.9. A comparison of concept tasks (six dimensional) built from categories that are, or are not, linearly separable. The use of six dimensions allows greater concept cohesiveness and perhaps greater learnability.

relation. The clearest failure of the independent cue model is the single case of poor category structure. Both models perform well for more structured category tasks. (However, even with better structure, these tasks remain so difficult that more than half the subjects never reach learning criterion). Medin, et al., (1983) used the better-structured category task in four conditions. The context model accounted for 95%., 92%, 16%, and 88% of the variance in classification performance. The independent cue model accounted for 89%, 93%, 47%, and 92% of the variance over the same four conditions. So, over nine conditions using the better-structured task, a multiplicative exemplar model and an analytic independent cue model predict subjects' categorization performance about equally well.

Thus category size and structural ratio are possible determinants of holistic exemplar storage or analytic abstraction. Of course such claims are empirical (though they are operationalized with some difficulty). For example, Fig. 10.9 shows stimuli for an LS/NLS comparison using six-dimensional stimuli. Using such stimuli one could test the multiplicative exemplar model using better-structured, more learnable categories (structural ratio = 1.83).

I believe that tracing the relationship of category structure to holistic and independent cue models is important for several reasons. First, even young children learn concepts like gangbusters, and many of these categories have strong family-resemblance structure (Kemler Nelson, 1984; Rosch & Mervis, 1975; L.B. Smith, 1981). So to explore more thoroughly concept learning in the natural ecology, one might consider tasks of greater learnability. Second, some doctrine of abstract ideas has had a central if contentious place in philosophy and psychology for 100's of years—the strongest description of the status of abstracted representations will come from sampling broadly the whole space of concept tasks, not just in the area of greatest difficulty, or fewest exemplars.

FURTHER CONCERNS

Analytic/Holistic Purgatory

As described above, several categorization models offer a strange processing world where separable dimensions interact, and selective attention weights enter dimensionless similarity calculations. How are we to understand this mixture of analytic and holistic processes? Three approaches may be useful.

Levels of Processing. One could distinguish analytic and holistic levels of processing during categorization decisions. For example, Smith and

Kemler Nelson (1984) described how multimdimensional stimuli, composed of separable dimensions, might be processed holistically at first, then quickly analyzed.

Likewise, one could differentiate early perceptual representations and distance calculations (both quite analytic in Medin's and Nosofsky's models), from the similarity calculator where the whole stimulus complex matters. Nosofsky seems to intend just this division of processing labor (see also chapter 11). Hintzman's (1986) MINERVA2 categorizer also combines an analytic stimulus comparator with exponential (multiplicative) activation. This seems to be a promising approach, although levels of processing may not be as distinct as models wish them to be.

Varieties of the Holistic Experience. Considering different senses of holistic processing might also help unpack mixed analytic/holistic processing. Integral dimensions show holistic processing in its strongest, propertyless sense—the separable, priviledged dimensions of most categorization tasks do not meet this criterion. And yet the dimensions interact, suggesting that processing is more than just smeared attention spread over independent properties. Perhaps there may be other, "weaker" senses of holistic processes that are appropriate to categorization. For example, the calculation of similarity could operate on objects represented in terms of differentiated properties, but output a dimensionless overall similarity that controlled performance and awareness (see chapter 12 for thorough discussion of these issues). By trying out different senses of holistic processing, one is led to a detailed consideration of how selective attention enters categorization, and of how dimensions blend, interact, or configure, or whatever.

Configural Effects/Emergent Properties. Finally, there is a large literature on dimensional interactions (e.g., Pomerantz, 1983, Chapter 3, this volume; Pomerantz, Sager & Stoever, 1977). It could provide an analogue to the nonintegral but nonindependent dimensions seen in categorization.

For example, perhaps dimensions configure in a categorization task, so that some emergent property of the whole guides classification. Shepard and Chang's (1963) description of categorization had this flavor. They noted that categories with reasonably good structure can be roughly partitioned in n-dimensional space by drawing a line (or n-1 surface) through the space. They speculate that the space somehow becomes polarized during categorization, rendering the relevant, "new " dimensional axis more salient, so that categorization becomes a division of stimuli into two clusters along that emergent dimension.

Perhaps so for their integral dimensions. However, one doubts that in typical categorization tasks, any new dimensional axes ever replace the dominant ones. Typically, configural effects depend on a rather exact combination of stimulus components, (e.g., parentheses in particular positions and orientations). Yet categorization shows dimensional interactions across stimuli and counterbalancing that should quickly root out occasional configural effects. Neither configuration nor emergent features seems likely as an analogue for dimensional interaction in categorization.

Attentionless Selective Attention?

Selective attention in categorization is usually linked to active strategies, hypothesis testing, and stateable concept rules (Brooks, 1978; Kemler Nelson, 1984). However, with the formal categorization models, another selective weighting beast appears on the scene. Sometimes the weightings on different attributes seem to be a quiet absorption of cue validity that does not rely on focal attention. For example, both Nosofsky and Medin find complex weighting schemes for attributes (e.g., Nosofsky, 1984; Medin et al., 1983). It is doubtful that subjects strategically build such elaborate schemes or consciously use them (see also chapter 11). In addition, subjects apparently optimally distribute attention in categorization tasks involving integral dimensions, which strongly discourage the use of focal attention to hypothesize about individual attributes (Nosofsky, 1987). This distinction between conscious and tacit attentional weights raises important issues.

First, just what is this cognitively quiet weighting mechanism? Is it a general conditioning of more informative cues to control responses (Estes, 1957, 1959) while uninformative cues become adapted and lose associative strength (Restle, 1955, 1957). Such automatic increases in trace strength needn't involve focal attention at all.

Second, what place is there for conscious hypothesis testing and verbalizable rules in categorization tasks? Here there are difficulties. If one emphasizes the *tacit* weighting mechanism, the conflict is that subjects often state rules that predict classification 100% of the time, and report on their hypothesis-testing procedures. Based on a variety of such considerations, Shepard, et al., (1961) ruled out quieter mechanisms that relied on conditioning of cues, or patterns of cues. Instead, they concluded that subjects must be abstracting, attending, formulating and testing rules.

But emphasizing the *conscious* weighting mechanism carries another set of risks. Subjects who analyze, test hypotheses, and state rules seem like categorizers of the old-school kind; abstractive, not exemplar storers, and testers of dimensional hypotheses, not users of interactive/ multiplicative similarity. Letting conscious rule search into categorization models risks letting in the things that exemplar models were deliberate alternatives to.

One possible resolution is that the tacit weighting mechanism is at work all the time, absorbing the statistical nature of the environment. Particularly clear or simple weighting schemes could then arrive into consciousness as hypotheses to confirm, or category rules to state. Here consciousness would just report the outcome of the tacit weighting procedure. Another possibility is that many hypotheses about individual attributes are consciously evaluated, but in difficult cases all succeed only minimally. Then, the tacit weights could represent the residue of many explicit hypothesis tests, all of which crashed, but some worse than others.

In any case, this discussion makes clear that there is a tension in categorization models between covert perceptual weights and overt conceptual hypotheses. It will be a valuable next step to explore this tension more fully.

A Developmental Perspective

Finally, I consider three ways in which this discussion bears on developmental trends from holistic to analytic processing in categorization.

The Impulsive or Incidental Young Learner. In perceptual tasks, several operations (e.g., speed, concurrent loads, etc.) scrape off adults' analytic bias to reveal holistic processing beneath, perhaps akin to children's impressionistic cognition. Does one predict, therefore, that children will be holistic categorizers?

The problem is that identical operations (speed and concurrent load) do not converge in categorization. This offers an opportunity to finetune our hypothesis about kids and holistic cognition. The question is whether incidental or speeded/impulsive conditions is the best analogue for child categorizers. Are children incidental concept learners, as they play or watch TV, who give no focal attention to the concept task? Then one would predict holistic categorization.

Or, children might be cognitively impulsive, with curiosity drawing focal attention to categories, but with processing hasty or unskilled. Speeded adults categorize analytically, as they seize any trait in a storm. Impulsive categorization by children could also be analytic. Smith and Kemler Nelson (1988) also point out that fallback modes of cognition can be holistic or primitively analytic. I do not prejudge this issue, but simply note this. Category tasks drive a wedge between incidental conditions and an impulsive approach. This makes it important to specify just what we mean by "impressionistic" cognition in children, before judging its holistic nature.

Tacit Selective Weighting and the Young Learner. Of children's holistic processing, we usually say: They lack the higher level strategies and hypothesis-testing procedures that allow selective attention and analytic rules, so they process holistically in a fallback mode instead.

But what if selective attention weights get adjusted through an unconscious conditioning of cues? Then the absence of conscious hypotheses would not imply the absence of selective weighting schemes. Children and adults might use exactly the same kinds of selective weighting mechanisms in categorization.

Efforts are now being made to relate children's classification to formal models (see chapter 11). Smith and Evans argue that there may be only one categorization mechanism, or similarity comparator, common to children and adults, and that development adjusts this common machine's parameters. By this view, if adults show a greater tendency to report conscious hypotheses and verbalize categorization rules, this might be because they explore more the workings of that machine and report its output. It seems quite possible that adults and children have the same tacit weighting mechanism at their disposal. But my own feeling is that there are categorization tasks where a classic adult–child difference will exist, with adults actively testing conscious hypotheses to feed their bias for analysis and rules, and with children weighting dimensions tacitly. This would represent a basic difference in approach to the task, not just a difference in access to and report on similar functions. Unfortunately, little is known that could decide the point. But clearly, the important tension between conscious and tacit weighting mechanisms surfaces in developmental models too.

The Special Status of Categorization Tasks. For various reasons, some described earlier, tasks of categorization and higher level rule discovery seem to particularly encourage selective attention and hypothesis testing. The implications of this for developmental trends in categorization are clear but significant. For example, L. Smith (1979) found that when children must discover an explicit rule, almost all developmental differences disappear—everybody looks analytic. As she says, "Wholistic similarity is the dominant perceptual relation, but this relation is not abstracted in a learning task" (p. 713). Thus, it seems likely that categorization tasks may show children at their adult, analytic best, that developmental holistic/analytic trends, if present (Kemler Nelson, 1984,

Ward and Scott, 1987) will begin sooner and end earlier than for perceptual tasks, so that categorization leads perceptual segregation in a kind of holistic-to-analytic horizontal decalage. This is another instance of the paper's central theme—that perception and categorization diverge in important ways, and that the balance is shifted toward selective attention in categorization. But the holistic/analytic distinction, so productive in discussions of perception, seems likely to inform discussions of categorization as well.

REFERENCES

Anglin, J.M. (1977). *Word, object, and conceptual development.* New York: Norton.

Bamber, D. (1969). Reaction times and error rates for "same"–"different" judgments of multidimensional stimuli. *Perception and Psychophysics, 6,* 169–174.

Broadbent, D.E. (1977). The hidden preattentive processes. *American Psychologist, 32,* 109–119.

Brooks, L.R. (1978). Nonanalytic concept formation and memory for instances. In E. Rosch & B.B. Lloyd (Eds.), *Cognition and categorization* (pp. 169–211). Hillsdale, NJ: Lawrence Erlbaum Associates.

Brooks, L.R. (1983). *On the insufficiency of analysis.* Unpublished manuscript, McMaster University, Hamilton, Ontario, Canada.

Brown, A.L., & DeLoache, J.S. (1978). Skills, plans & self-regulation. In R.S. Siegler (Ed.), *Children's thinking; What develops?* (pp. 3–35). Hillsdale, NJ: Lawrence Erlbaum Associates.

Bruner, J.S., Goodnow, J.J., & Austin, G.A. (1956). *A study of thinking.* New York: Wiley.

Busemeyer, J.R., Dewey, G.I., & Medin, D.L. (1984). Evaluation of exemplar-based generalization and the abstraction of categorical information. *Journal of Experimental Psychology: Learning, Memory, and Cognition, 10,* 4, 638–648.

Estes, W.K. (1957). Of models and men. *American Psychologist, 12,* 609–617.

Estes, W.K. (1959).Component and pattern models with Markovian interpretations. In R.R. Bush & W.K. Estes, (Eds.), *Studies in mathematical psychology* (pp. 9–52). Stanford, CA: Stanford University Press.

Flavell, J.H. (1977). *Cognitive development.* Englewood Cliffs, NJ: Prentice-Hall.

Foard, C.F. & Kemler Nelson, D.G. (1984). Holistic and analytic modes of processing: The multiple determinants of perceptual analysis. *Journal of Experimental Psychology: General, 113,* 1, 94–111.

Garner, W.R. (1974). *The processing of information and structure.* Potomac, MD: Lawrence Erlbaum Associates.

Handel, S., & Imai, S. (1972). The free classification of analysable and unanalysable stimuli. *Perception and Psychophysics, 12,* 108/116.

Hintzman, D.L. (1986). "Schema abstraction" in a multiple-trace memory model. *Psychological Review, 93,* 411–428.

Homa, D., Sterling, S., & Trepel, L. (1981). Limitations of exemplar-based generalization and the abstraction of categorical information. *Journal of Experimental Psychology: Human Learning and Memory, 7,* 418–439.

Jacoby, L.L., & Brooks, L.R. (1984). Nonanalytic cognition: Memory, perception and concept formation. *Psychology of Learning and Motivation, 18,* 1–47.

Kemler, D.G. (1982). Classification in young and retarded children: The primacy of overall similarity relations. *Child Development, 53,* 768–779.

322

SMITH

Kemler, D.G. (1983). Holistic and analytic modes in perceptual and cognitive develop-
ment. In T. Tighe & B.E. Shepp (Eds.), *Perception, cognition, and development: Interactional analyses* (pp. 77–102). Hillsdale, NJ: Lawrence Erlbaum Associates.

Kemler Nelson, D.G. (1984). The effect of intention on what concepts are acquired. *Journal of Verbal Learning and Verbal Behavior, 23*, 734–759.

Kemler Nelson, D.G. (1988). When category learning is holistic: A reply to Ward and Scott. *Memory and Cognition, 16*, 79–84.

Kemler Nelson, D.G., & Smith, J.D. (in press). Analytic and holistic processing in reflection-impulsivity and cognitive development. In T. Globerson & T. Zelniker (Eds.), *Cognitive style and cognitive development*. Norwood, NJ: Ablex.

Kemler, D.G., & Smith, L.B. (1979). Accessing similarity and dimensional relations: The effect of integrality and separability on the discovery of complex concepts. *Journal of Experimental Psychology: General, 108*, 133–150.

Krueger, L.E. (1973). Effect of irrelevant surrounding material on speed of same–different judgment of two adjacent letters. *Journal of Experimental Psychology, 98*, 252–259.

Lockhead, G.R. (1972). Processing dimensional stimuli: A note. *Psychological Review, 79*, 410–419.

Medin, D.L., Dewey, G.I., & Murphy, T.D. (1983). Relationships between item and category learning: Evidence that abstraction is not automatic. *Journal of Experimental Psychology: Learning, Memory, and Cognition, 9*, 4, 607–625.

Medin, D.L., & Schaffer, M.M., (1978). Context theory of classification learning. *Psychological Review, 85*, 207–238.

Medin, D.L., & Schwanenflugel, P.L. (1981). Linear separability in classification learning. *Journal of Experimental Psychology: Human Learning and Memory, 7*, 5, 355–368.

Medin, D.L., & Smith, E.E. (1981). Strategies and classification learning. *Journal of Experimental Psychology: Human Learning and Memory, 7*, 4, 241–253.

Nosofsky, R.M. (1984). Choice, similarity, and the context theory of classification. *Journal of Experimental Psychology: Learning, Memory, and Cognition, 10*, 1, 104–114.

Nosofsky, R.M. (1986). Attention, similarity and the identification-categorization relationship. *Journal of Experimental Psychology: General, 115*, 1, 39–57.

Nosofsky, R.M. (1987). Attention and learning processes in the identification and categorization of integral stimuli. *Journal of Experimental Psychology: Learning, Memory, and Cognition, 13*, 1 87–108.

Pomerantz, J.R. (1983). Global and local precedence: Selective attention in form and motion perception. *Journal of Experimental Psychology: General, 112*, 516–540.

Pomerantz, J.R., Sager, L.C., & Stoever, R.J. (1977). Perception of wholes and their component parts: Some configural superiority effects. *Journal of Experimental Psychology: Human Perception and Performance, 3*, 422–433.

Reber, A.S. (1976). Implicit learning of synthetic languages: The role of instructional set. *Journal of Experimental Psychology: Human Memory and Learning, 2*, 88–94.

Reber, A.S. & Allen, R. (1978). Analogic and abstraction strategies in synthetic grammar learning: A functionalist interpretation. *Cognition, 6*, 189–221.

Rescorla, L.A. (1981). Category development in early language. *Journal of Child Language, 8*, 225–238.

Restle, F. (1955). A theory of discrimination learning. *Psychological Review, 62*, 11–19.

Restle, F. (1957). Theory of selective learning with probable reinforcement. *Psychological Review, 64*, 182–191.

Rosch, E., & Mervis, C.B. (1975). Family resemblances: Studies in the internal structure of categories. *Cognitive Psychology, 7*, 573–605.

Rosch, E., Mervis, C.B., Gray, W.D., Johnson, D.M., & Boyes-Braem, P. (1976). Basic objects in natural categories. *Cognitive Psycology, 8*, 382–439.

Shepard, R.N. (1964). Attention and the metric structure of the stimulus space. *Journal of Mathematical Psychology, 1,* 54–87.

Shepard, R.N., & Chang, J.J. (1963). Stimulus generalization in the learning of classifications. *Journal of Experimental Psychology, 65,* 94–102.

Shepard, R.N., Hovland, C.I., & Jenkins, H.M. (1961). Learning and memorization of classifications. *Psychological Monographs, 75.* (13, whole no. 517).

Shepp, B.E., Burns, B., & McDonough, D. (1980). The relation of stimulus structure to perceptual and cognitive development: Further tests of a separability hypothesis. In J. Becker & F. Wilkening (Eds.), *The integration of information by children* (pp. 113–145). Hillsdale, NJ: Lawrence Erlbaum Associates.

Shepp, B.E., & Swartz, K.B. (1976). Selective attention and the processing of integral and nonintegral dimensions: A developmental study. *Journal of Experimental Child Psychology, 22,* 73–85.

Smith, E.E., & Medin, D.L. (1981). *Categories and concepts.* Cambridge, MA: Harvard University Press.

Smith, J.D., & Kemler Nelson, D.G. (1984). Overall similarity in adults' classification: The child in all of us. *Journal of Experimental Psychology: General, 113,* 137–159.

Smith, J.D., & Kemler Nelson, D.G. (1988). Is the more impulsive child a more holistic processor? A reconsideration. *Child Development, 59,* 719–727.

Smith, J.D. & Shapiro, J.H. (in press). The occurrence of holistic categorization. *Journal of Memory and Language* .

Smith, L.B. (1979). Perceptual development and category generalization. *Child Development, 50,* 705–715.

Smith, L.B. (1981). Importance of the overall similarity of objects for adults' and children's classifications. *Journal of Experimental Psychology: Human Perception and Performance, 7,* 811–824.

Smith, L.B., & Kemler, D.G. (1977). Developmental trends in free classification: Evidence for a new conceptualization of perceptual development. *Journal of Experimental Child Psychology, 24,* 279–298.

Smith, L.B., & Kemler, D.G. (1978). Levels of experienced dimensionality in children and adults. *Cognitive Psychology, 10,* 502–532.

Trabasso, T., & Bower, G.H. (1968). *Attention in learning theory and research.* New York: Wiley.

Ward, T.B. (1980). Separable and integral responding by children and adults to the dimensions of length and density. *Child Development, 51,* 676–684.

Ward, T.B. (1983). Response tempo and separable-integral responding: Evidence for an integral-to-separable processing sequence in visual perception. *Journal of Experimental Psychology: Human Perception and Performance, 9,* 103–112.

Ward, T.B. (1988). When is category learning holistic? A reply to Kemler Nelson. *Memory and Cognition, 16*(1), 85–89.

Ward, T.B., & Scott, J.G. (1987). Analytic and holistic modes of learning family-resemblance concepts. *Memory and Cognition, 15*(1), 42–54.

11   *SIMILARITY, IDENTITY, AND DIMENSIONS: PERCEPTUAL CLASSIFICATION IN CHILDREN AND ADULTS*

Linda B. Smith
Paul Evans
Indiana University

INTRODUCTION

Is the transition from immature to more mature forms of psychological function one of quantitative change or qualitative change? This classic question in developmental theory can be asked about any developmental trend. Here, we ask about the trend from more holistic to more differentiated comparisons of objects. In particular, we ask the quantitative-versus-qualitative question about the well documented findings that, in perceptual classification tasks, young children classify objects by their overall similarity, whereas older children classify by identities on single dimensions. Does this trend reflect principally a change in the frequency, magnitude, or amplitude of a psychological variable or process? Or does the trend reflect a qualitative change—a change in the structure or organization of underlying processes?

Smith (in press, b has recently proposed a model, the weighted-imension-plus-identity model, that accounts for the developmental shift from overall-similarity to dimensional-identity classifications by positing only quantitative changes. In this chapter, we present the background evidence to be explained, an overview of the model (see Smith, in press, b for a more detailed presentation), and some new empirical evidence for some of the specific claims of the model. The weighted-dimension-plus-identity model has further important implications for the issues that organize this book—for the relation between attributes and wholes, for the nature of perceptual similarity, and for the question of what develops in the perception of multidimensional objects. Accordingly, in the final section of this chapter, we consider the insights and evidence on these issues raised by other contributors—and we consider how their various ideas and findings and the ones embodied in our model may be fit together. Particularly relevant are chapters 7, 9, 10, 12, and 13.

BACKGROUND

One principle of development is a trend from holistic to differentiated perception (Gibson, 1969; Vurpillot, 1976; Werner, 1948; Wohlwill, 1962). Ten years or so ago, several researchers (Shepp & Swartz, 1976, Smith & Kemler, 1977) reinterpreted this trend in terms of Lockhead's (1966, 1972) and Garner's (1970, 1974) distinction between integral and separable dimensions. According to this reinterpretation, development proceeds from holistic perception organized by overall similarity to differentiated perception organized by dimensions. The new claim is that holistic perception is not diffuse and unorganized. Rather, holistic perception is said to be highly organized by overall similarity relations, just as differentiated perception is highly organized by dimensions. The reinterpretation of the trend in terms of integrality and separability suggests a qualitative shift in perceptual organization with development.

One task that provides support for a shift from perception organized by overall-similarity to perception organized by dimensions is classification. In the typically used classification task, subjects are given small sets of objects and asked to group them. The sets are structured to pit an overall-similarity organization against a dimensional one. Figure 11.1 illustrates schematically the structure of such a set. The relations in this set can be described in two qualitatively distinct ways. By a dimensional description, objects A and B are identical on dimension X and different on dimension Y, and objects A and B both differ from object C on both dimensions. By the overall similarity description, objects B and C are very much alike (close in the multidimensional space) and very different (far) from object A.

When adults are given sets of objects to classify that are structured as in Fig. 11.1, and when the objects vary on separable dimensions such as color and shape or darkness and size, adults classify in a manner consistent with the dimensional description: They group together objects (i.e., A and B) that are identical on one dimension. When children under age 6 or so are given the very same sets to classify, they classify in accord with the overall-similarity description: They group together the objects that are most alike on both varying dimensions (objects B and C), even

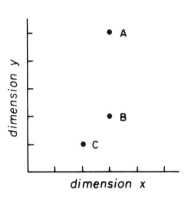

FIGURE 11.1 Schematic illustration of the structure of a triad
used to diagnose overall-similarity
(BC vs. A) and dimensional-
identity (AB vs. C) classifications.
Individual objects (A, B, and C)
are represented in terms of their
coordinates on two varying dimensions.

though they are not exactly alike on either dimension. This trend from
overall similarity to dimensional-identity classifications has been widely
replicated with a variety of separable stimulus dimensions. These results
have led some (e.g., Kemler, 1983; Shepp, 1983) to conclude that the
perceived structure of objects changes qualitatively so that the proper
psychological description of the stimulus for young children is the overall similarity description and the proper psychological description for
older children and adults is the dimensional one. In contrast, we suggest
that both descriptions are ultimately the same and that they stem from
the very same processing of objects and relations between objects.

This idea that there is a unitary account of overall-similarity and
dimensional-identity classifications derives from the now considerable
evidence that the developmental trend between the two kinds of
classifications is not all or none. Preschool children can, under certain
task procedures, compare and classify objects by identity on a dimension (e.g., Caron, 1969; Kemler, 1982; Odom, 1978; L.B. Smith, 1983;
1984, L.B. Smith & Kemler, 1978). Further, adults who are well able to
compare objects by single dimensions perform "holistically," comparing
objects by their overall similarity just as young children do, when performance is placed under severe time constraints or limited by the addition of a concurrent task or by stimulus complexity (J.D. Smith &
Kemler Nelson, 1984; L.B. Smith, 1981; Ward, 1983). Thus, both
young children and adults perceive both the overall similarity and separate dimensional relations that exist between objects. In this way, the
perceptions of children and adults are not qualitatively distinct. We suggest further that the perception of overall similarity and dimensional
identity are manifestations of the very same way of comparing objects.
The weighted-dimension-plus-identity model makes the claim that the
same perceptual machinery and processing leads to the perception of
both overall-similarity and dimensional-identity relations. For the pres-

ent, we limit our claims to the case when the underlying dimensions are (for adults) separable.

The Developmental Hypothesis

The model accounts for the developmental trend in the classification of separable stimuli by positing two areas of growth. The first is an increased ability to attend selectively to single dimensions when comparing objects. The second is the differentiation of identity as a special kind of sameness relation. The fact of a developmental increase in selective attention is both well known and well documented (e.g., Gibson, 1969; Shepp & Swartz, 1976; Smith, Kemler, & Aronfreed, 1975). The idea that identity relations come to take precedence over similarity ones is supported by a growing number of studies (Evans & Smith, in press; Keil & Batterman, 1984; Smith, in press a). The suggestion is that early in development, objects are represented as being merely more or less alike and that identity is simply very strong similarity. Later, however, identity emerges as a special and particularly valued kind of similarity (see Smith, 1979; Smith, in press b).

The involvement of these two areas of growth—in selective attention and in the value of identity—is also suggested by a logical analysis of the classification task. Given a stimulus set structured as depicted in Fig. 11.1, overall-similarity classifications and dimensional-identity classifications differ objectively in two ways. One difference involves selective attention. The number of dimensions contributing to the within-group similarity in the overall-similarity classification is two, but the number of dimensions contributing to the within-group similarity in the dimensional-identity classification is one. The second difference concerns the kind of within-group similarity. In the overall similarity classification, the objects grouped together are just similar. In the dimensional-identity classification, the objects are not *just* similar; rather, they are (part) identical.

These two factors—number of dimensions and kind of similarity— are orthogonal as depicted in Fig. 11.2. One can attend to both dimensions and classify by overall similarity (BC vs. A) or by overall, that is, absolute, identity (A vs. B vs. C). Or, one can attend selectively to a single dimension and classify by similarity on one dimension (on x, AB vs. C or on y, BC vs. A) or one can selectively attend and classify by identity (on dimension x, AB vs. C). Notice that individual classifications fall in more than one cell in this 2×2 scheme. The BC-versus-A classification (see Fig. 11.1) is a similarity classification given attention either to all dimensions or to any one. This is necessarily so;

for two objects to be similar on all varying dimensions they must be similar on each one alone. The AB versus C classification (see Fig. 11.1) is both a one-dimensional identity classification and a one-dimensional similarity classification. This is also necessarily so; similarity includes identity, and thus two objects that are identical on a single dimension are also similar on that dimension. We suggest, however, that the trend from predominantly BC versus A classifications to AB versus C classifications is in fact a trend from overall similarity to one-dimensional identity classifications. Our point is that this trend involves two separate trends: from overall to one-dimensional and from similarity to identity. We turn now to the weighted-dimensions-plus-identity model that instantiates these claims.

THE MODEL

The model has four parts: (a) the representation of objects; (b) the calculation of similarities between mentally represented objects; (c) the valuing of perceived similarities for the purpose of classifying objects; and (d) the construction of a particular classification.

Representation of Objects

We propose that at a preconscious level, separate features and dimensions are separately processed and put together to form the represented whole object. We illustrate this notion in Fig. 11.3. Represented wholes are both built from and represented in terms of their constituent attrib-

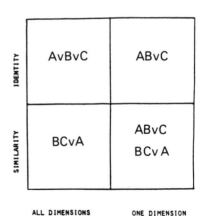

FIGURE 11.2. A 2 × 2 characterization of possible classifications of the triad illustrated in Fig. 11.1.

utes. (See Smith, in press, b for more details). We make this claim about the initial processing of separate features and dimensions and the formation of represented wholes regardless of the developmental level of the perceiver; objects are *universally* represented in terms of constituent attributes and features. However, the products of feature analyses and the internal structure of represented wholes are not immediately available to experience. Rather, it is the represented whole *as a whole* that is perceived. In terms of the representation in Fig. 11.3, one cannot get inside the represented whole, inside the parentheses, without some mental effort.

Perceived Similarity

The represented whole is the unit of perceptual comparison. We suggest that represented whole objects are most easily and most rapidly compared to each other as wholes. The first and easiest comparison between objects yields information about how much alike two objects are but does *not* yield information about the *dimensions* of likeness. Relative to the representation in Fig. 11.3, one would first experience the three objects as differing by a fair amount, but one would not have knowledge of the specific dimensions of similarity and difference. According to the model, to know that the three objects all differ on dimension x requires selective attention to x.

According to the weighted-dimension-plus-identity model, objects are compared by calculating their perceived similarity across *all* dimensions. Similarity is simply a measure of how much alike two objects are and does not in and of itself specify the separate contributions of specific

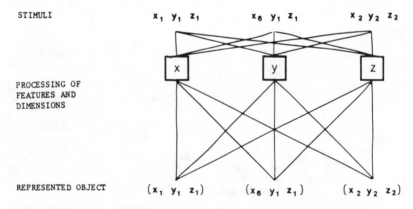

FIGURE 11.3.   The building of represented whole objects from the prior processing of separate dimensions.

dimensions to that similarity. However, the perceived similarity between objects will vary with how attention is distributed to the constituent dimensions. Further, perceived similarity can yield information about a single dimension, if in the calculation of similarity that dimension is weighted to the virtual exclusion of all other dimensions. Within our model, the differential weighting of dimensions is the only means through which subjects can *experience* separate dimensions of similarity. Further, our view is that the differential weighting of dimensions requires attention.

We formally instantiate these ideas in the function we use to calculate perceived similarities. Following Nosofsky (1984a, 1984b), we use an exponential decay function: The similarity between objects i and j is:

$$S_{ij} = e^{-\sum_{k=1}^{N} w_k d_{ij(k)}} \tag{1}$$

where $d_{ij(k)}$ is the difference between objects i and j on dimension k, N is the number of dimensions, w_k is the weight accorded to dimension k, $0 < w_k \leqslant 1$ and $\sum_{k=1}^{N} w_k = 1$. Perceived similarity thus varies from not alike at all (0) to identity (1). Note that this formula yields a measure of dimension*less* overall similarity. For perceived similarity to yield information about a specific dimension of similarity, that dimension must be accorded all the weight in the calculation of similarity. To know that the objects in Fig. 11.3 differ on dimension x, the weighting scheme must be $W_x = 1$ and $W_y = W_z = 0$.

Here then is our first developmental claim: Because the differential weighting of dimensions takes mental effort, young children are less likely to differentially weight dimensions and are therefore less likely to have information about specific dimensions. Also, even when there is sufficient time and capacity available, younger perceivers may not differentially weight dimensions in their comparison of objects because they do not know that it would be strategically useful to do so. This point brings us to the next part of the model—valuing similarity.

Valued Similarity

In this part of the model, the perceived similarities are evaluated for the purpose of forming classifications. We suggest that for younger classifiers, similarity is just a matter of degree and good classifications are ones in which highly similar objects are grouped together. We suggest that older classifiers treat similarity more dichotomously; objects are the "same" and worthy of being classified together if their perceived similarity is close to identity and objects are "different" and not worthy of being grouped together otherwise.

These ideas are illustrated in Fig. 11.4, which shows the classifactory value of particular degrees of dissimilarity. The dotted line shows a situation in which the value of the dissimilarities for classifying is linearly related to the degree of perceived similarity. We suggest that this is the situation for young children—objects are more or less alike, and being "identical" is only being very much alike. The solid line shows a situation in which the value of the dissimilarities is sharply demarcated into two categories so that only dissimilarities at or close to 0 (i.e., similarities at or close to 1) are highly valued. We suggest that this is the situation that characterizes older classifiers. By our view, it is this categorical valuing of identity that provides the motivation for the differential weighting of dimensions. Because very few objects are absolutely identical, a highly valued level of similarity may not be found unless one attends selectively to single dimensions.

We model these notions about the value of perceived similarities via a power function where the valued similarity between objects i and j equals:

$$V_{ij} = (S_{ij})^P \tag{2}$$

where $1 < p < \infty$ and $0 < V_{ij} < 1$. Here, we have the second and final proposed developmental change: We propose that P increases with age; that is, that identity relations become increasingly special with development.

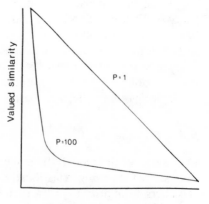

FIGURE 11.4. Valued similarity as a function of perceived difference for two levels of P. See equation 2.

The Goodness of a Classification

The valued similarities are used to construct classifications. We assume that when subjects are asked to classify, they try to produce a "good" classification. What is a "good" classification? Most models of classification use some sort of ratio rule to pick out the "good" classification of a set (see Medin & Schaeffer, 1978, and chapter 9 of this book for examples). The assumption is that a classification is good and likely to be produced to the degree that it is better than other possible classifications of the same set of objects. We suspect that this usual treatment of what is a "good" classification is not quite right. We suspect that there are stimulus sets with *no* "good classification." The valued similarities between *all* objects may be so high that none can be separated out, or the valued similarities between all objects may be so low that no two are worthy of being grouped together.

We define the goodness of a classification in terms of *all* possible classifications, including the two cases of "no" classification (all objects grouped together and each object grouped singly). More precisely, we define the goodness of a classification as equal to the combination of the valued similarities of the objects grouped together and the inverse of the valued similarities of the objects classified apart. The goodness of the A, B versus C classification (G(AB, C) is equal to the product of valued similarity of AB and the valued *dis*similarities (i.e., 1 minus the valued similarity) of AC and BC. This is:

$$G(AB,C) = V(AB) \times 1\text{-}V(AC) \times 1\text{-}V(BC). \tag{3}$$

The goodness equations for all the other classifications of the triad of objects shown in Fig. 11.1 is given in Table 11.1. The goodnesses of all the classifications of a set sum to 1.0; thus, our measure of goodness picks the "best" classification of a set but includes the possibilities of grouping all objects together and each object alone.

The Input to the Model

Within the model, the mental machinery by which objects are grouped is constant throughout development. The same calculations and processes underlie both overall similarity and dimensional identity classifications. At all developmental levels, perceived similarity is calculated across all dimensions at once. All that changes with development is the tendency to differentially weight constituent dimensions when

TABLE 11.1

The Goodness of the Five Possible Classifications of the Triad
is Illustrated in Figure 11.1. The Goodness of a Classification
is Equal to the Valued Similarity of the Items Grouped
Together Times the Value of the Similarity (1-Valued
Similarity) of the Items Grouped Apart.

$$G \ (AB \ vs \ C) = V_{(AB)} \times (1 - V_{(BC)}) \times (1 - V_{(AC)})$$
$$G \ (BC \ vs \ A) = V_{(BC)} \times (1 - V_{(AB)}) \times (1 - V_{(AC)})$$
$$G \ (AC \ vs \ B) = V_{(AC)} \times (1 - V_{(AB)}) \times (1 - V_{(BC)})$$
$$G \ (A \ vs \ B \ vs \ C) = (1 - V_{(AB)}) \times (1 - V_{(BC)}) \times (1 - V_{(AC)})$$
$$
\begin{aligned}
G \ (ABC) = \quad & [V_{(AB)} \times V_{(BC)} \times (1 - V_{(AC)})] \\
+ \ & [V_{(AB)} \times V_{(AC)} \times (1 - V_{(AC)})] \\
+ \ & [V_{(AC)} \times V_{(BC)} \times (1 - V_{(AB)})] \\
+ \ & [V_{(AB)} \times V_{(AC)} \times V_{(BC)}]
\end{aligned}
$$

comparing objects and an increased valuing of similarities at or close to identity.

Before we can use our quantitative instantiations of these claims to make predictions, we must specify the input to the quantitative model. Given some set of objects to be classified, say, various-sized circles of several shades of blue, structured as shown in Fig. 11.1, what do we input to the model as a description of the stimulus objects and their relations to each other? One possible solution that has been employed by others (e.g., Nosofsky, 1984a, 1984b) uses similarity judgments and multidimensional scaling techniques to obtain distances as descriptors of stimulus sets. We rejected this solution. It seems to us that the task of giving similarity ratings is a no more privileged measure of similarity than other tasks such as classification. Further, it is unlikely that the task of rating similarities is immune to the developmental differences we postulate in the differential weighting of dimensions and in the valuing of identity relations. In other words, our model might well be required to explain developmental differences in rated similarity (see Shepard, 1964).

Our solution to this problem was to assume only that stimulus differences vary from not discriminable to infinitely different and that the similarities in any classification set fall between these two endpoints. More precisely, given a triad of objects to be classified such as those shown in Fig. 11.1, we input to the model a specification of which objects share a value on which dimensions and a set of ratios of the distances between pairs of objects. All the predictions we report in this chapter are based on a 2:1 ratio given equal dimensional weights of the distances between the AB:BC pairs. Given a specification of the ratio of distances between pairs of objects and a specification of which objects share values on the specific dimensions, we next set all distances at 0 and increase the distances incrementally until the perceived similarity between all pairs of objects *given equal weighting* of all dimensions is close to zero. We then examine the effects of various dimensional weights and values of P on the goodness of the possible classifications over this range of distances. In other words, our model makes predictions across ranges of stimulus differences—from when the three objects depicted in Fig. 11.1 are on top of each other in the multidimensional space to when they are extremely far from each other.

The output of the model, then, is a set of curves of the goodness of various classifications over a range of magnitudes of stimulus differences. Because we do not know precisely the actual magnitudes of difference in any stimulus set, our predictions concern the *relative goodnesses* of various classifications (i.e., AB vs. C as compared to BC vs. A) and changes in the relative goodness of classifications with changes in the magnitude of stimulus differences in a set. Importantly, the goodness of a classification as output from the model probably does not map directly onto the expected frequency of a classification. From our calculated goodnesses we predict only the relative ordering of frequency of classifications in performance.

Quantitative Predictions

Our developmental claim is that there are two orthogonal developing processes—differential weighting of dimensions and the valuing of similarity. In this section, we predict the goodnesses of all possible classifications of the triad shown in Fig. 11.1 as stimulus differences vary from not discriminable to very different. We consider the predictions from the model for the four cases (see Fig. 11.2) resulting from the combination of nondifferential versus differential weighting of dimensions with the nonvaluing versus high valuing of identity. The predictions for the four cases are shown in Fig. 11.5. For these illustrative predictions, we consider our two developmentally varying parameters, the dimensional weights (W_i) and the power (P) of the valuing function at their virtual limits. See Smith (in press b), for a more detailed consideration of intermediate values. The case of equal weighting of dimensions and a nonvaluing of identity is hypothesized to be characteristic of the young child, and the case of selective attention and a high valuing of identity is hypothesized to be characteristic of older children and adults. We consider these two cases first.

The Young Child: $W_x = .50$, $P = 1$.   By our conceptualization, panel 1 of Fig. 11.5 describes the young child: equal weighting of the varying

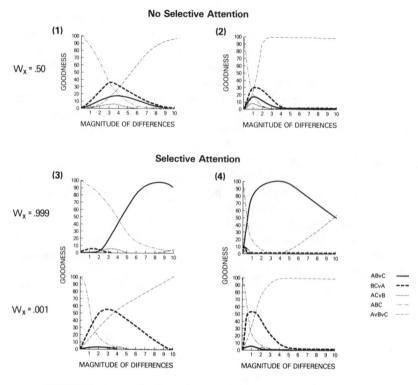

FIGURE 11.5. Predicted goodnesses of classifications for four cases resulting from various combinations of dimensional weights (W_x) and powers (P) of the valuing function.

dimensions and no special treatment of similarities close to identity. Under this description, children should produce overall-similarity classifications across the midrange of stimulus differences and overall-similarity classifications should always outnumber dimensional-identity ones. At the lowest magnitudes of stimulus difference, young children should, however, be strongly tempted to group all objects together, and at large magnitudes of stimulus difference, they should be tempted to group each object by itself.

The Adult: $W_x = .999$, P = 100. Panel 4 of Fig. 11.5 illustrates the case we think descriptive of adult classifiers. Here, two sets of curves are relevant—one set depicts the goodnesses of the various classifications given selective attention to dimension x ($W_x = .999$); the other shows the expected goodnesses given selective attention to dimension y ($W_x = .001$). We assume that adults selectively attend to each dimension in turn and classify by the dimension that yields the classification with the highest goodness. Given the triad depicted in Fig. 11.1, then, adults should selectively attend to dimension x and produce the dimensional-identity classifications across a wide range of magnitudes of difference as the only good "classification" by dimension y consists of grouping each object singly. As shown in the figure, however, dimensional identity classifications may give way to classifications of each object singly at extreme magnitudes of stimulus difference. This decline is expected at extreme differences *only* if selective attention is not perfect. If selective attention is perfect (e.g. if W_x = 1.00), then the dimensional identity classification is the best classification across the entire range (see Smith in press b, for a fuller discussion of predictions under cases of imperfect selective attention.)

Selective Attention Without the Valuing of Identify (W_i = .999, P = 1).
Panel 3 of Fig. 11.5 illustrates the possibility of classifying by a single dimension but without any special valuing of identity. This case, then, corresponds to the case illustrated in the lower right cell of Fig. 11.2. Again we assume that subjects attend to each dimension in turn and then classify by the dimension yielding the best classification. Given a triad structured as in Fig. 11.1, subjects should sometimes attend to dimension x and produce the AB versus C classification and sometimes should attend to dimension y and produce the BC versus A classification. In other words, subjects should sometimes produce what looks like classifications by dimensional identity and sometimes produce what looks like classifications by overall similarity. However, in both cases, the classifications are actually the *one-dimensional similarity* classifications. According to the model, which dimension is attended to and which classification is produced (AB vs. C or BC vs. A) depends on the magnitude of stimulus difference. At low levels of stimulus difference, selective attention to dimension y yields the best classification, that is, the BC versus A. At higher magnitudes of stimulus difference, selective attention to dimension x yields the best classification, that is, AB vs. C.

This case of selective attention without the valuing of identity is an important possibility for several reasons: First, although the magnitude of stimulus difference has not been systematically considered in theorizing about the categorization of multidimensional stimuli, there are hints in the literature that it matters. Specifically, young children are somewhat more likely to produce what look like dimensional identity classifications when the stimulus differences are large (Kemler & Smith, 1979; Smith, 1979), just as would be expected if they attended selectively to single dimensions but did not value identity. Second, Aschkenasy and Odom (1982) have criticized the hypothesized trend from *holistic* overall-similarity classifications to analytic dimensional classifications on the grounds that "true" overall similarity classifications have not been unambiguously demonstrated. They suggest that both older and younger children selectively attend to single dimensions but that young children consistently attend to dimension y. In other words, the developmental trend may be from one *dimensional* classification strategy, classifying by single dimensions, to another, classifying by *the* dimension on which there is an identity. This alternative hypothesis highlights the need to make precise claims about the developmental trend. Virtually all studies to date have employed classification sets structured as in Fig. 11.5 but without systematic variation in the magnitudes of stimulus difference, and as we shall see, such studies have led to some incorrect characterizations of the developmental trend.

Nonselective Attention and the Valuing of Identity.   Panel 4 of Fig. 11.5 illustrates the futility of the final combination of factors—nonselective attention but a high valuing of identity relations. Given the standard classification set as illustrated in Fig. 11.1 in which the only identity relations are *part* identities, there is no point to valuing identity unless one can selectively attend to the dimensional parts of objects.

The Magnifying Effect of Valuing Identity.   Before considering empirical evidence, one last aspect about the model—the relation between the valuing function and the magnitude of stimulus difference—merits discussion. The principal effect of a high valuing of identity is a magnification of stimulus differences. It is for this reason that selective attention must be near perfect given a high valuing of identity for the dimensional-identity classification (or any classification other than each object singly) to be good. When identity is highly valued, even "small" stimulus differences "count" for a lot in the determination of goodness. When identity is valued, small differences "count" as if they were large differences. This magnifying effect of valuing identity is illustrated in Fig. 11.6, which shows that increasing P pushes the curves leftward, both when selective attention to x is near perfect and when it is perfect.

This fact within our model raises the possibility that what develops is not, as we propose, an increased valuing of identity relations when classifying. One could argue that what develops is the scale of the psychological similarity space—that it expands with development. Developmental changes in discriminability and in stimulus generalization gradients are certainly consistent with this view (Gibson & Gibson, 1955; Mednick & Lehtinen, 1957). We do not, however, think that changes in discriminability can, themselves, account for the developmental data. There may be some amount of expansion of the psycholog-

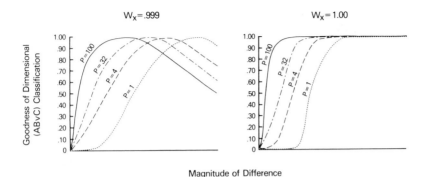

FIGURE 11.6. Predicted goodnesses of the dimensional-identity classification as the power of (P) of the valuing function increases for near perfect ($W_x = .999$) and perfect ($W_x = 1.00$) selective attention to dimension x.

ical similarity space with perceptual learning and development and perhaps also with capacity allocated to the task of discriminating between stimuli (indeed, we believe there is), but such an expansion is probably not of the magnitude of the developmental effects in classification tasks. Further, in most classification tasks, the stimulus differences are highly discriminable for all subjects. Our characterization of P as a *strategy* to value identity in classification tasks also implies that it may be abandoned at will with changes in task context. Task context should not alter the discriminability of stimulus differences in the psychological similarity space.

EVIDENCE

Magnitude of Difference

A fundamental prediction of the model is that the magnitude of stimulus difference matters. Perceptual similarity and what constitutes a good classification depends on the absolute differences between stimulus objects. Indeed, as illustrated in Fig. 11.5, it is the pattern of performances across a range of stimulus differences that allows one to distinguish between particular combinations of weights and P values. Accordingly, the first experiments on the model (Smith, in press b), examined the classifications of children from 2 to 8 years of age and adults across sets that varied widely in the magnitude of stimulus differences in the sets.

The structures of the classification sets used in one experiment are shown in Fig. 11.7. The actual objects were circles varying in color and size. Consider first, the middle set, or standard set. The color and size values used for these triads were identical to values used in other free classification experiments (Smith, 1983), and the magnitudes of difference are typical of those used in the literature. Specifically, the colors varied from light green to dark green and the sizes of the circles varied from 3 ¼ cm. to 6 ¾ cm. Importantly, even the smallest one-dimensional differences in this set were highly discriminable even to 2-year-olds. The discriminable set was constructed by decreasing the distances between the individual objects so that the smallest one-dimensional differences were *just* discriminable for the youngest children. The extreme set was constructed by expanding the differences in the standard set. The largest difference, that between objects A and B on dimension y were increased to a "nominal" level. For example, when y was color, the difference was that between light green and dark pink; when dimension y was size, the difference was between 3 ¼ cm. and 9 cm. Note that in this extreme set, the overall similarity pair (B and C) differ by more than the dimensional-identity pair (A and B) in the standard set. Both children and adults were given instances of each type of triad— intermixed and in random order—and asked to "put the ones together that go together."

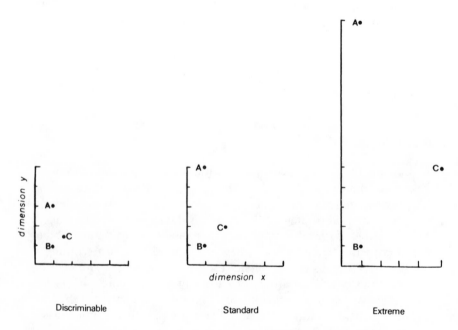

FIGURE 11.7. Experimental triads from Smith & Evans (1987).

Figure 11.8 shows the results. The two- and 3-year-olds' classifi-cations fit the pattern predicted by the model (see Fig. 11.5) given equal weighting of the two dimensions in the calculation of similarity and the nonvaluing of identity. Overall similarity classifications rise and then fall with increases in stimulus difference and are never exceeded by dimen-sional-identity classifications. Further, for these youngest children there is a considerable tendency to group all objects together when the differ-ences are small and each object singly when the differences are great. Children at these two age levels thus seem to produce true overall simi-larity classifications.

The performances of the 4- and 5-year olds fit those predicted by the model under the assumptions of selective attention to a single dimen-sion but no (or little) valuing of identity. The 4- and 5-year-olds shift from what *look like* "overall similarity" classifications to what *look like* "dimensional identity" with increases in the magnitude of stimulus dif-

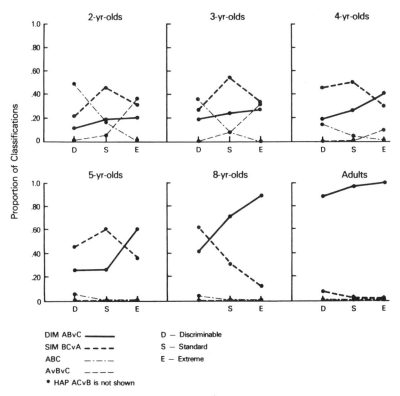

FIGURE 11.8. Mean proportions of the various classifications of the triads depicted in Fig. 11.7 by children and adults.

ferences. This is the pattern expected if children classify by *similarity* on a single dimension as illustrated in quadrant 3 of Fig. 11.5.

The performances of the 8-year-olds and adults also suggest selective attention but differing degrees of valuation of identity. The adults' performance fits that expected by (virtually) perfect selective attention and a high valuing of identity. Perfect selective attention is suggested by the fact that dimensional-identity classifications do not decline with increased magnitudes of stimulus difference. The 8-year pattern also fits that expected given selective attention and some valuing of identity. Indeed, the 8-year-old curves fall nicely between that of the 5-year-olds and the adults. Recall (Fig. 11.6) that increasing the power of the valuing function has the effect of pushing the goodness curves leftward. The 4- and 5-year olds', 8-year-olds', and adults' performances seem related in just this way, and suggest that a major change in this age range is the special treatment of identity in classification tasks.

The results of this experiment thus emphasize the importance of examining performance across a wide range of stimulus differences. If we had used only the standard set, we would have obtained the usual result in the literature—2-, 3-, 4- and 5-year-olds produce overall similarity classifications and 8-year-olds and adults produce dimensional-identity classifications. By considering the standard set alone, we obtain what looks like a monolithic qualitative shift in the structure of classifications. But clearly such a conclusion is wrong. Two- and 3-year-olds and 4- and 5-year-olds are not doing the same thing. The pattern of results indicates that 2- and 3-year-olds classify holistically but 4- and 5-year-olds classify by similarity on one dimension.

Dimensional-Similarity Classifications

In a recent experiment, we found corroborating support for a trend from *overall*-similarity to *dimensional*-similarity to dimensional-identity classifications. Children and adults were given sets of six objects to classify; again, the objects varied in color and size. The sets were structured as in Fig. 11.9. Three possible kinds of classifications were of interest: (a) dimensional identity classifications—AB vs. DC vs. FE or AC vs. BE vs. DF; (b) overall similarity classification—AB vs. CE vs. DF; and (c) *dimensional*-similarity classifications—AB vs. CDEF or ABCE vs. DF. The results are shown in Fig. 11.10. Three- and 4-year-olds principally produced the overall-similarity classification. Adults principally produced the dimensional-identity classification and virtually never produced the dimensional-similarity classification. Five-year-olds, in contrast, often constructed the one-dimensional similarity classification. These children

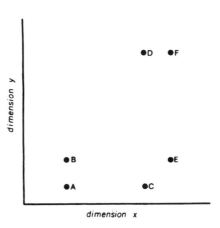

FIGURE 11.9. Structure of a classification set used to distinguish a overall-similarity classification (AB vs. CE vs. DF) from dimensional-similarity classifications (AB vs. CDEF or DF vs. ABCE) and from dimensional-identity classifications (AB vs. DC vs. EF or DF vs. BE vs. AC).

often attend to one dimension but apparently do not require an identity on that dimension to form a group. Performances on control sets showed that there were no developmental differences in the tendency to produce 2 versus 4 or 2 versus 2 versus 2 classifications. Rather, the developmental trend appears to be from classifying by overall similarity, to at least sometimes classifying by *one*-dimensional similarity to classifying by one-dimensional identity.

Absolute Identity

Our finding that older preschoolers selectively attend but do not value identity might seem to suggest that the comparison of objects on one dimension at a time emerges prior to a special emphasis on identities. However, we think the correct story is that both developing abilities emerge at about the same time but are not executed together. Older preschoolers seem to value identity as long as it is absolute identity and selective attention is not required. This idea was first suggested by Evans and Smith's (in press) finding that older preschoolers (5-year-olds) are much more likely than younger ones to produce absolute identity classifications (see also Smith, in press, a in press, b, 1987). For example, if we give children (and adults) sets containing a red square, a red-orange square, a blue square and a blue-green square, very young children (2-year-olds), older children, and adults will group the two reddish ones together and the two bluish ones together. If, however, we add an identical copy of each square so that there are a total of eight, dramatic developmental differences result. The youngest children will put all four reddish ones together in one group and all four bluish ones in the other group. Five-year-olds and adults, in contrast, will tend to group by ab-

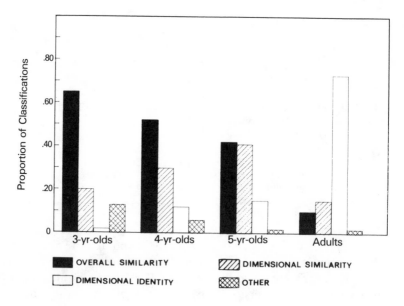

FIGURE 11.10.   Mean proportion of classifications by children and adults of classification sets structured as shown in Fig. 11.9.

solute identity: the two red ones versus the two reddish-orange ones versus the two blue ones versus the two blue-green ones. For the older children and adults (see Evans & Smith, in press) mere similarity is not a good enough basis to constitute a group when absolute identities are present.

Perhaps the best evidence for a shift in the valuing of identity would be developmental changes in similarity ratings. Unfortunately, we cannot (yet) obtain reliable similarity ratings from very young children. We do, however, have some preliminary evidence from eight 4-year-olds and ten 6-year-olds. We gave the children pairs of objects that differed by various amounts on one dimension (size or color) and asked them to rate how well they "matched" by moving a pointer along a board from an unhappy face (do not match at all scored as 0) to a happy face (exactly alike scored as 20). The children's ratings are shown in Fig. 11.11. Both 4-year-olds' and 6-year-olds' ratings of similarity decline with the magnitude of difference. But there is a much steeper drop from absolute identity to the smallest difference for 6-year-olds than for 4-year-olds. In terms of the model, the power of the valuing function becomes greater with age. Between 4 and 6 years and perhaps beginning even sooner (see Smith, in press b), identity becomes an increasingly special kind of similarity.

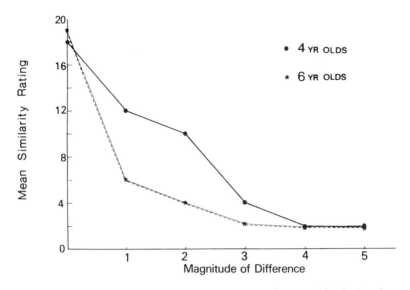

FIGURE 11.11. Mean similarity ratings by 4- and 6-year-olds of pairs of objects that were identical or that differed by increasing amounts on one dimension.

Summary

The evidence supports our claim of two distinct areas of growth: selective attention to dimensions when comparing objects, and the special emphasis on identities (part or whole) when classifying. Growth in the two areas appears concurrent, although initially they may be executed separately. Thus, older preschoolers both classify by single dimensions without showing a preference for part-identity and yet also treat absolute identity as distinct from overall similarity. We think there is an intimate, mutually reinforcing relation between comparing objects on one dimension at a time and the valuing of identity. On the one hand, the emergence of absolute identity clearly prepares the way for the special valuing of part-identities given selective attention. Further, the search for part-identities when there are no absolute ones presumably motivates the comparison of objects on single dimensions. On the other hand, a well developed ability to attend selectively and find part-identities may enhance the cognitive value of identity relations over mere similarity ones. Absolute identity seems too restricted a basis for forming categories and thus would seem to have little advantage as a dominant relation over overall similarity. Whatever its source, an emerging specialness of identity makes good cognitive sense given the logically powerful properties of equivalence relations: reflexivity, transitivity, and symmetry.

IMPLICATIONS AND SPECULATIONS

Our major claims are:

1. Separate features and attributes are processed and analyzed and then put together to form represented wholes.
2. Once formed, these wholes operate as units and cannot be pulled apart. Objects are compared one whole to another; perceived similarity is calculated across all constituents at once.
3. The perceived similarity between one represented whole to another may vary, however, with changes in the weights assigned to individual constituents.
4. The value of perceived similarities for particular tasks may also vary with development such that perceived similarities are treated more or less continuously or dichotomized into the categories of identity and difference.

We have shown that these four claims are sufficient to account for the developmental trend from overall-similarity to dimensional-identity classifications. We suggest that two aspects of comparing multidimensional objects are variable throughout development—the assignment of weights in the calculation of perceived similarity and the value associated with identity as a separate kind of similarity—and variation in these is all that is needed to account for the trend from overall similarity to dimensional identity classifications with separable stimuli. There is no need to posit changes in the units of perception nor in how objects are represented.

By proposing a specific detailed model, we were able to show that both overall-similarity and dimensional-identity classifications are explainable in the same way. By proposing a specific quantitative model, we have also clarified the kinds of data than can and cannot usefully distinguish so-called holistic and analytic perception. First, ostensive overall-similarity classifications may be based on quite unequal weightings of the dimensions. Selective attention without a high valuing of identity may lead to apparent "overall similarity" classifications at certain magnitudes of stimulus difference. Second, magnitude of stimulus difference matters. It is insufficient to show simply more overall similarity or more dimensional-identity classifications. If one wants to conclude something about how "holistic" perception is from classification performance, then the structure of classifications must be examined across a range of stimulus differences.

The model also has broader implications for a number of the issues that motivated this book. We consider these next.

Qualitative Versus Quantitative Change in Development

We began this chapter by asking whether the developmental trend from overall-similarity to dimensional-identity classifications of stimuli varying on separable dimensions reflected developmental differences in *kind* or *degree*. In terms of the actual structures of the classifications produced, there would seem to be a difference in kind. But we have shown that one model can explain both kinds of classifications. The processing that underlies overall-similarity classifications does not differ in kind from that which underlies dimensional-identity classifications, but only in degree—in the degree to which dimensions are differentially weighted and in the degree to which the identity relation is accorded a special status. Further, the developmental changes are likely to be truly continuous; it is not that the child goes from never attending selectively to single dimensions to always doing so perfectly (see Smith, in press b), or from not valuing identity at all to always valuing identity highly. Rather, with age children may simply become more and more likely to compare objects on one dimension at a time, more likely to classify by identity, and more likely to do both at the same time.

The proposal offered here thus fits perfectly with Kemler Nelson's description (chapter 12) of weak-holistic processing. In her view, weak-holistic processing consists of the calculation of overall similarity from independent *dimensional* specifications of objects. This is precisely what we propose to be true *across* developmental levels. By our view, everyone is a weak-holistic processor. Note, also, that we posit no sharp contrast between holistic and analytic processing. They are both the same. They both consist of the calculation of similarity across all represented dimensions; the only differences are in the degree to which dimensions are differentially weighted and whether identities (either part or whole) are particularly valued. We suggest that there is only more or less of the same thing. There is only one machine, one perceptual mode, not one "holistic" mode and another "analytic" mode.

This conclusion does not imply that there are no qualitative differences. Although there may be no qualitative differences in the machinery that underlies perception, there are, perhaps, qualitative differences in the products of perception. Although based on the very same ma-

chinery, the experience of two objects being mostly alike and the experience of two objects being exactly alike in some specified way may be
best thought of as qualitatively distinct kinds of experience. Intro-
spectively, this seems to be the case. The experience of the similarity between a collie and a shepherd seems different in kind from the experience that a cup and car are the very same red. By our view, children and
adults do differ in the frequency with which they weight one dimension
to the exclusion of all others and thereby gain information about similarities on specific dimensions. Thus, there may be qualitative differences in *what* is experienced, albeit none in the mechanisms that cause
those perceptions.

Parts and Wholes in Perception

When we perceive an object, such as a large yellow cup, we perceive it
both as a unitary whole and a conjunction of separate parts. A classic
question has been which of these percepts is primary? Is the whole built
from the parts, or are the parts derived from the whole? Treisman
(1986) has argued that there are two different answers: one for the
coding involved at preconscious levels of processing, and one for the
structure of experience. We embody these two answers in our model; at
the preconscious level, represented wholes are built from parts, but at
the level of experience, parts must be derived from the wholes. The
classification tasks that we have considered in this chapter involve the
conscious comparison of objects and thus in these tasks, *at all developmental levels*, whole object comparisons are simpler. However, in other
tasks that tap the preconscious analysis of features and the buildings of
represented wholes, we would expect to find, as Treisman and Gelade
(1980) did, that attributes and features are prior to the whole.

Within this framework, then, the correct characterization of the developmental trend is not, just as the computational steps are not, from
whole to parts. The developmental trend is most likely primarily one of
greater flexibility and efficiency in the use of developmentally constant
machinery. In tasks involving the conscious comparison of objects, such
as classification, the lesser efficiency and flexibility of the young child
will manifest itself in a greater likelihood of comparing objects by their
similarity on all dimensions equally. In tasks tapping preconscious
stages of processing, the lesser efficiency and flexibility of the young
child will manifest itself in a perhaps lesser likelihood to correctly represent whole objects. There is evidence for a trend from representing parts
to wholes in infancy that may reflect precisely growth in the construction of represented wholes (see Aslin & Smith, 1988, for a review of the

relevant literature). The trend in development, and in computation, may be from unconnected parts to their representation as constituents of wholes to the systematic comparison of wholes in terms of the constituent dimensions.

This suggested trend from "features" to "represented wholes" to "dimensions," *is not* a suggestion that infants perceive features, children perceive wholes, and adults perceive dimensions. Our claim is that the basic nature of processing is the same throughout development: Features are analyzed and combined into represented objects that are compared to each other. We suggest that this is so at all developmental levels. We also suggest that each step becomes more facile with development. In any task designed to measure any step, the younger perceiver is likely to have greater difficulty than the older perceiver. If the task measures the preconscious building of represented wholes from features, the younger perceiver may appear *less* holistic than the older one. If the task measures the comparison of represented wholes, the younger perceiver may appear *more* holistic than the older one.

Are There Changes in What Is Represented?

In the model, we posit developmental changes only in how objects are compared—in the differential weighting of dimensions and in the valuation of identity. We posit no changes in features or in their representation, and we do not think such developmental changes are likely *major* factors in the developmental trend with *separable* dimensions. However, a complete account of the perception of objects (and events) will have to include developmental changes in features and their representation. There are clear changes in feature analyses in infancy, in, for example, visual acuity, in stereopsis, in temporal resolution (see Aslin & Smith, 1988, for a review). There are also changes in the represented dimensions. The representation of object size, for example, undergoes reorganization as stereopsis emerges (see Aslin & Smith, 1988).

Perceptual representations may also change beyond infancy. The human perceptual system is highly flexible, and sensitive to the effects of experience, either via general exposure or specific learning (see Gibson & Gibson, 1955). One possible source of perceptual learning is the formation of new units at the level of perceptual representation, perhaps through a process of extracting task-relevant correlations between sensory primitives. Something of the sort must be the case in speech perception. The representation of speech appears to shift from acoustic to language-specific (e.g., phonemic) units in early childhood (see, e.g., Jusczyk, 1985, 1986; Walley, in press). The very units with which the

sounds corresponding to "ball" and "cup" are represented change with
development and depend on the specific language learned. In terms of
our model, then, the dimensions across which the perceived similarities
are calculated change with development. Note that by our view, the
perceived similarity is calculated in the same way—across all *represented*
features—however, in the case of speech, the represented features
change with development.

We do not believe that changes in which features are represented is a
major source of developmental differences. Except in the special case of
language and perhaps also special training with other stimulus sets, it
seems likely that infants beyond 6 months, children, and adults all represent most objects in mostly the same way (see Aslin & Smith, 1988).
And what our model shows is that one need not posit changes in representation to account for a shift from overall similarity to dimensional
comparisons of objects.

Integral Dimensions and Configural Dimensions

As pointed out in chapters 3, 5, and 8, the precise stimulus dimensions
matter. Not all dimensions are separable. Some are integral and some
configure. We think that such stimulus effects are easily incorporated
into the present model at the level of feature analysis and representation. Integral and configural dimensions both seem to represent cases of
different features at the levels of feature analyses and representation. Integral dimensions such as hue, saturation, and brightness are *psychological* dimensions, and are therefore clearly in the system. The issue is
where they are in the system. We think that these dimensions are part of
the feature analysis level but are not (usually, see Foard & Kemler Nelson, 1984) parts of object representations. Rather, only "color" as a global feature may be represented as a constituent dimension in the mental
description of objects. Our suggestion, then, is that hue, saturation, and
brightness are, in Kemler Nelson's terminology (chapter 12), strongly
holistic. We illustrate this notion in Fig. 11.12. Of course, one could propose that hue, saturation, and brightness are parts of object representations, but are perceived holistically because they cannot be differentially
weighted. However, such an account would leave unexplained why differential weights cannot be applied to these three represented dimensions but can be to other represented dimensions.

Configural effects definitionally consist of a discrepancy between the
represented (i.e., perceived) object and the simple conjunction of individual features. Whether the individual features exist at early levels of
analysis and are just not part of the represented object is an issue for

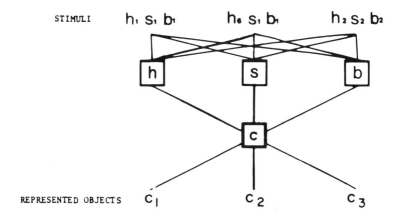

FIGURE 11.12. Illustration of the proposed discrepancy between hue (h), saturation (s), and brightness (b) as dimension at initial levels of processing and color (c) as the unitary dimension at the level of represented objects.

others (e.g., chapter 6) to resolve. The feature-analyses level we depict in Fig. 11.3 is clearly much more complicated than our illustration, and some cases of holistic processing may well be due to the "dimensions" under investigation not being part of the represented object. Again, however, we do not think that changes in the structure of representation play a major role in the *developmental* trend in classification.

Strategic and Non-Strategic Weightings of Dimensions

A question left unresolved in the current version of the model is whether there are any constraints on the distribution of dimension weights. The only cases we considered were the "default" equal weighting of all dimensions and the strategic weighting of one dimension to the exclusion of all others. Can one attend selectively to only two of three varying dimensions? This is clearly an empirical question. We suspect that the answer will be "yes, but not perfectly." Our hunch is that one can strategically attend to one dimension perfectly. And one can certainly *try* to split attention between two dimensions while excluding a third. But the processing demands may be considerable. We doubt that one could consciously, strategically employ weighting schemes between "splitting" attention and attending only to one (or perhaps several) dimensions. We doubt, for example, that one could *decide* to use a .6, .3, .1 weighting scheme.

Such intermediate weighting schemes may well be common but just not strategically deployed. Nosofsky (1984b), in his studies of adult category learning, has shown that adult subjects subtly distribute attention among component dimensions so as to optimize performance in a given category learning task. We suspect that the *nonstrategic* fine tuning of weights to fit particular categories is, in fact, an important part of natural category learning. On this point, we agree with J.D. Smith (chapter 10) and Ward (chapter 13). Although very young children may not strategically shift weights in laboratory classification tasks, they may nonstrategically but nonetheless systematically do so in more natural category learning tasks.

Landau, Smith, & Jones (in press) have reported evidence that points to this important possibility. In this study, 24-month-olds and 30-month-olds were asked to classify objects that varied in their shape, size, and texture. One task was a free classification task. Children were presented with a standard object and asked which one of two other objects was like it. In the second task, the standard object was named. The children were shown the standard and told, for example, "this is a Dax." They were then asked which of the two other objects was also a Dax. The results were quite straightforward. In the free classification task, the children attended to all dimensions and grouped together the two that were most alike. In the naming task, in contrast, the children attended to shape. They called by the same name objects that were the same shape. Just how dramatic this result was is illustrated in Fig. 11.13, which shows a sample trial drawn to scale. In the free classification task, the children grouped together a 2″ U shaped object and a 2″ slightly bent U shape. In the naming task, they grouped together a 2″ U shape and the identically shaped but 24″ object. In terms of the model, very young children differentially weight shape more heavily than texture and size when *naming* objects.

Perceptual Similarity

The model *and* the data suggest that perceptual similarity is not all relative. The absolute magnitudes of similarity matter. We wonder if perceived similarity is not relative at all but only *appears* to be because of varying weighting schemes (see Smith, in press b, for more on this point, also Shephard, 1964). Further, we suspect that adult performances provide a highly contaminated measure of similarity. Relevant to this latter point are recent findings reported in Evans & Smith (in press). We gave adults sets to classify in which there were dimensional identities and other sets in which there were no identities. The adults

FIGURE 11.13. Scale drawing of stimuli used by Landau, Smith, & Jones (1987).

readily produced overall similarity classifications when there were no part-identities—producing what, by the model, should have been for them not-very-good classifications as often as they produced the dimensional-identity classifications when such preferred classifications were possible. However, when asked to rate the "quality" of their own classifications, they rated the overall-similarity ones much lower than the dimensional-identity ones. The *best* classifications of the two different sets were not equally good. The problem, we think, is that when an experimenter asks, "which two go together," adults give the best answer. Adults, unlike the very young child, strive to meet adult expectations of task performance and try to avoid such "odd' classifications as grouping all objects together or each singly. Our view, then, is that Lockhead's demonstration (chapter 9) of the relativistic nature of similarity actually has very little to do with *perceptual* similarity. Lockhead's results may instead reflect something very lawful about how adults reason about relative similarity. If one is interested in the *perception* of similarity, the best subject population may be very young children. We suspect that a 2- or 3-year-old would not honor the "Golden Section."

CONCLUSION

The purpose of our quantitative model was to specify *in detail* what might be developing in perceptual classification tasks. Detailed accounts that may be empirically examined are critical to evaluating what this trend is about. There are lots of vague hypotheses in the literature, and it is not clear that they can account for the developmental evidence. The present model can. Further, the building of a detailed model brought new insights. By attempting a quantitative account, we discovered the critical importance of the absolute magnitude of stimulus difference. We discovered that apparent overall similarity classifications need not be based on *overall* similarity at all, but rather may be based on single-dimension similarity. We discovered that there are *two* developing abilities—the differential weighting of dimensions and the differentiation of identity as a special kind of similarity. And we learned that the apparent *qualitative* differences in the structure of overall similarity and dimensional identity may stem from solely *quantitative* differences in processing.

ACKNOWLEDGMENTS

This work was supported by Public Health Service Grants HD-19949 and HD-00589 and benefited from many discussions with Robert Nosofsky. Paul Evans is now at Princeton University.

REFERENCES

Aschkenasy, J.R., & Odom, R.D. (1982). Classification and perceptual development: Exploring issues about integrality and differential sensitivity. *Journal of Experimental Child Psychology, 34,* 435–488.

Aslin, R.N., & Smith, L.B. (1988). Perceptual development. In M.R. Rosenzweig & L.W. Porter (Eds.), *Annual review of psychology,* Volume 39, 435–474.

Caron, A.J. (1969). Discrimination shifts in three-year-olds as a function of dimensional salience. *Developmental Psychology, 1,* 333–339.

Evans, P.M., & Smith, L.B. (in press). The development of identity as a privileged relation in classification: When very similar is just not similar enough. *Cognitive Development, 3.*

Foard, C.F., & Kemler Nelson, D.G. (1984). Holistic and analytic modes of processing: The multiple determinants of perceptual analysis. *Journal of Experimental Psychology: General, 113,* 94–111.

Garner, W.R. (1970). The stimulus in information processing. *American Psychologist, 25,* 350–358.

Garner, W.R. (1974). *The processing of information and structure.* Potomac, MD: Lawrence Erlbaum Associates.

Gibson, E.J. (1969). *Principles of perceptual learning and development.* New York: Appleton-Century-Crofts.

Gibson, J.J., & Gibson, E.J. (1955). Perceptual learning: Differentiation of enrichment? *Psychological Review, 62,* 32–41.

Jusczyk, P.W. (1985). On characterizing the development of speech perception. In J. Mehler, & R. Fox (Eds.), *Neonate cognition: Beyond the blooming buzzing confusion* (199–229). Hillsdale, NJ: Lawrence Erlbaum Associates.

Jusczyk, P.W. (1986). Toward a model of the development of speech perception. In J.S. Perkell & D.H. Klatt (Eds.), *Invariance and variability in speech processes* (1–35). Hillsdale, NJ: Lawrence Erlbaum Associates.

Keil, F.C., & Batterman, N. (1984). A characteristic-to-defining shift in the development of word meaning. *Journal of Verbal Learning and Verbal Behavior, 23*, 221–236.

Kemler, D.G. (1982). Classification in young and retarded children: The primacy of overall similarity relations. *Child Development, 53*, 768–779.

Kemler, D.G. (1983). Exploring and reexploring issues of integrality, perceptual sensitivity, and dimensional salience. *Journal of Experimental Child Psychology, 36*, 365–379.

Kemler, D.G., & Smith, L.B. (1979). Accessing similarity and dimensional relations: Effects of integrality and separability on the discovery of complex concepts. *Journal of Experimental Psychology: General, 108*, 133–150.

Landau, B., Smith, L.B., & Jones, S.S. (in press). The importance of shape in early lexical learning. *Cognitive Development, 3*, ??–??.

Lockhead, G.R. (1966). Effects of dimensional redundancy on visual discrimination. *Journal of Experimental Psychology, 72*, 95–104.

Lockhead, G.R. (1972). Processing dimensional stimuli: A note. *Psychological Review, 79*, 410–419.

Mednick, S.A., & Lehtinen, L.E. (1957). Stimulus generalization as a function of age in children. *Journal of Experimental Psychology, 33*, 180–183.

Nosofsky, R.M. (1984a). Choice, similarity, and the context theory of classification. *Journal of Experimental Psychology: Learning, Memory and Cognition, 10*, 104–114.

Nosofsky, R.M. (1984b). Optimization of similarity relations in the categorization of multidimensional stimuli. Doctoral thesis, Harvard University, Boston, MA.

Odom, R.D. (1978). A perceptual-salience account of decalage relations and developmental change. In L.S. Siegal, & C.J. Brainerd (Eds.), *Alternatives to Piaget* (pp. 111–130). New York: Academic Press.

Shepard, R.N. (1964). Attention and the metric structure of the stimulus space. *Journal of Mathematical Psychology, 1*, 54–87.

Shepp, B.E. (1983). The analyzability of multi-dimensional objects: Some constraints on perceived structure, the development of perceived structure, and attention. In T.J. Tighe & B.E. Shepp (Eds.), *Perception, cognition and development* (pp. 39–74). Hillsdale, NJ: Lawrence Erlbaum Associates.

Shepp, B.E., & Swartz, K.B. (1976). Selective attention and the processing of integral and nonintegral dimensions: A developmental study. *Journal of Experimental Child Psychology, 22*, 73–85.

Smith, J.D., & Kemler Nelson, D.G. (1984). Overall similarity in adults' classification: The child in all of us. *Journal of Experimental Psychology: General, 113*, 137–159.

Smith, L.B. (1979). Perceptual development and category generalization. *Child Development, 50*, 705–715.

Smith, L.B. (1981). The importance of the overall similarity of objects for adults' and children's classifications. *Journal of Experimental Psychology: Human Perception and Performance, 1*, 811–824.

Smith, L.B. (1983). Development of classification: The use of similarity and dimensional relations. *Journal of Experimental Child Psychology, 36*, 150–178.

Smith, L.B. (1984). Young children's understanding of attributes and dimensions: A comparison of conceptual and linguistic measures. *Child Development, 55*, 363–380.

Smith, L.B. (in press a). From global similarity to kinds of similarity: The construction of dimensions in development. In S. Vosniadou & A. Ortony (Eds.), *Similarity and analogy*. New York, NY: Cambridge University Press.

Smith, L.B. (in press b). A model of perceptual classification in children and adults. *Psychological Review*.

Smith, L.B., & Kemler, D.G. (1977). Developmental trends in free classification: Evidence for a new conceptualization of perceptual development. *Journal of Experimental Child Psychology, 24*, 279–298.

Smith, L.B., & Kemler, D.G. (1978). Levels of experienced dimensionality in children and adults. *Cognitive Psychology, 10,* 502–532.

Smith, L.B., Kemler, D.G., & Aronfreed, J. (1975). Developmental trends in voluntary selective attention: Differential effects of source distinctness. *Journal of Experimental Child Psychology, 20,* 352–362.

Treisman, A. (1986). Properties, parts and objects. In K. Boff, L. Kaufman, & J. Thomas (Eds.), *Handbook of perception and performance* (pp. 35-1–35-70). New York: Wiley.

Treisman, A., & Gelade, G. (1980). A feature integration theory of attention. *Cognitive Psychology, 12,* 97–136.

Vurpillot, E. (1976). *The visual world of the child.* New York: International Universities Press.

Walley, A.C. (in press). Spoken word recognition by young children and adults. *Cognitive Development.*

Ward, T.B. (1983). Response tempo and separable-integral responding: Evidence for an integral-to-separable processing sequencing in visual perception. *Journal of Experimental Psychology: Human Perception and Performance, 9,* 103–112.

Werner, H. (1948). *The comparative psychology of mental development.* New York, NY: International Universities Press, Inc.

Wohlwill, J. (1962). From perception to inference: A dimension of cognitive development. *Monographs of the Society for Research in Child Development, 72,* 87–107.

12 THE NATURE AND OCCURRENCE OF HOLISTIC PROCESSING

Deborah G. Kemler Nelson
Swarthmore College

INTRODUCTION

Over the last fifteen years or so, there have been a number of interrelated claims about the conditions under which holistic processing is likely to occur. Even a brief list of some of the generalizations that have been proposed makes clear that they have spanned a number of different kinds of effects. In comparison with analytic processing, holistic processing has been said to occur relatively more often when:

(a) The stimuli that are being processed are composed of integral dimensions;
(b) The individuals doing the processing are young or intellectually retarded or characterized by an impulsive cognitive style;
(c) The conditions under which processing is occurring undermine resource-intensive modes of cognition or conscious problem-solving strategies.

What sets apart the preceding generalizations about (a) stimulus effects, (b) processor effects, and (c) contextual effects from some other claims about holistic processing is that they have come out of a shared conception and operationalization of what holistic processing entails. For example, I have excluded from this list the often-heard proposal that right-hemisphere processing is holistic because, generally, that claim does not rest on the same experimental operations or, it seems, on the same view of what holistic processing means. In fact, when shared operations are used, the right-hemisphere hypothesis receives mixed support at best (Trope, Rozin, Kemler Nelson, & Gur, submitted).

I believe that the understanding of holistic processing that unites the generalizations that I have mentioned is worthy of special attention, and that one of the reasons is that it is a particularly precise and, accordingly, useful understanding of "holistic." Still, it is absolutely clear that the distinction between analytic and holistic processing is not easy to demonstrate unambiguously even in the best of circumstances. Not surprisingly, every one of the three aforementioned proposals has generated some controversy, with counterclaims that the pattern attributed to holistic processing really stems from analytic processing of some sort.

The purpose of this chapter is to take a careful look at the usage of "holistic" and the kind of evidence that can count for holistic processing in the literature that I have demarcated. First, I provide a brief specification of what holistic processing has denoted and how it has been indexed. Then, I consider how well differentiated this usage is—operationally and also conceptually—from alternative views of how processing is occurring. Optimally, such an enterprise will provide a useful guide for further reflection and clarification and for further research in any of the several domains in which the attribution of holistic processing has been made.

THE PRIMACY OF OVERALL SIMILARITY RELATIONS

The series of three generalizations at the beginning of this chapter starts with the proposal about stimulus integrality for very clear historical reasons (and to give credit where credit is due). The sense of holistic processing that is the focus of this chapter has its roots in discussions of stimulus effects by Lockhead (1972) and by Garner (1974). These investigators (see also Shepard, 1964) have noted that different combinations of stimulus dimensions consistently elicit different patterns of perceptual processing. In particular, dimensions like saturation and brightness—the most studied example of integral dimensions—combine in stimuli that seem to be processed as global wholes. For integral stimuli as global wholes, the primary stimulus relation is overall similarity. By contrast, stimuli composed from separable dimensions—such as size and brightness—are processed primarily in terms of their dimensional components, and the predominant stimulus relations are property-specific. In the separable case, the stimuli are usually analyzed into their constituents, and these component properties serve as the units that guide processing. In the integral case, the component properties do not function as independent units, but combine instead into a whole, to be related to other stimulus wholes on the basis of global similarity. This description of the processing of integral stimuli is the starting point for the current understanding of holistic processing: It is processing guided by relations of overall similarity.

Many of the operations used to distinguish integral and separable dimensions—and, accordingly, holistic and analytic processing—do no more than pit the use of overall similarity relations against the use of relations based on constituent properties (e.g., dimensions). When overall similarity relations take precedence, processing is said to be holistic; and when component property relations predominate, it is said to be analytic. The idea is very simple and it can be exemplified in a number of ways. For example, one of the original operations high-lighted by Garner (1974) involves a simple unspeeded classification task, in which as few as three stimuli are presented. The subject is simply told to "put together the ones that go together." As Fig. 12.1 shows, the stimulus triad is structured so that the two stimuli most similar over-all (B and C) have no specific distinguishing properties in common. But one of these stimuli (B) does share a distinguishing property or dimensional component (e.g., same value of size or same value of color, etc.) with the third stimulus (A). By seeing which partition the processor selects, one assesses the relative importance of overall similarity versus dimensional relations, and infers from this the preferred mode of processing—holistic or analytic.

Partly due to its simplicity, the unspeeded classification operation has been widely used. In fact, it has contributed data relevant to each of the three generalizations with which I began this presentation (e.g., Handel & Imai, 1972; Kemler, 1982a; Shepp, Burns, & McDonough, 1980; L.B. Smith & Kemler, 1977; J.D. Smith & Kemler Nelson, 1984, 1988; Ward, 1980).

Holistic processing as processing characteristically guided by overall similarity relations has been indexed in other rather different ways. Kemler and L.B. Smith (1979) devised an operation that involves the categorization of stimulus pairs. Consider a set of stimulus pairs that differ—one pair from the other—both according to which particular (single) dimension has a value that is different within the pair and also according to the overall similarity within the pair (as created by the single difference). For example, if the stimulus space consists of variations in size and shade of gray, one subset would contain pairs of stimuli in which the stimuli are identical in every respect save size. Half of these pairs would consist of stimuli that differ by a relatively small amount in size (e.g., a pair containing a square that is 1 inch to a side and a square of the same color that is 1 ¼ inches to a side); half of them would contain stimuli that differ by a relatively large amount in size (e.g., a pair containing a square that is 1 inch to a side and a square of the same color that is 1 ¾ inches to a side). Complementing these small-difference/size and large-difference/size pairs, the other subset would contain pairs in which the stimuli differ only along the other dimension, shade of gray. Again, small-difference pairs (e.g., white and light gray squares of the same size) and large-difference pairs (e.g., white and dark gray squares of the same size) would be included in the subset.

To pit overall similarity against constituent property relations, the processor is induced to categorize the pairs either according to overall similarity, regardless of which particular dimension varies (i.e., all small-difference pairs vs. all large-difference pairs) or according to the specific dimension of difference, regardless of the amount of similarity (i.e., all size-different pairs vs. all shade-different pairs). Either ease of learning or ease of executing the two categorization schemes can be compared. This kind of operation was used successfully by Kemler and L.B. Smith (1979) to converge on stimulus effects, integrality and separability, and by J.D. Smith and Kemler Nelson (1984) to examine the contextual effect of speed stress.

A third paradigm that I discuss explores the implications of overall similarity versus specific property relations in category learning. Kemler Nelson (1984) suggested that holistic processing as attuned to overall similarity is better suited to learning categories that have a strong family resemblance structure (based on many characteristic attributes) than to learning categories based on a constituent defining attribute. The derivation depends on the fact that when a cluster of many characteristic attributes creates high similarity among members of the same category and low similarity among members of different categories, a learner at-

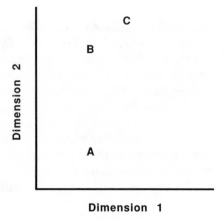

FIGURE 12.1. The structure of a triad of stimuli often used in free classification tasks. A, B, and C represent three stimuli. A and B have an identical value on Dimension 1 but differ appreciably on Dimension 2. Although B and C do not have a common value on either dimension, they are the most overall-similar pair of items in the triad. Adapted from J.D. Smith and Kemler Nelson (1984).

tuned to overall similarity relations (i.e., a holistic processor) will be in a good position to learn the categories. By contrast, when only one of many attributes is relevant to categorization, the similarity relations will not be particularly helpful in learning the categories, and, accordingly, the holistic processor will run into more difficulty.

This kind of argument can be applied to learning the categories whose structure is shown in the top panel of Fig. 12.2. In this particular case, the category learning task can be solved on two bases: (a) the individual may learn to respond on the basis of the single attribute that alone is criterial for category membership, that is, the leftmost attribute in the series; or (b) the individual may learn about the entire cluster of stimulus attributes, most of them only characteristic attributes, that form the family resemblance structure. Within this kind of task, the prediction is that conditions that prompt holistic processing will shift learning in the direction of the second kind of solution and away from the first.

The "critical test stimuli," shown in the middle panel of Fig. 12.2, can be inserted after learning is completed in order to figure out how a subject solved the problem. A learner who makes decisions on the basis of the single criterial attribute should classify the top stimulus (a) in Category I and the bottom stimulus (b) in Category II in line with the dictates of that criterial attribute. On the other hand, a learner attuned to the overall similarity relations of the family resemblance structure should tend to classify the top stimulus (a) in Category II and the bottom stimulus (b) in Category I. This is because stimulus a is more similar overall to the instances in Category II and stimulus b is more similar overall to the instances in Category I.

With this kind of paradigm, Kemler Nelson (1984) concluded that when learning is unintentional, family-resemblance-based processing—hence, holistic processing—is more likely among adults than when category learning is intentional. A variant of this paradigm was also used to argue that younger children, more than older children, are biased toward family-resemblance learning based on holistic processing under intentional conditions of learning (Kemler Nelson, 1984, Exp. 4). Moreover, L.B. Smith (1984), studying individual differences among adults, found that family-resemblance-based (hence, presumably holistic) category learning tended to occur more frequently in individuals who predominantly responded by overall similarity (hence, presumably holistically) in triad classification tasks.

All in all, the conceptualization of holistic processing as characterized by the predominance of overall similarity relations has been very productive. It has allowed us to go beyond the initial set of operations that were tied to stimulus integrality (Garner, 1974; Lockhead, 1972) to an expanded set of operations that maintain the same sense of what holistic

LEARNING TASK

Category I	Category II
0 0 0 1	2 2 2 1
0 0 1 0	2 2 1 2
0 1 0 0	2 1 2 2

FIGURE 12.2. A representation of the structure of the stimuli used in Kemler Nelson's (1984) study (Exp. 2) of category learning. Each stimulus is indicated as a string of four numbers, denoting the values of the stimulus on each of four attributes. Value 1 of an attribute is intermediate between values 0 and 2. Top: Six stimuli used during the category learning phase. Middle: Two "critical test" stimuli, inserted in the test phase. Bottom: Six "close instances," inserted in the test phase. The test stimuli help to distinguish between different bases for learning the original task. Adapted from Kemler Nelson (1988).

CRITICAL TEST STIMULI

(a) 0 2 2 2

(b) 2 0 0 0

CLOSE INSTANCES

(c) 0 0 0 2

(d) 0 0 2 0

(e) 0 2 0 0

(f) 2 2 2 0

(g) 2 2 0 2

(h) 2 0 2 2

processing entails. Both the pairs-classification paradigm and the category-learning paradigm just discussed are examples of such expanded operations. Moreover, the generation of new—but conceptually related—ways of indexing holistic processing is more than a methodological asset (i.e., allowing for more converging operations). As the preceding discussion of category learning suggests, the importance of overall similarity relations provides a link between holistic processing proposals and other significant psychological issues. Kemler Nelson (1984) has noted, for example, that holistic processing in early and unintentional category learning, that is, processing of wholes and generalization by overall similarity, should be conducive to the everyday learning of basic-level object categories. This derivation follows from Rosch and Mervis' (1975) view that basic-level categories are well differentiated by overall similarity because of a strong family resemblance structure based on correlated characteristic attributes—that, at this basic level, there is relatively high similarity between common category members and relatively low similarity between members of different categories. In addition, Keil's hypothesis of a characteristic-to-defining shift in the development of word meanings (e.g., Keil & Batterman, 1984) is highly consistent with the notion that the younger child is attentive to the overall similarity of category exemplars rather than to a principled basis for meaning (see also Carey, 1978), again a tendency that ties in with the developmental hypothesis about more holistic, *qua* overall-similarity-dominated, processing in younger children.

It appears, then, that the understanding of holistic processing as dominated by overall similarity relations has been central to a number of conceptual and experimental endeavors over the last decade or so. In the sections that follow, I consider this understanding in a critical vein. Two issues frame the bulk of the following discussion. The first issue is whether the grounds for inferring processing by overall similarity relations have been sufficiently convincing when the various generalizations about holistic processing have been made. This is largely an empirical issue. The second issue revolves around a more conceptually fundamental point. It calls for a critical examination of the sense of "overall similarity" relations needed to support an interesting understanding of holistic processing. Even when the case for overall similarity is made (the first issue), the attribution of holistic processing may not be justifiable (the second issue). The challenge that threads through the entire discussion is whether processing might be more appropriately described as analytic in the cases that holistic processing has been invoked instead. Only by responding to this kind of challenge can we sustain the holistic/analytic distinction in an account of the various stimulus, observer, or contextual effects mentioned at the beginning of this chapter.

OVERALL SIMILARITY
OR A DIFFERENT SELECTED PROPERTY?

Holistic processing as indexed by the use of overall similarity relations is often contrasted with analytic processing as indexed by a focus on a single stimulus property. With regard to the analytic case, the basic and simple idea is that analysis of the stimulus into its properties is a prerequisite for the selective use of one of the properties as a guide to processing. Thus, an individual who classifies the stimulus triads of Fig. 12.1 on the basis of the shared dimension (Dimension 1) (putting Stimuli A and B together) or who learns the categories of Fig. 12.2 by a rule based only on the first-mentioned attribute, which is defining for category membership, would seem to be processing in an analytic way. Such inferences would seem to be reasonably clearcut.

However, within these paradigms, there is more ambiguity in the inference of holistic processing. A moment's reflection reveals that the response patterns that would be taken to indicate the use of overall similarity relations and, hence, holistic processing could be due instead to selective analytic processing that is quite similar in kind to, but different in content from, the sort of selective analytic processing referred to earlier. In particular, the response patterns taken to indicate the use of overall similarity relations could arise because the individual is processing a different selected property from the particular one that the experimenter has singled out. In other words, the subject could be analytic and selective, but could fail to select exactly the same property that the experimenter defines as relevant. To count such an event as an instance of overall-similarity-based or holistic processing is plainly to commit an inferential error. Hence, an important issue is whether the generalizations about holistic processing with which we began are protected against this kind of alternative account, by which the processing in question is not attuned to overall similarity at all.

In the discussion that follows, I outline two versions of this challenge that have been raised in the literature, and I discuss the kinds of argument and evidence that have been used to bolster the holistic processing conclusion. The two cases constitute an interesting pair because they involve different experimental paradigms.

The triad classification task was the focus of Aschkenasy and Odom (1982), who specifically questioned the case for a developmental trend from holistic to analytic processing (e.g., Shepp et al., 1980; L.B. Smith & Kemler, 1977; Ward, 1980). What has been claimed is that older children are more likely than younger children to classify these triads (analytically) according to a particular dimension, and less likely than younger children to classify them (holistically) according to overall similarity relations. That is, by reference to Fig. 12.1, the older child is relatively more likely to classify A and B together (presumably because they share a value on Dimension 1) and the younger child is relatively more likely to classify B and C together, purportedly because they constitute the most similar pair of items. However, as Aschkenasy and Odom pointed out, B and C are also the two stimuli most similar on Dimension 2. Hence, if a subject were attuned preferentially to Dimension 2, that subject could group B and C together for an analytic reason, and might be mistaken for a holistic responder.

Is there any plausible reason why young children might be attuned particularly to Dimension 2, that is, to the dimension that does not permit an identity match within the triad? Unfortunately for the holistic proposal, such an alternative view of the observed effect can be formulated quite reasonably. Aschkenasy and Odom's principal argument is that young children are sensitive to fewer dimensions than older children, and particularly that young children are likely to focus selectively on what is for them the most salient dimension of the stimuli. If the most salient dimension for a child were Dimension 2, that child might focus inflexibly on Dimension 2, and put B and C together in the triad of

Fig. 12.1. Older children, attuned to both dimensions, presumably would be more able to switch flexibly between Dimensions 1 and 2, always selecting the dimension that permits an exact match within the class (Dimension 1 for the triad that is shown). Hence, the older child, but not the younger one, would produce just the analytic responses that the experimenter expected. Still, both would be analyzing.

To distinguish inflexible but dimensionally analytic classification from truly holistic (i.e., overall-similarity-based) classification (or from flexible and analytic classification), it is necessary to examine performance over a series of triads. Across the triads, the roles of Dimensions 1 and 2 in Fig. 12.1 need to be interchanged between the dimensions that are being varied in the stimulus set. For example, when the stimuli are composed from the dimensions of size and brightness, sometimes two stimuli in the triad should match on size and other times, they should match on brightness. Then, a dimensional preferrer, that is, an inflexible but analytic processor, would manifest a distinctive response pattern. For example, a size preferrer would always produce the dimensional classification when size is the dimension that permits a match, but would appear to produce the similarity classification (because Dimension 2 controls the response) when brightness is the matched dimension. By contrast, a truly holistic processor would produce the overall-similarity classification and a flexible analytic processor would produce the dimensional classification regardless of the type of triad.

What does the evidence suggest? First, it suggests that Aschkenasy and Odom's challenge was not without some foundation: The dimensional preference pattern does sometimes emerge in children's classifications (e.g., Shepp et al., 1980; J.D. Smith & Kemler Nelson, 1988). However, the evidence also fundamentally confirms the holistic processing proposal as a description of early classifications. It appears that the dimensional preference pattern may constitute an intermediate level of classification, preceded developmentally by a predominance of true overall-similarity classifications and followed developmentally by a predominance of dimensional responses that are flexibly adjusted to the dimensional roles. Indeed, it makes sense that the dimensional preference pattern—clearly analytic but still quite rigid—is developmentally earlier than the pure dimensional strategy (Kemler, 1983a). Accordingly, addressing the challenge presented by Aschkenasy and Odom leads to a more differentiated proposal about holistic and analytic processing. This kind of tripartite proposal may apply not only to developmental differences, but to other kinds of variables that systematically affect processing modes, such as the stimulus and contextual effects mentioned earlier, as well as other observer effects.

Quite recently, Ward and Scott (1987) resurrected the kind of issue

originally raised by Aschkenasy and Odom, but with reference now to
the category-learning paradigm. They pointed out that an inflexible but
analytic category learner could produce the same response pattern that
was taken by Kemler Nelson (1984) as evidence of family-resemblance
learning and hence the use of holistic similarity relations. Accordingly,
both the effect of intention to learn and the developmental effect that
were observed (Kemler Nelson, 1984) might be due not to the holistic/
analytic difference, but to a difference between inflexible and flexible
analytic learning procedures. The question they raise is whether the
subjects originally classified as "family-resemblance learners" were really attuned to the overall similarity relations created by the family resemblance structure or whether, instead, those subjects were trying to
learn the categories by attending to a specific selected stimulus
property—just one that was not created to be criterial by the experimenter.

Referring to Fig. 12.2, one can see how these quite different approaches to learning might be confused. As previously discussed, a subject who learns about the family-resemblance structure and generalizes
by overall similarity will respond in the test phase by categorizing the
top "critical-test" stimulus (a) in Category II and the bottom "critical-
test" stimulus (b) in Category I. This will contrast with the "critical-test"
responses of the analytic criterial-attribute learner, but, importantly, it
will be indistinguishable from those of an analytic subject who merely
responds on the basis of a selected but noncriterial attribute, such as any
of the three rightmost attributes listed in Fig. 12.2. A subject who is selectively focussing on any of the characteristic but not defining attributes
in the original problem will produce critical-test responses that are indistinguishable from the similarity-based family resemblance pattern.

It would seem to be absolutely critical to address this ambiguity in the
paradigm. Like the dimensional preference proposal of Aschkenasy and
Odom, the suggestion that subjects may respond selectively to a single
attribute that is not the experimenter's target and be misrepresented as a
result goes to the core of the paradigm. Such a response tendency is
clearly based on analytic rather than holistic processing, because it involves selecting out a single property of the stimuli. Thus, to confuse it
with the response tendency predicted by holistic processing as governed
by overall similarity is to undermine the usefulness of the paradigm as a
way to index holistic versus analytic processing.

Moreover, Ward and Scott make a plausible case that the very factors
that Kemler Nelson (1984) identified with holistic processing could be
promoting instead a tendency to respond according to a noncriterial attribute. Incidental learners or young learners, more than intentional
learners or older learners, may "get stuck" on a noncriterial (only char-

acteristic) attribute—because of rigid attribute preferences, for example, much like those posited by Aschkenasy and Odom. Stuck on such an attribute, they may achieve a problem solution by supplementing this single-attribute rule with the learning of exceptional instances or they may simply end up with an incomplete solution and guess on the instances that do not fit it. For example, by reference to Fig. 12.2, a subject who focussed on the right-most attribute would have to guess about the top category exemplars in the learning task or would have to learn their assignments in rote fashion, because these two stimuli have the neutral value, "1," on the right-most attribute.

Given the force of Ward and Scott's challenge, it is again fortunate that there are reasonably straightforward experimental operations for meeting it. Consider the stimuli called "close instances" in the bottom panel of Fig. 12.2. The name derives from the high similarity between each of these instances and an original category member. More importantly here, inserting the set of close instances in the test phase permits one to distinguish the response pattern of the noncriterial-attribute responder from that of the family-resemblance learner (Kemler Nelson, 1984, 1988; Ward & Scott, 1987). Whereas the latter, using overall similarity to the original stimuli, would be likely to classify the first three close instances in Category I and the last three in Category II, the selective noncriterial attribute learner would show a different pattern that is specific to the noncriterial attribute that has been singled out. For example, if it is the rightmost attribute, the subject would classify the first (c) and the last two (g and h) close instances in Category II and the other three close instances (d, e, and f) in Category I—simply following the dictates of that single attribute.

Ward and Scott (1987) showed that the single noncriterial attribute pattern occurred with some frequency within the category learning paradigm. For present purposes, however, the more critical question is whether that pattern, as opposed to the family-resemblance overall-similarity pattern, accounted for apparent incidental-versus-intentional learning effects or for developmental differences. Although some of Ward and Scott's findings suggest that it might, Kemler Nelson (1984, 1988) showed that the conclusion of more family resemblance learning when learning is unintentional survives the more stringent tests (even though about 10% of Kemler Nelson's adult learners may be showing the noncriterial attribute strategy of concern to Ward and Scott).

In fact, the tripartite proposal that emerged from the discussion of triad classification would seem to be consistent with these findings. For example, in a breakdown comparing incidental and intentional conditions in Kemler Nelson's Experiment 2, Table 12.1 shows that family resemblance learners were more likely under incidental than intentional

TABLE 12.1
A breakdown of the classifiable intentional and incidental learners in
Kemler Nelson's (1984) Experiment 2, according to the way they
learned. It shows the number of learners of each type, as well as
the percentage of all classifiable learners in each condition who
were of each type.

Type of Learner	Learning Condition	
	Intentional	Incidental
Family Resemblance	17 (39%)	24 (67%)
Noncriterial Attribute	5 (11%)	5 (14%)
Criterial Attribute	22 (50%)	17 (19%)

conditions; noncriterial attribute responders were about equally likely
in the two conditions, and criterial-attribute learners were more likely
in the intentional condition. Although the particulars of this pattern are
undoubtedly specific to the stimuli, stimulus structure, and the instructions used in the experiment, the overall tendency for the apparently
inflexible analytic subjects (the noncriterial attribute responders) to fall
somewhere between the holistic and the flexibly analytic learners is at
least suggestive. As before, the hint is that holistic processing is the most
"primitive" mode (i.e., primitive in the sense of being differentially associated with young children and nonstrategic learners), that flexible
analytic processing is the most resource-intensive mode (associated
with older individuals and strategic learners), and that inflexible analytic processing is intermediate in its cognitive status.

OVERALL SIMILARITY OR
THE WRONG DESCRIPTION OF THE STIMULI?

In a chapter entitled, "A psychophysical approach to dimensional integrality," Pachella, Somers, and Hardzinski (1981) raised an important
question about the appearance of holistic processing in a discussion of
the stimulus distinction between integrality and separability. The issue
was later elaborated by Cheng and Pachella (1984). At a fundamental
level, their question about holistic processing is a variant of the issues
that we have already considered: Are we mistakenly reaching the conclusion that processing is guided by overall similarity relations when,
instead, processing is organized around a different selected property of
the stimulus information than the one(s) that the experimenter has
defined as relevant? Pachella and his colleagues argued specifically that
the pattern of results typical of dimensional integrality (i.e., holistic pro-

cessing of stimulus dimensions) occurs when there is a psychophysical mismatch—that is, when the experimenter's description of the physical properties of the stimuli fails to coincide with the perceptual properties in terms of which the subject actually processes the information. An important implication of their view is that there exists at least one alternative description of the properties varied in the stimuli by which the response patterns taken to implicate holistic processing will disappear and the subject can be shown to be truly processing analytically in the current sense of the term. In short, holistic processing is said to constitute no more than an experimental artifact—although, to be sure, an informative artifact (informative in that the experimenter should now search for a more psychologically valid description of the stimuli).

A consideration of this position raises several issues that are important to treat in the current discussion of holistic processing. If the position is right—that is, if claims of holistic processing are specific to situations in which there is a discrepancy between the experimenter-defined and the processor-defined properties of the stimuli, then holistic processing in the sense discussed in this chapter is not a valid psychological phenomenon. The generalization from the position is that the basic notion of holistic processing as processing by overall similarity may not occur at all. Although their argument is addressed particularly to the phenomenon of stimulus integrality, that is, stimulus control of holistic processing, it is not difficult to see how, in principle, it can be extended to all the generalizations about holistic processing that we have been considering.

To understand how Pachella et al.'s argument may apply, consider again the triad classification task, schematized in Fig. 12.1. In that figure, the three stimuli are not only represented in terms of their psychological distances from one another (monotonically related to interpoint distances), but they are also shown in relation to two specific axes, representing two experimenter-defined dimensions. The latter feature conveys the ideas that stimuli A and B share a value on Dimension 1 and that no other two stimuli share a value on either of the two dimensions that the experimenter is explicitly varying. But suppose that the experimenter's dimensions are not the subject's. In that case, the drawn axes have no psychological counterpart. But, further, suppose that there are other axes that could be placed within Fig. 12.1 that do have psychological reality for the subject. For example, suppose that, from the subject's point of view, we should represent two axes that are rotated 45 degrees from the ones we actually drew. If this is true, then putting stimuli B and C together means putting together the only two stimuli that have a common dimensional value from the subject's point of view.

Note that, relative to the rotated axes, B and C share a value on one axis, and no other pair of stimuli does. But, relative to the axes that the experimenter has defined, the experimenter would wrongly infer responding by overall similarity if the subject classifies B and C together.

It is important to recognize that there is no logical way to eliminate the kind of alternative view offered by Pachella et al. (1981) and by Cheng and Pachella (1984). In principle, there are an infinite number of ways to describe the variables in stimulation, and so there is always the possibility that there exists for the subject another description of the properties of the stimuli than the experimenter's and that, by this description, the subject's processing can be seen to be analytic, that is, guided by these subject-defined properties. The in-principle argument becomes a convincing argument when the experimenter can discover what the subject's properties are, and, as Pachella et al. show, this can sometimes be done.

Following their arguments, I would suggest that there are some clear warning signs that we can heed to alert us to situations in which the relevant kind of mismatch exists. Even without any data, the investigator can sometimes consult his or her own intuitions to discover alternative ways of describing the psychological properties in the stimulus space that is being sampled. For example, rectangles varying in height and width can also be easily apprehended as rectangles varying in overall shape and in size. Here, if the experimenter chooses to describe the stimuli according to the former properties, but the subject processes them in terms of the latter properties (instead of in terms of their overall similarity relations), then calling the subject's processing "holistic" is unwarranted, according to the specific way that I am conceptualizing the holistic/analytic distinction.

As Pachella et al. pointed out, there is also an empirical warning sign. Often, when the subject's properties are not the experimenter's, then some indices of the similarity relations that the subject perceives among the stimuli, such as those provided by direct judgments of multidimensional similarity, cannot be described coherently in terms of the experimenter's dimensions (see also Krantz & Tversky, 1975). For example, two stimuli described as differing by a unit amount along two experimenter-defined dimensions might be apprehended by the subject as more similar to one another than either stimulus is to the stimuli that differ from it by a unit amount along only one of those experimenter-defined dimensions while being identical to it on the other. Here, one should entertain that from the processor's perspective, the two stimuli that the experimenter describes as different in two ways are similar in a property not acknowledged in the experimenter's description of the stimuli. (To avoid confusion, let me add that when the subject's similarity responses do not violate the experimenter's property descriptions in this kind of way, one should not necessarily conclude that the subject is analyzing the stimuli into those properties.)

This discussion may also bring to mind the phenomenon often described as "configural" dimensions in the entended literature on stimulus structure (e.g., Pomerantz & Garner, 1973; and chapters in this book). In light of what I have said so far, it should be clear that I do not take the response pattern sometimes taken to indicate such configural dimensions as necessarily arguing for any holistic processing in the sense that I am using the term. (See also Monahan & Lockhead, 1977.)

On a related point, it is important to distinguish between a frequent usage of "holistic" as implying the psychological importance of properties-of-the-whole from the current usage of "holistic" processing. By my usage, holistic processing is attuned to overall similarity relations rather than to any stimulus property, whether that property be a stimulus element or a property of a stimulus element or a property of the stimulus as a whole. This distinguishes the current sense of "holistic" from the best-known usages in the literature of the Gestalt psychologists. Symmetry of a form, for example, is a property of the form as a whole, rather than a property of any element of that form. But, according to the current usage, if the symmetry of a form or the pattern of a melody serves as a selective basis for processing the form or the melody, processing is said to be analytic rather than holistic. Analytic processing can permit the extraction of the melodic information from timbral information, for example. More generally, when the best candidates for psychologically real properties for the subject are properties of the whole, the stage is set—but the story is yet to be told about whether the subject processes in terms of these constituent properties (analytically) or in terms of overall similarity relations (holistically). (See also Monahan & Lockhead, 1977.)

This would seem to be a good time to state what should be already evident. The present discussion should certainly not be read as deprecating uses of the term "holistic" that are different from the one I am using. There are good reasons for counting some usages of "holistic' as better than others, but those reasons revolve around clarity. Thus, of course, I prefer any usage of "holistic" that is precise and that can be operationalized to one that is vague and *post-hoc*. Still, I believe that more than one construal of "holistic" in the current literature is clear and useful. My only concern in this discussion, then, is to keep distinguishable understandings apart. It appears that for "holistic' meaning attuned to a property-of-the-whole and "holistic" meaning attuned to overall similarity relations, we would be better served by using two different terms. (I will not propose them, however, because I have little confidence that they would stick. "Holistic" seems like just the right label for both kinds of phenomena, but for different reasons.)

Let me address now whether the kind of argument made by Pachella et al. (1981) and by Cheng and Pachella (1984) applies pervasively to the kind of evidence that has previously counted for the generalizations about holistic processing—in the current sense. Foard and Kemler Nelson (1984) undertook a set of studies on the conditions under which saturation and brightness, integral dimensions in that they are usually processed holistically, may be analyzed by adults. For present purposes, the crucial generalization is that we were able to identify some conditions that prompted analytic processing even for this best-known case of integrality. We commented:

> The demonstrations here that saturation and brightness, which so often show the holistic pattern, still do have psychological reality for perceivers under a diverse and coherent set of processing conditions strengthen the claim that those dimensions (and, we expect, hue) are the psychological constituents of color for our subjects. In the face of all the data, it is difficult to maintain, as Pachella et al. do, that the predominantly holistic pattern of the processing of integral dimensions is essentially an artifact. Psychological dimensions can be integral. Accordingly, one can maintain the interesting notion of holistic processing as the apprehension of complex stimuli in the character of unitary, unanalyzed wholes. (Foard & Kemler Nelson, 1984, p. 109)

Recently, Grau and Kemler Nelson (in press) have further answered the arguments of Pachella and his colleagues with evidence for the integrality of two auditory dimensions, pitch and loudness.

It seems also that the generalizations about processor effects and contextual effects are at least partially built on an empirical base where Pachella et al.'s alternative strains credibility. For example, with regard to the developmental trend from holistic to analytic processing, their argument would be that young children tend to process the same stimuli as older children in terms of a different set of properties than older children (and experimenters). Even if this is plausible in one or two cases in the literature, the evidence for the developmental trend now includes studies involving quite a few different kinds of stimuli. It seems most unlikely that, in all of these, there is an alternative psychological description of the stimuli that has special reality for the younger children. Moreover, in parallel to the argument of Foard and Kemler Nelson, the literature also contains demonstrations of contextual effects on children's processing, the bottom line of which is that young children (e.g., preschoolers), who most often process holistically, sometimes process analytically (e.g., Kemler, 1982b; L.B. Smith, 1979). It is certainly much easier and more coherent to understand these effects as due to conditions that facilitate or prompt analysis (e.g., lack of speed constraints; task demands that call for analysis), than to hypothesize that the conditions prompt the children to analyze differently, that is, into different stimulus properties. Finally, a systematic study of contextual effects on the processing of separable stimuli by adults (J.D. Smith & Kemler Nelson, 1984) makes a good case for the contextual generalization by revealing a very consistent pattern of when these stimuli are processed holistically—under speed stress (also Ward, 1983), divided attention, and impressionistic instructions. Again, the nature of the converging effects is far more easily identified with the tendency to analyze at all (the explanation originally favored) than with the tendency to analyze the stimuli into one set of properties or another (the kind of explanation the Pachella et al. treatment might suggest).

It appears, then, that some evidence for all three kinds of generalizations about holistic processing would seem to survive the test posed by Pachella and his colleagues, as long as our criterion is plausibility rather than logical proof. This does not mean, however, that one can casually dismiss their kind of argument across the board. Those who would claim holistic processing in the current sense need to be continually sensitive to the kind of caution that their treatment engenders.

IS OVERALL SIMILARITY NECESSARILY HOLISTIC?

I have deferred until now the issue that I find the most complicated and subtle to deal with. Up to this point, I have taken holistic processing to be equivalent to processing of overall similarity relations, and thus indexed appropriately by paradigms that distinguish the use of overall similarity relations from the use of a selected perceptual property. I have considered the inferential difficulties that arise because the subject's property may not be the experimenter's,—first, because the subject attends selectively to a property that the experimenter has taken to be irrelevant, and, second, because the subject attends selectively to a property that has not been considered at all in the experimenter's description of the stimulus. Still, up to now I have been able to stick with the relatively straightforward idea that what distinguishes analytic processing from holistic processing is selective attention to a property.

However, if selective attention is the whole story, then a holistic processing proposal is not distinguishable from a proposal by which processing is simply nonselective; the distinction between analytic and holistic processing is only a matter of the breadth of processing. Yet, for many of us who have invoked the holistic/analytic distinction in the domains I have been discussing, a more qualitative and more fundamental difference has been contemplated (if not always demonstrated—see Rust & Kendler (1987) and Wilkening, Hemmer, & Krämer (1983)). The understanding is that, in holistic processing, stimulus properties have no immediate psychological reality, that is, it is "property-less" processing (Kemler, 1983b). Then, a consequence, rather than a primary defining characteristic of holistic processing, is that selective attention to a property is absent: If the stimulus is not apprehended as a set of independent properties, but instead as a unitary whole, then it does not afford selective-property processing. Still, if we are to take the selection-attention test as one consequence rather than defining, we must provide other criteria by which holistic processing can also be detected. This is a highly demanding requirement, however.

At a conceptual level, I would propose that there are three different senses in which processing may be nonselective. Of these three, the first is clearly analytic. Nonselective but analytic processing would characterize a processing episode in which the individual attends to all the stimulus properties one-by-one as a basis for mental computations and making response decisions. Accordingly, when comparing two stimuli, the subject's response will be a function of all the stimulus attributes and, as a consequence, a function of their overall similarity. Still, overall similarity stands in a clearly secondary role; it is the observed outcome rather than the psychological basis for decision-making (Rust & Kendler, 1987).

The other two senses of nonselective processing elevate overall similarity to a primary role and, in so doing, imply holistic processing. I distinguish a weak and a strong form of nonselective holistic processing. In both, the stimulus representations that are accessed in processing are accessed as wholes, rather than as a concatenation of independent properties. Thus, wholes rather than properties are the primary unit of processing. When stimuli are compared, they are compared as wholes and the relation that is internally computed is their overall similarity. These holistic representations are not decomposed while doing computations and arriving at a response during the processing episode.

I would like to make clear that the understandings of nonselective holistic processing that I am contemplating do allow: (a) that the underlying representation of the stimulus may be as a set of properties, and (b) that this representation may be constructed out of property-specific perceptual activities at an earlier level of processing. So, for example, I do not find Treisman's suggestion (e.g., Treisman & Gelade, 1980) that separable properties must be glued together by focal attention in order to perceive an object to be incompatible with the conclusion that that object may be perceived as a holistic unit (and not decomposed) when it is classified or categorized or otherwise compared with another stimulus (see J.D. Smith & Kemler Nelson, 1984, for a relevant discussion). Moreover, if Treisman's account is correct, it would seem natural for the underlying representation of the object to preserve information about the properties from which it was constructed. However, although this information is preserved, it may not be accessed or even accessible to processes that operate on the representation of the object that has been formed. When it is not generally accessed, processing is holistic in the sense that I am considering. Incidently, I think that the developmental generalization of a trend from holistic to analytic processing almost demands the view that at some level in the system, information about the constituent properties is directly preserved. Without such a presumption, it is difficult—if not impossible—to account for how the child ever comes to analyze into the properties that he or she eventually does. Moreover, as has been pointed out innumerable times, even overall similarity relations have to be constrained in some way.

If I may digress for one additional point, it is to emphasize that the current notion of holistic processing entails some sense in which information about properties is preserved in the whole, whether or not such properties are directly represented or accessible. A holistic representation of a stimulus preserves some information about the properties in the sense that one stimulus whole is distinguishable from another stimulus whole even if the stimuli—from an investigator's point of view—differ in only one property. The fundamental point about the holistic mode is that property-specific information is not accessible: So, the holistic processor detects the unidimensional difference but does not apprehend it as a difference on a particular kind of property. For example, an infant who discriminates between a red circle and a blue circle gives no evidence of analyzing into properties such as color or of accessing properties in any way (Kemler, 1981). The infant as a holistic processor simply could be discriminating between two unanalyzed wholes that have nonidentical representations.

I go on now to distinguish between the weak and the strong versions of what nonselective holistic processing entails. By the weak form, overall similarity relations are computed over stimulus representations that maintain independent specifications of the constituent stimulus properties. In effect, the "overall similarity computer" takes as input a dimensionalized or property-specific encoding of the stimulus whole and computes overall similarity over these differentiated encodings. The strong form, by contrast, denies the psychological reality of properties even as input to the "overall similarity computer." On this view, overall similarity relations are directly apprehended between stimuli as unitary "blobs" (Lockhead, 1972), by analogy to the appreciation of distance between points in Euclidean space.

The analogy to Euclidean distance has played an important role in the understanding of the psychology of overall similarity in the previous literature on holistic processing. In his early discussions of the operations that converge on integrality and separability, Garner (1974) suggested that the metric that best describes psychological distance should be different when processing is holistic or analytic. In the present treatment, his proposal differentiates between the strong version of holistic processing and the other two cases. Garner noted that in direct-distance scaling studies, judgments of overall similarity are best fit by a Euclidean metric when the stimuli are integral (and presumably processed holistically), but that they are best fit by a city-block metric when the stimuli are separable (and presumably processed analytically). The sense of this difference is of considerable heuristic value. As Garner pointed out, the Euclidean metric—appropriate for integral stimuli—is unique among Minkowski metrics in being insensitive to the placement of axes in the multidimensional space. It is the metric that fits when there are no privileged axes in the space,—by analogy, when there is no privileged dimensional description of the stimuli. In contrast, the city-block metric does imply privileged axes and, accordingly, a privileged or psychologically real dimensional description at some level of processing.

In terms of the current attempt to distinguish three versions of nonselective processing, the Euclidean metric, carrying the general notion of no privileged axes, would be characteristic of the strong version of holistic processing. The city-block metric, with the implication of privileged axes representing the privileged psychological properties, whether they are generally accessible or not, would be compatible respectively with the account of analytic processing and with the weak version of holistic processing.

In several investigations (and in several different kinds of tasks), the privileged-axis criterion has served as the explicit guide to formulating operations sensitive to analytic and holistic processing (L.B. Smith & Kemler, 1978; Kemler, 1982a; Foard & Kemler Nelson, 1984).

The most straightforward of these was used in two studies by Foard and Kemler Nelson (1984) in their investigations of integrality. The stimuli were combinations of saturation and brightness that were presented in pairs. The difference between stimuli in some pairs conformed exactly to a dimensional axis; that is, the stimuli in these pairs differed in exactly one way—either in saturation or in brightness, but never in both ways. The difference between stimuli in the other pairs conformed exactly to a 45-degree rotated axis in the stimulus space; more simply, they differed in two ways, in both saturation and brightness. Adults were asked to judge whether the two stimuli in each pair differed in one way or two.

Despite the apparent simplicity of the task requirements (subjects were better than 90% correct when the stimulus dimensions were separable), subjects had a good deal of difficulty in this situation. In fact, in the first experiment reported, adults' performance with the integral dimensions of saturation and brightness was only 53% correct—no different from chance. Evidently, the subjects did not succeed in accessing the nature of the stimulus differences, that is, the properties underlying the stimulus differences, as the task requires. Furthermore, it was shown that individuals were not responding randomly either: As one might expect, if overall similarity is the primary relation that is accessible, our subjects "reinterpreted" the instructions as if to map "differ in one way" and "differ in two ways" into the interpretations, "similar overall" and "dissimilar overall." Thus, it appears that adults' processing of integral dimensions is sometimes (often, I would say—see also L.B. Smith & Kemler, 1978) holistic in the strong sense that I have defined in the current discussion. (In a second experiment, Foard & Kemler Nelson (1984) showed some ability to access the dimensional properties under conditions that prompt analysis.)

I know of no equivalent evidence for this strong version of holistic processing within the literature on processor effects. L.B. Smith and Kemler (1978) used the privileged-axis criterion in studies of speeded classification of size-and-brightness (separable) stimuli by kindergarten children. At this age, children often show a predominance of overall-similarity classifications with these stimuli in the unspeeded triad classification paradigm. Still, we found some evidence for privileged axes—that is, the psychological reality of the dimensions for the children at some level of classification processing. In addition, Kemler (1982a) detected statistical evidence for privileged axes conforming to size and brightness in still younger children, preschoolers, in the triad classification task (although, again, most classifications were based on overall similarity). Thus, the few relevant tests in the literature do not favor the strong version of holistic processing as characteristic of young children.

However, stimulus integrality does not seem to be a necessary condition for the strong form of holistic processing. Kemler Nelson (1984) presented evidence for this kind of holistic processing under incidental conditions of category learning, when attributes of cartoon faces were varied. It is likely that these attributes are separable. The pertinent comparison is somewhat different from those discussed already, although it is related to the distinction between Euclidean and city-block metrics introduced earlier.

Consider the two categorization tasks, adopted from Medin and Schwanenflugel (1981), that are schematized in Fig. 12.3. They are matched in important respects. Both involve learning three instances in each of two categories. Within each category, each kind of property takes on its characteristic value in two of the three instances. In neither task is a single attribute criterial for category membership (as was true, for example, in Fig. 12.2).

However, the categorization task on the left offers bases for solution that are unavailable for the task on the right. The so-called linearly separable categories on the left can be learned analytically by simply discovering the characteristic value of each independent attribute for each category and then using a majority rule to decide category membership. If an instance has at least two of the three values that are characteristic of the category, then it is a member. Each instance can also be learned by abstracting prototypes or central tendencies and then using an analytic computation of similarity as a basis for decisions. But note that neither of these procedures can apply successfully to solving the task on the right, where categories that are not linearly separable must be learned.

However, a strong version of holistic processing leads to the prediction that the task on the right should be the easier to learn. Suppose that a holistic processor learns the categorization tasks by encoding information about the category membership of specific whole exemplars and generalizing to others on the basis of overall similarity (e.g., Brooks, 1978; and particularly Medin & Schaffer, 1978). If the computation of overall similarity (more appropriately, overall dissimilarity), is based on a Euclidean metric, then the categories on the right are favored in two relevant ways. First, the average dissimilarity between members of the same category is less than within the linearly separable categories; and, second, the average dissimilarity between members of different catego-

LINEARLY SEPARABLE CATEGORIES		NOT LINEARLY SEPARABLE CATEGORIES	
Category I	Category II	Category I	Category II
0 0 1	1 1 0	0 0 0	1 1 1
0 1 0	1 0 1	0 0 1	0 1 1
1 0 0	0 1 1	1 1 0	1 0 0

FIGURE 12.3 A representation of two category learning tasks used in Kemler Nelson's (1984) Experiment 3. Adapted from Kemler Nelson (1984).

ries is greater than in the linearly separable problem. Accordingly, if the strong version of holistic processing holds, the categories that are not linearly separable should be the easier to learn in this case. Furthermore—and importantly for the present issues—the same prediction does not hold by the weak version of holistic processing: A subject who encodes whole exemplars and generalizes by similarity that is modeled by a city-block metric should not find the not-linearly-separable categories easier. By a city-block metric for similarity, the tasks are equal.

Kemler Nelson (1984, Exp. 3) presented the category learning tasks of Fig. 12.3, using cartoon faces as stimuli. It was found that subjects who learned without intending to learn (who acquired the categories under the cover task of judging stereotypy) showed the advantage in acquiring the not linearly separable categories, as predicted if they are holistic processors in the strong sense of the term.

If we can come up with distinguishing operations for the strong version of holistic processing, can we also convincingly discriminate between nonselective analytic processing and the weak version of the holistic processing proposal? This is a more difficult problem, because these two modes as I have described them have a good deal in common with one another. Recall that what differentiated them is that overall similarity is the primary psychological relation for weak holistic processing with property-information only as input to the similarity computer, whereas, for analytic processing, properties serve as the directly accessed units by which representations of stimuli are compared, and overall similarity is only a derived relation.

In our studies of speed effects on classification, J.D. Smith and Kemler Nelson (1984) provided what seems to me to be a relevant kind of comparison. We reasoned that if processing of the stimuli was sometimes holistic in at least the weak sense, then, under those conditions, subjects should be able to classify by overall similarity at least as fast as they could classify by dimensional relations. This follows from the assertion that overall similarity is directly accessed rather than derived when processing is (at least weakly) holistic. The best test involved arranging requirements for subjects to classify according to either an overall similarity rule or a dimensional rule, and comparing how accurately subjects could perform in the two cases. The requirement to classify one way or the other stands in contrast to the usual method of having subjects classify freely, according to whatever system they choose.

The results of two experiments suggested direct access to similarity when separable stimuli were classified at high speeds. Both experimental procedures started subjects classifying at slow speeds and gradually accelerated their performance. In Experiment 1, the results suggested a marginal advantage for the overall similarity rule over the dimensional rule at high speeds of classifying triads (even though the dimensional rule had the advantage at slow speeds). Experiment 2 showed an even more convincing advantage for the overall similarity rule at high speeds of classifying stimulus pairs. (This pair classification paradigm was described in an earlier section of this chapter.) We concluded:

> Most importantly, our results suggest that similarity responding to . . . separable stimuli need not be a secondary, subsequent mental recombination of dimensional values, though at low levels of training or speed it may be. If similarity classification is necessarily recombinatory, performance with a similarity rule should deteriorate with acceleration at least as fast as dimensional performance deteriorates. Certainly, recombinatory similarity classification should not show an advantage at high speeds because it is hard to imagine a secondary and derived process that would show a selective high-speed advantage over the elementary components on which it is based. The data suggest that adults have direct access to the overall similarity relations among separable stimuli. (J.D. Smith & Kemler Nelson, 1984, p. 146)

In the current terminology, processing was holistic in at least the weak sense.

Turning now to the category-learning task, can we distinguish weakly holistic from analytic nonselective processing? My thinking here is more tentative. It does seem to me that when the pattern of results suggests that the learner is nonselectively encoding whole exemplars rather than nonselectively coding information about the constituent dimensions,—the latter, as Spence (1936), for example, proposes—then there is at least a weak, but fundamental sense in which processing is holistic. When exemplars are learned, the stimulus as a whole is the immediate unit of processing, and transfer to new instances is based directly on overall similarity (even though overall dissimilarity may be better modeled according to a city-block metric, as opposed to the fit of the Euclidean metric to strong holistic processing). Such an understanding of how learning is occurring certainly smacks of the sense of holistic, as well as nonselective.

The earlier distinction between direct access to overall similarity (weak holistic) as opposed to derived access to overall similarity (analytic) also raises the possibility that we might want to tread the riskier ground of using consciousness among our criteria for when learning is holistic. Presumably, when overall similarity is only a derived relation, there is a rather plausible sense in which the processor could be conscious of actually undertaking the relevant computations of similarity by summing over properties. By contrast, direct access to similarity would be far less likely to carry with it a conscious appreciation of the underlying properties upon which the apprehension of similarity is based. This suggestion brings to mind my favorite informal examples of everyday holistic processing, which occurs when we immediately appreciate the resemblance between two people—or appreciate a dissimilarity in the appearance of the same person now and at some earlier time—and yet, crucially, we are unable to bring to consciousness the basis for that feeling of similarity or dissimilarity (Kemler, 1983b). Errors in the conscious process are striking evidence for this dissociation between the appreciation of (dis)similarity relations and the ability to reflect consciously on its basis. So, for example, we incorrectly infer that our acquaintance has shaved off the mustache that he never had, when instead he has gotten eyeglasses. Following this line of thinking back to categorization, we may want to talk of holistic processing in at least the weak sense when the individual cannot bring to consciousness the basis for a category decision. If so, I think that my ability to categorize musical works by composer is largely based on holistic processing. J.D. Smith and Kemler Nelson (1984) also mentioned this tie between holistic processing and an implicit, unconscious-of-origins mode of appreciating similarity: When classifying by overall similarity, as they did at high speeds, J.D. Smith and Kemler Nelson's subjects sometimes reported poor awareness of the system that they were using. Thus, it is sometimes tempting to refer to conscious experience as a possible index of holistic processing.

A LAST DISTINCTION: OVERALL SIMILARITY VERSUS IDENTITY RELATIONS

There is a feature of processing that is orthogonal to the issues that have just been raised, and that I would like to touch on here, near the end of this chapter—partly for the sake of completeness and also because it helps to put the earlier concerns in perspective. In the last section, the central focus was on how overall similarity is computed. Is it appreciated totally apart from underlying properties (strongly holistic), by computations over underlying properties without general access to those properties (weakly holistic), or by derived computations over underlying properties that serve as the primary and accessed units of processing (analytic)? Now, I point out what has not been an issue, namely the degree to which overall similarity is appreciated—the amount of spread of similarity, shall we say. In the way that I am understanding "holistic processing," some use of overall similarity relations is presumed—for example, as a basis for the processor's relating discriminable stimuli. In fact, this spread based on overall similarity underlies much of the power that has been attributed to holistic processing within the literature I am considering. For instance, it accounts for why young children as holistic processors can still form classes systematically and can extend what is learned about category instances to new exemplars.

Still, closely related to this notion of holistic processing is another processing mode that may be of some psychological importance, and that also has some claim to the sensible use of the term "holistic." It is a processing mode in which identity, rather than similarity, is the relation that has psychological reality. Such a mode would be manifested by a processor who cannot systematically classify in the same group any stimuli that are discriminably different. It also would be characteristic of a processor who does not transfer from learned instances in categorization except when the new instance is encoded indistinguishably from a known instance.

In the literature, this kind of proposal has sometimes been mentioned. For example, this would seem to have been the notion that Cohen (e.g., Cohen & Gelber, 1975) had in mind when he talked about "compounding" in young infants: The infant who encodes the green circle and the red square as "compounds" would not be expected to generalize at all to a green square or to a red circle. Also, Tighe and Tighe's (1978) developmental hypothesis concerning perceptual differentiation sometimes seems to assume these kinds of compounds in young children. Their prediction of "subproblem independence" in discrimination learning tasks is based on the lack of generalization from what is learned about one stimulus to a stimulus that differs from it in any way. However, this strong prediction of an "identity" mode of processing in preschool children has recently been questioned (Rust & Kendler, 1987). Importantly, the very same recent evidence leaves a holistic processing proposal untouched. The way in which overall similarity is computed (and, accordingly, the pattern of its multidimensional spread) is central to a discussion of holistic processing, but always some use of overall similarity (i.e., some generalization between wholes) is presumed. In my view, it remains to be seen whether the identity mode of processing is ever the best description of the nature of processing. Because human beings, even very young ones, seem to be such ready generalizers, it would seem that holistic processing is far more likely to be a pervasive mode.

CONCLUDING REMARKS

The considerations that have threaded through this chapter highlight several features of the present conception of holistic processing. Holistic processing is said to occur: (a) when the psychological attributes of the stimulus are processed nonselectively, (2) when those psychological attributes are not directly accessed in making comparisons between stimulus representations, and instead, (c) comparisons are carried out through computations of the relations of overall similarity between representations of stimulus wholes. I have tried to show that empirical evidence for such holistic processing is possible to obtain, and that, in some important cases, it has been obtained convincingly. Thus, in my view, the various challenges that have been mounted to a proposal of holistic processing do not undermine the psychological reality of holistic processing when the entire literature is entered into the picture. This is not to say that the challenges I have considered do not apply validly to particular paradigms or studies. It is to say that the strategy of seeking converging evidence (Garner, 1974) has paid off in making the inference of holistic processing the most parsimonious and most plausible way to account for the variety of systematic empirical observations that have been made.

Brooks (1978) pointed out quite convincingly that nonanalytic or holistic processing has failed to get the respect that it deserves as a powerful cognitive tool. Historically, holistic processing has also been evaluated negatively as a scientific concept,—often criticized for its vagueness, shifting meanings, and *post-hoc* appearances. It seems to me that research and commentary of the last 15 years have done much to turn these states of affairs around. Such a claim is implicit in the content of this chapter.

There are two different kinds of convergence that reinforce many of the generalizations about holistic processing that have been under consideration. One kind arises from the repeated attempts to test generalizations about particular stimulus, observer, or contextual effects through a number of different kinds of experimental operations. This strategy of seeking converging operations was fundamental to this literature from its inception; Garner's (1974) discussion of stimulus separability and integrality was based on the recognition of such convergences. So, for example, integral dimensions—as distinguished from separable dimensions—were said to be those that lead to: (a) unspeeded classifications based on overall similarity, (b) interference in speeded classification when the dimensions are varied orthogonally, (c) facilitation in speeded classification when the dimensions are correlated, and (d) judgments of multidimensional similarity that are best accommodated by a Euclidean model of interstimulus distance (Garner, 1974). Indeed, since 1974, this list has been enlarged (e.g., Kemler & L.B. Smith, 1979; L.B. Smith & Kemler, 1978; Foard & Kemler Nelson, 1984). The strategy of seeking converging experimental operations has also been used across studies of some observer and contextual effects. For example, the case for a developmental trend from more holistic to analytic processing can call on the first three operations just named (e.g., Shepp, 1978), and, in addition, several new ones (e.g., Kemler, 1982b; Kemler Nelson, 1984; L.B. Smith, 1979).

The second kind of convergence that has strengthened the current literature on holistic processing is produced by forging conceptual links between different stimulus, observer, and contextual effects. Put simply, there is a sensible fit between the generalizations that, relative to analytic processing, holistic processing is more typical of: (a) difficult-to-analyze stimuli than easy-to-analyze stimuli, (b) younger children than older children, (c) individuals of subnormal intelligence than individuals of normal intelligence, (d) impulsive individuals than reflective individuals, and (e) conditions that undermine cognitive resources than conditions that allow or encourage resource-intensive processing. Together these generalizations would seem to converge on the common conclusion that holistic processing is the more primitive and also the more basic cognitive mode (see J.D. Smith & Kemler Nelson, 1984; Kemler Nelson & J.D. Smith, in press). I suggest that this confluence of stimulus, observer, and contextual influences on holistic processing is at least as encouraging and as provocative as each of the individual effects by itself.

REFERENCES

Aschkenasy, J.R. & Odom, R.D. (1982). Classification and perceptual development: Exploring issues about integrality and differential sensitivity. *Journal of Experimental Child Psychology, 34,* 435–448.

Brooks, L.R. (1978). Nonanalytic concept formation and memory for instances. In E. Rosch & B.B. Lloyd (Eds.), *Cognition and categorization* (pp. 169–211). Hillsdale, NJ: Lawrence Erlbaum Associates.

Carey, S. (1978). The child as a word learner. In M. Halle, J. Bresnan, & G. Miller (Eds.), *Linguistic theory and psychological reality* (pp. 264–293). Cambridge, MA: Cambridge University Press.

Cheng, P.W., & Pachella, R.G. (1984). A psychological approach to dimensional separability. *Cognitive Psychology, 16,* 279–304.

Cohen, L.B., & Gelber, E.R. (1975). Infant visual memory. In L. Cohen & P. Salapatek (Eds.), *Infant perception: From sensation to cognition* (pp. 347–403). Vol. 1. New York: Academic Press.

Foard, C.F., & Kemler Nelson, D.G. (1984). Holistic and analytic modes of processing: The multiple determinants of perceptual analysis. *Journal of Experimental Psychology: General, 113,* 94–111.

Garner, W.R. (1974). *The processing of information and structure.* Potomac, MD: Lawrence Erlbaum Associates.

Grau, J.W., & Kemler Nelson, D.G. (in press). The distinction between integral and separable dimensions: Evidence for the integrality of pitch and loudness. *Journal of Experimental Psychology: General.*

Handel, S., & Imai, S. (1972). The free classification of analyzable and unanalyzable stimuli. *Perception and Psychophysics, 12,* 108–116.

Keil, F.C., & Batterman, N.A. (1984). A characteristic-to-defining shift in the development of word meaning. *Journal of Verbal Learning and Verbal Behavior, 23,* 221–236.

Kemler, D.G. (1981). New issues in the study of infant categorization: A reply to Husaim and Cohen. *Merrill-Palmer Quarterly, 27,* 457–463.

Kemler, D.G. (1982a). Classification in young and retarded children: The primacy of overall similarity relations. *Child Development, 53,* 768–779.

Kemler, D.G. (1982b). The ability for dimensional analysis in preschool and retarded children: Evidence from comparison, conservation, and prediction tasks. *Journal of Experimental Child Psychology, 34,* 469–489.

Kemler, D.G. (1983a). Exploring and reexploring issues of integrality, perceptual sensitivity, and dimensional salience. *Journal of Experimental Child Psychology, 36,* 365–379.

Kemler, D.G. (1983b). Holistic and analytic modes in perceptual and cognitive development. In T. Tighe & B.E. Shepp (Eds.), *Perception, cognition, and development: Interactional analyses* (pp. 77–102). Hillsdale, NJ: Lawrence Erlbaum Associates.

Kemler, D.G., & Smith, L.B. (1979). Accessing similarity and dimensional relations: The effects of integrality and separability on the discovery of complex concepts. *Journal of Experimental Psychology: General, 108,* 133–150.

Kemler Nelson, D.G. (1984). The effect of intention on what concepts are acquired. *Journal of Verbal Learning and Verbal Behavior, 23,* 734–759.

Kemler Nelson, D.G. (1988). When category learning is holistic: A reply to Ward and Scott. *Memory and Cognition, 16,* 79–84.

Kemler Nelson, D.G., & Smith, J.D. (in press). Analytic and holistic processing in reflection-impulsivity and cognitive development. In T. Globerson & T. Zelniker (Eds.), *Cognitive style and cognitive development.* Norwood, NJ: Ablex Publishing.

Krantz, J.R., & Tversky, A. (1975). Similarity of rectangles: An analysis of subjective dimensions. *Journal of Mathematical Psychology, 12,* 4–34.

Lockhead, G.R. (1972). Processing dimensional stimuli: A note. *Psychological Review, 79,* 410–419.

Medin, D.L., & Schaffer, M.M. (1978). Context theory of classification learning. *Psychological Review, 85,* 207–238.

Medin, D.L., & Schwanenflugel, P.L. (1981). Linear separability in classification learning. *Journal of Experimental Psychology: Human Learning and Memory, 7,* 355–368.

Monahan, J.S., & Lockhead, G.R. (1977). Identification of integral stimuli. *Journal of Experimental Psychology: General, 106,* 94–110.

Pachella, R.G., Somers, P., & Hardzinski, M. (1981). A psychophysical approach to dimensional integrality. In D.J. Getty & J.H. Howard (Eds.), *Auditory and visual pattern recognition* (pp. 107–126). Hillsdale, NJ: Lawrence Erlbaum Associates.

Pomerantz, J.R., & Garner, W.R. (1973). Stimulus configuration in selective attention tasks. *Perception and Psychophysics, 14,* 565–569.

Rosch, E., & Mervis, C.B. (1975). Family resemblances: Studies in the internal structure of categories. *Cognitive Psychology, 7,* 573–605.

Rust, K.J., & Kendler, T.S. (1987). Lower level encoding: Holistic or nonselective? *Developmental Review, 7,* 326–362.

Shepard, R.N. (1964). Attention and the metric properties of the stimulus space. *Journal of Mathematical Psychology, 1,* 54–87.

Shepp, B.E. (1978). From perceived similarity to dimensional structure: A new hypothesis about perceptual development. In E. Rosch & B.B. Lloyd (Eds.), *Cognition and categorization* (pp. 135–167). Hillsdale, NJ: Lawrence Erlbaum Associates.

Shepp, B.E., Burns, B.B., & McDonough, D. (1980). The relation of stimulus structure to perceptual and cognitive development: Further tests of a separability hypothesis. In F. Wilkening & J. Becker (Eds.), *The integration of information by children* (pp. 113–145). Hillsdale, NJ: Lawrence Erlbaum Associates.

Smith, J.D., & Kemler Nelson, D.G. (1984). Overall similarity in adults' classification: The child in all of us. *Journal of Experimental Psychology: General, 113,* 137–159.

Smith, J.D., & Kemler Nelson, D.G. (1988). Is the more impulsive child a more holistic processor? A reconsideration. *Child Development, 59,* 719–727.

Smith, L.B. (1979). Perceptual development and category generalization. *Child Development, 50,* 705–715.

Smith, L.B. (1984). *Holistic and analytic processing: Insights from individual differences.* Paper presented at the 25th Annual Meeting of the Psychonomic Society, San Antonio, TX.

Smith, L.B., & Kemler, D.G. (1977). Developmental trends in free classification: Evidence for a new conceptualization of perceptual development. *Journal of Experimental Child Psychology, 24,* 279–298.

Smith, L.B., & Kemler, D.G. (1978). Levels of experienced dimensionality in children and adults. *Cognitive Psychology, 10,* 502—532.

Spence, K.W. (1936). The nature of discrimination learning in animals. *Psychological Review, 43,* 427–449.

Tighe, T.J., & Tighe, L.S. (1978). A perceptual view of conceptual development. In R.D. Walk & H.L. Pick, Jr. (Eds.), *Perception and experience* (pp. 387–416). New York: Plenum.

Treisman, A.M., & Gelade, G. (1980). A feature integration theory of attention. *Cognitive Psychology, 12,* 97–136.

Trope, I., Rozin, P., Kemler Nelson, D.G., & Gur, R.C. (submitted). Information processing of the separated hemispheres of callosotomy patients: Does the analytic-holistic distinction hold?

Ward, T.B. (1980). Separable and integral responding by children and adults to the dimensions of length and density. *Child Development, 51,* 676–684.

Ward, T.B. (1983). Response tempo and separable-integral responding: Evidence for an integral-to-separable processing sequence in visual perception. *Journal of Experimental Psychology: Human Perception and Performance, 9,* 103–112.

Ward, T.B., & Scott, J.G. (1987). Analytic and holistic modes of learning family-resemblance concepts. *Memory and Cognition, 15,* 42–54.

Wilkening, F., Hemmer, K., & Kramer, D. (1983). *An integration-theoretical approach to the separability hypothesis.* Paper presented at the meetings of the Society for Research in Child Development, Detroit, MI.

13 ANALYTIC AND HOLISTIC MODES OF PROCESSING IN CATEGORY LEARNING

Thomas B. Ward
Texas A&M University

INTRODUCTION

The tendency to divide objects in the world into categories is one of the most basic and pervasive aspects of human cognition. As such, categorization and concept learning have received an enormous amount of research attention. Some of that research has focussed on the structure of both natural and artificial categories, whereas some has focussed more on the processes and procedures used by humans as they attempt to learn concepts and make category decisions.

This chapter is concerned with interrelations between category structures and processes. More specifically, it is concerned with the possibility that there may be naturally occurring matches between structures and processes that facilitate real world category learning. There are several recent trends in the categorization literature that are particularly relevant to this issue. The first is a growing interest in the structure of natural categories in which category membership is based not on a single criterial attribute, but on clusters of correlated attributes or a family-resemblance principle (e.g., Mervis & Rosch, 1981; Rosch & Mervis, 1975). The second trend is a growing interest in *nonanalytic* forms of cognition (Brooks, 1978; Jacoby & Brooks, 1984) and in the related idea that nonanalytic or holistic modes of processing may facilitate the learning of family-resemblance category structures (e.g. Kemler, 1983; Kemler Nelson, 1984). The third trend is the tendency to view the child as a holistic processor (e.g. L. Smith & Kemler, 1977; Shepp,

Burns, & McDonough, 1980), and to view that mode of processing as well suited to learning family-resemblance category structures (e.g. Kemler Nelson, 1984). The final trend is a growing interest in implicit or incidental category learning (e.g. Fried & Holyoak, 1984; Lewicki, 1986; Reber, 1976) and in the related idea that incidental learning conditions may foster a holistic mode of processing that is well suited to learning natural categories (e.g. Kemler Nelson, 1984; Ward & Scott, 1987).

The primary goal of the research described in this chapter is to examine the interrelations across these domains of research. The results of the studies conducted in the present research program thus far provide a new perspective on the nature of the convergence among these trends. The discussion that follows relates those findings to others in the literature and suggests new directions that research should take to define further the nature of the links between family-resemblance category structures, analytic and holistic modes of processing, developmental differences, and differences in the learner's intent. The first section is concerned with children's concept learning, whereas the second is concerned with intentional versus incidental learning. The final section provides the rough outlines of a model designed to integrate the findings described in those two sections.

ANALYTIC AND HOLISTIC CONCEPT LEARNING IN CHILDREN

Children's concept learning provides an interesting paradox. On the one hand, young children (i.e., those 5 years of age and under) tend to perform relatively poorly in laboratory studies of concept learning (see e.g. Kendler, 1979; Tumblin & Gholson, 1981). On the other hand, they seem to acquire information about real world categories with remarkable speed and efficiency. The challenge to theorists of concept learning is to account for this apparent discrepancy in rate of learning.

One rather uninteresting resolution is to suggest that the discrepancy is more apparent than real and that children learn concepts just as slowly in the real world as they do in the laboratory. That is, the apparent discrepancy may be based on noncomparable measures across the domains, our inability to accurately measure the rate of real world learning or some other extraneous factor. A more interesting possible resolution emerges if we adopt as a working hypothesis that the discrepancy is real. Whether right or wrong, the hypothesis provides a vehicle and a framework within which questions regarding age-related changes in concept learning can be asked.

Assuming that the discrepancy in rate of learning is real, one possible resolution concerns the extent of the match between the child's preferred mode of processing and the structure of the categories that the child is required to learn. There is considerable evidence that, under many circumstances, young children adopt a more holistic approach to tasks than do older children or adults (Smith & Kemler, 1977; Shepp, et al., 1980, Ward, 1980). Children seem especially attuned to the overall appearance of objects. This holistic mode of processing may cause difficulty in the laboratory because most of the concepts that children are asked to learn in the laboratory are highly analytic and require a focus on specific stimulus dimensions (e.g., red versus green or red square versus yellow circle) (see, e.g. Tumblin & Gholson, 1981). In contrast, natural categories in the real world are thought to have a family-resemblance structure (see e.g., Rosch, 1978). Category members do not possess single defining attributes. Rather, they share bundles of characteristic attributes with different members of the category each having a slightly different bundle of such attributes. The result of such a structure is that the members of natural categories tend to be more similar in an overall sense to one another than they are to members of any other category. Therefore, such categories may be uniquely suited to the young child's holistic mode of processing because analysis into separate attributes is not necessary to determine category membership (see Kemler 1983; Kemler Nelson, 1984; Medin, 1983, L. Smith, 1979).

Tests of the Structure-Process Match Hypothesis

The possibility that children's preferred holistic mode of processing is perfectly suited to learning the real world categories that they must acquire is a very important and interesting one. However, there have been very few reported attempts to test this possibility empirically. One way to test the issue is to attempt to simulate the family-resemblance structure of natural categories in the laboratory. The materials described in Tables 13.1 and 13.2 provide an example of one such attempt. The ma-

TABLE 13.1
Coding Scheme for Faces in Concept Learning Task

Level	Attribute/Type			
	Hair (H)	Mustache (M)	Ears (E)	Nose (N)
1	straight	clipped	small	tall-thin
2	wavy	medium-length	medium	medium
3	curly	handlebar	large	short-fat

TABLE 13.2
Example of the Structure of a Family-Resemblance Problem.
The Faces Denoted are Ones That Would Be Presented During Learning.

Category A					Category B				
Face	Hair	Must.	Ear	Nose	Face	Hair	Must.	Ear	Nose
1.	1	1	1	2	5.	3	3	3	2
2.	1	1	2	1	6.	3	3	2	3
3.	1	2	1	1	7.	3	2	3	3
4.	2	1	1	1	8.	2	3	3	3

terials are cartoon faces that vary along the attributes of hair, mustaches, ears, and noses. The formal structure of two contrasting categories is shown in Table 13.2, and a coding scheme for interpreting the entries in that table is shown in Table 13.1. Note that the members of Category A have the characteristic values of straight hair, clipped mustache, small ears, and a tall-thin nose, whereas the members of B have the opposite characteristics. Note also that each member of those respective categories possesses a different bundle of those characteristic attributes, and that no single feature can serve as a defining or criterial attribute. Finally, assuming an equal salience for all four attributes, the faces within a category are overall more similar to one another than they are to faces of the contrasting category. Thus, the categories have a strong family-resemblance structure. In using these materials in the laboratory, there are two relevant questions. The first is whether or not young children readily learn such categories. The second is, assuming that children do readily learn such categories, do they do so by way of a holistic mode of processing?

Kemler Nelson (1984) provided data that are particularly relevant to the first of these questions. She conducted a series of experiments using cartoon faces divided into the types of categories described in Table 13.2. In one study (Experiment 4), she found that kindergarteners learned such category structures as rapidly as fifth graders. Thus, the answer to the question of whether young children will readily learn family-resemblance-type concepts in the laboratory appears to be yes.

Ward and Scott (1987) also used cartoon faces in an attempt to determine whether young children's success with categories of the type described in Table 13.2 was based on their use of a holistic mode of processing. They reasoned that two different types of approaches could lead to rapid learning of such categories. Pilot testing had revealed that the faces within a given category were perceived as more similar to one another than to members of the opposing category. Thus it would be possible for an individual to learn the appropriate category assignments for the faces by adopting a holistic or nonanalytic mode of processing and comparing faces in terms of their overall similarity. Presumably, in making such comparison, the individual could treat each face as a single holistic entity rather than as a collection of features. Likewise the person would not abstract some prototypical representation of feature values, but would make comparisons in terms of individual known exemplars.

The second approach, however, is a more analytic one that involves a focus on single attributes and can be termed attribute-plus-exception. For example, the learner could selectively attend to any one of the four attributes. This approach would facilitate learning about the characteristic values of that particular attribute for the contrasting categories and thus could lead rapidly to correct responding for six of the eight faces. This approach would also allow the person to identify the remaining two faces by the presence of the noncharacteristic value of the attended attribute. Presumably then, the person could learn that those two faces were exceptions to the analytic rule and must be considered separately. Note that because the approach will work equally well with any of the four attributes, the child need not be "analytic" in the sense of discovering the one correct experimenter-defined attribute but merely analytic in the sense of choosing any one attribute on which to focus.

A third approach that was not described in detail by Ward and Scott is also possible. This third approach would also be an analytic one in that the individual would selectively attend to a single attribute. However, the selective weighting of that one attribute would not occur to the total exclusion of the other attributes as in the more rule-based attribute-plus-exception approach. Rather, category decisions would be based on the similarity of an item to known exemplars, with that similarity being computed from some weighted combination of matches and mismatches on all attributes. The approach would be analytic in the sense that a single attribute (e.g., hair) would receive more attention than the other three and would thus figure more heavily in similarity computations and category decisions. It is important to note that this selective weighting exemplar approach differs sharply from the holistic exemplar approach just described. Both involve category decisions that are based on similarity to known exemplars; however, a holistic mode of processing would not allow selective weighting of any given attribute in computing similarity. Thus, although exemplar models are often linked with "nonanalytic" forms of cognition (see e.g., Jacoby & Brooks, 1984), only the holistic model and not the selective weighting exemplar model can be viewed as consistent with the holistic mode of processing that is often attributed to young children (see Smith & Evans, this volume). Any evidence for selective attention, whether complete as in the case of the attribute-plus-exception model or partial as in the selective weighting model would imply that children are not adopting purely holistic approaches.

Ward and Scott's (1987) Study 2 was designed to determine whether young children are any more likely than adults to exhibit holistic modes of learning. Participants were given 48 learning trials with the items depicted in Table 13.2. Transfer items of the type shown in Table 13.3 were used to determine the mode of learning adopted, and converging measures of reaction time and errors were also used. Faces T1 and T2 in Table 13.3 are the prototypic examples of categories A and B and should be identified as members of categories A and B, respectively, regardless of the learner's approach. If the person has adopted a nonanalytic mode and focused on holistic, overall appearance in attempting to learn the concept, then faces T3, T5, T7, and T9 should be called A, and T4, T6, T8, and T10 should be called B, because that would be consistent with the global (unweighted) similarity relations among the stimuli. In contrast, if a person adopted an analytic approach (either attribute-plus-exception or selective weighting), and attempted to learn the concept by focusing on hair, for example, then that individual should place T3 in category B, and T4 in category A, even though T3 has more features in common with members of A and T4 has more features in common with members of B. Such a classification would violate the principle of holistic, overall similarity but would be consistent with an analytic focus on or selective weighting of a single attribute. Similar predictions could be made for an analytic focus on any one of the other three attributes. During transfer, each of the test items T3–T10 was presented twice, and thus 16 trials were relevant for classifying learners into groups. Fifteen of those 16 responses had to be consistent with the use of a given attribute for the individual to be classified as an analytic, single attribute

TABLE 13.3
Example of Test Items for Problem Shown in Table 13.2

Face	Hair	Must.	Ear	Nose	
T1	1	1	1	1	(Category A Prototype)
T2	3	3	3	3	(Category B Prototype)
T3	3	1	1	1	
T4	1	3	3	3	
T5	1	3	1	1	
T6	3	1	3	3	
T7	1	1	3	1	
T8	3	3	1	3	
T9	1	1	1	3	
T10	3	3	3	1	

learner. Likewise, 15 of 16 responses had to be consistent with overall appearance responding for the person to be classified as a holistic learner.

The convergence of reaction time and error measures on analytic modes of learning can be described as follows. Assuming that the individual is attempting to learn the concept on the basis of one attribute, that attribute will lead quickly to the correct answer on six of every eight learning trials. The remaining two trials would presumably require more time because the learner can no longer rely on the information available from the favored attribute and must either guess or check the values of the other attributes. (In the selective weighting exemplar model, more time might be required because items in question would be less similar to stored exemplars because they differ on a heavily weighted attribute). In either case, reaction time should be longer on those two trials. Finally, an individual should continue to make errors for the two ambiguous faces for some minimum number of trials after achieving perfect performance on the other six faces. So, for example, an individual who focused either fully or mostly on hair as an attribute should learn to correctly categorize the three members of A that have straight hair (faces 1–3) and the three members of B that have curly hair (faces 5–7) in Table 13.2 relatively quickly. The individual should exhibit longer reaction times and more errors to the other two *ambiguous* faces (4 and 8). Note that the faces that are assumed to be ambiguous depend on the attribute on which the learner has focussed. To summarize, transfer items were used to identify the specific attribute on which an individual appeared to focus. This allowed a determination of which faces ought to be *ambiguous* for that individual and thus provided the opportunity to look for convergence with reaction time and error measures.

The participants in the study were 40 college students recruited from psychology classes at Texas A&M University and 24 5-year-olds recruited from preschools. The mean age of the children was 5 years, 2 months.

The original learning items were each presented twice during transfer, and a criterion of 12 of 16 correct on those faces was used to classify an individual as a *learner*. All 40 of the adults and 21 of the 24 children were identified as learners. Of those individuals, 26 of the adults and 11 of the children were identified as single-attribute learners based on the procedures described earlier. The proportion of such learners is somewhat higher for adults (see Figure 13.1), but assignment to the different learning groups was found to be independent of age group, $X^2 = .91$, p > .25. Thus, the predominant mode of learning appeared to be an analytic one for both age groups. The data thus far are consistent with either

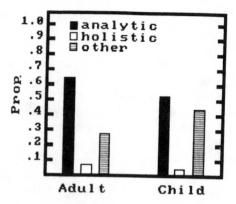

FIGURE 13.1. Proportion of children and adults identified as analytic, holistic, and other types of learners. The data are from Ward and Scott (1987).

version of analytic processing and a differentiation of the two models is considered in a later section of this chapter.

For the adults, the number of individuals identified as using the attributes of hair, mustache, ears, and nose was 4, 11, 3, and 8, respectively, whereas the comparable numbers for children were 0, 8, 0, and 3. In contrast to the adult group in which some individuals focused on each of the four attributes, the children exhibited attribute learning only with the more central features (nose and mustache) of the faces.

For both age groups, errors and reaction times converged on the assignment of individuals to the analytic learning group. For adults, 18 of the 26 individuals made their last learning trial error on one of the two ambiguous learning faces, and of the 13 who made errors during transfer, 9 made those errors only on ambiguous faces. For children, 10 out of 11 made their last learning trial error on an ambiguous face and 10 out of 11 made errors only on the ambiguous faces during transfer trials. All distributions are significantly different from what would be expected by chance, $p < .05$. For adults, mean correct reaction time was significantly longer for the ambiguous faces (1.80 sec.) than for the other faces (1.42 sec.), $F(1,24) = 13.49$, $p < .01$, and the same was true for children (3.03 vs. 2.36 sec.), $F(1,10) = 16.10$, $p < .01$.

Because degree of learning might be related to the individual's approach to the task and because a lax learning criterion (12 out of 16) was used, it was important to compare the performance of perfect learners (16 out of 16) to those who only met the more lax criterion. The proportion of analytic versus holistic learners did not differ across those two groups, $\chi^2 = 1.71$, $p > .20$, nor did the convergence of reaction time and learning trial errors.

Along with Edward Vela and Sally Hass, I have conducted a series of studies to examine these issues further. We have recently conducted a very similar study with a different set of materials to determine whether or not the results obtained would generalize to materials other than the faces. The materials used in this study were cartoon "bugs" that varied in the attributes wing size, facial expression, number of body stripes, and antenna length. Each of those attributes had three levels and, in a formal sense, the learning and transfer items can be represented exactly as the items depicted in Tables 13.2 and 13.3 by simply replacing the label "hair" with "wings" and so on.

The participants in the study were 24 5-year-olds and 36 adults. They received a total of 48 learning trials and 36 transfer trials. The procedures for determining learning criterion, analytic versus holistic mode, and convergence of reaction time and errors were the same as described previously.

Seventeen of the children and 35 of the adults were identified as learners. Of the child learners, 8 were identified as analytic, single-attribute learners, whereas of the adults, 28 were identified as analytic (see Figure 13.2). In contrast to the study with cartoon faces, the proportion of analytic learners among the adults was significantly higher than that among children, $\chi^2 = 5.82$, p < .05. Thus, to some extent, the age effects observed depend on the set of materials presented. However, it should also be noted that none of the children and only one adult exhibited purely holistic patterns of transfer performance. As was true for the faces, reaction time and errors converge on the idea of analytic learning for both children and adults. Correct reaction time to the ambiguous and other bugs was 3.37 and 2.44 seconds respectively, for children and 1.40 and .89 seconds respectively, for adults.

Across the studies described so far, approximately half of the individuals tested appear to have learned appropriate category assignments by focussing all or most of their attention on a single attribute. This should not, however, be taken to mean that the remaining half of the partici-

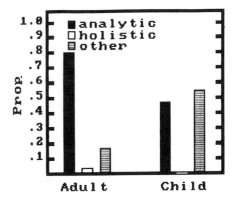

FIGURE 13.2. Proportion of children and adults identified as analytic, holistic, and other types of learners. The data are from a follow-up to Ward and Scott (1987) with bugs as stimuli.

pants adopted purely holistic approaches. First, across both studies, only one 5-year-old and four older individuals exhibited purely holistic patterns of transfer performance. Second, many of the individuals who did not use a single attribute appeared to use some other analytic-type strategy, such as a disjunctive rule. Considering the test items shown in Table 13.3, a disjunctive rule of the form straight hair or clipped mustache or both for category A and curly hair or handlebar or both for category B would result in the following pattern of transfer responses. T7 and T9 would always be assigned to A and T8 and T10 would always be assigned to B. T3, T4, T5, and T6 would be assigned randomly (i.e., 50% of the time to A and 50% to B) because the two attributes provide conflicting information regarding category membership. A number of individuals exhibited these patterns.

We have conducted a third study that examined the tendency of individuals in intermediate age ranges to exhibit either analytic or holistic modes of learning. The participants tested were 28 first graders and 20 third graders. The materials were the cartoon faces as described for the first study. Of the first graders, there were 23 learners and 10 showed analytic patterns of learning. Of the third graders, there were 19 learners and 10 showed analytic patterns. The proportions of analytic learners did not differ significantly (see Figure 13.3), and as in the two studies described previously, reaction times and errors confirmed the assignment of individuals to the analytic learning group. Correct reaction time to the ambiguous and other faces was 2.60 and 2.01 seconds for first graders and 2.21 and 1.49 seconds for third graders. This study also included additional transfer items to better assess disjunctive rules, and we found that three individuals in each age group were clearly analytic in that sense.

The studies just described provide little support for the contention

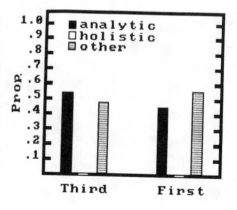

FIGURE 13.3. Proportion of first- and third-graders identified as analytic, holistic, and other types of learners. The stimulus materials were faces.

that children approach concept learning tasks (at least the intentional ones used in these studies) with a holistic mode of processing. Thus, the proposed match between the child's assumed holistic mode of processing and the structure of natural categories has little support. This result is not entirely unexpected because young children exhibit higher levels of analytic responding when rule learning is emphasized (L. Smith, 1979), and they have often been found to exhibit hypothesis testing in concept learning studies (see Tumblin & Gholson, 1981). Preschoolers' hypotheses are by no means as sophisticated as those of older children or adults, and they often take the form of response sets regarding particular dimensions rather than predictions regarding those dimensions (see Tumblin & Gholson, 1981). One of the major age-related changes seems to be the tendency to alter hypotheses in the face of disconfirming information. Thus, children may be as analytic as adults in the sense that their responses are based on single features, and yet still not apply strategies as effectively. The implication is that there is no necessary link between the use of sophisticated strategies and the tendency to focus on a single attribute in performing a task nor between more primitive modes and the tendency to focus on overall appearance (see e.g., L. Smith, 1983).

An Alternate Matching Hypothesis

The results to date suggest an alternate hypothesis about young children's relative success in learning both laboratory and real world family-resemblance categories. Consider again the category structure depicted in Table 13.2, which was set up to mimic several important properties of natural categories. One property is that several characteristic attributes are present that are reasonably (although not perfectly) predictive of category membership. The reason for the young child's relative success in dealing with laboratory concept learning tasks of the type shown in Table 13.2 (see e.g., Kemler Nelson, 1984) may not be that they approach the task holistically. Rather, it may be that learning tasks induce analytic processing (i.e., attention to single features) and that any single attribute on which the child decided to focus would provide enough information to accurately classify 75 percent of the faces. By analogy, a child's tendency to focus on single attributes (or a small number of attributes) of objects in the real world may provide enough information to achieve categorization performance at well above chance levels given the assumed family-resemblance structure of natural categories. So, for example, a child who focused on wings, or feathers, or a beak, or egg-laying would be correct in categorizing most instances of birds and would correctly reject most noninstances. Thus, there may be a match between the child's approach to category learning and the structure of natural categories that facilitates real world learning. But the match may be between the child's tendency to focus on salient component attributes and a natural category structure that provides a number of partially valid salient characteristic features rather than between a holistic approach and a strong similarity structure.

The preceding account also provides an alternate explanation of the young child's relatively poor performance in many other laboratory tasks of concept learning. The child may be at a disadvantage, not because of a holistic approach to a task that requires analysis, but because of an analytic approach that is not readily modified. By this account, the young child should be at a disadvantage in the situation in which an experimenter determines a single attribute as the critical one and in which no other attributes provide category-relevant information. The child may selectively weight an irrelevant attribute and be resistant to modifying that weighting. The exception to this is a situation in which the experimenter-chosen attribute is highly salient for the child (see e.g., Suchman & Trabasso, 1966). In this case, the child fortuitously selects the correct feature.

When interpreted within the framework just described, the findings to date bear an interesting relation to those of Keil and Batterman (1984), who report a characteristic-to-defining shift in children's word meanings. That is, younger children tend to rely on characteristic features in determining whether an instance is an exemplar of a category, whereas older children rely on defining features (e.g., palm trees vs. surrounded by water for the category "island"). Although not the interpretation favored by Keil and Batterman, it is possible that one or two of the characteristic features of the categories that they studied are highly salient for young children. Thus, children are initially captured by one of those features and, only over time, are the children willing to modify their "hypotheses" about the relevance of that feature and thus come to adopt the initially less salient defining feature as the correct one on which to focus. It would be of interest to examine the salience of the various features of the first exemplars that children encounter. That is, the features need not be the most salient across all exemplars, but only need be salient across the ones that the child encounters first (cf. Mervis & Pani, 1980, regarding the importance of first encountered exemplars). One potential qualifier on this interesting link is that the characteristic-to-defining shift occurs at different ages for different domains, whereas the ineffective use of analytic hypotheses in the laboratory may be strongly age-dependent.

Resolving Discrepancies:
Task Factors and the Importance of Parts

If children are viewed as behaving analytically in the way that they learn categories, it becomes necessary to explain the discrepancy between that analytic mode of processing and the more holistic responding that they exhibit in many classification tasks (e.g., L. Smith & Kemler, 1977). One way to explain the discrepancy is to suggest that explicit rule learning instructions induce a more analytic mode in which the child attempts (albeit ineffectively) to find a rule to predict category membership. In the more ambiguous classification tasks, the child relies on the simpler preferred holistic mode. In contrast, adults attempt to find rules whether explicitly instructed to do so or not. Thus, they behave analytically in both classification and learning tasks.

A second way to interpret the category learning versus classification task performance differences is related to the stimulus materials used. Classification tasks typically vary the *qualities* of objects (e.g. size, color), whereas the concept learning tasks used in the present research program have varied the *parts* of objects (e.g. ears, noses, wings, etc.). Intuitively, the parts of objects seem more separable from the whole than do the qualities and thus it is reasonable to expect more analysis when parts rather than qualities are varied (see Shepp, this volume).

Related to this *part* versus *quality* distinction is Tversky and Hemenway's (1984) observation of the importance of parts as features that differentiate members of basic level categories. If children are inclined to process the parts of objects, and if basic level categories tend to have a number of salient characteristic parts, then such a coincidence would greatly facilitate the child's learning of such categories. Indeed, Mervis and Greco (1984) have argued that children must be able to attend to parts, rather than just integral wholes, if they are to form basic level categories.

Because parts appear to be extremely important to the differentiation of categories at the basic level (Tversky & Hemenway, 1984), and because basic level terms are acquired early in language learning, it becomes important to determine whether parts are accorded a special status in the processing shown by young children. That is, are young children any more likely to process the parts of objects analytically than they are to process other types of attributes analytically?

The suggestion that young children are inclined to process parts and that basic level categories are differentiated by way of parts might help to explain the young child's seemingly efficient real world category learning. Even with such a fortunate link between a mode of processing and a category structure, it would appear necessary to specify some constraints on the parts that the child selectively processes. Of all the many parts to which a child may attend, how does the child come to attend to characteristic features that are useful for category differentiation?

One possible answer to that question is based on the link between form and function. Not only do basic level categories appear to have a strong part structure, those characteristic parts have distinct specifiable functions (Tversky & Hemenway, 1984). Thus, one way that the child's selection of parts may be constrained is that only those parts that have some functional significance for the child are selected. So, for example, if a child understood that legs served the function of locomotion, the child might attend to those parts in making a category discrimination. Attending to such a part might allow information regarding quantity (e.g., two- vs. four-legged) or quality (e.g., the shape of a rabbit's legs vs. those of a dog) to be encoded. This idea is consistent with "top-down" selection of parts rather than "bottom-up" (see Kosslyn, Heldmeyer, & Glass, 1980). It is concerned with the tendency of the individual to bring prior knowledge to bear on category learning tasks.

A question arises immediately as to how a child acquires the functional significance of the part. One possibility is that adults label significant parts for children. In fact, work reviewed by Anglin (1977) indicates that references to body parts occur quite regularly in adults' speech to children. Another possibility is that, through experience, the child discovers the unique functions of certain parts (e.g., the wheels of a toy car). Finally, it is possible that the infant's apparent sensitivity to relative coherence in kinetic stimuli (see e.g., Bertenthal, Proffitt, Kramer, & Spetner, 1987) facilitates learning about the parts of objects that move. In the current phase of this research program, the emphasis is on how the child's knowledge about particular parts impacts on the features that are selected from presented exemplars rather than with the way in which that knowledge is acquired. However, the latter is a longer-term goal that must be met in order to understand concept acquisition fully.

Parts Versus Other Attributes in Category Decisions

There are a number of functional parts that occur regularly in young children's speech, and chief among these are body parts (e.g., leg, hand, eye, etc.) (see Anglin, 1977). Thus, these types of parts can be used initially to construct various types of category contrasts. However, parts are certainly not the only useful attributes for discriminating basic level categories. For example, work summarized by Rosch (1978) indicates that similarity or dissimilarity of overall body shape may be another important factor.

With these ideas about task demands and stimulus attributes in mind, several students and I are conducting a series of labelling studies. The studies are still going on, but preliminary data from a portion of the subjects in one study can be described. The groups whose data are reported were 4- and 5-year-olds, 13-year-olds, and college students.[1] In contrast to the studies described previously in this chapter, there was no explicit learning phase in which participants were given feedback. Rather, participants were shown either one or two items and were given nonsense words as labels for the items. They were then shown other items and were asked to decide if the new items should also be assigned those labels. The study was designed to simulate a situation in which an adult would provide a child with a label for some object. For example, an adult might point to a dog and say to a child, "That is a dog." The relevant issue here is what information the child stores as a result of the experience. Which attributes, either singly or in combination, does the child encode as properties of dogs in general? Which attributes, if any, does the child consider essential in assigning future instances to the category of *dog*?

Several recent labelling studies have attested to the young child's relative sophistication in understanding the significance of different types of labels (see e.g., Markman, 1987; Taylor & Gelman, 1988). For example, even very young children appear to interpret labels that contain articles (such as "a vibble") as common nouns that constitute category names for the labelled object. Nevertheless, it is still important to determine what aspects of the labelled object the child encodes as being relevant for category membership. Does the child encode single attributes, combinations of attributes, overall appearance, or some other properties?

Four sets of materials were created with two intended to be "animate" and two intended to be "inanimate." The members of each set varied in terms of the number of parts, shape or parts, body shape, and body size. Variations along those dimensions were intended to be roughly equally discriminable. For each of the four sets of materials, there were two levels of each of those four attributes and thus there were 16 possible variants within a given set. For one set of animate items, the parts that varied were the legs. The members of the set could

---

[1]Ward, Vela, Peery, Lewis, Bauer, and Klint (in press) have recently reported results from the four- and five-year-olds and college students described here, additional subjects in those age ranges, and a group of seven-year-olds.

have either three or five legs (number), and those legs could have either hooves or claws at the end (shape of parts). The body shape could be angular or rounded. For the other animate set, the part variations were the number (2 vs. 4) and shape (round or angular) of wings. The body shape was either straight or wavy. One inanimate set looked somewhat like scooters and varied in the number (2 vs. 4) and type (smooth versus coglike) of wheels. The body shape was either rounded or angular. The other inanimate set looked somewhat like airplanes and varied in terms of number (2 vs. 4) and type (broad versus tapered) of wings. The body shape was either sleek or bulging. Example items from each of the sets are shown in Figs. 13.4a–d.

Each participant received labels and made judgments for each of the four sets of materials. Order of presentation was counterbalanced so that

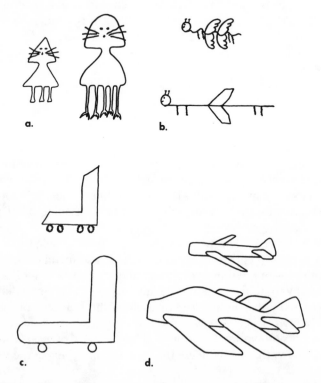

FIGURE 13.4. Stimulus materials used in labelling study. The materials depicted in a and b were created to simulate animate creatures and the materials depicted in c and d were created to simulate inanimate objects.

each of the four sets occurred equally often in each of the four possible presentation positions. When animate items were presented, participants were told a story about a child who wanted a particular type of pet. When inanimate items were presented, they were told a story about a child who wanted a particular type of toy. They were instructed to help the child find all (and only) instances of the desired pet or toy.

There were two modes of presentation. In the *single* mode, the participant was shown a single item from one of the sets and was given a label for that item (e.g., "This is a vibble"). The participant was then shown all 16 possible variants from that set one at a time in a random order (including a duplicate of the labelled item). The participant was instructed to decide for each variant whether or not it was an instance of the desired pet or toy (e.g., "Is this a vibble? Is this the type of pet that the boy wants?"). In the *dual* presentation condition, the participant was shown two items at opposite extremes on all four attributes for a given set. The participant was given a different label for each of the two items (e.g., "This is a vibble and this is a morkel."). He or she was then shown the 16 possible variations one at a time and was asked to decide whether each one was an instance of one or the other or neither of the labelled items.

Responses to each of the 16 variants were used to identify the attribute(s) that each participant judged as relevant to category membership. For each set of materials, there were four possible single attribute rules (e.g., all items with the same number of legs receive the same label), six possible dual attribute rules (e.g., all items with the same number and shape of parts receive the same label), and four triple attribute rules (e.g., items with the same number and shape of parts and the same body shape receive the same label).

In all age groups, slightly more than half of the participants could be clearly identified as using one of those rules. Figures 13.5a–d show the proportion of those individuals who showed patterns consistent with the different types of rules for each of the types of material illustrated respectively in Figs. 13.4a–d. Preliminary analyses revealed no differences between the *single* and *dual* presentation conditions nor between the 13-year-olds and college students. Thus, the proportions shown are for both older groups combined and for both presentation conditions combined.

As can be seen in Fig. 13.5, the predominant types of rules for the young children involved single attributes. Subsequent comparisons indicated that the children who showed single attribute patterns were approximately equally divided across the four types of single attribute variations. Thus, there is no compelling evidence that children are focussed

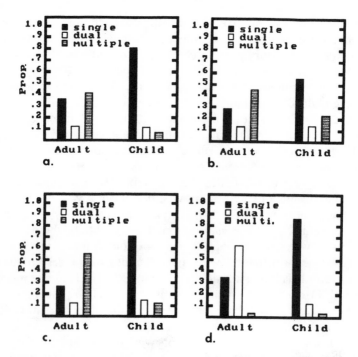

FIGURE 13.5. Proportion of adults and children identified as using some type of rule who could clearly be classified as single-, dual-, or multiple-attribute responders. The data shown in panels a–d correspond respectively to the materials shown in Figs. 13.4a–d.

on parts to the exclusion of other types of attributes. However, there is also no evidence that the children are focussed on holistic overall appearance.

In contrast to young children, the predominant rule for older individuals was a triple-attribute type for three of the four sets of materials. More specifically, the triple-attribute rules involved the number and shape of parts as well as the body shape. In effect, the older individuals allowed that members of a category could be of different sizes but they must have the same number and type of parts and the same body shape. Across the first three sets of materials, the older individuals were significantly less likely to exhibit single attribute rules and significantly more likely to exhibit this particular triple attribute rule than were young children, $\chi^2 = 12.73$, p < .01, $\chi^2 = 4.05$, p < .05, and $\chi^2 = 14.70$, p < .01 for the materials illustrated in Figures 13.4a–c, respectively. Ward, et al. (in press) also found that seven-year-olds used triple-attribute rules more than the younger children.

The results are intriguing in that they may tell us something about the individual's understanding or conception of what constitutes an organism or artifact or about the individual's tendency to bring that knowledge to bear on the task at hand. Through many years of experience, the older individuals have learned that size (within some reasonable range of variation) is irrelevant to category membership, whereas the other three attributes manipulated here are all relevant. For example, horses have four legs, hooves, and a particular body shape. An organism with six legs or claws at the end of the legs or with a considerably different body shape would not be identified as a horse even if it matched a horse prototype on all other attributes. In contrast, newborn and adult horses vary considerably in size, but are still considered to be members of the same category.

For young children, category membership appears to be less restrictive. A match on any of several attributes appears to be enough to place items in the same category. Perhaps their concept of what constitutes an organism is not sophisticated enough to include the idea of a match on several relevant attributes. On the other hand, the concept may be developed, but the tendency to apply that knowledge to new situations may be limited. In either case, the child would be expected to show either under- or over-generalizations, depending on the particular single attribute attended and the exact categories involved.

For the fourth set of materials, young children predominantly used single attribute rules, whereas the older individuals used dual attribute rules, $\chi^2 = 17.20$, $p < .01$. The dual attribute rules always involved the number of parts and the body shape. One possible interpretation of this finding is that the variation in part shape was not salient enough to be considered relevant to category membership. However, the fact that older individuals were more likely than young children to use multiattribute rules is also consistent with the results for the other three sets of materials.

The findings from this labelling study are consistent with the first three studies in showing that young children often process single attributes in making category decisions. There is no evidence from any of these studies that is consistent with the idea that young children judge category membership holistically. Again, the results are consistent with a very different interpretation of the young child's success with real world categories. That success may be based not on a tendency to process holistically but on a tendency to process some small number of attributes combined with a category structure that provides many characteristic attributes that can serve as partially valid cues for category membership.

ANALYTIC AND HOLISTIC MODES IN
INCIDENTAL LEARNING

An issue that is directly related to the question of analytic versus holistic modes of learning in young children concerns the modes of processing that occur during incidental versus intentional learning. The question is, when individuals of any age learn incidentally rather than intentionally, do they behave less strategically and thus adopt a more primitive holistic mode of processing (Kemler Nelson, 1984; Ward & Scott, 1987)? As with previous suggestions regarding children's concept learning, this question is based on the idea that a holistic mode of processing is cognitively less developed or strategic than an analytic one. Because much of our learning about the world both as children and as adults occurs incidentally as a result of interacting with objects, this question also raises the issue of a link between the natural mode of processing adopted in real world settings and the structure of the material to be learned.

In contrast to the fact that much of human concept learning occurs incidentally, most of our scientific knowledge regarding concept learning has been generated from studies in which subjects are given explicit instructions to learn a concept. To the extent that incidental and intentional concept learning operate according to similar principles, the laboratory studies of intentional learning can be informative with respect to real world knowledge acquisition. However, to the extent that they operate according to different principles, laboratory results may be at best uninformative and at worst misleading with respect to real world concerns.

Recently, a debate has arisen as to the similarity of learning principles across incidental and intentional learning conditions (Kemler Nelson, 1984; Ward & Scott, 1987), and the issues raised parallel those described earlier regarding age differences. Ward and Scott (1987) have argued that there is no compelling evidence for differences across the two types of learning situations. In contrast, Kemler Nelson (1984) has reported data that support the idea that incidental learning conditions induce less strategic behavior in adults and thus evoke more holistic processing than do intentional learning conditions.

Ward and Scott (1987) reported analytic learning under incidental conditions, whereas Kemler Nelson (1984) reported holistic learning. Both Ward and Scott (1987) and Kemler Nelson (1984) had participants learn the category membership of cartoon faces under intentional and incidental learning conditions. In the intentional condition, participants were asked to learn which faces belonged in the category "firemen" and which belonged in the category "doctor." They were shown a single face on each trial, responded with label "firemen" or "doctor," and were given feedback. In the incidental condition, participants viewed a pair of faces from one of the categories (e.g., "firemen") and were asked to indicate which of the two faces best fit their stereotype of that category. They were not explicitly instructed to learn which faces were members of a given category. Afterwards, all participants were tested on their knowledge of the category membership of the original items and on novel faces designed to determine whether subjects had learned by way of particular attributes or by way of holistic overall appearance. The structure of the original learning categories can be illustrated by way of the example problem in Table 13.4, and the structure of the transfer items used by Ward and Scott is shown in Table 13.3.

Kemler Nelson (1984) reported data that appear to show that incidental learners were more likely than intentional learners to process holistically. In contrast, Ward and Scott (1987) found that participants in the incidental condition were no more likely than those in the intentional condition to focus on overall appearance. The incidental learners were however, less likely than intentional learners to learn by way of the criterial attribute and more likely to learn by way of one of the noncriterial but characteristic attributes. (The parallel to Keil and Batterman's finding of a characteristic-to-defining shift as described earlier may also apply here, and may illustrate a basic feature of incidental concept learning.)

One interpretation of the discrepancy between the Kemler Nelson and the Ward and Scott results concerns the nature of the incidental learning tasks used in those two studies. In the incidental condition of the Ward and Scott study, the two members of the category pair were presented side by side until the participant made a response. Such a presentation format would certainly be expected to foster a comparison of the attributes of the presented stimuli, and thus lead to analytic learning. In contrast, Kemler Nelson presented one member of the pair for a few seconds and then removed that member and presented the second member. Such a presentation format forces the participant to respond

TABLE 13.4
Example of the Structure of a Family-Resemblance Problem. The Faces
Denoted are Ones That Would Be Presented During Learning.

Category A					Category B			
Face	Hair	Must.	Ear	Nose	Face	Hair	Must.	Ear	Nose
1.	1	1	1	2	4.	3	3	3	2
2.	1	1	2	1	5.	3	3	2	3
3.	1	2	1	1	6.	3	2	3	3

from memory and may encourage the storing of holistic properties (see, e.g., Brooks, 1978). Regardless of the exact interpretation of the discrepancy, however, it is clear that incidental learning conditions do not lead invariably to holistic modes of processing.

The important point here is that there are likely to be varieties of incidental concept learning. Rather than asking whether or not incidental learning conditions lead to holistic modes of processing, it may be more productive to ask what properties of incidental tasks lead individuals to selectively store information about particular attributes of presented stimuli. We have begun a series of studies designed to examine this issue. The working hypothesis adopted is that the learner's intent will be found to be less important than the procedures demanded by the orienting task in determining what is learned. One set of incidental tasks that we have been using represents an attempt to integrate Gati and Tversky's (1984) work on similarity judgments with ideas about exemplar storage in category learning.

Gati and Tversky have observed that both the distinctive and common features of objects are processed in making similarity judgments. Their work also indicates however, that particular stimulus and task factors can influence the relative weighting of common and distinctive features. This latter observation suggests that similarity judgment tasks may provide very useful incidental learning situations for testing our working hypothesis. As an example, there are two aspects of the cartoon faces used in the present studies that should lead to relatively greater weighting of distinctive features; they are pictorial materials, and their baseline similarity is quite high (see, e.g., Gati & Tversky, 1984). Thus, when participants are given the incidental task of judging the similarity of the faces, they should selectively weight the distinctive features of those faces over their common features. The result of that increased weighting should be that more information is stored about those distinctive features than about the common features. Therefore, when asked to make categorization decisions about the faces after performing a similarity judgment task, participants' decisions should be more heavily influenced by distinctive than by common features.

As a preliminary test of these ideas, Sally Hass, Edward Vela, and I had college students perform an incidental task with the cartoon faces structured as shown in Table 13.4. The study had a 2 x 2 design. As one factor in the design, participants were asked to make either similarity or dissimilarity judgments for pairs of faces. As the second factor in the design, the members of any given pair of faces were either from the same category (Within-Category condition) or from different categories (Cross-Category condition). All participants made 48 judgments. For the Within-Category group, 24 judgments involved pairs of doctors and

24 involved pairs of firemen. For the Cross-Category group, all 48 judgments were of pairs that included one doctor and one fireman. Participants were not instructed to try to learn which faces belonged in which category. They were simply asked to judge the similarity (or dissimilarity) of each pair of faces on a 9 point scale. The faces appeared atop uniforms, and thus, information about category membership was available to the participants during the judgment task.

The predictions of the study can be described by reference to the category structure shown in Table 13.4. In that example problem, hair is a critical attribute. (In practice, four such problems were created so that each attribute could serve as the critical one.) Note that in the Within-Category condition, any given pair of faces being judged will always be identical on the critical attribute. In contrast, in the Cross-Category condition, any given pair being judged will always differ on the critical attribute. Put differently, the critical attribute will function as a *common* attribute in the Within-Category condition and as a *distinctive* attribute in the Cross-Category condition. When given a surprise transfer test, participants in the Cross Category condition should exhibit more categorization decisions based on the critical attribute and participants in the Within-Category condition should exhibit more categorization decisions based on one of the other attributes.

It is important to note that the terms *distinctive* and *common* are being used in a slightly different way than in Tversky and Gati's work. In their view, distinctive features are features that are present in one member of a stimulus pair and not in the other. In our case, distinctive features are those attributes that always differ between members of the pair being judged. Nevertheless, it is reasonable to assume that the importance of distinctive features that Tversky and Gati observed in judgments of pictorial materials is an indicator that in judging pictorial materials participants attend more to differences between the items than commonalties across the items. It is this greater attention to differences, or distinctive features, that leads to the prediction described heretofore.

The reason for examining similarity versus dissimilarity judgments is that Gati and Tversky have observed that common features are more emphasized in the former, whereas distinctive features are more emphasized in the latter. Thus, it might have been expected that type of judgment would interact with the condition (Cross vs. Within). There was, however, no effect of the type of judgment and no interaction of judgment with condition. Thus the results reported next are collapsed across judgment type.

Consistent with the results of Ward and Scott (1987), the majority of individuals exhibited transfer performance on the items shown in Table 13.3 that was consistent with an analytic approach. In that sense, the present results provide additional evidence against a necessary link between incidental learning and holistic processing. More importantly, however, the type of attribute used varied systematically with condition. In the Within-Category condition, 7 individuals showed evidence of focussing on the critical attribute and 13 appeared to focus on one of the other three attributes. In contrast, in the Cross Category condition, 18 individuals focussed on the critical attribute and 9 focussed on one of the other three attributes. The distributions are significantly different, $X^2 = 4.63$, $p < .05$.

The fact that the critical attribute was more prominent in the Cross-Category conditions provides at least suggestive evidence that the attributes that are weighted heavily in performing incidental learning tasks are the ones most likely to be stored and used in later category decisions. This idea is elaborated further in the next section of this chapter.

As noted, the incidental–intentional learning debate is actually part of the larger question of whether holistic modes of processing are more primitive or less well developed than analytic modes (see e.g., J. Smith & Kemler Nelson, 1984, Ward, 1983; Ward, Foley, & Cole, 1986; Ward & Vela, 1986; Wilkening & Lange, in press). Despite considerable evidence in favor of the claim that holistic processing is primitive, it is becoming apparent that less cognitively sophisticated individuals do not always process information more holistically than cognitively advanced individuals. As an example, Ward and Vela (1986) have shown that young children actually make more analytic responses than adults do in classifying materials varying in the dimensions of hue, saturation, and brightness (see also Wilkening & Lange, in press). Therefore, there is no necessary link between holistic responding and more "primitive" modes of processing. Rather, a given level of holistic responding is the result of a particular type of observer interacting with a particular type of stimulus material. Likewise, the results of the present studies provide no evidence for a necessary link between holistic responding and primitive modes of processing.

MODEL CONSIDERATIONS

The question arises as to the type of category learning model that can best account for the results obtained in the present program of research. With the exception of the labelling study, one of the most prevalent findings across the studies is that individuals of all ages appear to focus heavily on single attributes. Thus, a purely holistic, unweighted exemplar model is inadequate. However, because of the structure of the categories used in the first three studies, a focus on a single attribute is not enough to achieve perfect performance. Therefore, because many individuals did achieve perfect categorization performance with the original learning items, a simple, single-attribute rule-based representation also cannot account for the results.

One possible interpretation of the results is that individuals developed a mixed representation of the category with a portion being rule based (to deal with the members that have the critical feature) and a portion being exemplar based (to deal with the exceptions that fail to satisfy the rule). However, such a mixed representation may be unnecessary and, at least in some situations, incorrect. Ward and Scott's (1987) reaction time data from adults learning with the cartoon face stimuli are relevant to this issue. The relevant comparisons can be seen by considering the test items in Table 13.3. All of the items T3–T10 are relevant to categorizing an individual as an attribute learner, but certain items are critical test items because they pit the given attribute against all of the others. As an example, if a learner appears to be focussed on the attribute of hair, then faces T3 and T4 are critical test items because they pit categorization by the value of the hair attribute against categorization by all of the other attributes. That conflict is not present for faces T5–T10 for a hair learner. If the learner is operating from a rule-based representation for categorizing such faces, then there is no reason to predict a difference in reaction time for critical test faces as opposed to other test faces, because the rule would be equally well satisfied in all cases. However, certain pure exemplar models would allow a prediction of a reaction time difference. Exemplar models hold that category decisions are made on the basis of the relative similarity of an exemplar to the members of the contrasting categories (see e.g. Medin & Schaffer, 1978); and under all but the extreme condition of complete weighting of the hair attribute and zero weighting of all of the other attributes, T3 is less similar overall to the exemplars of category B than are T6, T8, and T10, and T4 is less similar to the exemplars of category A than are T5, T7, or T9. Across several studies involving the faces (see Ward & Scott, 1987), adults identified as analytic learners had significantly longer reaction times to critical test faces than to other test faces. This indicates that the individuals selectively attended to certain attributes that led them to make particular categorization choices, but that the selective attention was not so complete as to be consistent with a rule-based representation.

The way in which these reaction time findings can be interpreted within an exemplar model involves the related ideas that (a) the probability of retrieval of a known exemplar is a direct function of its similarity to the test exemplar, and that (b) a test exemplar will be assigned to a category if it retrieves some critical number of exemplars of that category before retrieving some critical number of exemplars from a contrasting category (see, e.g., E. Smith & Medin, 1981). Presumably, lower similarity of T3 to members of B and T4 to members of A could slow this process if the process is viewed as a serial one.

Reaction time was not measured in the labelling study described earlier in this chapter. Thus, it is not possible to verify whether the decisions of the single-attribute responders were influenced by variations on any of the other attributes. However, there are also no data from that study that are inconsistent with an exemplar-type model.

Although the results are consistent with a weighted feature exemplar model, they do not necessarily support it uniquely. Other types of models may be consistent with the results. However, one value in using such an exemplar model is that it might be possible to represent a continuum of concept learning performance from a "pure" nonanalytic exemplar mode with equal weighting of all features to a pure analytic rule-based mode in which a single feature is weighted to the exclusion of all others. In this way, it may be possible to view a variety of otherwise diverse concept learning situations within a single coherent system (see Medin, 1986). It is also possible to view the effects of observer differences, stimulus manipulations, strategy differences, attentional factors, and so on, as shifting performance along that continuum rather than shifting performance to some other type of model or representation. Certain stimuli and/or tasks may allow an identification of the boundary conditions for such a model.

Within the model adopted here, each stimulus presentation is viewed as an episode and each episode is assumed to result in a memory trace. Those individual traces can be characterized in terms of a set of feature values. Thus, the model can best be characterized as a member of a family of models that Estes (1986) has termed *array models*. The array is assumed to contain an entry for each episode, although not all entries are assumed to have complete, veridical information for every feature. Specifically, if an individual performing an intentional learning task tests a hypothesis about a given feature or selectively attends, the probability of storing the value of that feature is higher than the probability of storing the values of the remaining features. Likewise, if an incidental orienting task requires or encourages the learner to attend to a given feature, that feature is more likely to be stored. This last point highlights the most important assumption of the model, which is that the basic processes of trace storage and retrieval are the same whether learning occurs under intentional or incidental conditions. That is, an experience with an exemplar results in a trace (i.e., an entry in an array of feature values) whether that experience occurs under intentional or incidental learning conditions, and the probability that a feature is stored veridically is related to the extent of the learner's attention to that feature. Attention to particular features can be biased by factors such as hypothesis testing during intentional learning or task demands during incidental learning. A related assumption is that the trace storage and retrieval processes operate according to the same principles whether the learner is a young child or an adult. The knowledge base and cognitive abilities of the learner as well as the demands of the task may affect the features that are heavily weighted, but there is no necessary link between "primitive" (e.g., young and incidental) processors and holistic modes of storage, retrieval, or comparison.

Category decisions are assumed to be based on the similarity of the test item to stored exemplars, but it is recognized that this exemplar-based computation of similarity is more a description than an explanation. Similarity is in turn based on the features that the learner considers to be relevant to the task (see Murphy & Medin, 1985). Thus, the immediate goal of the present research program is not to provide evidence (either quantitative or qualitative) in favor of this exemplar model over other types (e.g., prototype models such as those described by Reed, 1972, or Homa, 1984), but to examine the stimulus, task, and observer factors that lead individuals to selectively weight particular features of presented exemplars in category learning and decision making.

The results of the studies conducted to date provide important information regarding the nature of category learning and also suggest future directions for research in the area to take. It is clear that 5-year-olds can and do behave as analytically as adults in intentional category learning tasks, as evidenced by their use of single attributes in making category decisions. However, there is no evidence from these studies that would suggest that children are analytic in the sense of optimally weighting the dimensions of the exemplars. Studies to examine this issue should be conducted using category structures that require differential weighting of several partially informative attributes.

It is also clear from the studies to date that incidental learning conditions do not necessarily result in less analytic processing. Rather, it appears that a variety of modes of processing may occur in either intentional or incidental conditions. Within the framework adopted here, each experience with an exemplar, whether under intentional or incidental conditions, constitutes an episode and results in the formation of a memory trace. The information that the learner is required to process in performing a task is hypothesized to have more of an impact on the nature of the trace than whether or not that individual is intentionally trying to learn about category membership. The results reported in the preceding section of this chapter provide some tentative support for that hypothesis.

A common theme throughout the preceding results is the idea that there may be observer, task, and stimulus factors that determine the features that are encoded and weighted heavily in making category decisions. However, it is clear that simple relationships (e.g., children are more holistic, incidental conditions result in less analysis) are not to be found. Studies must be designed to provide more systematic information about the factors that do determine the weighting of features relative to one another and to the whole. As Murphy and Medin (1985) have noted, a shortcoming of most models of category learning is that they fail to provide an adequate account of conceptual coherence, that is, the "glue" that holds categories together. That is, most models assume that similarity is an important determinant of category membership, and, given the appropriate set of features, it may be possible to show for many categories that the exemplars of the group are more similar to one another than they are to members of a contrasting category. However, most models fail to specify the criteria by which we can determine which features are relevant; which features are to be included (and to what extent) in computations of similarity. Studies must be designed to examine some of the factors that affect the nature of the "glue" by way of their effect on the way individuals selectively weight particular features or relations among features. The results of the labelling study reported earlier in this chapter suggest that the individual's knowledge base may exert a profound effect on the features that are encoded as being relevant to category membership. Other influential factors may include perceptual abilities that individuals bring to the concept learning task, strategic and executive control factors that can result in modifications of the initial weightings, the nature of the stimulus features or dimensions used, the predictive value of the information provided by particular features, and task factors that affect the way in which the individual processes information.

It is important to note that the position argued here is not that any set of results can be produced. Rather, it is proposed that the varieties of learning observed will be related in systematic and predictable ways to stimulus, task, and observer factors operating interactively with one another.

STIMULUS LIMITATIONS

The research described in this chapter has been focussed primarily on observer and task factors. Stimulus factors have been given somewhat less attention. The results to date, which indicate a large amount of analytic processing, may therefore apply only to a limited range of stimuli. It is conceivable that by simulating more of the properties of natural categories in the laboratory, higher levels of holistic processing will be observed. Two aspects of real world categories that may be particularly important to examine in this regard are featural variability and configural properties.

Featural Variability

Attributes that are characteristic of the members of real world categories exhibit a great deal of variability from one category exemplar to the next. For example, dogs possess the characteristic attribute of fur, but the length, color, and texture of that attribute varies greatly across different dogs. Such variability may affect the individual's reliance on that attribute for category learning and decision making. Thus, an important goal for future research is to simulate the variability of real world category attributes in the laboratory. As one example of this approach, real faces could be used as category exemplars. Although category members could be set up to share the attribute of blue eyes, for example, the exact shade of blue would vary from one face to the next.

A related goal is to differentiate between variability of an attribute within a category and variability between categories (see also Lockhead, this volume). The prediction is that the less variability of the attribute within the category and more variability across categories, the more likely individuals are to use the attribute in learning category membership. This would help to explain why both children and adults behaved analytically with the cartoon faces and bugs. That is, the attributes varied considerably across categories but not within a category. Such a structure may make the individual attributes salient enough that they are processed even by children who have holistic processing tendencies.

Configural Properties

Another property of real world categories that has yet to be explored fully is that certain types of attributes tend to co-occur. For example, the attribute of wings occurs much more often with feathers than with fur. After extended experience with such co-occurrences, we may begin to treat otherwise separate attributes more holistically. In addition to such learned configurations, there may also be perceptually-based configural properties that are not dependent on experience.

One goal for future research is to examine the effects of both perceptual and conceptual configural properties on analytic and holistic processing during concept learning. Examples of configural properties that would be particularly informative to investigate are the racial and ethnic group membership as well as the attractiveness of faces. Other interesting properties would be naturally occurring correlations between animal parts of particular sizes and shapes. Perhaps when parts violate previously learned correlations (e.g., giraffe's neck) they are weighted heavily in determining category membership.

SUMMARY AND FUTURE DIRECTIONS

The present studies have been concerned with the factors that determine the weighting of features in category learning by individuals of different ages operating under different learning conditions. The assumption is that an understanding of those factors is necessary for achieving an understanding of the glue that holds categories together.

One of the longer range goals that must be met in coming to understand categorization is to specify the environmental input (e.g. parent labeling, direct observation), stimulus factors (e.g. bottom-up gestalt factors such as those examined by Kosslyn, et al., 1980), and perceptual processing abilities (e.g. sensitivity to relative coherence, Bertenthal, et al., 1987), which affect the salience of the various features of objects for children. More importantly, it is necessary to specify how those factors interact with one another and with the child's growing knowledge base and increasing tendency to apply that knowledge base in acquiring and using categories. A related goal is to specify the environmental, perceptual, and knowledge-based factors that determine adults' selection of object parts and qualities in both learning and making decisions about category membership. Finally, an important goal is to develop a single coherent model within which both developmental and adult findings can be interpreted. As currently envisioned, such a model would be exemplar-based but also would allow for a variable amount of control over the features that are included in the exemplar traces and in category decisions. The selective weighting and storage of stimulus features might occur as a result of testing hypotheses or applying "theories" in intentional learning or responding to processing demands or tendencies in incidental learning. Such a model, with its emphasis on exemplar-based categorization, would also be compatible with the current trend toward examining the links between differentiation (e.g. stimulus identification, episodic memory) and categorization (e.g. concept learning) processes (see, e.g., Hintzman, 1986; Nosofsky, 1984; Richards & Goldfarb, 1986).

ACKNOWLEDGMENT

This chapter is based on work supported by the National Science Foundation under Grant BNS-86-08916.

REFERENCES

Anglin, J.M. (1977). *Word, object, and conceptual development*. New York: W.W. Norton.
Bertenthal, B.I., Proffitt, D.R., Kramer, S.J., & Spetner, N.B. (1987). Infants encoding of kinetic displays varying in relative coherence. *Developmental Psychology, 23*, 171–178.
Brooks, L.R. (1978). Nonanalytic concept formation and memory for instances. In E. Rosch & B. Lloyd (Eds.), *Cognition and categorization* (pp. 169–211). Hillsdale, NJ: Lawrence Erlbaum Associates.
Estes, W.K. (1986). Array models for category learning. *Cognitive Psychology, 18*, 500–549.
Fried, L.S., & Holyoak, K.J. (1984). Induction of category distributions: A framework for classification learning. *Journal of Experimental Psychology: Learning Memory and Cognition, 10*, 234–257.
Gati, I., & Tversky, A. (1984). Weighting common and distinctive features in perceptual and conceptual judgments. *Cognitive Psychology, 16*, 341–370.
Hintzman, D.L. (1986). "Schema abstraction" in a multiple-trace memory model. *Psychological Review, 93*, 411–428.
Homa, D. (1984). On the nature of categories. In G.H. Bower (Ed.), *The psychology of learning and motivation* (pp. 49–94). Orlando, FL: Academic Press.
Jacoby, L.L., & Brooks, L.R. (1984). Nonanalytic cognition: Memory, perception, and concept learning. In G.H. Bower (Ed.), *The psychology of learning and motivation: Vol. 18* (pp. 1–48). Orlando, FL: Academic Press.
Keil, F.C., & Batterman, N. (1984). A characteristic-to-defining shift in the development of word meaning. *Journal of Verbal Learning and Verbal Behavior, 23*, 221–236.
Kemler, D.G. (1983). Holistic and analytic modes in perceptual and cognitive development. In T.J. Tighe & B.E. Shepp (Eds.), *Perception, cognition, development: Interactional analyses* (pp. 77–102). Hillsdale, NJ: Lawrence Erlbaum Associates.
Kemler Nelson, D.G. (1984). The effect of intention on what concepts are acquired. *Journal of Verbal Learning and Verbal Behavior, 23*, 734–759.
Kendler, T.S. (1979). The development of discrimination learning: A levels-of-functioning explanation. In H.W. Reese & L. Lipsitt (Eds.), *Advances in child development and behavior* (pp. 83–117). New York: Academic Press.
Kosslyn, S.M., Heldmeyer, K.H., & Glass, A.L. (1980). Where does one part end and another begin? A developmental study. In F. Wilkening, J. Becker, & T. Trabasso (Eds.), *Information integration by children* (pp. 147–168). Hillsdale, NJ: Lawrence Erlbaum Associates.
Lewicki, P. (1986). Processing information about covariations that cannot be articulated. *Journal of Experimental Psychology: Learning, Memory, and Cognition, 12*, 135–146.
Markman, E.M. (1987). How children constrain the possible meanings of words. In U. Neisser (Ed.), *Concepts and conceptual development: Ecological and intellectual factors in categorization* (pp. 255–287). Cambridge, MA: Cambridge University Press.
Medin, D.L. (1983). Structural principles in categorization. In T.J. Tighe & B.E. Shepp (Eds.), *Perception, cognition, and development: Interactional Analyses* (pp. 203–230). Hillsdale, NJ: Lawrence Erlbaum Associates.

Medin, D.L. (1986). Comment on "Memory storage and retrieval processes in category learning". *Journal of Experimental Psychology: General, 115*, 373–381.

Medin, D.L., & Schaffer, M.M. (1978). Context theory of classification. *Psychological Review, 85*, 207–238.

Mervis, C.B., & Greco, C. (1984). Parts and early conceptual development: Comment on Tversky and Hemenway. *Journal of Experimental Psychology: General, 113*, 194–197.

Mervis, C.B., & Pani, J.R. (1980). Acquisition of basic object categories. *Cognitive Psychology, 12*, 496–522.

Mervis, C.G., & Rosch, E. (1981). Categorization of natural objects. *Annual Review of Psychology, 32*, 89–116.

Murphy, G.L., & Medin, D.L. (1985). The role of theories in conceptual coherence. *Psychological Review, 92*, 289–316.

Nosofsky, R.M. (1984). Choice, similarity, and the context theory of classification. *Journal of Experimental Psychology: Learning, Memory, and Cognition, 10*, 104–114.

Reber, A.S. (1976). Implicit learning of artificial grammars. *Journal of Verbal Learning and Verbal Behavior, 6*, 855–863.

Reed, S.K. (1972). Pattern recognition and categorization. *Cognitive Psychology, 3*, 382–407.

Richards, D.D., & Goldfarb, J. (1986). The episodic memory model of conceptual development: An integrative viewpoint. *Cognitive Development, 1*, 183–219.

Rosch, E. (1978). Principles of categorization. In E. Rosch & B. Lloyd (Eds.), *Cognition and categorization* (pp. 27–48). Hillsdale, NJ: Lawrence Erlbaum Associates.

Rosch, E. & Mervis, C.B. (1975). Family resemblances: Studies in the internal structure of categories. *Cognitive Psychology, 7*, 573–605.

Shepp, B.E., Burns, B., & McDonough, D. (1980). The relation of stimulus structure to perceptual and cognitive development: Further tests of a separability hypothesis. In F. Wilkening, J. Becker, & T. Trabasso (Eds.), *Information integration by children* (pp. 113–145). Hillsdale, NJ: Lawrence Erlbaum Associates.

Smith, E.E., & Medin, D.L. (1981). *Categories and concepts*. Cambridge, MA: Harvard University Press.

Smith, J.D., & Kemler Nelson, D.G. (1984). Overall similarity in adults' classification: The child in all of us. *Journal of Experimental Psychology: General, 113*, 137–159.

Smith, L.B. (1979). Perceptual development and category generalization. *Child Development, 50*, 705–715.

Smith, L.B. (1983). Development of classification: The use of similarity and dimensional relations. *Journal of Experimental Child Psychology, 36*, 150–178.

Smith, L.B., & Kemler, D.G. (1977). Developmental trends in free classification: Evidence for a new conceptualization of perceptual development. *Journal of Experimental Child Psychology, 24*, 279–298.

Suchman, R.G., & Trabasso, T. (1966). Stimulus preference and cue function in young children's concept attainment. *Journal of Experimental Child Psychology, 3*, 188–198.

Taylor, M., & Gelman, S.A. (1988). Adjectives and nouns: Children's strategies for learning new words. *Child Development, 59*, 411–419.

Tumblin, A., & Gholson, B. (1981). Hypothesis theory and the development of conceptual learning. *Psychological Bulletin, 90*, 102–124.

Tversky, B. & Hemenway, K. (1984). Objects, parts, and categories. *Journal of Experimental Psychology: General, 113*, 169–193.

Ward, T.B. (1980). Separable and integral responding by children and adults to the dimensions of length and density. *Child Development, 51*, 676–684.

Ward, T.B. (1983). Response tempo in separable and integral responding: Evidence for an integral-to-separable processing sequence in visual perception. *Journal of Experimental Psychology: Human Perception and Performance, 9*, 103–112.

Ward, T.B., Foley, C.M., & Cole, J. (1986). Classifying multidimensional stimuli: Stimulus, task and observer factors. *Journal of Experimental Psychology: Human Perception and Performance, 12*, 211–225.

Ward, T.B., & Scott, J.G. (1987). Analytic and holistic modes of learning family resemblance concepts. *Memory & Cognition, 15*, 42–54.

Ward, T.B., & Vela, E. (1986). Classifying color materials: Children are less holistic than adults. *Journal of Experimental Child Psychology, 42*, 273–302.

Ward, T.B., Vela, E., Peery, M.L., Lewis, S.N., Bauer, N.K., & Klint, K.A. (in press). What makes a vibble a vibble? A developmental study of category generalization. *Child Development*.

Wilkening, F., & Lange, K. (in press). When is children's perception holistic? Goals and styles in processing multidimensional stimuli. In T. Globerson & T. Zelniker (Eds.), *Cognitive style and cognitive development*. Norwood, NJ: Ablex.

AUTHOR INDEX

340, 343, 344, 348, 349, 350,
352, *354, 355,* 359, 360, 361,
364, 373, 376, 377, 383, 384,
385, 386, 387, 389, 397, 399,
418
Snodgrass, J. G., 20, 21, 36, *52*
Somers, P., 368, 372, *385*
Souther, J., 21, 42, *52*
Spence, K. W., 380, *386*
Spetner, N. B., 400, 416, *417*
Spottswood, P., 237, *264*
Sterling, S., 312, *321*
Stoever, R. J., 61, *88,* 179, *202,* 317,
322
Strobe, W., 292, *293*
Stroop, J. R., 66, *89*
Suchman, R. G., 398, *418*
Sutliff, D., 176, *201*
Swartz, K. B., 203, *232,* 241, 261,
265, 298, *323,* 326, 328, *355*
Sykes, M., 23, *52*

T

Takane, Y., 282, 284, *294*
Taylor, M., 401, *418*
Tharp, D. A., 244, *265*
Thorslund, C., 292, *294*
Tighe, L. S., 382, *386*
Tighe, T. J., 382, *386*
Tipper, S. P., 24, *50*
Torgerson, W. S., 208, *233,* 236, *265*
Townsend, J. T., 20, 21, 36, *52*
Trabasso, T., 300, *323,* 398, *418*
Treisman, A. M., 19, 20, 21, 23, 24,
42, 48, *52,* 59, *89,* 203, 226,
233, 348, *356,* 374, 375, *386*
Trepel, L., 312, *321*
Trope, I., 358, *386*
Tumblin, A., 388, 389, 397, *418*
Tversky, A., 208, 231, *233,* 235, 237,
265, 266, 292, *295,* 370, *385,*
399, 400, 408, *417, 418*
Tversky, B., 399, 400, *418*

V

Van der Heijden, A. H. C., 21, 25,
39, 40, 41, *51, 52*
Vela, E., 236, *266,* 401, 404, 410,
419
Vernon, M. D., 165, 166, *202*
Virzi, R. A., 20, 24, *51*
von Helmholtz, H., 92, *119*
Vurpillot, E., 171, 172, *202,* 326, *356*

W

Wall, S., 20, 25, 26, 32, 48, *50*
Walley, A. C., 349, *356*
Ward, L. M., 168, 170, 171, 172, *202*
Ward, T. B., 204, 205, 210, *233,*
236, 241, 242, 251, 256, 257,
261, 262, *266,* 307, 308, 321,
323, 327, 352, *356,* 359, 364,
365, 367, *386,* 388, 389, 390,
392, 395, 401, 404, 406, 409,
410, 411, *418, 419*
Weiner-Ehrlich, W. K., 208, 209,
210, *231,* 237, 239, 244, *264,*
266
Weintraub, D. J., 13, 14, *17*
Weisstein, N., 179, 181, 182, *202*
Werner, H., 326, *356*
Wertheimer, M., 9, *17,* 165, 166, *202*
Weyl, H., 138, *161*
Whitlock, D., 176, *200*
Wilkening, F., 374, *386,* 410, *419*
Williams, A., 179, 181, 182, *202*
Wing, H., 268, *295*
Wiser, M., 130, 134, *161*
Wohlwill, J., 213, *233,* 326, *356*
Wolfe, J. M., 170, 171, *201*

Y

Young, F. W., 282, 284, *294*
Yund, E. W., *160,* 162

Z

Zelnicker, D., 20, 33, *50*

SUBJECT INDEX

A

Analytic processing, *see* Holistic processing
Asymmetric interference, 69–70, 215, 225, 249–250
Attention
  see, Selective attention
  see, Divided attention
  see, Perceptual grouping

C

Categories
  Aristotelian definition, 267–269
  ill-defined, 300–301
  linearly separable, 303–306, 313–316
  and multidimensional stimuli
    with rectangles, 281–284
    with words, 284–289
  relations between, 274–275
  structured, 269–270
  variability, 274–275
Categorization
  for intervals of space and time, 276–277
  for loudness, 278–280
  for tone durations, 277–278

Category learning
  analytical model of, 410–414
  development of, 319, 360–363, 366–368, 376–381, 388–405
  incidental vs. intentional, 307–309, 406–410
  matching hypothesis, 397–398
  structure-process match hypothesis, 389–397
  Holistic views of, 300–306
  as a fallback mode, 307–311
City-block metric, *see* Euclidean metric
Classification, *see* Tasks
Configural stimuli, 225, 317–318, 371, 415
  see also Developmental trend
  relation to local/global precedence, 168–170, 197–200
  Type N configurations, 168–170, 199
  Type P configurations, 168–170, 199
Configural superiority effect, 61
Context (exemplar) model, 302–305